Our special thanks to Ann Reynolds, Chancellor of the City University of New York;
Joseph S. Murphy, former Chancellor of the City University of New York;
Jay Hershenson, Vice Chancellor for University Relations;
and Ernesto Malavé, Budget Officer
for their generous support in the reproduction of **CENTRO**

Blanca Vázquez
Editor

Juan Flores
Roberto P. Rodríguez-Morazzani
Amílcar Tirado Avilés
Associate Editors

Néstor Otero
Blanca Vázquez
Art Direction

Erica González
Alida Rodríguez
Daniel Cotté Sánchez
Production Assistants

Cover
Néstor Otero
Slave document courtesy of the Schomburg Center for Research in Black Culture

Inside Cover Spread
Ricardo Alcaraz Díaz

Inside Back Cover Spread
Máximo R. Colón

Thanks to
José Dejesus
Pedro Juan Hernández
Diana Lachataniere
Tony Vélez, photographic reproduction

ISBN 1-878483-55-2

APRENDER A LUCHAR, LUCHAR ES APRENDER
© 1996 CENTRO DE ESTUDIOS PUERTORRIQUEÑOS
Hunter College, City University of New York
695 Park Avenue, New York 10021
212 772-5689
FAX 212 650-3673
E Mail: bvazquez@shiva.hunter.cuny.edu

CENTRO

FOCUS *EN FOCO*
Race and Identity

Table of Contents	Page
Editorial	4–7
Un hombre (negro) del pueblo: José Celso Barbosa and the Puerto Rican "Race" Toward Whiteness **Miriam Jiménez Román**	8–29
Domestic Work and Racial Divisions in Women's Employment in Puerto Rico, 1899–1930 **Elizabeth Crespo**	30–41
Policing the Crisis in the Whitest of all the Antilles **Kelvin Santiago-Valles**	42–57
AfroPuerto Rican Cultural Studies Beyond *cultura negroide* and *antillanismo* **Juan A. Giusti Cordero**	56–77
PORTFOLIO **Héctor Méndez Caratini**	78–81
Negar lo negro sería gazmoñería: Luis Palés Matos, Margot Arce and the Black Poetry Debate **Magali Roy Fequiere**	82–91
Afro-Puerto Rican Radicalism in the United States: Reflections on the Politcal Trajectories of Arturo Schomburg and Jesús Colón **Winston James**	92–127
Jugando en el Norte: Caribbean Players in the Negro Leagues, 1910–1950 **Adrian Burgos, Jr.**	128–149
Beyond the Rainbow: Mapping the Discourse on Puerto Ricans and "Race" **Roberto P. Rodríguez-Morazzani**	128–149
Pan-Latino/Trans-Latino: Puerto Ricans in the "New Nueva York" **Juan Flores**	170–186
PORTFOLIO **Gloria Rodríguez**	187–189
The Racialization of Latino Caribbean Migrants in the New York Metropolitan Area **Ramón Grosfoguel and Chloé Georas**	190–201
Boricuas from the Hip Hop Zone: Notes on Race and Ethnic Relations in New York City **Raquel Z. Rivera**	202–215
Puerto Rican Underground **Mayra Santos**	216–231
Review of *Boricuas: Influential Puerto Rican Writings, An Anthology* **Juan Flores**	232–234
Bibliography on Puerto Ricans and Race	235–238

EDITORIAL

Breaking Silence

The issue of "race" and Puerto Rican identity has been a complex and enigmatic one, most characteristically met by silence and dismissal. From *"la gran familia puertorriqueña"* to the "rainbow people," the image of Puerto Ricans intent on building and affirming a unified national culture has meant an official denial of racial divides and hierarchies. To the extent that they have any salience for Puerto Ricans, race matters are claimed to be externally generated and imposed from outside, that is, the U.S. framework.

Yet neither in Puerto Rico nor in the diasporic communities in the U.S. is racism expressed or experienced as something external. A history of uninterrupted colonial subordination has involved the racialization of Puerto Rican experience at multiple levels, with the migration and generations of life in U.S. settings adding new dimensions to that racializing process. Central to the racialization of Puerto Ricans is the reality of colonial power and the internal articulation of power as manifest in Puerto Rican social and political struggles.

Historically and in everyday life, race/racism is experienced in multiple ways, both in Puerto Rico and in the diaspora. The social devaluation of blackness, which is itself a form of denial through distancing, is rampant in Puerto Rican popular and elite culture, in historical narratives and political discourses, in social practices of all kinds, and in everyday speech. Traditionally, the silence over these aspects of Puerto Rican history and culture has been accompanied by their folklorization and a paternalistic sense of "inclusion."

In more recent writing and discussion, since the 1970s, issues of race and racism have been confronted more directly than in previous scholarship. There has been a growing awareness of the central importance of these issues for the concept and construction of Puerto Rican identity, as well as other identity formations along the lines of social class, gender and sexuality. The work of writers such as Samuel Betances, Isabelo Zenón Cruz, Angela Jorge and José Luis González did much to help break the traditional silences by showing that the direct confrontation with our racial selves alters drastically the terms of the discussion of our identity as Puerto Ricans. In the two decades since that opening of the discourse, some important intellectual and cultural work has gone to rewriting Puerto Rican history and re-mapping social relations with these issues of race and identity in view.

■ *Ricardo Alcaraz Díaz*

The works gathered herein raise questions and indicate new trends and interpretations in discourses of race and identity within a Puerto Rican context. The idea of "whitening" Puerto Rican society and the world of work are themes discussed in articles by Miriam Jiménez-Román and Elizabeth Crespo. Juan Giusti Cordero and Magali Roy Fequiere use literature as a vehicle for the discussion of racial themes, especially the themes of *cultura negroide* and *antillanismo*. Contemporary treatments of race as manifested in Puerto Rico are discussed by Kelvin Santiago-Valles and Mayra Santos.

Issues of race and identity go hand in hand with the migratory experience of Puerto Ricans, particularly to the United States. Different manifestations of this are presented in the works of Adrian Burgos, Jr., Juan Flores, Ramón Grosfoguel and Chloé Georas, Winston James, Raquel Z. Rivera and Roberto Rodríguez-Morazzani.

With this special double issue of *CENTRO* we offer a contribution to this ongoing effort to break the silences, old and new, surrounding the question of Puerto Ricans and race/racism. ■

Rompiendo el Silencio

El tema de lo racial y la identidad puertorriqueña ha sido uno complejo y enigmático, que se ha caracterizado por el silencio y la negación. El intento de construir y afirmar una imagen puertorriqueña como una cultura nacional unificada, desde "la gran familia puertorriqueña" hasta el concepto de pueblo arcoiris ("rainbow people"), ha significado la negación oficial de unas divisiones y jerarquías raciales. Los asuntos raciales, en la medida en que éstos tienen alguna prominencia para los puertorriqueños, se les atribuye un origen externo generados e impuestos por los Estados Unidos.

Sin embargo, tanto en Puerto Rico como en los comunidades puertorriqueñas en las Estados Unidos, el racismo expresado o experimentado no es una condición externa. Una historia de continua subordinación colonial ha envuelto la racialización en múltiples niveles de la experiencia puertorriqueña. A este proceso de racialización se le ha añadido una nueva dimención producto de la migración y de varias generaciones de puertorriqueños viviendo en los Estados Unidos. Fundamental para este proceso de racialización ha sido la realidad del poder colonial y la articulación interna de poder según se manifiesta en las luchas políticas y sociales puertorriqueñas.

La cuestión racial y el racismo, tanto en Puerto Rico como en la diáspora, se ha dejado sentir históricamente y en la vida diaria de múltiples maneras. La devaluación social de la negrura, la cual implica en sí una forma de negación a través del distanciamiento, es rampante en la cultura puertorriqueña, tanto en su vertiente popular como en la elitista, en la narrativa histórica y el discurso político, en las prácticas sociales de todas clases y en la conversación cotidiana. El silencio sobre estos aspectos de la historia y la cultura puertorriqueña tradicionalmente ha estado acompañado por su folklorización y por un sentido paternalista de "inclusión."

Actualmente los temas de raza y racismo están siendo confrontados en una forma más directa que lo expresado en los escritos y discusiones previas a 1970. Se ha desarrollado una creciente conciencia de la importancia central de estos temas para el concepto y construcción de la identidad puertorriqueña, así como para la formación de otras identidades de clases sociales, género y sexualidad. Los trabajos de Samuel Betances, Isabelo Zenón Cruz, Angela Jorge y José Luis González han contribuído grandemente a romper el silencio tradicional al mostrar que la confrontación directa con nuestras concepciones raciales altera drásticamente los términos de la discusión de nuestra identidad como puertorriqueños. En los dos décadas desde que se abrió el discurso ha estado en progreso un importante trabajo intelectual y cultural re-escribiendo la historia puertorriqueña y re-articulando las relaciones sociales con estos temas de raza y de identidad.

Los trabajos recogidos en este número levantan interrogantes e indican nuevas interpretaciones en cuanto a la discusión del tema racial e identificación en el contexto de los puertorriqueños. La idea de "blanquear" la sociedad puertorriqueña y el mundo del trabajo, en su aspecto racial, son tomas discutidos en los trabajos de Miriam Jiménez-Román y Elizabeth Crespo. La literatura representa otra avenida para la discusión del tema racial, particularmente en lo que se refriere a la cultura negroide y el antillanismo. Estos temas son discutidos en los trabajos de Juan Giusti Cordero y Magali Roy Fequiere. Los trabajos de Kelvin Santiago-Valles y Mayra Santos presentan discusiones contemporáneas del tema racial según se manifiestan en Puerto Rico.

La discusión del tema racial y la identidad de los puertorriqueños es el tema que acompaña la experiencia migratoria de los puertorriqueños, particularmente hacia los Estados Unidos. Diversas manifestaciones de esta situación quedan recogidas en los trabajos de Adrian Burgos, Jr., Juan Flores, Ramón Grosfoguel y Chloé Georas, Winston James, Raquel Z. Rivera, y Roberto P. Rodríguez-Morazzani.

Con este volúmen doble del CENTRO *ofrecemos una contribución a los esfuerzos de romper los silencios, viejos y actuales, que rodean el debate de los puertorriqueños y la raza/ racismo.* ■

■ *"Baile de Bomba."*
Héctor Méndez Caratini

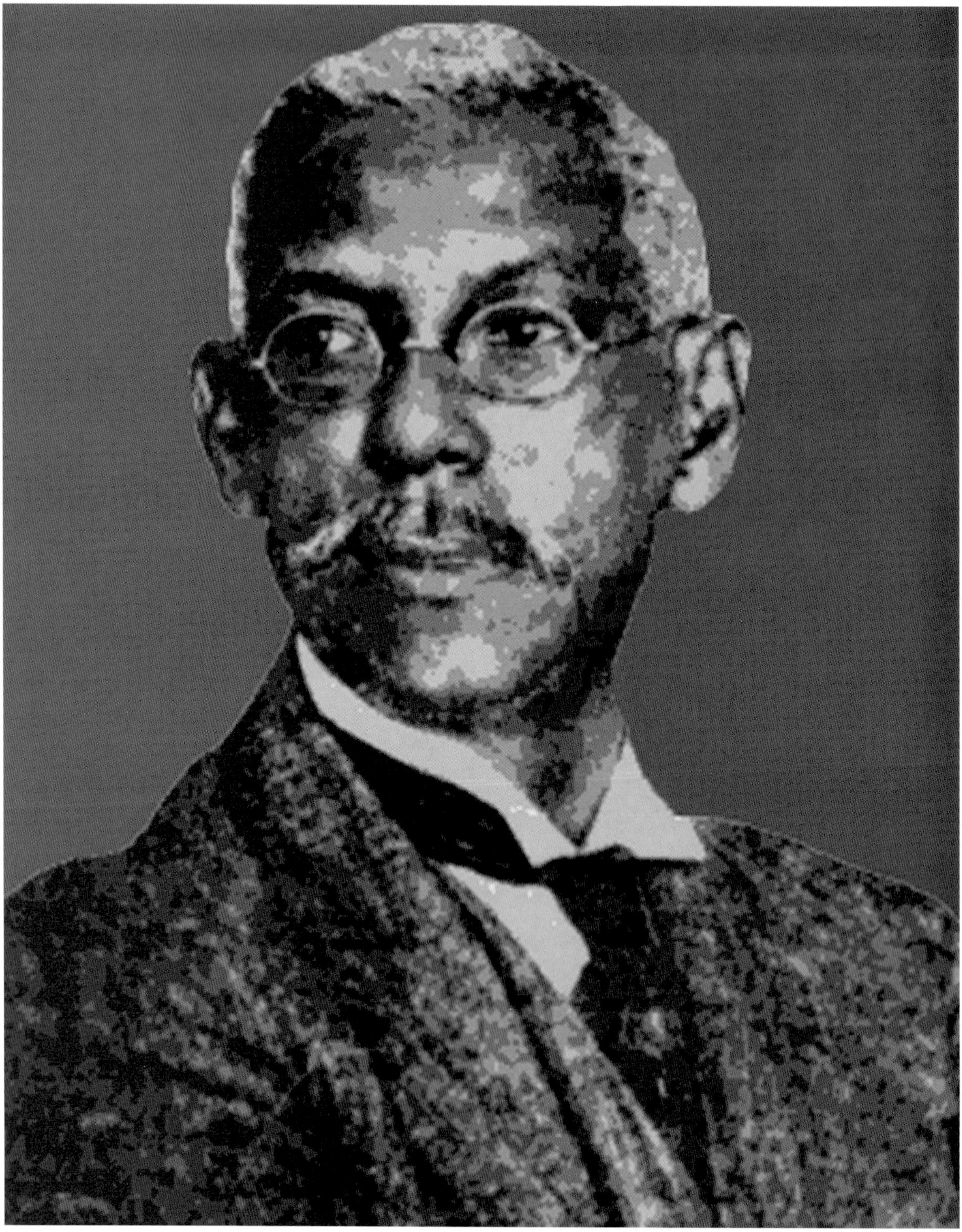

Un hombre (negro) del pueblo:
José Celso Barbosa and the
Puerto Rican "Race" Toward Whiteness

MIRIAM JIMENEZ ROMÁN

It has long been part of official ideology and popular lore that racism does not exist in Puerto Rico, indeed cannot exist given the overwhelming "racial" mixture that defines the Island's people. The biological and cultural fusion of the Indian, Spaniard and African, it is claimed, has created a distinct Puerto Rican "Creole" society where the social (and more specifically, the cultural) takes precedence over the "racial" and where the nation is presented as a homogeneous whole. Neither black nor white, Puerto Ricans are described as the quintessential "rainbow people," a nation of mestizos free of the "racial" concerns and conflicts so rampant in the United States. If there should be any acknowledgment of racial *prejudice*[1] it is with the caveat of its being merely a survival or "vestige" of slavery or, more commonly, of its coming to the Island as a recent, foreign (read United States) import. Always, there is the insistence on the uniquely non-hostile nature of "race relations" in Puerto Rico.

Juxtaposed to this mestizo construct is a widely accepted belief in the superiority of "whiteness,"—and its corollary, the inferiority of "blackness"—popularly expressed in the notion of *"mejoramiento de la raza"* [improvement of the race]. Thus in 1995, on the occasion of the 122nd anniversary of abolition, Luís Díaz Soler, author of the only comprehensive study of slavery on the Island[2] emphasized the small population of "negros"(sic) during the 19th century and the Spanish "tolerance" for intermarriage which encouraged widespread mestizaje, and breezily predicted that "in two centuries, there will hardly be any blacks in Puerto Rico."[3] In the same article, anthropologist and cultural promoter Ricardo Alegría offered his own prediction consistent with the argument that Puerto Rico is the "whitest" of the Antilles: in the race toward whiteness the Dominican Republic will come in second

---

MIRIAM JIMENEZ ROMAN is curator at the Schomburg Center for Research in Black Culture and a doctoral candidate at the State University of New York at Binghamton. A version of this paper, was originally presented before the Latino and Latin American Student Association (AELLO) of the Graduate School of the City University of New York in April 1994. *"Muchas gracias* to Gabriel Haslip-Viera, Amílcar Tirado Avilés and María Sosa for their helpful suggestions—good looking out!"

■ José Celso Barbosa, *Centro de Estudios Puerttorriqueños Library and Archives*

and Cuba will finish dead last. Such "predictions" are neither new or unusual; rather, they have been a mainstay of the race discourse for the past century, presented as the "final solution," without any apparent awareness of the racist implications of such a formulation. From this perspective, *mestizaje* is only laudable—or even acceptable—as a transitional phase and not, as the "rainbow people" construct would seem to suggest, as an end in itself.

That racist expressions and practices continue to coexist alongside its almost adamant denial is a testament to the often contradictory nature of racism itself. Racism, as it is manifested in Puerto Rico, and much if not all of Latin America, is indeed different from that which operates in the United States or South Africa. But for Latin Americans generally, and for Puerto Ricans specifically, difference is typically translated into its non-existence/absence. For most of this century Puerto Ricans have compared themselves (and been compared) with the giant to the North and, finding neither Jim Crow segregation nor lynchings, they have declared themselves free of racism. Despite the changes brought about by the civil rights movement of the sixties and seventies which have significantly reduced the more overt expressions of racism in the United States, this ideology of racial harmony continues to hold sway and most Puerto Ricans continue to object to any suggestion that, in matters of "race," the two countries are more alike than dissimilar. This stance, then, serves to buttress all the other distinctions which the colony asserts, over and against the metropole. Puerto Rican racial exceptionalism has rested on the implicit view that there is only one kind of racism, one way of being racist, with the United States serving as the primary point of reference.[4]

With rare exceptions,[5] students of "race relations" in Puerto Rico have not been immune to this United States-centric perspective on "race." In an attempt to capture different manifestations of what is essentially the same phenomenon, some have taken recourse in the term "social race," as though "race" were anything other than a social construction.[6] As a social construction it has been adaptable to the particular exigencies of the moment, taking on innumerable guises, responding to local, regional and international demands and influences. Yet this range of possibilities, across time and space, actually makes visible certain consistencies and continuities. That Puerto Ricans continue to express derogatory notions about people of visible[7] African ancestry is far from an aberration; they are quite simply expressing the commonplace truisms on matters of "race" as constructed in their particular context(s). In Puerto Rico, these truths have been articulated within a colonial context spanning 500 years and imposed by two "white" imperial powers, with an almost seamless continuity in the transition.

For Puerto Ricans "race" has always functioned on various levels simultaneously and often in contradiction to one another. There is the institutionally sanctioned and popularly reinforced belief in distinct races with identifiable, essential traits, with a corresponding notion of a "multiracial" society whose citizens enjoy harmonious relations, not least because of their evolutionary trek toward "whiteness." On the other hand there is the idea of homogeneity articulated through the rhetoric of "*la gran familia puertorriqueña*," a "race" of mestizos that shares a common culture, language, and history. Trapped between the desire to demonstrate the capacity for self-governance to their colonial overlords and the equally strong striving for national unity and cultural dignity in the face of colonial domination, Puerto Ricans have opted for ambiguity and general avoidance whenever the subject of "race" comes up. As with gender, sexuality, and class, "race" is an issue that threatens the core beliefs of the "family" paradigm, the pillar of much of Puerto Rico's national rhetoric, both anticolonial and annexationist.

Until recently, the discussion of "race" among the Island's political and intellectual elite (whatever their racial classification or political sympathies) has offered up seemingly incompatible arguments based on remarkably similar premises and arriving at predictably similar conclusions. Flowing through all the narratives is a reluctance to acknowledge the existence of racism as anything but an aberration attributable to the baser instincts of a few ignorant, misguided individuals. Interestingly, these "individual" culprits have included "whites," "pretenders to whiteness," and "upstart Negroes"—suggesting the pervasiveness of the very racism which is being denied.

Certainly what is most problematic about the prevailing constructs is that they don't allow for protest from those that are excluded because in theory there is no exclusion. Those who have protested racially motivated exclusions and injustices and demanded full and dignified membership in *"la familia"* have been labeled overly sensitive, as suffering from an inferiority complex, or unwitting victims of an imported, i.e., alien racial ideology. In a society which devalues blackness, black Puerto Ricans are trapped in the paradoxical situation of being doubly silenced, largely absent from the family portrait and yet prohibited from mentioning the slight under penalty of even greater ostracism. In such a climate it is hardly surprising that few black voices have been raised in protest, or that even those rare attempts at articulating the lived experience of racism have been suppressed or ignored. More commonly, though, black Puerto Ricans have struck an accommodationist chord, downplaying "race" in the interest of national unity, eager to demonstrate their Puerto Ricanness by acquiescing in the very racist ideology that denies them full membership.

What follows is a preliminary discussion of the positions regarding "race" taken by a few prominent members of the Island's national elite, with special attention to the writings of the illustrious political leader, José Celso Barbosa (1857–1922). Barbosa appears as a unique figure in several respects. In a society where African ancestry and Blackness are not understood to be necessarily the same thing, and where phenotype, i.e. appearance, determines "race," Barbosa was unequivocally *un negro*. Of very humble working class origins, Barbosa directly experienced his "race" during the last quarter century of Spanish rule, achieving notable success despite overwhelming social and economic obstacles. During the first decades of United States rule Barbosa was the epitome of the "self-made man," exercising considerable political power within the limited spaces available to the national elite. Barbosa, whose personal experiences left him with few illusions about the social and political system bequeathed the Island by Spain, was a fervent admirer of the republican democratic ideals represented by the United States, and actively struggled to make Puerto Rico a state—at a time when de jure segregation ruled the South and lynching was the national pastime. Most significantly, Barbosa left a record of his experiences and opinions regarding "race," publishing numerous newspaper articles over a span of 25 years, most aimed at explaining the seeming incongruity of a black man wanting political annexation to an openly racist country.

But while Barbosa is unique in his straddling of colonial regimes, his crossing of class lines, and in the documentation that he left behind, in the final analysis his position is quite representative of the contradictions faced by many of those who are both black and Puerto Rican. Throughout his life Barbosa operated under many of the same constraints which still function to silence black Puerto Ricans today. The opinions he put forth were already informed by ideas which would be refined and become officially inscribed during the cultural debates of the 1930s, a period of social, economic and political crises on the Island. Most glaringly, since he directly experienced both regimes, Barbosa would precede La generación de los treinta in his selective remembrances of life under Spanish colonialism, ultimately succumbing to the same line of defense against the perceived threats of United States racism and colonialism: the cultural distinctiveness of Puerto Ricans. Because "memories" of Spanish colonialism play such a crucial role in Barbosa's discussions of "race," and continue to serve as the basis for subsequent postulations, it is first necessary to briefly examine the historical context out of which springs the "race" discourse articulated by these, and other, men in twentieth century Puerto Rico.[8]

■ *Historical Background*

Far from being a recent import, Puerto Rico was racialized at birth. The Spanish conquerors rationalized the enslavement and extermination of the native Taínos by reference to their "infidel" status, their physical weakness and their lack of "civilization." As is the case with the rest of the Americas, estimates as to the number of indigenous peoples at the moment of contact are varied, fragmented and often exaggerated. For Borikén the numbers range from (an unlikely) high of one million people to a low of 16,000.[9] We find much greater consensus among chroniclers and later scholars as to the fate of the Taínos: within a century of the conquest their numbers had been decimated.

Over 90 percent of the approximately 10 million enslaved Africans brought to the Americas during the more than three centuries of the transatlantic slave trade were taken to Latin America and the Caribbean. The Island of Puerto Rico received approximately one percent (about 100,000), certainly a small figure when compared to Brazil's 38%, or even to the 4.6% received by what is now the territory of the United States. But this seemingly paltry figure takes on greater significance when we consider the small size of the Island (3500 square miles) and the overwhelming presence of Africans relative to the various other ethnic groups who have populated Puerto Rico through the years.[10] The territory now encompassing the United States, more than one thousand times the size of Puerto Rico, received fewer than five times as many enslaved Africans. In addition to receiving proportionately greater numbers of enslaved Africans, Puerto Rico's small size and settlement patterns (the first Spanish towns were established in the southwest and northeast, and by the mid–18th century the Island's population was "so scattered" that houses could be found "everywhere"[11]) also encouraged a greater dispersal of its black population.

The *ladino*, i.e. Christianized African, slaves who first accompanied the Spanish conquerors were initially used as domestic servants and then, as the supply of Indian labor continued to dwindle, as miners alongside the Taínos. Just as had occurred in the earliest colony in Hispaniola, *ladino* slaves joined with Taínos and escaped the Spanish settlements. The so-called *bozales*, enslaved Africans who were brought directly from the Niger-Congo region to the Island beginning with the first Royal license in 1519, also engaged in organized rebellion in alliance with the Taínos and the *ladinos*. The intimacy of these relations during the first years of Spanish settlement has led at least one student of the subject to observe that any indigenous cultural survivals present today are probably traceable to this early period of isolated fugitive communities of Africans and Taínos. In any event, as an identifiable group, the Taínos had all but disappeared by the 17th century,[12] while *bozales* continued to arrive for another 200 years and Spanish adventurers, repelled by the miserable conditions on the Island and seduced by the promise of wealth on the mainland, continued to leave. Rebellion and subversion of Spanish authority was a mainstay of the developing nation, as reflected at every level of Island society, from the frequent escapes from slave-worked plantations[13] to the resentment of the *criollos*,[14] who increasingly identified their interests as distinct from those of Spain.

Concern with the racial composition of the Island was evident from the earliest years of colonization. A 1581 report on the Island population listed more than twice as many Blacks, *mulatos* and mestizos as there were whites. Almost 200 years later, the French naturalist, André Pierre Ledrú, observed that "pure whites without mixture of strange blood are extremely rare."[15] Despite earnest attempts in the 19th century to rectify what was considered a dangerous imbalance of the "races" through the promotion of European immigration to the Island, the colony's first three centuries resulted in a population predominantly composed of people classified as *negro* and *mulato* or *pardo*. European immigration never approached the numbers of black people who, taking advantage of the Spanish offer to accept slave runaways from rival European powers, escaped from the British (and to a lesser extent, Dutch and Danish) colonies and settled as free men and women on the Island.

The elaborate racial caste system developed by the Spanish showed an obsessive concern with, and dependence on, lineage as a means of controlling their colonies.[16] Membership in a particular *casta* not only determined one's standing within the pecking order but also one's relations with the other castes. Despite the complexity of its classification and terminology the caste system essentially established the superiority and authority of Spaniards. Anyone who was not a Spaniard, or could not claim some affiliation with "Spanish blood,"—which was extended to include its "civilizing" culture—was, by definition, inferior and powerless.

In Spain's attempt at imperial consolidation, "Hispanization" was encouraged; *bozales*, for example, became *negros criollos* within one generation. Accepting the Spanish language and Roman Catholicism did not, however, protect Creole slaves from the abuses of their masters. Notwithstanding what is considered the most "benevolent" of the European slave codes, slave owners acted with impunity, whipping, maiming and even killing their slaves for real or imagined infractions. Slaves were scarce and expensive but the fear of rebellion was greater, and demonstrations of force and authority were a fundamental means of maintaining discipline and obedience. The denigration of Africans and their descendants was the other essential aspect of this control. The chronicler Iñigo Abbad y Lasierra described a scenario that was commonplace in the mid-18th century:

> ...there is nothing more ignominious on this Island than to be black, or to be descended from them: a white man insults any of them, with impunity, and in the most contemptible language; some masters treat them with unjust rigor....[17]

Free Blacks, and *pardos (mulatos* and other *castas)*, as descendants of slaves, were legally and socially discriminated against. Representing the vast majority of the Island's population, they were restricted in the work they could do, in their freedom of movement, the places they could attend and live in, whom they could marry, the bearing of arms, their access to institutions, the clothing they could wear—in short every aspect of their lives was carefully regulated.[18] White apprehension that such discriminatory treatment could lead to possible alliances between free and enslaved Blacks and *pardos* is evident in the legislation of the 19th century dealing with slave insurrections; these always included penalties against free Blacks and *pardos*. The steady stream of newly enslaved Africans (many entering through the contraband trade which defied the Crown's regulatory decrees) and the frequently "brutal intimacy"[19] inflicted on the enslaved women by the slave owners, substantially increased the numbers of those classified as *pardos*. *Pardos* were thus stigmatized for both their origins as Africans and as illegitimate offspring. Within the context of a rigid patriarchal morality prescribed by the Catholic Church and enforced by the State, *pardas* were particularly vulnerable, regarded as naturally lacking in moral rectitude, and therefore as the instigator, rather than the victim, of (white and black) male and (white) female aggression. Almost all *pardos* and *pardas* were free,[20] albeit only conditionally; ultimately they were not *blancos*, their loyalties were never certain, and they were not deemed deserving of the same considerations as *blancos*.

Most prevalent among *blancos* was the belief that *pardos* were suspect and had to be watched. We thus find that even in the (ostensibly) Church-based segregated *"cofradías"* and *"hermandades"* that were common throughout the Island well into the 19th century, the officers were always *blancos;* Blacks and *pardos* could not aspire beyond simple membership.[21] As representatives of the Spanish Crown and primary beneficiaries of the colony's resources, Spaniards were not only the most privileged *blancos*, but all so classified automatically were assured deference from the other castes. The Código Negro Carolina, issued in the late 18th century, specifically referred to the necessity of establishing "the most severe subordination and discipline" toward the white population "as the fundamental basis of the colonies' domestic policy." The order read further that "...all blacks, whether slave or free, and *pardos* to the first, second, or third degree on, shall be submissive and respectful to all white persons as though each were their very master or owner."[22]

Because deference was not limited to matters of social etiquette but included access to employment, goods and services, the "rewards" of whiteness made it a much sought-after classification. In an attempt to control the forging and "fixing" of documents so prevalent in the colonies, the Church and state periodically passed regulations establishing the criteria for membership in one or another caste. None was guarded more closely than the classification as *blanco*, even as its legitimacy was clearly being regarded with increasing suspicion. By the mid-18th century visitors reported that Puerto Rico had "a lack of families of refined and pure ancestry" and that even among the scant white families there were few "without mixture of all types of bad blood."[23]

Bringing in "good blood" included receiving Europe's adventurers and vagabonds into established, but "tainted" families. As reported by the 18th century chronicler Abbad y Lasierra, deserting sailors were assured a warm welcome by the Islanders who would "offer them their daughters for wives, even when the prospective new members of the family have no other clothes than the ones which they are wearing, and no other title to commend them than that of sailor or ship boy; since the titles of *Spanish* and *white* constitute in themselves an extensive property and an evident mark of nobility...."[24] The very desirability of "whiteness" thus functioned to make it a difficult to regulate and unreliable signifier.

Cross-caste marriages particularly for women, often the best course for attaining upward caste mobility[25]—were discouraged but occurred with enough frequency to expose ever greater contradictions in the caste system itself. In 1757, for example, clerics were instructed in how to register births, marriages and deaths in the two parish ledgers, one for *blancos* and another for *negros* and *pardos*, free or enslaved. In the event of a cross-caste marriage between a *blanco* and a *pardo* whose parents were free, it was to be registered in the "white" ledger. If either parent had been a slave, and the *pardo* was male, the marriage would be listed in the "black" ledger; if it was the female, then the marriage would be in the "white" book.[26] Any children of the marriage would then be classified according to the ledger in which the marriage had been registered. These regulatory prescriptions suggest a certain receptivity to *pardas* legalizing their unions with *blancos* and can be seen as both an accommodation to the popular preference for "colored" women as (fetishized) sexual partners (a preference which had much to do with their numerical preponderance), and as indicative of the greater value placed on the male's racial caste position. Thus the private woman, and the product of her womb, is defined by the public man.

When the biological and the social collided, adjustments were made to accommodate both in the interest of maintaining the political and ideological status quo. Because these practices were well-known, the "whiteness" of *blancos* was continually under scrutiny and contestation. "Whiteness," clearly referring to more than just "blood," or even appearance, required other signifiers, other "proofs" of one's superiority that were consistent with notions of origins, and indeed served to reinforce them. For the *criollos*, education and training, available exclusively to the wealthy, reinforced the notion of their superiority over the lower castes while simultaneously establishing their capacity to rule. It is to these "high(er) sentiments" that Ramón Emeterio Betances, 19th century revolutionary and abolitionist, seems to be referring in a letter to his sister regarding another sister's marriage in 1879:

> You, as a person of the world, know the preoccupation with color that exists in certain circles.... When the marriage of doña Ana and don Pepe was confirmed, since there were many envious parents ... they brought up the family's African blood-something that no Betances with any common sense has ever denied....It is thus well understood that we are dark-ish, and we don't deny it; but as Luís Betances says: All the more honorable! And let it also be understood that if we had had different mothers, I would have renounced my own in order to be the son of yours, since she knew to give birth to a person of such high sentiments as yours....[27]

The "darkish" Betances writes his letter during a crucial period in the consolidation of the Puerto Rican nation. Less than two decades earlier the criollos, frustrated by the limitations placed on their access to the Island's potential wealth (and many with similar "darkish" skeletons in their own family closets), had organized a revolt and seized the mountain town of Lares, declaring the Republic of Puerto Rico. The anti-slavery movement, long linked to the independence movement, had succeeded in obtaining its abolition in 1873, and five years later all of Puerto Rico's remaining 37,000 slaves were unconditionally freed.[28] Although the Lares revolt was quickly suppressed, the independence struggle against Spain would continue for another two decades, under the leadership of men such as Betances, Roberto Henna, Sotero Figueroa, many living in exile in Europe and the United States.

It was also a period of increasing receptivity in Europe and the United States to racialist formulations based on distorted interpretations of Darwin's theory of evolution. The biological essentialism already evident in the concept of *pureza de sangre* (however ambiguously applied) provided a receptive base for the progression of deterministic notions (such as social evolution, positivism, naturalism and social Darwinism) that would flourish into the 20th century. These ideas, articulated and reproduced in the interest of the European dominant classes, were developed as a way of explaining already existing social relations under imperialism, slavery and capitalism as "natural." But while the social Darwinists were speaking of purity of race, industry and progress, Puerto Rico was a poor, agrarian colony of "colored people," precisely the type of mongrel "race" being classified as inferior, and regarded as "the problem."

Betances, exiled in Paris, was cognizant of and directly addressed the developing racialist theories of the times. In 1882, a Parisian magazine published a series of articles by Leo Quesnel which recounted his experiences in Cuba and Puerto Rico, where he claimed to have confirmed the inferiority of people of African ancestry and concluded that this "explained" the backwardness of Haitians. A group of Haitian intellectuals quickly put together a collection of rebuttals to Quesnel's "malevolent appraisals and calamitous assertions."[29] In a letter that serves as prologue to the book, and which he defiantly signs "El Antillano," Betances dismisses the perpetrators of such racist ideology by asserting a "higher moral ground":

> "That is why we see with surprise that writers whose articles are accepted in respectable publications wallow in hasty, as well as unjust and injurious criticisms. We would be indignant at their insults if we weren't so inclined to laugh at their ignorance." [30]

The *criollo* elite had insisted on their equality with Spaniards and their ability to rule autonomously, but there was never any question as to who would rule this proposed new nation. Thus, these "scientific" new ideas could be received by an Island intellectual elite as viable rationalizations for their continued position of privilege in the social hierarchy.

Before this national project could be realized, the invasion by the United States in 1898 made even more urgent a reconfiguration of the national identity. The North Americans promptly re-named the Island "Porto Rico," and, holding out the promise of industry and prosperity, proceeded to assume its pre-ordained "destiny" as one of the most "advanced races" and bring "enlightened civilization" to the "natives." [31] At the same time, it was necessary to make these inferior "colored people" as palatable as possible to "whites" in the United States, who were not expected to welcome the burden of more "Negroes" among them.

It is interesting that only two years earlier, in the infamous case of Plessey vs. Ferguson, the U.S. Supreme Court had rejected the plea of a Louisiana octoroon that his seventh-eighths "white blood" should qualify him for a seat on a railroad "white" car. The historic decision firmly established the legitimacy of white supremacy and the inferiority of those known to have the slightest trace of African ancestry. Both the new colonizers and the elite of the twice-colonized Puerto Rico had reason for concern over the Island's racial composition and the implications for future relations; from the beginning, it was in their common interest to downplay the issue of "race" and to minimize the black presence on the Island.

The resulting efforts were wrought with incongruities. One of the earliest colonial reports on conditions in Puerto Rico, *Our Islands and Their People* (1899), offered a wealth of photographic proof of Puerto Rican "coloredness"—along with a text that disputed the evidence: Puerto Ricans were described as pertaining to three "distinct types, or races": "Spanish," "white or light mulatto," and "pure-blooded Africans," the latter group described as "few" in number and essentially confined to "a colony at one end of the Island."[32] Apparently concerned that even a "few" Blacks might be cause for alarm, the author reassured his readers, "[b]ut the African race is declining, and will eventually either disappear or be amalgamated with the white race."[33]

In 1900, a Puerto Rican delegation led by José Julio Henna called on the Congress "of the most enlightened, inventive and powerful of all nations" to permit a civil government on the Island for its "one million intelligent Christians, almost eighty percent of whom are Caucasians."[34] Apparently not convinced that Puerto Rico was "white" enough, in 1901, a (presumably) "white" Spaniard wrote to the Island's Civilian Governor proposing that the immigration policy then under consideration encourage the departure of two Blacks and *mulatos* for every white that left, since Puerto Rico already had too many of the former and should rid itself of them posthaste. In addition, he recommended that the entry of Blacks to the Island be forbidden, while that of whites encouraged.[35]

Coming at the matter from different directions, colonizer and colonized converged in their shared values and beliefs regarding the economic and political superiority of the United States, and either implicitly or explicitly attributed it to biology. Where there was disagreement it was in the social sphere, articulated by the national elite in terms of Spain's "ancient civilization," the foundation for Puerto Rico's superior culture. Indeed, as a colony of a "really white" imperial power, with a different language and different racial codes, Puerto Rican "culture" would have to serve double-duty: the Island's superior "culture" also accounted for its "flexible" racial attitude which seemed so incomprehensible to the North Americans. The banner of the "cultural" homogeneity of Puerto Ricans would also be raised whenever internal social tensions and contradictions threatened to surface. It would provide the moral higher ground that exempted Puerto Ricans from accepting a United States construction of race that basically disenfranchised a whole people.

■ *Barbosa: Un hombre (negro) del pueblo*
For José Celso Barbosa, founder and leader of the Republican Party, this emphasis on "culture" helped resolve what would appear to have been a fundamental contradiction: his support for annexation to the United States and his being *un negro*.

Born free, poor, and black in 1857, the son of a sporadically employed Puerto Rican brickmason and a Venezuelan who had immigrated to the Island as a young girl, Barbosa was able to study at the Island's only secondary educational institution, thanks to the dogged determination of his aunt and despite the obvious hostility of his teachers and fellow students.[36] The victim of frequent humiliations,[37] Barbosa managed to graduate from the colony's Jesuit seminary and soon thereafter left the Island to pursue further studies in the United States. This was already a distinctly different route than that taken by his more affluent classmates, who were able to follow the Island elite tradition of a European university education. At the University of Michigan at Ann Arbor, where he obtained his medical degree in 1880, Barbosa enjoyed an active intellectual and social life (including the attentions of a German girlfriend) and, reportedly, "did not find that cloud of racial prejudices which he had left behind" on the Island.[38]

Certain particularities about Michigan appear to have made a profound impression on Barbosa during his years at the University. In the mid-1800s that state was the site of strong labor and socialist activity, generated in large measure by the recently arrived German, Irish and Dutch immigrants. The Granger Movement, which sought to correct economic abuses against farmers, was still at its peak. More significantly, Michigan had been pro-Union during the Civil War and remained firmly committed to the Republican Party until 1882 when it was defeated by the Greenback Party, a union of farmers and mining and lumber workers.

Although Michigan's black population never rose above one percent throughout the 19th century, the state's black residents included a large number of highly educated and successful African-Americans, and the community exerted significant economic and political influence in certain counties. By 1880 Blacks were being elected into office in those towns where they represented the majority of voters. A relatively tolerant racial climate led to the repeal, in 1883, of Michigan's anti-miscegenation laws, and two years later to passage of a series of laws banning discrimination in public accommodations. Since Barbosa had left Michigan by 1880 it is safe to conclude that, along with imbibing the ideas of the times, he also personally experienced racial segregation. Certainly he would leave the United States identifying the Republican Party as the savior and future hope of the black masses.

Returning to Puerto Rico, Barbosa began his medical practice, joining the ranks of the neglected colony's professional class which clamored for greater political and economic autonomy from Spain. He became a member of a Masonic lodge, a crucial site (as in the rest of the Americas) for subversive political activity, and joined the Partido Autonomista. A staunch anti-monarchist, by 1897 Barbosa had become the principal figure among Los Ortodoxos, a group which proposed a government which represented the "will of the people"—under the leadership of the educated vanguard, as opposed to hereditary rule by the Creole elite. Emphasizing the need for popular democracy and social equality, Barbosa attained considerable influence among the urban working class, many of whose leaders were also black.[39]

Barbosa's medical practice, which included the dispensing of free services to San Juan's indigent, also flourished—although he was not officially licensed to practice medicine by the Spanish authorities until 1890 when he was subjected to a grueling series of exams by a hostile medical court that included one member who refused to wear his robes "for a colored man." After passing these exams he was admitted to El Ateneo, the Island's first institution to offer post-secondary instruction, where he taught medicine (including classes in midwifery), and soon was serving on its Board.

In addition to his political and pedagogical activities, Barbosa was one of the founders, in 1893, of the Island's cooperatist movement and a regular contributor to the Island newspapers. All indications are that he was also an avid reader who kept abreast of events in Europe as well as the United States. His readings included the writings of W.E.B. DuBois and Booker T. Washington and he appears to have been a subscriber to (though not a sympathizer of) *The Messenger*, until 1922 one of the most widely circulated of the radical black publications in the United States. He also read *The Crisis*, the official organ of the National Association for the Advancement of Colored People. Like other black Puerto Ricans, Barbosa demonstrated a keen interest in "Negro literature and history," and necessarily filled much of this need with material produced in the United States.

Barbosa and his party played a key role in Puerto Rico's transition from Spanish to United States colony, serving as counterforce to the Creole elite's political aspirations. Most notably, during the period of *las turbas republicanas* ("the Republican mobs") that extended from 1900 to 1904, Barbosa's sympathizers among the urban poor and recently arrived peasants launched an often violent campaign against the (till then) dominant Federal Party, which led to the resounding defeat of the Federales in the municipal elections of 1902. Barbosa continued to enjoy the patronage of the United States colonial government, serving on the advisory Executive Council (1900–1917) and as a senator (1917–1921) until his death.[40]

A founding member of the Island's Republican Party, Barbosa often expressed a concern for the urban professional and working classes and advocated a "modernization" process which would free the Island of the sociopolitical practices left behind by Spain.[41] In addition to his more overt emphasis on the evils of hereditary class privilege, Barbosa implicitly racialized the political discourse by accusing Luis Muñoz Rivera of having been an accomplice and instrument of the Spanish government, suggesting that victory for the Federales would be a return to rule by *los blancos or los de la otra banda*.[42]

Unlike Muñoz Rivera, and despite his own *de facto* leadership, Barbosa refused to assume the presidency of the Republican Party. In like fashion, Barbosa never took on the directorship of the newspaper, *El Tiempo*, the Republican Party daily which he founded in 1907. This pattern of exerting power from "behind the scenes" would characterize Barbosa's entire career; with seeming approval, his daughter would say of Barbosa that he always managed to "rise above pettiness and focus on principle and political ideals," gaining people's respect by always "remaining in his place."[43]

Barbosa thus negotiated a fine line between a defensive "racial pride" and accommodation to the colonial status quo, both under Spain and the United States. This balancing act would result in a string of contradictions as he wrestled to speak as a Puerto Rican, as a black man, and as an accomplice of the United States colonial regime. Barbosa did indeed "stay in his place," in the sense that he maintained a non-confrontational stance throughout his life, but he was situated in a number of "places" which continually shifted and only rarely converged. Outspoken in his attacks against racial and class privileges while the Island was still under Spanish rule, Barbosa seems to have fallen victim to the same historical amnesia (albeit to a lesser degree) that would afflict other Puerto Ricans once under United States colonial rule. In a 1896 article, for example, Barbosa wrote of his "struggles" against "the Spanish Catholic Jesuits" and "the Yankee professors" who hindered the educational aspirations of "a son of the people" because he lacked "a false dossier of pure blood."[44] Less than ten years later, Barbosa would insist that "the color problem does not exist in Puerto Rico.... has never germinated in Puerto Rico," and recall the Spanish policy of "purity of blood" as "a mere formality."[45]

What would remain consistent in Barbosa's writings was a belief in privilege based on merit, and not on "an accident of birth." Thus, under Spanish rule, Barbosa would assert his own demonstrated superiority over "those who are truly inferior" because they owe everything they possess "to the capricious luck of their name."[46] Years later he would claim that under United States tutelage, "...superiority is manifested, not in one's race, nor in the greater or lesser quantity of coloring material in the skin. Superiority depends on the quantity of gray matter, on the refinement of the cerebral circumvolutions, on education, on will, on moral preparation, on the environment,...essential factors for individual and collective superiority."[47]

■ *En Nuestro Terreno: Barbosa on "Race"*

The bulk of Barbosa's writings on race issues were originally published in the Republican Party newspaper *El Tiempo*, between 1915 and 1920, and correspond to specific and politically significant events surrounding the First World War. In 1917, the United States would confer citizenship on Puerto Ricans, a step in the direction advocated by Barbosa's Republican Party. Growing dissatisfaction on the Island was finding expression in a more militant labor movement; the Socialist Party, founded less than two years before, had easily garnered 12% of the vote in the 1917 elections, attracting many former members of the Republican Party. By 1920, it was apparent that the United States had no interest in fulfilling the political and economic aspirations of the Island's people. Increasing racial tensions in the United States—most notably the wholesale lynchings and riots which marked the aftermath of the war—had also made Puerto Rican membership in the Union extremely unlikely, and for many sectors, clearly undesirable.

In the series of articles written before 1917 Barbosa is primarily concerned with reassuring other Puerto Ricans—and particularly other Blacks—that they have nothing to fear from the United States, and that any danger of racism resides closer to home. Indeed, despite his frequent claims regarding the nonexistence of racism on the Island, the articles were invariably motivated by denigrating statements made about him by other Puerto Ricans and Barbosa actually offered numerous examples of his personal tribulations. He was usually careful, however, to direct attention away from *los americanos* and point the finger of any possible blame at individual Puerto Ricans. Thus in the articles published under the title *"En nuestro terreno"* [In Our Land], a direct reply to the many accusations launched against him as "a traitor" to his "race," Barbosa identifies racism as an internal problem, one that need not be imported because it already exists. Insisting that he had always been treated with respect and consideration by North American colonial administrators, Barbosa charges "certain Puerto Rican whites" with having conspired against him "because Barbosa was black."[48] Letters, petitions, delegations and affidavits were all produced to destroy his reputation, "[a]nd it was natives who engaged in such infamy. And it was white Puerto Ricans who thus tried to humiliate Barbosa." At the same time he argued that under statehood, the laws of Puerto Rico would be made by Puerto Ricans and they alone would be responsible for assuring that "race prejudice" not "become a problem." On race matters, Barbosa thus upholds the myth of racial equality while simultaneously holding the Island's "whites" and the masses of "quasi whites" explicitly accountable for whatever racial problem might exist.

For Barbosa, it is these pretenders to whiteness who pose a potential problem "for the race" and for the country as a whole. Seeing in the history of Blacks in the United States "an inspiration to men of color who must feel pride in the progress they have attained," Barbosa contrasts them to Blacks in Latin America, whom he accuses of being the real "race traitors":

> ...In the countries of South America, in the Antilles, and even in Europe, people of black blood have won high distinction, both political and civic, and have shone in the arts and literature. But they have moved in an environment of tolerance that has accepted them as equals, and once they have risen they have ceased being

exponents of the African race and gone on to occupy a position of high distinction in the proclaiming of the great Latin culture, confusing themselves within the heterogeneity that is called *Latin civilization*. Transforming their descendency through amalgamation, through crossing, they have succeeded in being classified as of the white race, and in thus they cannot be presented as exponents of the advancements and progress of the African race."[49] (emphasis in original)

In a surprising twist, Barbosa actually finds cause for celebrating racism "because it gives blacks the opportunity to win in the battle, and demonstrate that, face to face, against a white race...[they] have advanced in all the spheres of life."[50] In a stance that attempts to accommodate local national integrity against the perceived threat of incorporation into an openly racist society, Barbosa insists that, in the United States, any obstacles to black advancement, any violation of the Constitution, has been carried out by the individual states and not by the federal government. Ironically, "state's rights," traditionally utilized by the South to maintain Jim Crow segregation, is invoked by Barbosa as a guarantee against Jim Crow segregation.

Never disputing the superiority of "legitimate whites," Barbosa instead appeals to the finer instincts, culture and refinement of Island "whites," calling for a higher moral position against those "dwarfs, upstarts of the white race, fresh from ethnic evolution, white of skin, dark of mind, shameful descendants of that race they scorn." The "genuine, direct representatives of the [white] race...." are above the pettiness bred by feelings of inferiority and "...give faith to their purity [of blood] in their distinguished manners, their respect and high regard for other classes." The "ignorant masses," who, fueled by the "envy of inferiority" deride Blacks and attempt to "confuse" themselves with "pure whites," are the real problem. In an accommodationist mode reminiscent of the North American black leader Booker T. Washington's 1895 Atlanta Speech,[51] Barbosa assures his readers of his belief in the separation of public and private life. Subscribing to a "stay in your place" bootstrap mentality of individual "improvement" that will ultimately prove one's worth to "legitimate whites", Barbosa is careful to stress that in his view "social mingling" is neither appropriate nor desirable. Indeed, he points to this willingness of Blacks to "stay in their place" as the reason for Puerto Rico not having a race problem:

> Since there is no *color problem* in political life, or in public life, and since the colored element has never attempted to cross or erase the social line, *the color problem* does not exist in Puerto Rico.[52] (emphasis in original)

Barbosa thus presents us with contradictory messages: On the one hand, he praises black people in the United States for having achieved as a "race," going so far as to see racism against them as ultimately being no more than a challenge, an opportunity to struggle and overcome obstacles. Simultaneously, Barbosa warns Blacks in Puerto Rico against any such race-based approach to equality. The color problem will not exist in Puerto Rico "...if the colored element manages to avoid, by all possible means, any race struggle; any linking of their rights to questions of race; or demands for benevolence for racial reasons, or consider as a favor the acts of justice made to colored men."[53]

Consistent with his elitist class perspective, Barbosa is convinced that, in the final analysis "class" will prevail and that having demonstrated their intelligence, cultural refinement and ability, Blacks will be recognized as equal by similarly intelligent, cultured and able whites. He cautions Puerto Rican youth, and especially those "of color" who study in the United States, not to become tainted by the prejudices that will surround them there. He seeks assurance that such ideas not be imported into the Island, arguing that, for the good of the Fatherland, "they should accept all that is good about that country and reject all that is bad." Ultimately, though, there is no need to fear that foreign ideas will take root in a Puerto Rico which has never known a race problem.

> Thus, the men of color of Puerto Rico can remain calm and satisfied under the new sovereign because the Americans cannot, even if they tried, act against that element,

nor will it be possible to import the color problem as long as the Puerto Ricans, by their expressed will, do not permit it.[54]

The series of six articles published by Barbosa in 1919 on "the problem of race in the United States" reflects new concerns. Most evidently, they are a reaction to the growing labor militancy on the Island. But Barbosa was also writing in the aftermath of the Congressional debates in 1916 regarding the extension of citizenship to Puerto Ricans, sessions which left no doubt as to the low esteem in which the Islanders were held. The more sympathetic congressmen argued that the majority of Puerto Ricans were white and therefore deserving of citizenship. More common though, were the sentiments of Representative Joseph G. Cannon who asserted that "really 75 to 80 percent of the population...was pure African or had an African strain in their blood," and that given this inferior foundation there was little that could be expected by way of capacity for self-rule.[55] For a black man who had himself argued that the "masses" of Puerto Ricans were "quasi-whites," Barbosa found little space for maneuvering in the racially loaded debates. He could hardly assert his own "Africaness" when even a "strain" of it was cited as a deficiency, nor could he, in a climate that posed the redemptive powers of "whiteness" as the only avenue toward self-determination, refute claims to the "whiteness" of Puerto Ricans.

For many Puerto Ricans the First World War offered an opportunity to demonstrate their mettle to their colonizers, whether as proof of capacity for self-rule or of worthiness for equal incorporation into the United States. More difficult to defend was the drafting of Puerto Ricans into the segregated United States Army. The initial plan to ship Puerto Ricans to segregated training camps in the United States was successfully challenged by the Island's Republican Party. After some conflict with members of the Union Party who argued for segregated camps in Puerto Rico, Barbosa proposed his usual hands-off solution: two training camps-one for whites and one for coloreds—and allow the men themselves to select their camp.[56] While his proposal resolved the immediate problem, it also made manifest both the racism among Puerto Ricans and the ability of the United States to impose their "race problem" on the Island.

Barbosa's writings offer ample evidence of his comprehensive knowledge of United States racial history as well as current events. Defending a broad spectrum of black leadership, which encompassed both Booker T. Washington and W.E.B. DuBois, he wrote sympathetically about the community's historic struggles for racial dignity and equal rights, and expressed confidence in their eventual success. At times explicitly identifying as a member of "the African race," Barbosa was careful also to establish distinctions between the conditions in the United States and those in Puerto Rico. Ultimately, the situation in the United States was one which Puerto Ricans should follow as "mere spectators, even when we become part of the American nation."[57]

But Barbosa's other agenda in these articles was to discredit the radical labor movement that threatened the status quo both in the United States and Puerto Rico, and to reaffirm the legitimacy of class distinctions. Denouncing the International Workers of the World and other "Bolsheviks" and "anarchists," Barbosa warns that the failure to resolve "the race problem" in the United States will make such radical organizations attractive to disenfranchised Blacks but his call is for reforms that will stave off more fundamental change. Segregated housing, for example, is "logical, natural," and only a problem when laws restrict access to property which is within one's financial means.[58] Barbosa claimed that even lynching is defensible when the culprit has assaulted or insulted a woman of any color, but particularly if the perpetrator is "of a lesser social condition than the victim."[59] In contrast to the hereditary privilege sanctioned under Spain, Barbosa poses earned class privilege as more democratic, attainable through individual effort. Again, "race" is relegated to secondary importance, as a problem that plagues the United States but which will be resolved through the good graces of good people who uphold the tenets of the presumably "color blind" Constitution.

Returning to his earlier attack on the color consciousness of the "masses" who have pretensions to whiteness, while continuing to deny the existence of any "race" problem, Barbosa is caught in the contradiction and finally falls back on an evolutionary argument, citing widespread racial mixture as the surest path to resolving any problem that might exist.

> The race problem does not exist here.
> That problem is resolving itself through the evolution of the black race.
> Here, the black race has been mixing with the other races; and today every man of color in Puerto Rico is a conglomerate of *blue blood, Indian blood*, and African blood and through evolution, depending on the predominance of one of those parts, and the fading of pigment, Blacks have evolved; from black to mixed, *mulato* or white.
> And the black Black continues to disappear.
> And evolution will continue, and the problem will be resolved (emphasis in original).[60]

Operating within the confines of a colonial and racist structure, Barbosa could ultimately not sustain his posture as a "race man" without endangering his legitimacy as a Puerto Rican. As an annexationist, for him to insist on the prevalence of racism on the Island would be to fall victim, once again, to accusations of having become a *piti-yanki*, a tool of alien domination intent on creating problems where none exists.[61] Instead he succumbed to the pressures of an ideology that left him, and all those who had not sufficiently "evolved," silenced and, increasingly, invisible.

■ *Defining "el pueblo": From Barbosa to Tomás Blanco*

The achievements of this "man of the people" have been memorialized throughout the Island. His name appears on street signs, public schools and parks, and he is commonly held up as a shining example of Puerto Rican racial democracy, as proof that neither poverty nor color are obstacles to success. And yet Barbosa's biographer offers the opinion that this reserved and noncombative man who never swayed from his expressed political principles was actually among the most vilified: "I doubt that in our history there has ever been a man more rudely fought and slandered than José Celso Barbosa."[62] That many of Barbosa's difficulties were directly attributable to racial discrimination makes this assessment all the more striking, coming as they do from none other than Antonio S. Pedreira. In 1934, three years before writing those words, the renowned professor and founder of the University's Department of Hispanic Studies had published *Insularismo: Ensayos de interpretación puertorriqueña*, considered "the classic, and in many ways, pioneering, statement on Puerto Rican identity," which glorified the Spanish past and directly blamed its "backwardness" on its biological "fusion."[63] *Insularismo* is thus premised on precisely those ideas of racial determinism and the inferiority of indigenous and African peoples (as opposed to the superiority of Europeans) which plagued Barbosa for most of his life.

The idea of Pedreira as Barbosa's biographer is nothing less than intriguing, although it suggests the very intangibility of the racial discourse in Puerto Rico that a man who bemoaned the African character of Puerto Rico's population should write a largely laudatory account of the life of a black compatriot. And yet Pedreira demonstrates, in his admiration for Barbosa, the practical viability of holding racist ideas about a group and simultaneously excluding certain individuals from that group. So that Barbosa *es negro pero....* (Barbosa is black but....) and his achievements serve to prove the rule of black inferiority; he is viewed as an exceptional black man. Ostensibly an example of the very "racial" tolerance that both Pedreira and Barbosa insisted existed on the Island, *Un hombre del pueblo* actually exposes the lie of the idealized Spanish rule and the racial tolerance it attempts to project.

Similar discordance with reality would plague much of the work produced by Pedreira's peers as well, most notably in the essay *"El prejuicio racial en Puerto Rico"* published by Tomás Blanco in 1942, and until recently considered an authoritative discussion of "racial prejudice" on the Island.[64] Already a celebrated author, two years earlier Blanco's *Prontuario histórico de Puerto Rico* had received the award from the Instituto de Literatura Puertorriqueña, bastion of the old Creole elite. It was a fitting tribute to one of their own, a member of the new generation which seemed doomed to inherit neither material nor social wealth. La Generación del treinta would dedicate itself to legitimizing and exalting their predecessors and securing their own future with an ideological vengeance. Speaking for this generation, Blanco will define the Puerto Rican essence as white, Western, Catholic and Spanish.

For Tomás Blanco, independence for the Island is the only way to remain true to this essential Puerto Rican character, and he argues that United States racial views make for a fundamental incompatibility between the two nations. His essay is a study in contrasts, with a benign, innocent Spain counterpoised to the cold and calculating United States. To maintain this dichotomy Blanco plays fast and loose with historical facts, selectively presenting a picture of the old regime that omits any of the complex relations that characterized it. His analysis of contemporary relations between the "races" is then interpreted on the basis of this distorted history.

Blanco's essay dealt with what he considered "virgin" territory, presumably because "[i]n Puerto Rico we still do not know very well what racial prejudice is."[65] This is due to the Puerto Rican tendency to confuse it with "social conventions" that are "not based on skin color or purity of blood, but on individual social status determined by wealth, prestige, culture, education, etc."[66] Acknowledging that the confusion "is natural" given the close correlation between the "disinherited classes" and "colored blood" and that "recognizable African ancestry is among us a shameful obstacle," Blanco moves immediately from these discussions of "social conventions" to the central premise of his essay:

> The United States, and especially those of the South, offer us the most genuine case of the unquestionable existence of prejudice. The prejudice which exists in the United States can thus serve us as a point of comparison, as a specimen for contrast and reference, in attempting to clarify whether genuine racial prejudice truly exists in our Island.[67]

Like Barbosa before him, Blanco sets up the United States as the benchmark for racism. Like Barbosa, Blanco concludes that racism does not exist in Puerto Rico. While Barbosa left open the possibility of its existence, Blanco is convinced that the very nature of Spanish culture makes its existence untenable. To support his position he offers examples that include the lack of correlation between racial terms in the two countries; the more humane treatment of enslaved Africans and their descendants under Spain; and the absence of *de jure* discrimination.

Like subsequent commentators on "race relations" in Puerto Rico, Blanco focuses on slavery, even while emphasizing that Puerto Rico had a relatively small enslaved population. Absent from his discussion is the situation of those (classified) free Blacks and *pardos* who made up the majority of the population throughout the Island's first 350 years. Instead, Blackness and slavery are strictly correlated; if all the Blacks were slaves and there were few slaves, then there were few Blacks.

His discussion on the contemporary manifestations of racism follows the same track. Jim Crow, anti-miscegenation laws, and lynchings are contrasted to the rampant miscegenation and social fraternization which he defines as the rule in Puerto Rico, acknowledging only the isolated incidence-always attributable to North American influence-of racial discrimination. Echoing Barbosa, Blanco dismisses these incidences as the acts of ignorant individuals, and blames racist practices on "pretenders to whiteness." Such practices, according to him, are "foolishness" *(ñoñerías)* engaged in by "persons with certain doubts about their own whiteness."[68] More importantly, any "ill-feeling" that might exist within certain social classes in Puerto Rico is "much more comical, but incomparably less bestial" than the racism of the United States. Consistent with Blanco's tendency to blame the "Other," he also singles out Puerto Rican women, with their "social scruples," as more inclined to practice racism than are men.[69]

For much of his essay, Blanco insists on the significance of miscegenation both as a cultural heritage of racial equality and as a form of immunity against racism. But he also argues for the essential "whiteness" of Puerto Ricans, taking umbrage at the North American suggestion that "Puerto Ricans are black" and that even those of Spanish genealogy are not really "white." Comparing Puerto Rico to the Southern states in direct contradiction to his earlier rejection of the validity of such parallels—Blanco studies the census data at his disposal, and concludes:

> The comparison of these figures cannot permit the conclusion that our Island is black. But conceding that all censuses contain explicable and human errors, and that among the three-fourths of our inhabitants who appear white there is a very small number with a dose or two of colored blood, our people could never seriously be considered as a black community. First, because there is little pure black blood on our Island, and second, because our general culture is white and western, with very few and minor non-Spanish influences.[70]

Blanco precludes any objections to his analysis by discrediting anyone who disagrees as either unauthentically Puerto Rican, emotionally disturbed, culturally deviant, or intellectually deficient. Having determined that racial prejudice is not *really* a problem, he is unsympathetic to any suggestion that it *is* a problem. Puerto Ricans who claim otherwise are tacitly guilty of intellectual acquiescence "to alien judgments," and suffering from a "colonial mentality."[71] In a lengthy final footnote, Blanco refutes the comments of two black critics of his essay by reiterating the "social," as opposed to "racial," nature of prejudice in Puerto Rico and insisting that they could not have experienced the racism that they reported. Blanco also describes one of the two critics as light-complexioned, implying that he is one of those "emotionally disturbed mulattos" who have already been discredited.

Blanco's essay would become the canon on "race relations" in Puerto Rico. Future writers would report on the correlation between class position and color, the personal "prejudices" of certain "individuals" and the negative stereotypes associated with Blackness—and yet insist on the absence of "real" racism on an Island that was "whiter" than any other in the Caribbean, and getting "whiter" by the year. Even among those who acknowledged the discrimination experienced by black Puerto Ricans and professed sympathy for their plight, we find observations such as those expressed by two social scientists at the University of Puerto Rico, who analyzed census data for the period 1860–1935, and concluded that "the colored race will have finally disappeared from Puerto Rico in a period of 75 to 100 more years."[72] The noted linguist Manuel Alvarez Nazario seems particularly wedded to the Blanco construct, prefacing his oft-cited study of African influences in Puerto Rican Spanish with a lengthy disclaimer as to their significance. Alvarez Nazario establishes the "Spanish foundations" of Puerto Rican culture, and the "ideal fraternization of the races," to explain "the minor quantitative and qualitative importance of words of African or Afro-American roots in the Hispanic-Puerto Rican vocabulary."[73] Like Blanco before him, Alvarez Nazario's efforts were rewarded with honors from the Instituto de Literatura Puertorriqueña.

■ *Discovering Zenón and the Consequences*

The ideas postulated by Barbosa and Blanco were not seriously challenged until the early 1970s when the Civil Rights and Black Power movements made many of the fundamental premises of the Puerto Rican racial discourse no longer tenable. With the collapse of de jure segregation in the southern United States, Puerto Ricans could no longer point to lynchings and Jim Crow as characteristic of the "authentic" form of racism. Even more significant was the impact of the Black Power movement, with its emphasis on racial pride and an "in your face" militancy that proclaimed the legitimate right to protest assaults on black dignity.

One of the first serious challenges to the notion of harmonious "race relations" on the Island appeared in 1974, with the publication of Isabelo Zenón Cruz's two-volume study, *Narciso descubre su trasero: El negro en la cultura puertorriqueña*.[74] Beginning with its provocative title, Zenón's book was a stunning indictment of racism in Puerto Rico, a compendium of historical facts, anecdotal accounts, and ironic commentary on a broad range of topics (theory, politics, education, sports, religion, literature, language, folklore and the arts) which seemingly left little room for rebuttal. A university professor of Spanish literature, Zenón was, like Barbosa, an educated and accomplished black man *"del pueblo"* who was influenced by the ideas of his day. Where Barbosa cited Booker T. Washington and W.E.B. DuBois, Zenón would look to Frantz Fanon and Eldridge Cleaver for inspiration and guidance.

Zenón not only documented a long list of abuses perpetrated against Blacks, collectively and individually,—he named names, citing the Island intellectuals, the University of Puerto Rico, each of the Island's major political parties, and the Left, generally, as guilty of repeated acts of discrimination and blatant racism. His intent was no less than to demonstrate that "the black Puerto Rican has always been a second-class Puerto Rican," victim of a "repugnant alienation" that has been "constant, systematic, and all-encompassing."[75] Arguing that within the context of a racist society race assumes primary significance for Blacks, Zenón simultaneously insisted on the Puerto Ricanness of the Island's black population and rejected any notion of *"la gran familia puertorriqueña"* that denied this integral membership in the national whole:

> The black man and woman has not "mixed with us" nor do they "live physically and spiritually with us," because neither the black Antilleans in general nor the black Puerto Rican in particular are strangers in their Caribbean or Boricua land. The French, English or Italian has "mixed with us" but not the black man or woman because they, just like the whites and Indians, are *us*.[76]

Clearly, Zenón was challenging the very meaning of what constitutes "us," but in so doing he is caught between apparently antithetical claims: the Puerto Ricanness of the Island's Blacks (which makes their "race" irrelevant) and Blackness of *all* Puerto Ricans (which makes racism "impossible"), over and against the particularizing of the situation of those deemed "too black" (which makes "race" and racism a very relevant reality.) Put another way, either Blacks are just another shade of Puerto Rican, like any other, or Blacks are distinctive, different—and in their uniqueness, no longer *really* part of the national whole. Or at the very least, "they" are a problematic part the collective "us."

In keeping with his strong attention to popular cultural expressions, Zenón begins his study by making reference to two oft-repeated derogatory adages in a defiant disclaimer:

> *"no lo voy a hacer ni a la entrada ni a la salida. Entiendase bien, no sólo. Porque lo haré a lo largo de toda la disertación. Tampoco derramaré únicamente el caldo. Se volcarán cosas más cálidas y sustanciosas."*[77]

This opening statement dramatically contextualizes Zenón's voice within the racial discourse, and attests to his vulnerability as a black man exposing the myth of Puerto Rican racial harmony. He fully expects to be dismissed as a troublemaker, capable only of making a mess of things and undeserving of serious attention. Thus Zenón is acknowledging—if not actually predicting—that the very racism he is attacking can also be employed to si-

■ *Barbosa at the University of Michigan*

lence him. Indeed, he was not far off the mark: save for a rash of newspaper and magazine articles immediately after the release of the book's first volume, there was little serious engagement of the "hot and substantial things" put forth by Zenón. Predictably sympathetic noises were made by most commentators, while some expressed outrage that such a book had ever seen the light of day. But barely a dent was made in the image of Puerto Ricans as "essentially white" (or, at least, "white enough"), and of Puerto Rico as a place basically unhampered by racism.[78]

Like the two black critics silenced by Tomás Blanco in a footnote, Zenón has met a similarly dismissive fate. The revisionist scholarship of the past two decades has largely failed to address directly either historical or contemporary racism and its role in Puerto Rican society. Indeed, the continued emphasis on slavery and musical expression as the fundamental definers of Puerto Rican "Blackness" has left unchallenged the broader understanding of what constitutes the "real" Puerto Rican nation. In a similar vein, the few discussions of "race relations" continue to project a cozy image of harmony and color-blind fellowship. For example, in her sole reference to Isabelo Zenón, (ironically enough, confined to a footnote) sociologist Clara Rodríguez concedes only that

> *it is possible* that in Puerto Rico, the degree of race consciousness *may be* positively related to the degree of visibility. Thus, there *may be* a gradient in which the lighter or less visible one is, the less the perception and experience of discrimination and prejudice in Puerto Rico. Similarly, the greater the visibility, the greater the experience.[79] (emphasis added)

What the "visibly" black man or women "experiences" is racism, and it makes him or her "invisible" as a Puerto Rican. For the black Puerto Ricans who have periodically dared to dispute the fictional image of the homogeneous and harmonious *gran familia* construct, that experience with racism has included further exclusion. So-called racial mixture, far from eliminating racism, has made invisible those whose faces still say "Africa," and thus made them complicit, for the sake of "the family," in their continued subordination. In the race toward "whiteness," black Puerto Ricans have been denied full and dignified membership in *la familia*, their presence—as so concisely portrayed in Fortunato Vizcarrondo's *¿Y tu agüela 'ónde ehtá?*—confined to the kitchen when company comes.[80] ∎

ENDNOTES

1 In Puerto Rico, "racial prejudice" is popularly conceived of as simply a matter of personal predilection, without any acknowledgment of the racist (usually negative) stereotypes that inform the preference. It is commonly understood and accepted, for example, that "straight hair" (*pelo lacio*) is preferable to very curly or "kinky" hair; indeed the latter is considered "bad hair" (*pelo malo*) that must be "fixed." Similarly, most other phenotypic features that are identified with "Blackness" are deemed inferior; by extension, it is believed that the bearers of these inferior physical traits are "naturally" imbued with inferior intellectual and emotional characteristics.

2 Luis M. Díaz Soler, *Historia de la esclavitud negra en Puerto Rico*, Río Piedras: Editorial Universitaria, 1970.

3 Díaz was clearly referring to the number of *slaves* and not to the population classified as Black or *mulato* which, in fact, made up the majority of the island's inhabitants until the 1860 census. Díaz and Alegría's remarks are contained in Peggy Ann Bliss, "Black, White, Puerto Rican All Over," *The San Juan Star*, March 22, 1995, pp. 30-31.

4 For a discussion of the exceptionalist logic that informs Latin American racial discourse see Michael Hanchard, "Taking Exception: Race and the Limits of Liberal Nationalism in Cuba, Mexico and Brazil," paper presented at the Latin American Studies Association 1992 Conference.

5 The most significant among these "exceptions" is the two-volume study by Isabelo Zenón Cruz, *Narciso descubre su trasero*, Humacao, Puerto Rico: Editorial Furidi, 1974. Other challenges to the myth of racial harmony in Puerto Rico include Maxine W. Gordon, "Race Patterns and Prejudice in Puerto Rico," *American Sociological Review*, 1949; Samuel Betances, "The Prejudice of Having No

Prejudice," *The Rican*, Winter 1972, pp. 41-55, Spring 1973, pp. 22-37; Martin Sagrera, *Racismo y política en Puerto Rico: La desintegración interna y external de un pueblo*, Río Piedras, Puerto Rico: Editorial Edil, Inc., 1973; and Luis Nieves Falcón, "La ruta del legado colonial," in *La Tercera Raíz: Presencia Africana en Puerto Rico*, San Juan: Comisión Puertorriqueña para la Celebración del Quinto Centenario del Descubrimiento de América y Puerto Rico, 1993.

6   An example is the following explanation given by sociologist Clara Rodríquez: "On a social level...Hispanics have a different conception of race, one that is as much cultural or 'social' as it is racial." In *Puerto Ricans: Born in the U.S.A.*, Boston: Unwin Hyman, 1989, p.66.

7   One is "Black" in Puerto Rico depending on the degree of conformity to the stereotype of the "pure African," i.e., having physical features which include tightly curled hair, broad nose, full lips, and dark skin color. Even when all the phenotypical criteria seem to fit the stereotype, few Puerto Ricans (past or present) identify, or are identified by Puerto Ricans, as African. Traditionally, those who were perceived as "too black" were suspected of being "from the islands," i.e. from other (usually English-speaking) Caribbean countries, and thus, not authentically Puerto Rican. More recently, however, and as a consequence of the growing numbers of people from the Dominican Republic who have settled on the island, Black Puerto Ricans are increasingly identified specifically as Dominicans.

8   Regrettably, I have not been able to discover any early writings by women that directly address questions of "race" and racism in Puerto Rico. Indeed, sensitivity to the subject is so great that one of the few contemporary accounts, included in a feminist anthology (Angela Jorge, "The Black Puerto Rican Woman in Contemporary American Society," in *The Puerto Rican Woman*, Edna Acosta-Belén, ed., New York: Praeger Publishers, 1979, pp. 134-141) was eliminated from the Spanish translation published in Puerto Rico. See Edna Acosta-Belén, ed. *La mujer en la sociedad puertorriqueña*, Río Piedras: Ediciones Huracán, 1980.

9   Francisco Moscoso, *Tribu y clases en el Caribe antiguo*, San Pedro de Macorís, República Dominicana: Ediciones de la Universidad Central del Este, 1986, pp. 408-410.

10 I make this observation fully cognizant of the prevailing argument which "explains" the apparent "whitening" of Puerto Rico by focusing on the 19th century open-door policy adopted by Spain to encourage European immigration to the island. During the period 1812 (just prior to enactment of the *Cédula de Gracias*), and 1846 (when Puerto Rico experienced its greatest population increase of 64%), there is, in fact, an insignificant growth in the number of those classified as "white": this group goes from representing 47% of the total, to comprising 48.8% of the island's inhabitants. *Pardos* and *negros*, free and enslaved, continued to maintain their numerical and proportional dominance until 1860, when "whites" represented 51.5% of the total population. The relative insignificance of European immigration is suggested by Picó, who calculates that if we accept the most inflated figures for Puerto Rico's population of "indios," (1.4% of the island's total in 1802) their descendants are "potentially greater than those of 19th century minority immigrant groups." See Fernándo Picó, *Historia general de Puerto Rico*, Río Piedras: Ediciones Huracán, 1988, p.57.

11 As reported by Fray Iñigo Abbad, *Noticias de la historia geográfica, civil, y política de Puerto Rico*, originally published in Madrid in 1788 and reprinted in Kal Waggenheim and Olga Jiménez de Waggenheim (eds.) *The Puerto Ricans: A Documentary History*, Princeton and New York: Markus Weiner Publishers, p. 27.

12 A by-product of minimizing the African/Black presence has been the exaggeration of the Taíno presence. Documentation on the Indian population is clearly unreliable, as the following suggests: the official Spanish census of 1530 reported 1,148 "indios" on the island; the historian Fernándo Picó reports that the 1802 census counted 2,300 "indios"—all residing in the southwestern town of San Germán, the first of the Spanish settlements. If we consider the devastating consequences for the Taínos of close contact with the Spaniards, it is highly unlikely that any Indians would have survived almost 300 years in San Germán, and no where else. Picó reports that after 1802 "indios" were counted as "pardos." op cit., p.57.

13 During the period 1795-1873 there were over twenty planned slave rebellions, most along the northern coast of Puerto Rico. Much more commonplace was *cimarronaje*, the escape into the hinterland or to distant towns where a Black man or woman could "disappear" among the general population. See Guillermo A. Baralt, *Esclavos rebeldes: conspiraciones y sublevaciones de esclavos, 1795-1873*, Río Piedras: Ediciones Huracán, 1981.

14 The very term *criollo* would reflect this growing national Puerto Rican identity. Originally used to denote the children of Spaniards born on the island, by 1788, when the first comprehensive history of Puerto Rico was published, Europeans were designated simply as *blancos* or "*hombres de la otra banda*" [men of the other band] and *criollo* had come to refer to the islander, i.e. the native Puerto Rican. See "Criollos" and "Blancos," in Waggenheim and Jiménez de Waggenheim, op cit., p.33

15 André Pierre Ledru, *Viaje a la isla de Puerto Rico*, (translated by Julio L. De Vizcarrondo), San Juan: University of Puerto Rico, 1935, p.75.

16. The caste system operated throughout the Spanish colonies, although it took different forms. In Puerto Rico, there were fewer caste terms than those used in South America, which probably reflected the absence of Indians on the island. The most commonly used terms, both in official documents and in daily life, were *blanco/a*, *mulato/a*, *pardo/a*, and *negro/a*. One caste term that underwent an intriguing reconfiguration is "*jíbaro*," defined in the early 18th century as someone descended from any of the following combinations: *calpamulo/a* and *indio/a*; *africano/a* and *indio*; *calpamul/a* and *albarazado/a*; *lobo/a* and *chino/a*; *barcino/a* and *indio/a*; *tente en el aire* and *lobo/a*. Each of these terms (with the exception of *indio* and *africano*), in turn, referred to other caste combinations; conspicuously absent—or very far in the background—is any reference to European ancestry. Still, since the late 18th century, a Puerto Rican *jíbaro* has been understood to be "White."

17. In Waggenheim and Jiménez de Waggenheim, op cit., p.34.

18. ibid., pp. 261-272.

19. Term used by Michael Jiménez in his discussion of relations between Colombian peasant women and landowners, quoted in Hanchard, op. cit., p. 12.

20. Until the early 19th century, manumission was a common practice of the slaveowners who fathered children with enslaved women and this has been hailed as an indication of the benevolence of the Spanish slave system. David Brion Davis in *Problems of Slavery in Western Culture*, offers a more persuasive explanation: "Such planters [who freed their mixed children and grandchildren] were unmoved by the plight of slaves or by the degraded position of their mulattos. Always one's own children or grandchildren deserved special consideration, for they were far superior to others of their class; they were of good character and had benefited from Christian training." (p.281) Economic imperatives, however, were able to override even these egocentric motivations; once slave labor became of fundamental importance for the developing sugar plantations of the 19th century the frequency of manumissions declined significantly,

21. López Cantos, in Jalil Sued Badillo and Angel López Cantos, *Puerto Rico Negro*, Río Piedras: Editorial Cultural, 1986, p.292.

22. López Cantos, p.245

23. López Cantos, p.244.

24. Quoted in José C. Rosario, *Historical Development of the Jibaro of Puerto Rico*, San Juan: University of Puerto Rico, 1935, p.75.

25. Denied education and confined to the private world of the family, women had few opportunities for improving their situation beyond marital/sexual alliances.

26. In the town of Utuado, Pedro Avilés and Andrea Cruz had ten children during the first decades of the 19th century; the marriages of two sons and one daughter were listed in the parish's registry for *pardos* while two other sons had theirs registered in the ledger for *blancos*. Fernándo Picó, *Amargo café*, Río Piedras: Ediciones Huracán, 1981, p.113. Utuado, traditionally perceived as a "White town"— as are all towns in the mountainous interior—was founded in 1739 by a group which "possibly" included a majority of *pardos libres*, i.e. free mulattos. See Picó, *Historia....*, p.108.

27. Parts of this "letter to Demetria" (1879) are quoted in Robert H. Todd, "La vida gloriosa de Ramón Emeterio Betances," *El Mundo*, 11 de abril de 1937, and in Luis M. Díaz Soler, op. cit., p.369.

28. The decree abolishing slavery in Puerto Rico, approved by the Spanish courts on March 22, 1873, did not bring immediate emancipation. Slaves were required to enter into labor contracts with their masters, another property owner or the state, for a period of no less than three years; their full political rights would not be recognized until 1878. See Díaz Soler, *Historia de la esclavitud....*, pp.344-345.

29. Letter to Jules Auguste, published in *Les détracteurs de la race noire et de la Republique d'Haiti*, (Paris: Marpon et Flammarion, 1882), and reprinted in Ramón Emeterio Betances, *Las antillas para los antillanos*, San Juan de Puerto Rico: Instituto de Cultura, 1975, p.96. The Haitian intellectuals included Jules Auguste, Dántes Sabourin, Arthur Bowler, Clément Denis, and Louis-Joseph Janvier.

30. ibid., p.100.

31. These sentiments, expressed by Major General Nelson A. Miles, commander of the invading forces, just four days after the landing of the U.S. troops, would continue to characterize the North American attitude toward its new colony. For full text of Miles' proclamation, see "To the Inhabitants of Puerto Rico," in Waggenheim and Jiménez de Waggenheim, op cit. pp. 95-96. For a discussion of the "Othering" of the "natives," see Kelvin A. Santiago-Valles, *"Subject People" and Colonial Discourses: Economic Transformation and Social Disorder in Puerto Rico, 1898-1947*, Albany: State University of New York Press, 1994.

32. William S. Bryan, ed. *Our Islands and Their People, as seen with Camera and Pencil*, New York: n.d., Thompson Publishing Co., 1899, p.297.

33 ibid., p.287

34 Henna expresses particular outrage that "the heterogeneous, rowdy and primitive" Hawaiian islanders, and the Mexican "greasers" of New Mexico should enjoy civil and political rights denied to Puerto Ricans. One of the most important leaders of the exiled anti-colonial movement, Henna had worked in political clubs alongside a number of Black Puerto Ricans in New York City, among them Sotero Figueroa and Arturo Alfonso Schomburg. The document, signed by other prominent Puerto Ricans, was originally published as *Appeal of the People of Puerto Rico to the People of the United States*; it has been translated as *"Al pueblo norteamericano,"* in Aarón Gamaliel Ramos, ed. *Las ideas anexionistas en Puerto Rico bajo la dominación norteamericana*, Río Piedras: Ediciones Huracán, 1987, pp. 65-72.

35 Ramón de Castro Rivera's letter elicited a strongly worded response from the radical labor leader, Ramón Romero Rosa. See "A los negros puertorriqueños," originally published in *La Miseria*, March 29, 1901, in History Task Force/Centro de Estudios Puertorriqueños, *Sources for the Study of Puerto Rican Migration, 1879-1930*, Hunter College of the City University of New York, n.d., p.30.

36 Barbosa studied at the Roman Catholic Seminario Conciliar de San Juan where, according to his biographer, he was "one of the few students of color who warmed those benches." (p.16) In an 1896 response to a particularly virulent racist attack ("No está en la cierto," *El País*, 29 de septiembre de 1896), Barbosa writes that he "opened the doors" of the Seminary, suggesting that he was the first "hombre de color" to study at that institution. Biographical information is primarily taken from Antonio S. Pedreira, *Un hombre del pueblo: José Celso Barbosa*, San Juan de Puerto Rico: Imprenta Venezuela, 1937.

37 Reminiscent of an oft-quoted story regarding the onset of Puerto Rican bibliophile and lay historian Arturo Alfonso Schomburg's interest in Black history (in reply to his questions about Black achievements a teacher presumably scoffed that Black people had no history,) Pedreira describes a classroom scene in which a priest asks his students what careers they plan to pursue. When Barbosa volunteers that he wants to be an attorney, the Jesuit laughs and replies, "You must mean a jailhouse lawyer!" Years later the same priest explained to the successful physician that the remark had been meant to "motivate" him in his studies. See Pedreira, p.19.

38 The first African American was admitted into the University of Michigan in 1869. In 1875, Barbosa was the first Puerto Rican to attend and, in 1903, the first to receive an honorary Master of Arts degree from the University at Ann Arbor.

39 The Carroll Commission Report described their meeting with representatives of Puerto Rico's labor movement; seven of the nine leaders were "colored men." Henry K. Carroll, *Report on the Island of Porto Rico*, Washington, D.C.: Government Printing Office, 1989, p.51.

40 For an analysis of the first years of colonial politics under United States domination, see Mariano Negrón Portillo, *Las turbas republicanas, 1900-1904*, Río Piedras: Ediciones Huracán, 1990.

41 The Republican Party attracted many Black Puerto Ricans to its ranks, including the attorney and teacher Eugenio LeCompte, who studied with Booker T. Washington and W.E.B. DuBois; Eulalio García Lascot, who received his medical degree at Howard University; and the labor leader, attorney, and writer Pedro Carlos Timothée, who corresponded with Arturo Alfonso Schomburg.

42 See note 14, above.

43 Pilar Barbosa de Rosario (comp.), *Problema de Razas: Documentos para la historia*, San Juan de Puerto Rico: Imprenta Venezuela, 1937. See Introduction, pp. 7-8,14.

44 Barbosa is already expressing, in 1896, his "enthusiasm for democratic principles, the only ones which have been able to help us to partly realize the beautiful dreams and beloved illusions of an awakened spirit." For full text, see "No está en lo cierto," ibid., pp. 25-28.

45 "El problema del color," originally published in *El Tiempo*, July 30, 1909, ibid., p.33.

46 "No está en lo cierto," ibid., p.26.

47 "Negrofobia," originally published in *El Tiempo*, July 28, 1920, ibid., p.19-20.

48 In his writings Barbosa often referred to himself in the third person. While this may have been simply a stylistic preference, it seems feasible that his language offered an aura of objectivity he deemed necessary when discussing issues as sensitive as racism and annexation.

49 *Problema de razas*, p.12.

50 ibid., p.21

51 Washington's speech included the following lines: "In all things that are purely social we can be as separate as the fingers, yet one as the hand in all things essential to mutual progress.... The wisest among my race understand that the agitation of questions of social equality is the extremist folly, and that progress in the enjoyment of all privileges that will come to us must be the result of severe and

constant struggle rather than of artificial forcing." For full text, see *Vital issues: The Journal of African American Speeches*, Vol. iv, No.3, 1994, pp. 34-36.

52 Problema de razas, p.31-32.

53 ibid., p.31-32.

54 ibid., p.38

55 Quoted in Gladys Jiménez-Muñoz, *"A Storm Dressed in Skirts:" Ambivalence in the Debate on Woman's Suffrage in Puerto Rico, 1927-1929*, 1993, mss., p.89.

56 Puerto Rico contributed more soldiers to the war than 25 states. The 375, Puerto Rico's "colored" Regiment, received the financial and personal support of Barbosa and other Black Puerto Ricans. For an interview with Barbosa's Daughter, Pilar, see Peggy Ann Bliss, "The island deals with race bias during WWI," *The San Juan Star*, Sunday Magazine, July 14, 1991, pp. 20-21.

57 *Problema....*, p.106

58 *Problema....*, pp. 131-132.

59 *Problema....*, p.157.

60 ibid., p.142

61 *Piti* is most probably a corruption of the French "petite."

62 *Un hombre del pueblo....*, p.

63 Juan Flores, "The Insular Vision: Pedreira and the Puerto Rican Misere," in *Divided Borders: Essays on Puerto Rican Identity*, Houston: Arte Público Press, 1993, p.55.

64 Blanco actually presented his essay before the Institución Hispano-Cubana de Cultura in Havana in 1937, the same year that Pedreira's biography of Barbosa was completed. See Tomás Blanco, *El prejuicio racial en Puerto Rico, con estudio preliminar de Arcadio Díaz Quiñones*, (Río Piedras: Ediciones Huracán, 1985) for the full text and a discussion of the central ideas of Blanco's essay.

65 ibid., p.105.

66 ibid.

67 ibid.

68 ibid., p.126

69 ibid., p.129

70 ibid., p.133. Similar claims have, of course, been made since then, sometimes in the least expected of places.

71 ibid., p.139.

72 José Colombán Rosario and Justina Carrión, *El Negro: Haití, Estados Unidos y Puerto Rico*, San Juan: Universidad de Puerto Rico, 1940, p.141.

73 Manuel Alvarez Nazario, *El elemento Afronegroide en el español de Puerto Rico: Contribución al estudio del negro en América* (San Juan de Puerto Rico: Instituto de Cultura Puertorriqueña, 1974, [1961]), p.229.

74 Isabelo Zenón Cruz, *Narciso descubre su trasero: El negro en la cultura puertorriqueña*, Humacao, Puerto Rico: Editorial Furidi, 1974. The title, according to Zenón, refers to his understanding that "the attempt to alienate the black man(sic) has been integral: both his(sic) body and 'soul' have been clumsily deprecated; they have converted the black man(sic) into a strange Narcissus who, far from discovering his face, discovers his behind." p.343.

75 ibid., p.24

76 ibid., p.47

77 ibid., p.21.

78 Two years after Zenón's *Narciso*, the island's medical establishment published, "as a special contribution to the celebrations...[around] the Centennial of the Abolition of Slavery," a book by Dr. S. Arana-Soto, which testily dismisses any suggestion that anything other than racial harmony reigns in Puerto Rico. Reiterating many of the arguments contained in Blanco's essay, Arana-Soto concludes that "The black [man or woman] is accepted, but not welcome: what more does [he or she] want? The important thing is to be accepted." *Puerto Rico: Sociedad sin razas*, San Juan: Asociación Médica de Puerto Rico, 1976, p.33.

79 Zenón, p.78.

80 Fortunato Vizcarrondo, *Dinga y Mandinga (Poemas)*, San Juan de Puerto Rico: Instituto de Cultura Puertorriqueña, 1976.

Domestic Work and Racial
Divisions in Women's Employment
in Puerto Rico, 1899 – 1930

ELIZABETH CRESPO

The analysis of domestic work forces us to look at the inequalities of race and gender and leads to an examination of the multiplicity of experiences that have configured the history of women and work.

Scholarship on women and work in Puerto Rico during the early decades of this century has focused on the dramatic increase in women's labor force participation, in particular on women's work in the needle and garment industries.[1] Little attention has been paid to domestic service,[2] which was the main source of employment for women during the first two decades of this century.[3] In fact, in 1899, 78 percent of employed women were domestic service workers, and in 1930, domestic service was still the source of employment for 30 percent of women who worked for wages or their equivalent.[4] Research on this topic and other realms of women's work may point to a much more diverse female labor force than is reflected by the literature on this period.

As we will see, the analysis of domestic work is also important because it was a much more significant source of employment for black than for white women. White women moved out of domestic work and into manufacturing at a much faster pace than black women did, preserving marked distinctions between the proportions of white and black women in domestic and manufacturing employment. The focus on domestic also work points to differences in the timing of the incorporation of black and white women into the labor force. The most dramatic growth in women's labor force participation rates during this period occurred among white women and among women who lived outside the major cities. Data presented in this paper will show that in the three largest cities of the Island, particularly in San Juan, black women had already been massively incorporated into the labor force by 1899. Differences in the experiences of black and white women have been given very little attention in Puerto Rican women's labor history. This essay contributes to fill this gap.

An analysis of census data between 1899 and 1930 offers a rare opportunity to examine racial differences in the labor force. After the census of 1930, data on occupations are not presented by race. While some censuses present data for black, mulatto, and white, the only racial classifications that were carried consistently through all four censuses were white

---

ELIZABETH CRESPO is Assistant Professor in the Department of Puerto Rican Studies at John Jay College of Criminal Justice, City University of New York. She was a Faculty Fellow at the Centro de Estudios Puertorriqueños during the spring of 1996. Thanks to the members of the Editorial Board of *CENTRO, Journal of the Centro de Estudios Puertorriqueños*, in particular to Amílcar Tirado Avilés, for their comments during the preparation of this paper.

and black (or colored). Consequently white and black are the racial categories used in this paper.

Definitions of white and black used by the U.S. Census are consistent with the prevailing notions of racial purity and impurity in America at this time. In the census of 1920, for example, the instructions were to "report as "black" all full-blooded Negroes and as "mulatto" all Negroes having some proportion of white blood."[5] Given these instructions, the distinctions between white, black, and mulatto made in the collection of data depended largely on the judgment of the enumerators. The category "mulatto" presented particular difficulties both in Puerto Rico and the United States. In the United States it was found that black enumerators classified a greater proportion of blacks as mulattos than did white enumerators. The latter were more reluctant to classify black people as mulattos, preferring to classify them as black.[6]

In Puerto Rico the census questionnaire was administered in Spanish, and the enumerators were Puerto Rican. Thus, the numbers of individuals placed in each category are based on the perceptions of blackness and whiteness that predominated in Puerto Rico at that time. Here a situation similar to the one above was observed in the census of 1899, where teachers (92 percent of whom were classified as white[7]) would categorize children as black even as those same children were reported as *mestizos* by their parents.[8] By identifying as black the children who were considered of mixed race by their parents, some white teachers may have been attempting to distance themselves and white students from mulattos and *mestizos*, whose skin color socially represented a threat to white notions of racial purity. On the other hand, the desire to whiten the family lineage may have been present on the part of children's parents.

López Cantos comments, in relation to 18th century Puerto Rico, that whites seemed to loath mulattos even more than they did blacks.[9] In terms of skin color mulattos approximated closely the social status of whites, but many were slaves. Whites felt the need to distance themselves from mulattos, who, many whites felt threatened the purity of their race because they aspired be integrated into white society and frequently falsified documents to do so. The detailed racial classifications in Puerto Rico reveal this social dynamic in which whites attempted to preserve notions of racial purity associated on the one hand and persons of mixed background aspired to "whiten the race" *(blanquear la raza)* on the other. This is one of the driving forces of the extensively detailed distinctions made according to tonalities of skin color, texture of hair, facial features, wealth, prestige, and context of the interaction, among others. It resulted in an exquisite demarcation of categories such as *negro, blanco, trigueño, trigueñito, indio, moreno, prieto, jabao*, etc.[10]

The process of "whitening" in Puerto Rico is revealed in the data from 1897–1940. The census of 1899 shows an increase of 2.8 percent in the white population, a 25.8 percent increase in the mulatto population, and a decrease of 21.6 percent in the black population in a period of only two years. Between 1899 and 1940 census numbers show a decline in the percentage of black and mulattos from 38 to 23 percent of the total population.[11] Although the census data have ambiguities and limitations as illustrated by the previous examples, the information reveals some interesting distinctions between black and white women in the labor force that are consonant with other historical data presented in this paper.

■ *Domestic work and constructions of "other" under Spanish rule*

To address the significance of the patterns of employment, it is important to describe first the social stigmas historically associated with domestic work. A review of this history reveals ways in which domestic labor has been tied to sexual exploitation and constructions of deviance associated with race, sexuality, religion, the supernatural, and women's traditional roles as healers.

During the first half of the sixteenth century the dream of many who migrated to the Caribbean from Spain was to live in an island rich with gold, fertile lands, a warm climate, and an abundance of slaves who would cultivate the land and serve them. This was not only the dream of the *hidalgos* from the upper echelons of Spanish society; in deed, it was the ideal of Spaniards of all social classes. In fact, according to the census of 1530, almost all

Spanish residents of Puerto Rico had slaves. Even poor Spaniards tried to reproduce the social status of the wealthy by owning slaves. Thus butchers, tailors, and barbers, people who it would seem could scarcely afford to own slaves, were in fact slave owners. In years of great economic hardship, very frequently many poor residents fled with their slaves and their debts. Although in Andalusian society people of many social strata had slaves, the proportion of slave owners in the Caribbean was much larger.[12]

Undoubtedly the idea of an abundance of female domestic servants was part of the paradise that Spaniards dreamed of reaching in the Caribbean. Domestic slaves were a sign of material privilege. Since the early days of Spanish colonization, black and indigenous women, both free and enslaved, and poor white women formed part of the pool of workers from which this labor was supplied. Nonetheless, enslaved women were the preferred source of labor.

Indigenous and black women slaves were used widely as domestic servants by their owners and were also bought to hire out as domestic workers. In fact, the use of domestic workers was so extensive that the Spanish crown considered it excessive because it created an environment in which lack of work and discipline enabled slaves to become too intimate with their masters, and consequently lazy and prone to vice.[13] The pervasiveness of this idea is illustrated by the fact that it was reproduced in texts by some Puerto Rican authors, particularly before the 1970s. These writers argued that slavery in Puerto Rico was benign because the majority of African slaves were domestic workers.[14]

Nevertheless, the historical record shows that the popular perception of slaveas as familiar, lazy. and steeped in comfort was deceptive. Domestic work performed by women involved cooking, cleaning, care of domestic animals, processing of food, and manufacture of household items. Domestic duties also entailed the role of wet nurse and nanny. Harsh working conditions were imposed on slaves, who were often severely and cruelly punished. Added to this mistreatment was the use of women slaves as sexual property. Rape was a form of establishing the power of the white man and the slave owner over black women. Daughters of slaves were reserved for the first sexual relations of the sons of their owners. Nevertheless, rape was not a term applied to slave women. The term used was prostitution or *"amancebamiento"* ("concubinage"). In this way, black women were seen as the initiators of sexual relations with white men and treated as savage and nonhuman. The perception of black women as animals eliminated, in the owners eyes, the possibility that their sexual exploitation could be considered rape.[15]

The Catholic church was aware of the sexual exploitation of black women and spoke of how slave owners *"usan mal del dominio que en ellas tienen"*[16] ("misused the control they had over them"), yet the church did not label it as such. Instead bishops expressed concern over the number of slave women who were *"amancebamientos."* Although a nominal fine was placed on slave owners, the burden of sexual relations was squarely placed on the slave women. The burden of responsibility was made especially clear when an ordinance was passed whereby slave women who died while giving birth to children conceived in sin would not receive a Catholic burial and those who accompanied her body would be excommunicato. In this way the myths that associating black women with promiscuity, immorality, voluptuousness, sexual potency, sexual freedom, and abandonment were used to dehumanize them and perpetuate their sexual exploitation with impunity. The bias against slave women perpetuated by these myths was also applied to free black and mulatta women. An example of this is found in the explicit extension of this ordinance to include free black and mulatta, but not white, women.[17]

Although racist constructions of black female sexuality allowed masters to exploit them sexually and reap the benefits of their labor, this otherness was also feared. black and indigenous women were seen as having the power to perform enchantments through sexual relations to harm their masters.[18] This was the flip side to their otherness, which assigned them the power of the supernatural. As a result, these women were feared and seen as a threat to the status quo.

Clerics were notoriously involved in the sexual exploitation of indigenous and black women in the Caribbean and Latin America. They either directly acquired women slaves as their personal servants or, under the guise of teaching women catechism or imposing penance for their sins, forced them to serve as laborers, mistresses, and prostitutes.[19]

Very often the sin that indigenous and black women were accused of committing was witchcraft. African and indigenous religious expressions were important targets of the Spanish Inquisition in the Caribbean. Men and women were accused of being sorcerers and were persecuted by both ecclesiastical and secular courts.[20] The persecution of practices labeled *"brujería"* ("witchcraft") and *"hechicería"* ("sorcery") had among its first victims freed black women. In 1578 the bishop of Salamanca requested the presence of the office of Inquisitor *"por la gran fama de hechicerías y grandes indicios de brujas que existían en la Isla"* ("because of the fame of witchcraft and great evidence of witches on the Island").[21] A number of years later, in 1591, the Inquisition ordered the burning of four black women slaves for having repeated the offense of holding religious activities in which they invoked the devil.[22]

To some degree these stigmas were tempered with the end of the Inquisition and the abolition of slavery. Nevertheless, these ideas continued to color the perceptions of domestic work and of poor, destitute, black, and indigenous women. To this day the images that associate black women with domestic work are used to establish differences between the status of black and white women.

Evidence of the continued presence of black women in domestic service is available in the 18th and 19th centuries. Although the data are not extensive, the presence of a growing number of women in San Juan, in particular black women, was noted in census data during the 18th century. Considering the limited economic opportunities for women it is assumed that many of them were domestic workers.[23]

More data are accessible for the 19th century. The census of 1846 indicates that four of five women who were listed as workers in San Juan were *parda*, mulatta or black. Many of them prepared food in establishments that catered to travelers, soldiers and sailors. Others were *mondongueras*, women who prepared *mondongo*, a tripe soup. These shops were considered suspicious by the authorities, who viewed them as potential meeting places for runaway slaves and other delinquents. While seamstresses tended to be of higher social status, many owning their own homes and earning higher wages, laundresses, servants, and cooks were most often of lower class and racial status. At least one third of laundresses were slaves. Some worked for the families that owned them while others also sold their services as a source of extra income. Some worked in military, state, or church institutions. Laundresses, who gathered at wells or springs to do their work, made colonial officials uneasy because as black women they were suspicious of subversive activities. They were also considered promiscuous since their business required them to be outside their house, enter the homes of clients, or pass through city streets unaccompanied. Often they were objects of verbal and physical sexual abuse.[24]

■ *Domestic work in early twentieth century Puerto Rico*

The information presented above on mid-19th century San Juan confirms the U.S. census data of 1899, which indicates that a large proportion of women in San Juan and Ponce, in particular black women, already formed part of the paid work force. Thus, one of the major changes in women's work during the first three decades of the 20th century in Puerto Rico was the rapid incorporation of women who lived outside the major cities, white women, and married women into the paid work force. As a result of the restructuring of the Island's economy, male workers were displaced while new sectors of women who had previously not worked for wages in large numbers increasingly became an important source of cheap labor. Labor force participation rates of women 10 years old and over climbed from 14 to 22.9 percent, while those of men declined from 83 percent to 69.5 percent.[25]

Notwithstanding the significance of this overall trend, we will focus our attention on the small but significant sector of women who at the turn of the century were already working for pay, primarily as domestic servants. Their importance goes beyond their numbers. The composition of this group is more revealing of its significance: 79 percent were single or widowed,[26] and a large proportion worked in the cities and were black. The proportion of women who worked in the cities was two and a half times larger than the proportion who worked in the rest of the Island. Here 26 percent of women worked for pay. In 1899, one-fifth of black women were already in the paid labor force, almost double the proportion of white women. The gap between the proportion of white and black women who worked outside the home increased steadily with age.[27] Although the proportion of black women in the labor force increased between 1899 and 1930, a more dramatic growth occurred among white women. While the percentage of black women ten years and older who worked in gainful occupations increased from 19 to 27 percent, the proportion of white women more than doubled rising from 10 to 21 percent.[28]

When we compare the growth in women's labor force participation in the cities with that of women in the rest of the Island, we find that the differences between the two localities gradually diminish during the period betwwn 1899 and 1930. Nevertheless, in 1930, the proportion of women working in gainful occupations in the cities remains approximately one and a half times higher thanthat of women working in the rest of the island. In 1899, 33 percent of women ten years and older in San Juan and Ponce worked for wages or an equivalent, compared with 13 percent in the rest of the Island. In 1930 the percentage of women workers in San Juan, Ponce, and Mayagüez had only risen slightly to 34 percent, while in the rest of the Island we observe a substantial increase to 21 percent.[29]

In the largest cities there were marked differences in the proportion of black and white women in the labor force. For example, in San Juan in 1899, 42 percent of black women ten years of age and over were in the labor force, compared with only 15 percent of white women. In 1930, the labor force participation rate of black women in San Juan was 40 percent, compared with 26 percent for white women.[30] The data for working women in Ponce and Mayagüez reveal a similar pattern, indicating that in the major cities black women's labor force participation rates did not increase during this period and were maintained at around 40 percent. In contrast, labor force participation rates for white women in the major cities almost doubled.

The data also show that labor force participation rates of white women in the cities were higher than those of their counterparts in the Island as a whole. In both 1899 and 1930 labor force participation rates for white women in the major cities were 5 percentage points higher than those of all white women in the Island.[31]

Moving from rural areas to the cities or from small Island towns to the capital often meant that women had to work as domestics because it was the kind of work most often available. As with many others, the woman who narrates her story below stopped working outside the home when she got married. Nevertheless, the economic hardship she encountered when her family moved to the capital forced her to start working outside the home once more.

> Cuando me casé en Comerío dejé de trabajar en el tabaco. Nos mudamos para San Juan y allí fue que empecé a trabajar lavando y planchando. Vinimos buscando ambiente. El esposo mío no encontraba trabajo allá y consiguió trabajo por acá. Primero él se quedaba por acá trabajando y después yo me vine. Yo cuando me mude pa'cá tenía dos hijos y estaba en cinta del hijo mayor varón. A veces las cosas se nos ponían un poquito difícil y yo me iba a las casas de los ricos a lavar y a planchar. Era lo único que yo sabía. Vivíamos en una barriada y dormíamos en el piso, y yo para ayudarlo, me fui a lavar y a planchar y a hacer lo que pudiera hacer.

> *When I got married in Comerío I stopped working in tobacco. It was when we moved to San Juan that I started washing and ironing. We came here (to San Juan) looking for better days. My husband couldn't find work and he found a job here. First he came then I followed. When I moved we had two children and I was pregnant. Sometimes things got a little hard and I would go to the rich people's houses to wash and iron. It was the only thing I knew how to do. We slept on the floor, so I would help my husband out by washing and ironing and doing whatever I could.* Inés, Interview by the author, San Juan, April 1996.

Some women moved to the cities because their husbands died or abandoned them. To provide for their children, they would leave them with a relative, move to the city, and live with the family they worked for. Work was arduous, and, as in the case narrated below, some girl children left behind also became domestic workers, although this is not reflected in statistics.

Mi mamá me dejó en casa de mi tía a los cinco años. Mi papá se volvió loco y quemó la casa, así que mi mamá tuvo mudarse a la ciudad a trabajar en una casa de familia. Ese era el único trabajo que podía conseguir. Venía a visitarnos de vez en cuando. Después de eso se vino para los Estados Unidos y no la vimos por cuatro o cinco años. Desde bien temprana edad yo hacía trabajo que cuando lo pienso, me doy cuenta de que era trabajo de adulta. Yo iba a lavar ropa al río y cargaba agua, porque no había agua en las casas en aquel entonces. Nadie me cree. Yo lo recuerdo, ¡yo hice eso! Planchaba con planchas de carbón. Hacía todo eso a la edad de nueve o diez años. Creo que como mi mamá me dejó con mi tía, ella me hacía trabajar así para aliviarle la carga un poco.

My mother left me at my aunt's house when I was five years old. My father went crazy and burned their house down, so my mother had to move to the city and work in the home of a family. That was the only work she could get. She came to visit us once in a while. After that she came to the United States and we didn't see her for four or five years. From a very young age I did work that when I think of it now, I realize it was adult work. I would wash clothes in the river and I carried water since there was no water in the houses then. Nobody believes me. I remember... I did that! I used to iron with the irons you put coal in. I did all that work when I was nine or ten years old. I think that since my mother left me with my aunt, my aunt would make me work that way in order to lighten her burden. Luz, Interview by the author, New Jersey, December 1992.

As we heard in the narration above, some women went to live and work in *"casas de familia"* ("family households") leaving their children to be raised by relatives. For other women the arrangement was to work in that household during the day and come home at night to continue cooking, cleaning, washing, and ironing for their own husband and children.

Mi papá murió cuando yo todavía no tenía dos años y entonces mi mamá quedó con diez hijos propios más los (hijos) agrega'os. Los otros hijos eran familia de mi papá y todos se agruparon a la familia de nosotros. Y entonces mi mamá siguió luchando con todos esos muchachos, trabajando ella y lavando y haciendo cosas domésticas en la casa. Ella se traía la ropa a casa y iba a la quebrada. Se lavaba con piedras, con paleta, con jabón de barra, to' eso. Se enjabonaba la ropa y se tiraba un rato al sol, entonces pues se enjuagaba con agua limpia, se traía a la casa y se tendía en los alambres. Ella no la planchaba, sólo la lavaba. La doblaba y la metía en un bolso así y la amarraba de paños como se hacía antes, la amarraba así bien dobladita y la llevaba al vecino. Eso lo hacía además de todo el trabajo de su casa con diez muchachos. Había que ir a traer una lata de agua en la cabeza pa' poder tomar agua y había que ir bien lejos a buscarla. Mi mama a las cinco de la mañana estaba trabajando. Yo veía a mi mamá tan afaná' que yo le dije no, yo no voy más a la escuela. Yo me quedo contigo para ayudarte en los quehaceres. Yo decía, un vellón que yo me gane, ayudo a mi mamá.

My father died before I was two years old so my mother ended up with ten children of her own plus the others she raised. The other children were from my father's family and all of them came over to our family. So my mother continued struggling with all those kids, working and ironing and doing domestic work at home. She would bring the clothes home and go to the stream. At that time washing was done with stones, with a paddle, with bar soap, all that. You had to soap the clothes, lay them out in the sun, then rinse them with clean water, bring them to the house and hang them on the line to dry. She didn't iron clothes, she only washed them. She would fold the clothes and put them in a bag and tie it with strips of cloth like it was done before. She would tie the carefully folded clothes and take them to the neighbor. She did this besides all the work at home with ten kids. She had to bring a can of water on her head so we had drinking water at home and she had to go far to get it. At five in the morning my mother was working. I saw she worked so hard that I said no, I won't go to school any more. I'll stay here with you and help with the household chores. I said, a nickel that I earn will help my mother. María, interview by the author, April 1996.

There were various types of domestic service workers, but in all four censuses between 1899 and 1930, the most common occupations listed under this category were servants and laundresses. In 1920, for example, 31,699 of a total of 32,482 female domestic and personal service workers were servants and laundresses.[32] This work was done for wealthier individuals, for whom the personal service workers performed duties such as washing, ironing, cooking, cleaning, and care of infants and elderly people. Some lived with their employer, others worked in their employers' house only during the day and some performed the work outside of the employers' home. The data indicate that only a small number of women performed these duties for institutions and commercial establishments. Some laundresses and ironers were hired in the embroidery and needlework industries.[33] Other occupations under the rubric of domestic and personal service included untrained midwives and nurses, and hairdressers and manicurists.

The relations between the employer and the domestic worker were characteristic of systems of servitude in many ways. Some women did not work for a wage, but for an equivalent, for example in the form of room and board. Additionally, domestic work was situated in an intermediate position between the spheres of the public and the private and resulted in women submitting to an unending work day. Domestic work for the most part was not subject to the increasing governmental regulations related to work hours, piece work, employment of children, wages and working conditions instituted during this period.[34] This was particularly true for those women who lived in their employer's home or worked on a day basis for individual families, but was also true for many who worked in institutions such as schools or hospitals:

Yo trabajaba en la lavandería de una escuela privada en San Juan y no nos íbamos hasta que no termináramos lo que había que lavar. Eso de horario de trabajo no existía y no nos pagaban más por los días más largos.

I worked in the laundry of a private school in San Juan and we didn't go home until we finished whatever needed to be washed. Fixed working hours did not exist and we were not paid extra for longer working days. *Luisa, interview by the author, San Juan, April 1996.*

Other women were paid by the dozen of clothes washed or ironed. In this case they had more control over the length of their paid work day, but their wages and working conditions also escaped supervision by the state.[35]

Many employers considered that domestic workers were their sexual property:

Muchos hombres se propasaban con las empleadas. Y como son don fulano y don fulano, había que quedarse calladitas. Además muchas tenían que decirle que sí porque si no, era irse y quedarse sin trabajo. En aquel entonces no es como ahora que todo sale a la luz pública. En aquel entonces la gente era más reservada.

Many men took undue liberties with their employees. Since they were Mr. So and So, we had to remain silent. Many had to consent because the alternative was to leave and lose the job. At that time it was not like it is now and everything comes out publicly. At that time people were more reserved. *María, Interview by author, Cayey, April 1996.*

Sí, yo tuve una sobrina que se fue a trabajar para una casa de familia y el marido, el dueño de la casa se propasó con ella. La hostigaba mucho. A veces la esposa del dueño decía que fue la muchacha la que lo provocó. Mi hermana la sacó de la casa donde trabajaba rápido. Muchas se quedaban calla'itas. Era como si eso fuera parte de la obligación. Eras sirvienta para lavar y planchar y para lo demás también. Muchas sí, a muchas les pasaba eso. Un montón. Era parte de las obligaciones aunque no se hablaba.

Yes I had a niece that went to work for a family, and the husband, the owner of the house, took advantage of her. He would really harass her. Sometimes the owner's wife would say that the girl had provoked him. My sister took her out of that house very quickly. Many did not speak out. It was as if that was part of your obligations. You were a servant to wash and iron and do other things as well. It happened to many. It was part of the obligations although it was unspoken. *Inés, Interview by author, San Juan April 1996.*

Often the boundaries between domestic servants and mistresses became quite blurred. In fact, various documents of the 16th through 19th centuries list *"concubina"* ("mistress") as an occupation along with washerwoman and cook.[36] It was not unusual for wealthy men or clerics to have mistresses who were also their domestic servants. This situation continued into the early 20th century as well.

Mis abuelos me criaron en los primeros siete años de mi vida. Mi mamá siempre estaba trabajando. Era de una familia muy pobre y no pudo ir a la escuela. Vivió una vida muy agitada. Se encontró a un hombre muy adinerado, casado, que la tomó como su concubina. En cierta medida ella se superó económicamente a través

TABLE 1

Percent of Gainfully Employed Women Workers
10 Years and Older by Occupations and Race, Puerto Rico, 1899–1930

Year	Black			White		
	Domestic Service	Manufacturing	All Other Occupations*	Domestic Service	Manufacturing	All Other Occupations*
1899	86.5	9.3	4.2	68.7	18.5	12.8
1910	70.0	18.5	11.5	48.1	27.9	24.0
1920	51.3	29.9	18.8	30.2	38.7	31.1
1930	44.7	44.5	10.8	23.2	55.8	21.0

*Includes clerical occupations, professional services, public service, trade, transportation, communication and agriculture. *Source: U.S. Bureau of the Census, Thirteenth Census of the United States: 1910, Occupational Statistics, Table IX*

de manipular a los hombres con quien ella vivía. O sea, que su situación económica mejoraba dependiendo del hombre con quien estaba. Ella parece que estaba muy consciente de eso, y utilizó su belleza, porque era una mujer guapísima, para atraer hombres y para poder económicamente sobrevivir.

My grandparents raised me until I was seven. My mother was always working. She came from a very poor family and did not go to school. Her life was very agitated. She found a very rich married man that took her as his mistress. To a certain degree she improved her economic position by manipulating the men with whom she lived. In other words, her economic situation improved depending on the man whom she was with. She seemed to be very conscious of that and used her beauty to attract men and survive economically. Rosa, Interview by the author, San Juan, August 1990.

Employment in domestic work declined rapidly, from 78 percent of the female work force in 1899 to 30 percent in 1930. On the other hand, the proportion of women in manufacturing increased dramatically, from 14 to 52 percent.[37] In spite of the overall decline in domestic work throughout these decades, such work continued to be a more important source of employment for black women than for white women.

As observed in Table 1, the percentage of black women employed in domestic work was approximately twenty points higher than that of white women in each census year. Although the importance of domestic work declined for both black and white women during this period, by 1920 it was no longer the most important source of employment for white women but continued to be for black women. In contrast, white women had more access to manufacturing jobs and to other occupations as well. In 1899 the percentage of white women who worked in manufacturing was twice as high as that of black women. Although this difference declined after 1899, in each census year the proportion of white women employed in this sector was approximately ten percentage points higher than that of black women.

On the highest end of the occupational queue racial divisions can also be observed. While 5.5 percent of white women were professionals, only 2.2 percent of black women were professionals in 1930. The most common occupations for both white and black women in this category were teachers and trained nurses.

The racial divisions in the work force described above were coupled with differences in illiteracy and poor health conditions. Data on Santurce in 1910 indicates that the proportion of domestic workers who could read and write was lower than the proportion of women in all other occupations except those who worked in trade, which was also a common occupation for black women. The percentage of surviving children, an important indicator of poverty and poor health, was smaller among domestic servants than in any other occupation.[38]

The first three decades of this century reveal a significant degree of racial division in women's work. Differences between white and black women are evident in the larger proportion of black women who worked for wages or their equivalent, and in the fact that high levels of participation in the paid work force occurred at an earlier date for black women. In addition a significantly larger proportion of black women were relegated to domestic service and were not able to move into manufacturing as rapidly as white women. Domestic work was the occupation most available to poor, immigrant, illiterate, and destitute women. The wages and working conditions of domestic workers were subjected to less regulation and supervision by the state, giving more opportunity for employers to exploit workers. Women who worked in the homes of their employers were particularly vulnerable to an unending work day. The low status of domestic work was also evidenced by the greater degree of poverty and the poorer health of these women. Physical proximity with their employers and the stereotypes associated with the sexuality of poor and black women made them very vulnerable to sexual abuse in the workplace. Racial divisions in the work force reinforced and confirmed the historical associations between domestic work, sexual exploitation, poverty, and blackness. ∎

ENDNOTES

1. On the needle work industry see for example: Lydia Milagros González García, *Una Puntada en el Tiempo, La industria de la aguja en Puerto Rico 1900-1929* (San Juan, Santo Domingo: CEREP - CIPAF, 1990); María del Carmen Baerga (Ed.), *Género y trabajo: la industria de la aguja en Puerto Rico y el Caribe Hispánico* (San Juan: Editorial UPR, 1993).

2. Domestic and personal service is the category used by the U.S. Census where much of the data for this paper was obtained. It does not include needle work done in the home. I use the terms domestic work and domestic service indistinctly.

3. References to domestic work during this period are made in Fernando Picó, "Las trabajadores del tabaco en Utuado, Puerto Rico, según el censo de 1910," *Homines* 10, no. 2 (agosto de 1986 a febrero de 1987): 173-186; Arlene Díaz Caballero, "Las trabajadoras asalariadas en Santurce," *Anales de Investigación Histórica* 1 (1988): 1-119. On women's work in the production of tobacco see Amílcar Tirado Avilés, "Notas sobre el desarrollo de la industria del tabaco en Puerto Rico y su impacto en la mujer puertorriqueña," *Centro Bulletin* 2, no. 20 (Winter 1989-1990): 19-29.

4. Gainful workers is the term used in the census for workers who worked for wages or their equivalent. U.S. Bureau of the Census. *Fifteenth Census of the United States: 1930, Occupation Statistics* (Washington: U.S. Government Printing Office, 1932).

5. Bureau of the Census, *Fourteenth Census, Vol. II -Population* 1920 (Washington, DC: U.S. Government Printing Office),16-17.

6. Ibid.

7. Departamento de la Guerra, *Informe sobre el Censo de Puerto Rico, 1899*. (Washington: Imprenta del Gobierno 1900) Table XXVI.

8. Departamento de la Guerra, *Informe sobre el Censo de Puerto Rico, 1899*, 89.

9. Jalil Sued Badillo and Angel López Cantos, *Puerto Rico Negro* (San Juan: Editorial Cultural, 1986) 262.

10. See paper presented by Doris Quiñones at the *Cuarto Congreso Puertorriqueño Sobre los Derechos Civiles*, San Juan, Summer 1995. (Forthcoming, Comisión de Derechos Civiles de Puerto Rico.)

11. Departamento de la Guerra, *Informe sobre el Censo de Puerto Rico, 1899*; U.S. Bureau of the Census, *Sixteenth Census of the United States: 1940* (Washington, DC: U.S. Government Printing Office). See Isabelo Zenon's comments on this in *Narciso Descubre su Trasero*.

12. Sued Badillo and López Cantos, *Puerto Rico Negro*, 86-88, 127, 131. The ownership of slaves by such wide sectors of society points early on to race as an important indicator of social status among all classes even when amongst the lower classes it was not supported by economic well being.

13. Sued Badillo and López Cantos, *Puerto Rico Negro*, 43-44.

14. Luis Díaz Soler. *Historia de la Esclavitud Negra en Puerto Rico (1493-1890)* (Madrid: Revista de Occidente, 1953). María Teresa Babín. *La Cultura de Puerto Rico* (San Juan: Instituto de Cultura Puertorriqueña, 1973).

15. An extensive discussion of this stereotype is presented by Bell Hooks, *Ain't I a Woman - Black women and feminism* (Boston: South End Press, 1981). See also Barbara Bush, *Slave women in Caribbean Society, 1650-1838* (Bloomington: Indiana University Press, 1990) 11-22.

16. Angel López Cantos, "Historia de una extraña normativa," *Revista del Instituto de Cultura Puertorriqueña* 28, no. 68, (julio - septiembre 1975): 10.

17. Ibid.

18. María Cadilla de Martínez, "La campesina de Puerto Rico". In Eugenio Fernández Méndez (ed.) *Antología del Pensamiento Puertorriqueño, 1900 - 1970*. (San Juan: Editorial Universitaria UPR, 1975) 659; Ruth Behar, "Sexual witchcraft, colonialism, and women's powers: Views from the Mexican inquisition". In Asunción Lavrin (Ed.), *Sexuality and marriage in colonial Latin America* (Nebraska: University of Nebraska Press, 1989) 178-206; Celsa Albert Batista, *Mujer y Esclavitud* (Santo Domingo: CEDEE) 52, 55; Bush, *Slave women in Caribbean Society, 11-22*.

19. Irene Silverblatt, *Moon, Sun, and Witches - Gender Ideologies and Class in Inca and Colonial Peru* (New Jersey: Princeton University Press, 1987) 138-147. Sued Badillo and López Cantos, *Puerto Rico Negro*, 149-50.

20. Ibid., 41.
21. Ibid., 152.
22. Ibid., 153.
23. Félix V. Matos Rodríguez, *Street Vendors, Pedlars, Shop-Owners and Domestics: Some Aspects of Women's Economic Roles in Nineteenth-Century San Juan, Puerto Rico (1820-1870).* In Shepherd, Brereton and Bailey (eds.) *Engendering History- Caribbean Women in Historical Perspective* (New York: St. Martin's Press, 1995) 178.
24. Ibid., 181-189.
25. Bureau of the Census. *Fifteenth Census of the United States: 1930, Occupation Statistics* (Washington: U.S. Government Printing Office, 1932) Table 1. In the United States this same percentage change took 60 years: 13.1 percent in 1870 to 22.0 percent in 1930. U.S. Bureau of the Census, *Sixteenth Census of the United States: 1940, Comparative Occupation Statistics for the United States, 1870 to 1940* (Washington, DC: United States Government Printing Office, 1943) 9.
26. One of the dramatic changes in the composition of the female labor force in the next three decades is the incorporation of married women into the work force although I do not focus on this aspect in this paper.
27. Departamento de la Guerra, *Informe sobre el Censo de Puerto Rico, 1899.* (Washington: Imprenta del Gobierno 1900) 98.
28. Departamento de la Guerra, *Informe sobre el censo de Puerto Rico, 1899*, Table XXIV; U.S. Bureau of the Census, *Fifteenth Census of the United States, Occupations,* Table 6.
29. Bureau Of The Census. *Fifteenth Census of the United States: 1930, Occupation Statistics, Puerto Rico*, Tables 1,2, 4, 5; U.S. Bureau of the Census, *Thirteenth Census of the United States: 1910, Occupation Statistics*. Table V; U.S. Department of War, *Informe sobre el censo de Puerto Rico, 1899*, Table XXIV.
30. Bureau of the Census, *Fifteenth Census Of The U.S. 1930* (Washington, DC: Government Printing Office); U.S. War Department, *Informe Sobre El Censo De Puerto Rico, 1899* (Washington, DC: Government Printing Office).
31. Bureau of the Census, *Fifteenth Census of the U.S., 1930* (Washington, DC: Government Printing Office); U.S. War Department, *Informe Sobre El Censo De Puerto Rico, 1899* (Washington, DC: Government Printing Office).
32. Bureau of the Census, *Fourteenth Census of the US: 1920* (Washington, DC: Government Printing Office) Table 10.
33. *Report of the Governor of Porto Rico, 1929* (Washington: Government Printing Office, 1930) 754.
34. The only mention of regulations applied to domestic service workers found in the Annual Reports of the Commissioner of Labor between 1900 and 1930 was a reference to Section 1487 of the Civil Code that provided indemnification for domestic servants hired for a fixed time if a master dismissed a servant without sufficient cause. *Annual Report of the Governor of Porto Rico, 1929, 739.* In spite of the observed absence of regulations, various reports by the Commissioner of Labor document cases of domestic workers who requested the intervention of the department of labor in relation to claims that employers refused to pay them. For example see *Report of the Governor of Porto Rico, 1920-21* (Washington: Government Printing Office, 1921) 503.
35. While attempts were made to prohibit and/or regulate piece work in the needle and embroidery industries during this period, the author found no evidence of this in domestic work. *Annual Report of the Governor of Porto Rico*, years 1900-1930.
36. Sued Badillo and López Cantos, 35, 284.
37. US Bureau of the Census, *Fifteenth Census of the United States: 1930, Occupation Statistics*, Table 3; US Bureau of the Census, *Fourteenth Census of the United States: 1920, Occupations*, Table 26.
38. Díaz Caballero "Las trabajadoras asalariadas en Santurce," 73-75. Similar findings were reported by Fernando Picó, "Las Trabajadoras del Tabaco en Utuado," *179.*

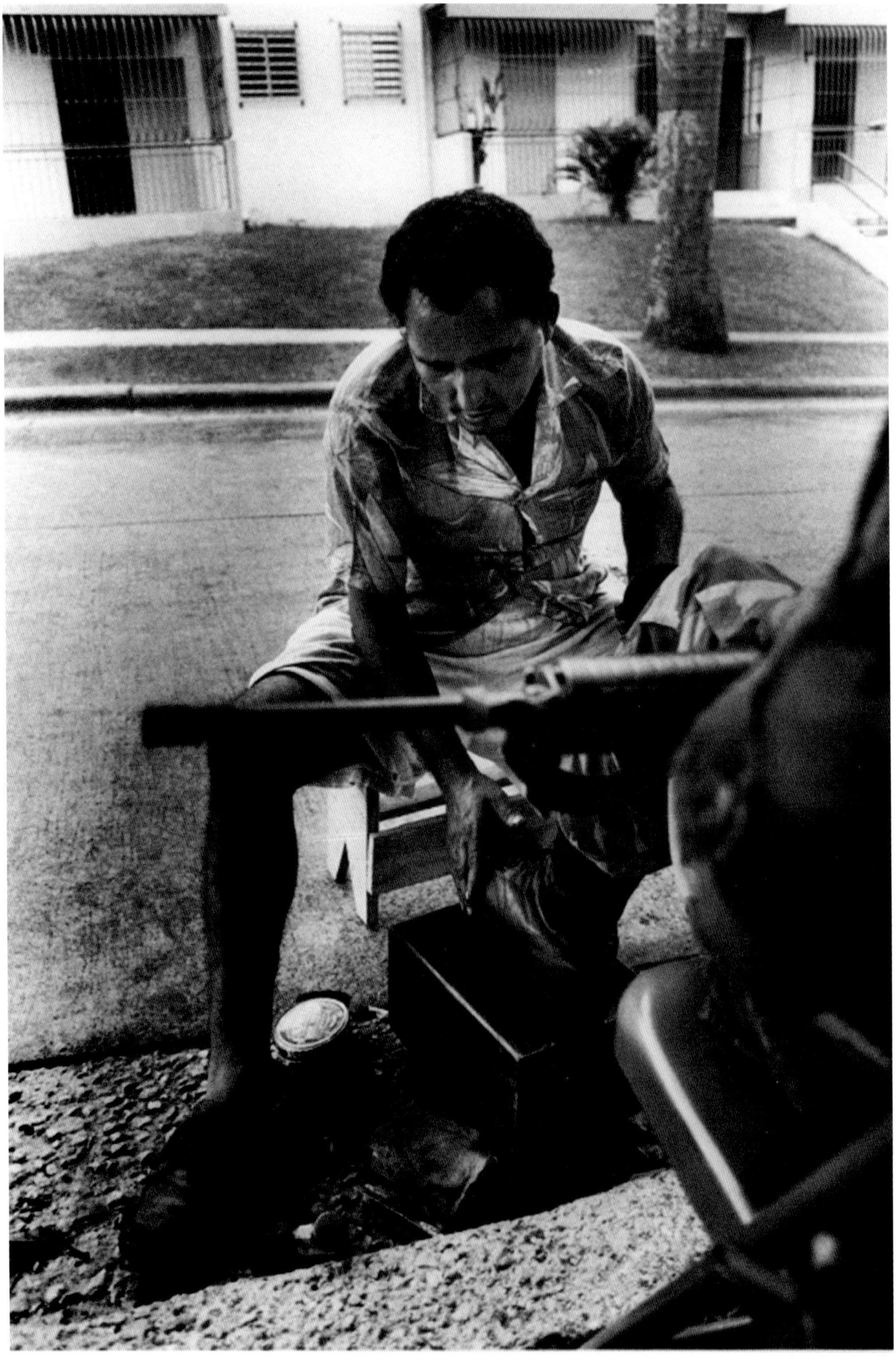

Policing the Crisis in the Whitest of all the Antilles

KELVIN SANTIAGO-VALLES

Distracted by its own abstractions, Puerto Rico is still searching for the body it desired and never had. (...) The problem is, Puerto Rico no longer has a mirror to look into... The body in Puerto Rican terms has always been a metaphor, a territory defined by opposition.
Félix Jiménez[1]

¿Cómo se lucha en contra de algo que no existe? Si somos incapaces de ser racistas ("el que no tiene dinga...") entonces, ¿qué nombre le ponemos a las ofensas y opresión que viven aquellos cuyas caras todavía dicen "África"?
Miriam Jiménez Román[2]

Puerto Ricans have a checkered history that crystallized in the nineteenth century, directly affecting racial taxonomies, attitudes, and identities among all of us to this very day. "Blackness" and anyone kindred to it is usually designated and experienced as "strange," "exotic" and/or "suspicious." More than any formal claim to explicit "ethnic" uniqueness, those uncommon Puerto Ricans self-defining themselves as "black" or "dark-mulatto" do so because they live an inferiorizing social distance with respect to light-mulattoes and whites in/from the Island, toward U.S.-European Americans, and toward other lighter-skinned Latin Americans and Caribbean peoples.[3]

It is largely an unwritten history and complex contemporary social analysis. Few Puerto Ricans of African descent explicitly identify themselves as such,[4] particularly among the poor masses, despite—or because of?—a long past of discrimination and a present of brutal (though furtively racialized) police persecution. Such is the reality summarized and explicated in this essay.

■ Historical Background
Similar to some countries in the rest of Latin America since the Conquest, there were as many as sixteen—and in a few cases, even more—different racial categories in Puerto Rico.[5]

KELVIN SANTIAGO-VALLES is associate professor of sociology, Africana studies, and Latin American and Caribbean area studies at Binghamton, State University of New York.

■ *Ricardo Alcaraz Díaz*

Nineteenth century census figures for the local population, however, list only three main racial classifications: *"blanco,"* *"mulato,"* and *"negro."* Grouped together, the latter two categories—often known as *"pardos"* and/or *"morenos"*—fluctuated between 56 percent (1820) and 38 percent (1899) of Puerto Rico's inhabitants. Five decades after the U.S. colonial regime replaced Spanish rule, the Island's combined nonwhite population had declined officially to 23 percent (1950).[6] This was the last time the colonial government—local or federal—formally used racial categories within Puerto Rico.

Again, as elsewhere in Latin America and the Caribbean, greater income, influence, and education could and can transform the darker-skinned into lighter-skinned persons. As U.S. anthropologist Raymond Scheele concluded in his early 1950s study of prominent families in the Island, "an individual is 'whiter' in proportion to his wealth. Anyone who is accepted into the upper class is considered non-Negro, despite his physical appearance."[7]

Although the Island's laboring majorities come from all races, the "native" propertied and educated classes tend to be exclusively white. They are still entrusted with varying degrees of control over the principal political organizations, financial resources, and local government authority of the colonial order. Within the colonizers' racial categories, however, even rich "criollo" or Creole whites cannot escape being classified as racially inferior together with the rest of the "native" population.[8]

Slavery was, of course, the most salient historical factor behind this first taxonomy. Until its abolition in 1873, slavery predominated in the sugar-cane coast and lowland valleys. Although captives had also worked in lesser numbers in the coffee- and tobacco-producing hill country, there was no necessary correspondence between these slave concentrations and the settlement patterns of *"pardos libres"* ("free coloreds").[9] *Pardos libres* or *"trigueños"* (literally: "wheat hued") tended to settle in the central mountain range where most Puerto Ricans (mainly peasants) lived well into the mid-twentieth century.

From the sixteenth to late-eighteenth centuries, important segments of this peasantry have been of mixed racial heritage: maroons of both sexes settled and intermingled with fugitive galley prisoners, former soldiers, and the minute remnants of the aboriginal population. Yet, until the 1940s and like the majority of the Creole-white rural population, many non-white hill tenants or non-white peasants migrating to the mountain-valley towns tended to differentiate themselves from the coastal population—seen as more identifiably "African"—by, among other things, attempting to pass for "white" or "near white."[10]

During the 1930s and 1940s, these racial transmutations were canonized within official cultural memory and historiography when renowned "native" intellectuals affirmed that "the Spanish race" had prevailed in Puerto Rico because it had weakened and assimilated all other races. For example, in 1937 the renown "native" philologist Augusto Malaret remarked that Puerto Rico was the "whitest of all the Antilles," among other things, because the African component within the Island's general culture and gene pool was insignificant and overwhelmingly negative.[11] From the 1950s to 1970s, other prominent scholars echoed this same viewpoint,[12] while in 1988 the colonial Governor of the Island (as usual, a white, propertied Creole) declared in an official visit to Madrid that—given "our people's…common Hispanic roots"—African contributions to Puerto Rico's culture were "a mere rhetorical identification."[13]

Between the 1940s and the 1960s, several Island scholars challenged such views. Historian Tomás Blanco argued that in 1942 only about 40 percent of the Island's population could be considered predominantly white. While in 1965 sociologist Juan Rodríguez Cruz found that the amount of race mixing in Puerto Rico probably reached as much as 70 percent of the population.[14]

Furthermore, the entire national-cultural palimpsest, on which Puerto Rican-ness was being inscribed and reinscribed massively, continued to bear the distinct, historical emblems of African ways and meanings. Such is the case of the copious and profound Africanisms in the inflection, morphosyntax, and vocabulary of Puerto Rican spoken-Spanish developed by the overwhelming majority of the Island's inhabitants—who, ironically, still perceived themselves as "white" or "near white." Similarly emblematic yet contradictory examples may be found in the various musico-folkloric genres (e.g., the *bomba, plena, seis,* and *danza)* created and adopted by this very same population over the preceding four centuries.[15]

■ *Current Socioeconomic Context*

Like other peripherical areas under U.S.-capitalist hegemony, postwar Puerto Rico went from agro-monoculture to being a light-industry enclave for cheap factory labor. The appeal of low-waged but better-educated labor was enhanced by urban-based industrial programs and increased public services in Puerto Rico, which coincided with labor shortages in the U.S. Northeast. This resulted in large-scale migratory movements and demographic dislocations between 1940 and 1970: countryside to city within Puerto Rico, and from the Island to the United States. The entire process was compounded by an expanded official culture (Creole and North American) of rapidly spreading schooling, radio, print media, and television.

Between the mid–1960s and the late 1970s, light-industry factories began being unevenly displaced by high-tech, capital-intensive plants, coinciding with massive waves of social unrest. The shift towards capital-intensive industry accelerated with the expansion of new social-control measures. Despite the fiscal constraints of the following decade, such regulatory measures have continued unevenly during the 1980s and early 1990s.

On one side of the social divide stood the heirs of the previous Creole elites—again, almost completely white and light mulatto. This aristocracy was composed of the junior partners of the new U.S. corporate investors and the upper strata of the rapidly expanding bureaucracy; and an overlapping ensemble of highly skilled professionals, technicians, and/ or managerial personnel spreading across all economic sectors. However restricted, the offspring of the old black/dark-mulatto intelligentsia also found a niche within this technocracy. The transition almost exclusively applied to non-white male professionals and/ or bureaucrats, their female counterparts being primarily limited to the petty professions (e.g., public school teachers, social workers, nurses, and so on) and academia. Such burgeoning—and gendered—social mobility was inclined to estrange the upper reaches of this non-white middle class from their racial kin among the new indigent majorities.

On the other side, a more socio-racially heterogeneous, much younger, no longer rural populace was growing. By the late 1960s, the group comprised two thirds of Puerto Rico's population. The latter unevenly blurred (phenotypically and culturally) with the Island's *gente de color.* Though still below poverty level, this laboring mass was more literate and media-conscious and had higher social expectations than their predecessors. Most now lived in the public housing projects (called *caseríos* or *residenciales),* as well as in the shanty towns and laboring-poor suburbs, that–along with older, sometimes semirural, pardo-libre communities,—were collectively known as *barrios.* All were rapidly being absorbed by the urban sprawl.

This socio-racial amalgam is still composed of three groups: a nucleus of unskilled industrial workers whose initial growth ended by the mid-1970s, when capital-intensive industry expanded; a larger and unstable fusion of impoverished petty professionals, semiskilled clerical employees, unskilled wage-workers, and/or independent laborers in all service sectors; and a swelling, formally nonemployed sub-proletariat (the latter two groups tended to overlap). People of color, especially young males, appear to be overrepresented among many of these social sectors—the subproletariat, in particular.

Although between 1950 and 1990 men continued to comprise most of the employed population, their labor participation rates plummeted during this period as those of women laborers steadily rose. Official unemployment rates oscillated between 15 and 30 percent (both sexes) during this period, while all data indicate that it was mainly male laborers who increasingly were not even bothering to look for jobs in the legal labor market. The proportion of officially nonemployed people climbed from a little less than a third of the entire population in 1950 to almost half in 1985. As in the rest of the postwar Caribbean, these were the elements involved in most social strife since the late 1960s: wildcat strikes (1968–1973, 1978–1983), squatters movements (1966– 1972, 1979–1983), riots, youth vagrancy, social violence, theft, and the uneven rejection of traditional-party loyalties.[16]

■ *Political Affiliations and Struggles for Racial Equality*
Transforming the colony's population and broadening the reach of institutional culture entailed a corollary metamorphosis in the Island's electorate. Although the pro-U.S.-commonwealth Partido Popular Democrático (PPD) was the chief promoter of the postwar transformation, the rural-based PPD did not reap its electoral benefits: it failed to grasp the novel traits of the emergent impoverished majorities—both social and racial. Local election results still depended on how Puerto Rico's elites secured the support of the impoverished "native" majorities. However, winning elections depended less on the Creole-white and light-mulatto, mountain peasantry than on the darker, more mulattoized urban barrios attracting impoverished country-folk.

Simultaneously, the new non-white middle strata focused more on the remnants of the older, more formal patterns of socio-racial discrimination than on the concerns of most *gente de color*. Between the 1950s and early 1970s racial-justice efforts in Puerto Rico usually reflected the middle-class background, careerist aspirations, and masculinism of the black/dark-mulatto—and mostly male—leadership of such struggles. Historically and among the general population, women of color were the ones who placed and continue to place the highest value on obtaining a profession as a way of counterbalancing the existing racial discrimination.[17] Nevertheless, the gendered imbalances within these struggles for racial equality might explain why among the already few educated, well-known Island blacks and dark-mulattoes it was primarily the men who reached prominence within politico-public and upper-professional circles in Puerto Rico.

The colony's newly created Civil Rights Committee (later it was titled Civil Rights Commission) investigated still recurring but more isolated cases of straightforward racism in fraternities, private academies, professional schools, elite sports, and some high visibility jobs. Although the 1959 Committee report confirmed the persistence of explicit bigotry in Puerto Rico, it did not issue any recommendations, a futile exercise that was repeated by legislative boards a few years later.[18] Perhaps the most scholarly, thorough, and astounding—in its civic honesty—was the Civil Rights Commission's 1972 study and report prepared by Eduardo Seda Bonilla.[19] As before, all of these findings fell largely on deaf ears within government circles because the more blatant, older, and traditional examples of racism tended to disappear—however slowly.

Between the 1970s and early 1990s this middle-class stratum of color and their white supporters have fostered and created varied "culturalist" expressions of "black affirmation." Examples include university symposia, literary presentations, modern dance performances, and sculpture and graphic arts exhibitions. A few "culturalist" efforts have attempted to bridge the gap between the black/dark-mulatto intelligentsia and the cultural production and social concerns of the *gente de color* in the *barrios*.[20]

Several young, black and dark-mulatto women in Puerto Rico have distinguished themselves in this type of activity, among them Mayra Santos Febres, Ana I. Rivera Lassens, Rayda Cotto, Celia M. Romano, and Marie Ramos Rosado. The greater exclusion of middleclass women of color in the Island from the traditional-political prominence and technocratic high-profile mentioned above might account for their seeming overrepresentation within "black affirmation" academic pursuits, arts, and literature. Some of these women organized themselves into the "Unión de mujeres puertorriqueñas negras" ("Union of Black Puerto Rican Women"). A number of them both promoted and participated in the "Primer Encuentro de Mujeres Negras de Latinoamérica y del Caribe" (First Meeting of Black Women from Latin America and the Caribbean), held in Santo Domingo in July of 1992.[21]

Meanwhile, the destitute majorities became alienated from the PPD administration due to coercive urban-renewal programs, spreading police intervention, expanding but decaying public services, rising social hopes, and increased social imbalances. By the mid-1960s, the more racially mixed urban poor became disaffected from the political party system in general and from the governing party in particular (the PPD). This explains their tendency to support new political formations and play one mainstream colonialist party against another, and/or to participate in the growing social unrest.

The prime beneficiary of the postwar social transformations was the new, pro-U.S.-statehood, and neo-populist Partido Nuevo Progresista (PNP), organized during the mid-1960s. After the PPD's landslide victories of 1952–1964, for a generation—from 1968 through 1992—this party and the PNP have practically alternated in controlling the colony's local administration, each time winning by scant margins. The PNP's rhetoric opportunistically emphasizes the mobilization of the indigent urban masses. It has successfully equated the erasure of all social—and racial?—inequalities in Puerto Rico with transforming the Island into a state of the U.S. federal union: therein the PNP slogan, "Statehood is for the poor!"

■ *New Settlement Patterns and Old Solidarities*

In the Island, there is still a tendency to identify the multiracial population in the shanty towns, *caseríos*, deteriorating laboring-poor suburbs, and the adjacent semirural localities as being of African descent. Despite existing governmental reforms, this demographic distribution was confirmed in the 1950s, among other things, by Caplow, Stryker, and Wallace research on the colony's capital city. The study found that the beach-front, tourist, and high-class districts "had by far the lowest proportion of non-whites" of 1950, while "the New Suburbs, not yet urbanized"—i.e., where the poorest warrens were located—"had the highest." The authors concluded: "Segregation by color, although not unknown in San Juan, occurs by blocks or by neighborhoods." By the 1960s and early 1970s, anthropologist Helen Safa observed that even the poor themselves "tend to associate black and poor."[22]

Social services and public infrastructures deteriorated between the 1960s and the 1980s while sources of legal income (particularly factory jobs) shrank. This indigent urban mass thus reinstituted older forms of cooperation within new and more socioracially mixed (mulatto-ized) patterns of communal reciprocity. Safa says that, exchanges of "labor and skills in the repair and improvement of their homes" comprise "one of the main avenues of cooperation among men in the shantytown." The principal compensation assumes "the form of food and drink and, of course, the expectation that these favors will be reciprocated." According to this U.S. anthropologist, "The few possessions shantytown families own are usually shared with others." These are gendered patterns of solidarity: "Women borrow small articles like cups of sugar or electric irons, while men exchange tools and cooperate in the repair of their homes." Such patterns are also age-graded: "Even food is shared. Some old men living alone in the shantytown depend almost completely on neighboring families for their meals, for which they contribute nothing."[23]

There is still an extreme dearth of even the most descriptive and cursory demographic, economic, and socio-cultural research specifically focusing on black and dark-mulatto Island "natives." One of the few recent studies suggests that it is mainly older poor women living in historically *pardo-libre*, semirural communities who fare the worst. These non-white women interviewees reported, however, that race rather than age was the greatest factor in determining the substandard quality of their lives.[24]

Roy Bryce-Laporte's 1968 investigation of former slum residents shows that reciprocal-aid practices accompanied this impoverished mass when they were resettled to *caseríos* and/or to laboring-poor suburbs. Such networks of solidarity included "mutual economic and protective assistance, visiting and confidential exchanges, care in times of sickness and emergency," in addition to "disciplining of children, borrowing and sharing, and decisionmaking on some subjects of common concern." Practices of this sort linked each family/community participant within a lattice of interdependent relationships so dense that, in order to "understand how individual members or individual units survived, it was necessary to know how they related to other units and operations of and within the network."[25]

■ *Musical expressions*

As in the past, Islanders of African descent were fundamental to Puerto Rican musical production, stemming directly from the Cuban/Puerto Rican/U.S.-African-American cultural fusions of the interwar period. Subsequently, this process was decisively marked by the huge Puerto Rican migration to the United States (1940–70), by both the post–1959 Cuban migrations and the post-mid1970s Dominican migrations to Puerto Rico, and by the subsequent cyclical flows of Puerto Rican labor between the Island and the U.S. mainland. This was how the mambo-, big-band-, and new-plena waves of the 1950s and early 1960s engendered the *salsa* wave of the late 1960s to the present, as well as the *merengue* and rap waves of the 1980s and 1990s.

Musical excellence in composition and/or interpretation were gateways out of poverty and discrimination—in the Island and in the U.S. ghettoes—but primarily for male *salseros*. And of these musicians, few had formal or institutional training; most of them come from the slums and *barrios* of New York City or San Juan. Quantitatively and qualitatively, Puerto Ricans in general and Island black and dark-mulatto men in particular were the main song writers, performers, and vocalists of the principal salsa bands in the United States-Caribbean circuit of the 1970s and 1980s. One of the factors making this an almost exclusively male-dominated art form and social-mobility mechanism was the variously stringent interdiction on having women playing the drums, the most prominent instruments in all Afro-Hispanic-Caribbean musical genres.[26]

Many of these Puerto Rican musicians, particularly men of color, never completely deserted their socio-racial roots. Sometimes it was a conscious effort to remain "authentic," mining these U.S.-ghetto and Island urban-indigent spaces for inspiration and feedback. Other times it was a matter of giving back to these communities—and to relatives and neighborhood friends—some of the recognition bestowed upon their progeny. However, these barrios were also the last refuge of the once successful *salsa* musician crushed by unfair recording contracts, drugs, and/or the criminal justice system.[27]

There have been other ways in which this urban music has personified the growing socio-racial polarization among Island Puerto Ricans. Such is the case of the violent clashes unfolding in concerts, streets, and school lots between U.S.-[white-] rock music advocates (known as *rockeros)* and salsa fans (known as *cocolos*) during the late 1970s to mid-1980s. Historically, in the Spanish-speaking Caribbean *cocolo* is one of several derisive terms used for people of African descent. In contemporary Puerto Rico, *cocolos* are the mostly non-white adolescents and young adults from the *barrios* of Puerto Rico and the U.S. mainland. The *rockeros*, instead, comprise primarily white, middle-class and rich youths: the children of the Island's Creole elites.

■ *The Criminalization of Subsistence Activities*

This period also witnessed an increase in the illegalization of survival practices (collective and individual) among the more non-white destitute majorities in urban, suburban, and semirural settlements. Kurt Back's 1962 social-psychology study of *caserío* occupants in Puerto Rico indicates that "the residents frequently tapped power lines and hence did not have to pay for utilities" and that, in general, those interviewed "mentioned a great amount of extralegal activity."[28] In the early 1980s, British historian Raymond Carr commented: "The social alienation of the lumpenproletariat, of which disadvantaged blacks constitute a significant section, is expressed…in deviance and delinquency."[30] Regulated or not by extra-legal and informal social-control mechanisms, these are the social class, racial, and geographical spaces officially identified with illicit drug sales, squatting, resisting police evictions, participating in unreported incomes, shootouts, the underground lottery, etc.

To a great extent, the key issue is not whether crime statistics are quantitatively higher among the urban impoverished population in general and among its growing *gente de color* elements in particular. I agree with Stuart Hall and colleagues, when, in the case of the United Kingdom during the 1980s, they remark:

> Black youth are clearly involved in some petty and street crime in these areas, and the proportion involved may well be higher than it was a decade earlier. …The question is not, precisely, how many, but why? What is the meaning, the significance, the historical context of this fact? This crime index cannot be isolated from other related indices if we really wish to unravel this puzzle. When examined in context, these various indices point to a critical intersection between black crime, black labour and the deteriorating situation in the black areas. Even these must be

contextualised, by setting them in their proper framework: the economic, social and political crisis into which the society is receding.[31]

The local mass media and the Creole intelligentsia (of all political stripes, formally anticolonialist or not) have failed to see the structural logic, however disturbing, and much less the racial undertones, of this explosive social polarization. Instead, they have issued copious alarmist writings diagnosing such behavior as the "growing disease" of "a community against itself."[32] Few realize that the expansion of subaltern literacy levels and access to the mass media have flowed directly opposite the waning access to the growing social wealth created in the Island among the dispossessed "native" majorities.

The mentioned illegalities should be understood, among other things, as a response to the multiplication of gross and frequently, although tacitly, racialized social inequalities. One of the injustices that has provoked considerable resistance among the destitute masses is the land-use policy of the colonial government—local as well as federal—, in turn, fueled by the activities of corporate speculators and ravenous real-estate developers. Increasingly, such schemes have placed residents in older, *pardo-libre* communities outside the law, while at the same time forcing a growing number of urban-poor families to unlawfully seize unused stretches of land because these laborers are unable to afford legal housing. In both cases, forced evictions are the ultimate official threat and/or actual practice. There have already been several notorious instances of this type of "cautionary tale," where the local police has brutally crushed the resistances of predominantly black/dark-mulatto, indigent residents. In 1980, the black, laboring-poor mother Adolfina Villanueva was gunned down by patrolmen while she defied an eviction in the Medianía Alta sector of the historically maroon municipality of Loíza. The "Villa Sin Miedo" squatters settlement—in whose organization poor women once again played a leading role—was razed by anti-riot platoons during a police assault and shootout two years later.[33]

Another outstanding example of criminalized responses to existing social inequalities stems from the local wage market's declining capacity to even attract—much less absorb—the spreading number of mostly destitute, more racially mixed (i.e., non-white), and disproportionately male youths. A case in point is the underground or illegal economy. In Puerto Rico, and contrary to its U.S. counterpart, illicit economic activities predominately involve laboring-poor, young men. They are the ones primarily absorbed by these burgeoning, now structurally fundamental, and volatile sources of income, whose most profitable endeavors are the distribution of controlled chemical substances, stolen goods in general, and firearms in particular.

Such activities, in turn, have been closely related to two factors negatively affecting postwar patterns of community solidarity, especially among increasingly mulatto-ized, urban, and indigent sectors. On the one hand, there is the increasingly perilous but lucrative nature of these leading, but by no means exclusive, sectors of the underground economy. On the other hand, there is the characteristically masculinist bravado of the maleyouth bands operating both within and outside of penal/juvenile institutions and fighting to control illicit operations at a neighborhood level. Although drawing on patterns of traditional *machismo* prevalent in Puerto Rico's society as a whole and in dispossessed urban localities in particular, such vicious competition to some extent has strained the community and family networks of reciprocity that the Island's illegal subsistence practices have historically depended on for protection, regulation, and support. This situation has undoubtedly informed the rising rates of local and domestic violence in general, especially of the battering of woman, within the *barrios*. A few of the bands themselves–the "Ñetas" being the prime example—have attempted to counteract some of this social cannibalism by enforcing strict autonomous controls against indiscriminate violence.

From the late 1970s to the early 1980s the estimated volume of the underground economy oscillated between 3.5 to 4 billion dollars. The latter sum meant that more than a quarter of the Island's gross production went to the outlawed sectors of the economy at this time. Puerto Rico's illegal economic activities seem to be 50 percent to 100 percent greater than their U.S. equivalent and involving at least 500,000 Island laborers during the 1980s.

This amounted to a little over half of Puerto Rico's active labor force: almost 25 percent of the entire population of employment age, both sexes.[35]

Government officials and advisors admit that unlawful practices such as the underground economy greatly weaken the hold of legal structures (local and federal) over the impoverished urban majorities in Puerto Rico.[36] In 1986, the consciously mulatto, Puerto Rican writer, and social critic José Luis González reached similar conclusions but from an opposing historical perspective. "Puerto Rico is undoubtedly living....a state of insurgency," he says. "Only that here" the Creole-white elites mistake "this insurgency...for a simple rise in delinquency." For González, the "state of insurgency" is escalating into a veritable—and racialized—civil war,

> ...whose real nature will be eminently *social* because this war will involve a confrontation, not only between socioeconomic interests, but also between the cultural interests of the two contending sectors within Puerto Rican society. Add to this the racial ingredient of the conflict and one can see that the current and seemingly inconsequential strife between "cocolos" and "rockeros" is only a preview of a historical and much more serious confrontation.[37]

■ *The Circuitous Racialization of Crime*

Consequently and similar to what was happening in Great Britain during mid-1970s, in Puerto Rico at this time, as in the United States, there was a

> synchronization of the race and class aspects of the [economic] crisis. Policing *the blacks* threatened to mesh with the problem of policing *the poor* and policing *the unemployed:* all three were concentrated in precisely the same urban areas—a fact which of course provided that element of geographical homogeneity... The ongoing problem of policing the blacks had become, for all practical purposes, synonymous with the wider problem of *policing the crisis*.[38]

In Puerto Rico, this racialization was being executed by the Creole institutions directly administering the colony and responsible for maintaining law and order.

But how can this be officially documented, given the absence of regular census statistics on Puerto Rico's racial subdivisions since 1950? One analytical alternative is to examine the Island police's continuing use of racial (or "color") taxonomies as part of its regular criminal/delinquent identification procedures. Nevertheless, practically all of the criminological studies during this period, whether informed by Puerto Ricans or not, have simply omitted any reference to,[39] or have explicitly disclaimed the pertinence of,[40] the police's race/color identification system.

The 1988 Nevarez-Muñiz and Wolfgang juvenile-delinquency study of a 1970 cohort in the San Juan Greater Metropolitan Area is one rare example to the contrary. Despite repeated disavowals and unlike similar work from the 1950s to the present, the authors cite and use the explicitly racial classifications employed by the police, the courts, and social services themselves: "*blanco,*" "*trigueño,*" and "*negro.*" Within their already defined delinquent cluster, these groupings were 54 percent *blanco*, 38 percent *trigueño*, and 8 percent *negro*.[41]

The study reflects the received official Creole perception that those living in Island *barrios*—in particular, black males—were more inclined to be classified as criminals and delinquents. But although Nevarez-Muñiz and Wolfgang would present it otherwise, they give ample proof of how punitive agencies in the Island have singled out black and dark-mulatto poor-urban young males for a disproportionate amount of police identification and persecution.

According to this study, *negros* supposedly had almost twice the recidivism rates of *blancos*. More than twice as many male *negros* became delinquents by age 14 than their *trigueño* and *blanco* counterparts. Among male juveniles, *negros* were seen as more apt to commit severe crimes—particularly violent crimes (44 percent)—versus 36 percent of all *trigueños* and 32 percent of all *blancos*. *Negros* were reported also as having the highest rates of illicit drug use.

Hence, male-adolescent negros were more likely to be referred to the courts (72 percent) than *trigueños* (68 percent) or *blancos* (61 percent). Since the court system issued much harsher sentences to recidivists than to first-time juvenile offenders, *negros* were more prone to be locked up within juvenile detention centers or psychiatric units (14 percent), than *trigueños* (11 percent) and *blancos* (5 percent).

Although young women only made up 17 percent of all those classified as delinquents (both sexes), the non-white members of the female population were also criminally identified at disproportionately higher levels that were comparable to those of their male *(negro* and *trigueño)* counterparts.[42]

In this sense, between the 1970s and early 1990s, Puerto Rico too, saw what Stuart Hall and co-workers have called a "synchronization" of race, poverty, and unemployment, "all three" being "concentrated in precisely the same urban areas." Meanwhile, policing has expanded on a much larger scale and with far more serious results. From early 1993 to the present the colony's PNP Governor has mobilized the militia-reserve units of the U.S. Army (or National Guard) to carry out joint police raids and to regularly patrol the public housing projects and laboring-impoverished suburbs. This troop deployment has transformed these areas into militarily occupied zones, formally and indefinitely under a state of siege.[43]

Such political and administrative practices suggest that, since the electoral base of Creole[-white] officialdom continues to be partly composed of the urban, non-white, destitute, and unemployed masses, then the local elites cannot maintain the openly racist discourses of the early twentieth century. But since the crisis requires policing and since the already mentioned race-slums-unemployment-crime "synchronization" still exists, being of African descent continues to be the absent referent in the way this "geographical homogeneity" is both imagined and regulated.

■ *The Contradictory Mass Responses to the Racialization of Crime*
As in the past, impoverished populations in the Island have reproduced racist inscriptions of social "threat." With the enormous influx of Dominican workers (legal and undocumented) into Puerto Rico since the mid–1970s, this mass-based racism has also meant envisioning Dominicans—who tend to be darker-skinned than most Puerto Ricans—as members of an "inferior race." Such practices have gone from mistaking black and dark-mulatto Puerto Ricans for Dominicans (and sometimes provoking the arrest of the former for failing to produce the "appropriate immigration papers") to graffiti calling for the murder of Dominicans residing in Puerto Rico.[44]

Young, impoverished Puerto Rican *gente de color*, unlike their Black-British counterparts, have not produced an Island equivalent of an openly "ethnically distinct class fraction" from the 1970s to the early 1990s. Instead of any explicit and frank "ethnic consciousness" in its principal forms of organization, the latter mainly adopted the form of bands or gangs outspokenly identified with the localities where certain individuals resided or are confined. The group leaders are "young black school-leavers...most exposed to the winds of unemployment." Such was the case of specific Río Piedras *caseríos* in the case of the "Manuel A. Pérez" clique; San Juan's former La Princesa jail where the legendary dark-mulatto convict, martyred social bandit, and prisoners-rights activist Carlos Torres Iriarte (a.k.a., Carlos La Sombra) organized the "Ñetas" or "Asociación de Confinados" (Convicts Association) and later the state penitentiary—one of the association's multiple current strongholds; public housing projects in Ponce where the "Avispas" operated; or entire urban centers such as the "Mayagüez" band whose name corresponds to that of the third largest city in the Island, and so on.[45]

Yet there may be also a paradoxical undercurrent of self-identification locating these barrios and/or detention units themselves as distinct, Puerto Rican *negro/trigueño* spaces. The groundwork for such a consciousness is partially being laid by the media coverage and police interdiction practices described above. Perhaps more important, though, since the late 1960s and early 1970s to the present, such self-identification seems to be surfacing with the growing imbrication of two processes. On the one hand, there are the illegal survival practices of these impoverished youths in Island cities and U.S. ghettoes. On the other hand, there are the unevenly explicit Africanist-Antillean and Afro-U.S.-Latino, musico-cultural production of *salsa, merengue*, new *bomba-plena*, rap/hip-hop, as well as the partially candid Afro-Caribbean mix of semireligious initiations and habitual rituals, including *santería, espiritismo*, and *palo-mayombe*. Both the musical expressions and the rituals are extremely popular among the urban-poor in general and the gangs in particular; they even have pockets of adherents among the Island's middle-class.[46] This trend continues unabated up to the present, although it has not assumed openly self-conscious expressions.

■ Conclusion

In a 1988 study of one *pardo-libre barrio*, the Creole historian and Jesuit priest Fernando Picó, remarked that today Island officialdom and the propertied, educated minorities "continue believing that their problem is drugs and crime and not the existing social conflicts resulting from racial discrimination and unequal opportunities."[47] As the bleak conditions of the Island's growing, mulatto-ized poor merges with the socioeconomic predicament of the destitute majorities, solving one situation cannot be separated from solving the other. This cannot be done without confronting the penury, racist policing, and socio-cultural under-evaluation being endured and resisted (however paradoxically) by these subaltern populations. ■

ENDNOTES

1. Jiménez, F., "The Body Rican," *The Village Voice* (August 29, 1989): 18.

2. Jiménez Román, M. "No se trata de la naturaleza: 'raza' e identidad en las Américas," paper presented at the conference "Nuestra tercera raíz: la presencia africana en los pueblos de América," October 21, 1992, Mexico City, pages not numbered.

3. E.g., Barbosa, J.C., *El problema de razas*, Imprenta Venezuela, San Juan, 1937, pp.19–21; Rosario, J.C. and Carrión, J., "Problemas Sociales: El negro: Haití-Estados Unidos-Puerto Rico," *Boletín de la UPR*, vol.10, no.2, December, 1939, pp.127–134; Picó, I., "Entrevista de LA HORA: El racismo en Puerto Rico," *La Hora*, 8 September 1972, pp.10–11; Santos, M., "A veces miro mi vida," *Diálogo*, October, 1993, p.42.

4. E.g., Romano, C.M., "Yo no soy negra," *Piso 13*, vol.1, no.4, August, 1992, p.3.

5. Anonymous, "El Jíbaro," in Morales, J.P. (ed), *Misceláneas Históricas*, Tipografía La Correspondencia de Puerto Rico, San Juan, 1924, pp. 51–54; originally published in *Almanaque de aguinaldo*, 1876.

6. U.S. War Department, Report on the Census of Porto Rico-1899, Government Printing Office, Washington, D.C., 1900, pp.57–58; Zelinsky, W., "III. The Negro Population Geography of Cuba and Puerto Rico," *Journal of Negro History*, vol.34, no.2, April, 1949, p.211; U.S. Census Bureau, Seventeenth Census of the United States; Printed Report No.53: Puerto Rico, Government Printing Office, Washington, D.C., 1951, p.8.

7. Scheele, R., "The Prominent Families of Puerto Rico," in R.H. Steward (ed), *The People of Puerto Rico*, University of Illinois Press, Urbana, 1956, p.425.

8. Sereno, R., "Cryptomelanism: A Study of Color Relations and Personal Insecurity in Puerto Rico," *Psychiatry*, vol.10, no.3, August, 1947, pp.265, 268. I have examined this situation in: Santiago-Valles,K., "Subject People" and Colonial Discourses: Economic Transformation and Social Disorder In Puerto Rico, 1898–1947, State University of New York Press, Albany, 1994.

9. Zelinsky, "The Negro Population," p. 214; Picó, F., *Vivir en Caimito*, Ediciones Huracán, Río Piedras, 1988, pp. 118–119.

10. Manners, R.A., "Tabara: Subcultures of a Tobacco and Mixed Crops Municipality," in R.H. Steward (ed), *The People of Puerto Rico*, pp.129, 164; Wolf, E., "San José: Subcultures of

a "Traditional" Coffee Municipality," in *The People of Puerto Rico,* pp.227, 238, 258; Whitten, N.E., Jr., and Torres, A., "Blackness in the Americas," *Report on the Americas,* vol.25, no.4, February, 1992, p.21.

11. Malaret, A., *Vocabulario de Puerto Rico,* Imprenta Venezuela, San Juan, 1937, pp.15, 20. See also, Cadilla de Martínez, M., *La poesía popular en Puerto Rico,* Universidad de Madrid, Madrid, 1933, p.4; Pedreira, A., *Insularismo,* Editorial Edil, Río Piedras, 1971, p.35.

12. E.g., Babín, M.T., *Panorama de la cultura puertorriqueña,* Las Americas Publishing Co., New York, 1958, p.121; Figueroa, L., *Breve historia de Puerto Rico,* Vol.I, Editorial Edil, Río Piedras, 1971, p.15.

13. Quoted in Flores, J., "Cortijo's Revenge," *CENTRO,* vol.3, no.2, spring, 1991, p.11.

14. Blanco, T., *El prejuicio racial en Puerto Rico,* Editorial Biblioteca de Autores Puertorriqueños, San Juan, 1942, pp.51–59; Rodríguez Cruz, J., "Las relaciones raciales en Puerto Rico," *Revista de Ciencias Sociales,* vol.9, no.4, December, 1965, p.381.

15. Alvarez Nazario, L.M., *El elemento afronegroide en el español de Puerto Rico,* Instituto de Cultura Puertorriqueña, San Juan, 1974; López Cruz, F., *La música folklórica de Puerto Rico,* Troutman Press, Sharon, Connecticut, 1967, pp.47–122.

16. Ríos, P., "Export-Oriented Industrialization and the Demand for Female Labor: Puerto Rican Women in the Manufacturing Sector, 1952–1980," in Meléndez, E. and Meléndez, E. (ed), *Colonial Dilemma,* South End Press, Boston, 1993, pp.89–102; Silvestrini, B., *Violencia y criminalidad en Puerto Rico, 1898–1973,* Editorial Universitaria, Río Piedras, 1980, pp.113–132; Anderson, R., "The Party System: Change or Stagnation?," in J. Heine (ed), *Time for Decision,* North-South Publishing, Co., Lanham, Maryland, 1983, pp.3–26; Silén, J.A., *Apuntes: Para una historia del movimiento obrero puertorriqueño,* Editorial Cultural, Río Piedras, 1978, pp.163–200; Cotto, L., "The Rescate Movement: An Alternative Way of Doing Politics" in *Colonial Dilemma,* pp.119–130; Ferracuti, F., et al., *Delinquents and Nondelinquents in the Puerto Rican Slum Culture,* Ohio State University Press, Columbus, 1975.

17. Quesada, P. and Rivera Ramos, A.N., "La satisfacción de vida de la mujer envejeciente puertorriqueña blanca y negra en dos areas geográficas de Puerto Rico," in Rivera Ramos, A.N. (ed), *La mujer puertorriqueña: investigaciones psico-sociales,* Editorial Edil, Río Piedras, 1991, p.127.

18. Comité del Gobernador para el Estudio de los Derechos Civiles en Puerto Rico, *Informe al Honorable Gobernador,* San Juan, 1959; "Viewpoint," *The San Juan Star,* 23 December 1969, p.34; Zenón Cruz, I., *Narciso descubre su trasero: el negro en la cultura puertorriqueña,* Vol.I, Editorial Furidi, Humacao, 1974, pp.166–169, 176, 182–183, 194–195, 220–222, 234–236.

19. Seda Bonilla, E., "El prejuicio racial" in *La cultural política en Puerto Rico,* Centro de Investigaciones Sociales, Universidad de Puerto Rico, April, 1972, pp.103–189.

20. Monclova Vázquez, H., "Julio Axel Landrón: en dos tiempos," *Claridad,* 5–11 November 1993, p.19; López, R., "Africa en el balcón y su cultura religiosa de paso por la universidad," Diálogo, April 1994, pp.48–49; Routte-Gomez, E., "Wood cutter carves own niche for black dignity," *San Juan Star -Venue,* 26 September 1993, p.3; López, R., "La ocupación de los ritos en manos de Daniel Lind," *Diálogo,* December 1992, p.49; Fiet, L., "Notas hacia un teatro cultural," *Claridad,* 10–16 September 1993, p.26; "Bomba y plena para rato," *Diálogo,* March, 1994, pp.20–21; Ortíz Luquis,R., "Adolfina: un proyecto con su nombre," *Claridad,* 8–14 February, 1991, p.15.

21. María la de Calabó, "Entre sonera y sonero," *Claridad,* 19–25 January 1993, p.29; María la de Calabó, "Testimonio de Año Nuevo," *Claridad,* 11–17 January 1990, p.27; "Carnaval de Pasión," *Claridad,* 4–10 June 1993, p.44; Cotto, R., "La mujer negra en la música folclórica y popular en Puerto Rico," *Claridad,* 25 September-1 October, 1992, p.25.

22. Caplow, T., Stryker, S., and Wallace, S.E., *The Urban Experience,* The Bedminster Press, Totowa, New Jersey, 1964, pp.48,191; Safa, H.I., *The Urban Poor in Puerto Rico,* Holt, Rinehart, and Winston, New York, 1974, p.69.

23. Safa, *The Urban Poor,* p.17.

24. Quesada and Rivera Ramos, "Mujer envejeciente blanca y negra," p.125.
25. Bryce-Laporte, R.S., "Family Adaptation of Relocated Slum Dwellers in *Puerto Rico: Implications for Urban Research and Development,*" The Journal of Developing Areas, no.2, July, 1968, p.534.
26. Special monographic issue on salsa, J. Roberts (ed), BMI: The Many Worlds of Music, no.3, 1986, pp.32–39; Zenón Cruz, *Narciso* -Vol.I, pp.318–324; Cotto, "La mujer negra," p.25.
27. Brenes, R.L., "A puerta cerrada con Ismael Rivera," *CENTRO*, vol.3, no.2. spring, 1991, pp.56–61; Monclova Vázquez, H., ""Yo no estoy para jugar. Mejor me quito". Entrevista a Roberto Rohena," *Claridad*, 6–12 May 1994, pp.22–23; Rodríguez Juliá, E., *El entierro de Cortijo*, Ediciones Huracán, Río Piedras, 1983.
28. Back, K., *Slums, Projects, and People*, Duke University Press, Durham, 1962, pp.9–10, 32.
29. Carr, R.C., *Puerto Rico: A Colonial Experiment*, Vintage Books, New York, 1984, p.248.
30. Safa, *The Urban Poor*, pp.28–29, 41–56, 64–66, 81–86; Picó, *Caimito*, pp.85, 133–158; Otero, R., "Yo soy de Canales: entrevista a Cruz Rivera," *Piso 13*, vol.1, no.1, May, 1992, pp.2–3; Osorio, I., "Hablan los jóvenes del caserío," *Diálogo*, August 1993, pp.16, 18; Centeno, D., "Un llamado a valorar la opinión de los residentes," *Diálogo*, September 1993, p.14; Cotto, "The Rescate Movement".
31. Hall, S., et al., *Policing the Crisis*, The Macmillan Press, London, 1978, p.338, emphasis in the original.
32. E.g., Rodríguez, W., "Puerto Rico: sociedad enferma salud mental, gran serie no. 1," *El Nuevo Día*, 27 October 1977, p.3; Silva de Bonilla, R., "Un análisis de la violencia, el crimen y los criminales: anatomía de un quehacer ideológico de los científicos sociales en Puerto Rico," *Revista del Colegio de Abogados*, vol.42, no.2, May, 1981, pp.127–138; PC, "La criminalidad: síntoma de una crisis profunda," *Pensamiento Crítico-Documentos*, separatta, vol.9, no.49, May-June, 1986; Rivera Lugo, C. and Gutiérrez, P., "Puerto Rico, Puerto Pobre: los senderos de la desintegración social o el camino de la esperanza," *Diálogo*, February, 1993, pp.16–17; Colón Martínez, N., "Consenso frente a la criminalidad," *Claridad*, 28 January 3 February, 1994, p.11.
33. O'Reilley, P., "Town Without Fear: Making the Land Their Own," *No Middle Ground*, no.3–4, fall, 1984, pp.72–76; Brentlinger, J., *Villa Sin Miedo ¡Presente!*, Claves Latinoamericanas, Mexico, 1989; Del Valle, S., "Vecinos de Loíza enfrentan desahucio," *Claridad*, 31 December, 1993– 6 January, 1994, p.4; Archilla Rivera, M., "Expropiación de Las Picúas: legislatura defiende a los ricos," *Claridad*, 29 April 5 May, 1994, p.3.
34. López, R., "Una vuelta al punto: el negocio y la cultura de la drogas al detal," Diálogo, February, 1993, pp.14–15; Picó, *Caimito*, pp.133–158; Knudson, D.G., ""Que nadie se entere": la esposa maltratada en Puerto Rico," in Azize Vargas, Y. (ed), *La mujer en Puerto Rico*, Ediciones Huracán, Río Piedras, 1987, pp.139–154; Picó, F., *El día menos pensado: historia de los presidiarios en Puerto Rico (1793–1993)*, Ediciones Huracán, Río Piedras, 1994, pp.152–154.
35. Russell, T., "'Underground economy' Here is a Huge Activity," *Caribbean Business*, 21 April 1982, pp.1–2; Stewart, J.R., "Notes on the Underground Economy in Puerto Rico," *Puerto Rico Business Review*, vol.9, no.4, 1 July 1984, pp.23–30; Junta de Planificación, *Informe económico al Gobernador*, Oficina del Gobernador, San Juan, 1987, p.A-1.
36. Stewart, "Notes on the Underground Economy," p.30.
37. González, J.L., *Nueva visita al cuarto piso*, Libros del Flamboyán, Madrid, 1986, pp.46, 114, emphasis in the original.
38. Hall, S., et al., *Policing*, p.332.
39. E.g., Vales, et al., *Patrones de criminalidad en Puerto Rico*, n.p., Río Piedras, 1982; Silvestrini, *Violencia y criminalidad*; Peterson, J., *Evaluación de la estadística criminal de la Policía de Puerto Rico: años 1969–70 a 1973–74*, Departamento de Justicia, San Juan, 1974; Vales, P. (ed), *Justicia juvenil y la prevención de la delincuencia en Puerto Rico*, Oficina del Gobernador, San Juan, 1987.
40. E.g., Ferracuti, et al., *Delinquents*, p.126.

41. Nevarez-Muñiz, D. and Wolfgang, M., *Delincuencia juvenil en Puerto Rico: cohorte de personas nacidas en 1970,* Senado de Puerto Rico, San Juan, November 1988, pp.38–39, 41, 49, 83.
42. Nevarez-Muñiz and Wolfgang, *Delincuencia,* pp.39, 41–42, 43, 44, 50, 83–84, 87, 94, 96–97, 99, 154, 177–178, 183, 219, 222–223, 224, 226–227, 229–230, 265–266.
43. Archilla Rivera, M.Y., "Guerra contra los pobres y militarización del país," Claridad, 5–11 February 1993, p.4; Picó, F., "Criminalidad y violencia: mano dura contra la mano dura," *Diálogo,* February 1993, pp.12–13; del Castillo, N., "Militarización de los caseríos," *El Diario,* 24 June 1993, p.18; Picó, F., "Crisis de autoridad y la autoridad por la fuerza," *Diálogo,* August 1993, pp.16, 18; Martínez, A., "Una división especial para vigilar los residenciales," *El Nuevo Día,* 1 June 1994, p.15.
44. Vélez, J., La Border patrol," *Claridad,* 11 November 1993, p. 40; Guadalupe, R., "Del graffiti como medio de expresión racista," *Claridad,* 22–28 July 1994, p. 24.
45. Hall, et al., Policing, p.331, emphasis in the original; Picó, El día menos pensado, pp.151–153.
46. Muller, K.C., "Santeria," *Sunday San Juan Star Magazine,* 22 May 1983, pp.2–3; Flores, J., "Rappin', Writin', & Breakin'," *CENTRO,* vol.2, no.3, spring, 1988, pp.34–41; Fernández, W., "Sepia del Bajo Mundo: música al compás de La Perla," *Avance,* vol.2, no.75, 24–31 December 1975, pp.24–31; Nurse Allende, L., "Los Pleneros de la 23 Abajo: creando un nuevo concepto de la plena y la bomba," *Hómines,* vol.6, no.1, January-June, 1982, pp.251–255; Rivera, R.Z., "Rap Music in Puerto Rico: Mass Consumption or Social Resistance?," *CENTRO,* vol.5, no.1, winter, 1992–1993, pp.52–65; Alegría Pons, J.F., "Aspectos de la religiosidad popular en Puerto Rico," *Claridad,* 27 December-2 January 1992, pp.16–17; "Latin Empire: Puerto Rap," *CENTRO,* vol.3, no.2. spring, 1991, pp.77–85; Cámara, D., "Las iniciaciones rituales de Palo Monte o Mayombé como fuentes de conocimiento y evolución humana," *Africanías,* no.7, 1991, pp.3–4.
47. Picó, *Caimito,* p.14.

Toque de plenas callejeras, fotografía de Héctor Méndez Caratini ©

AfroPuerto Rican Cultural Studies:
Beyond *cultura negroide* and *antillanismo*

JUAN A. GIUSTI CORDERO

Approaches to the historical experience of Puerto Ricans of color have been overwhelmed by the urgency of confronting racism, against recurrent claims that Puerto Ricans uniformly practice "racial democracy."[1] The debate on racial prejudice in Puerto Rico has experienced "a profound repression."[2] Racism in Puerto Rico is "silken or rough,"[3] and it is often subtler and more complex, but no less toxic—especially among the upper strata—than in the U.S.[4] Much remains to be said about racism in Puerto Rico, with regard to its almost perverse semantic richness and strategic ambiguity, and to its prime location in matters of Puerto Rican national identity.[5] Yet phenotypical boundaries among Puerto Ricans are part of the larger whole that is the historical experience of Puerto Ricans of color.[6]

Here I attempt to go beyond the narrow categories and issues that have confined the discussion of race in Puerto Rican culture. At issue is the broader AfroPuerto Rican historical and cultural context, where patterns and practices of racism are embedded, infused with meaning, and interwoven with other aspects of AfroPuerto Rican and Puerto Rican social life.[7] It is those larger patterns that we need to bring to the fore.

■ *National culture and cultural context*
Some preliminary remarks on Puerto Rican national culture and on culture in general, are in order. The Puerto Rican understandings of race is condensed in the saying *"El que no tiene dinga, tiene mandinga."*[8] This refrain simultaneously recognizes the deep African dimensions of Puerto Rico while waving aside (or, perhaps, laughing away) further discussion. Whatever we may make of it, this intense ambiguity about race sets Puerto Rico apart from the U.S. and constitutes a dimension of its national culture.[9]

JUAN A. GIUSTI CORDERO is an assistant professor of history at the University of Puerto Rico, Río Piedras, where he teaches Caribbean and African history. His dissertation (State University of New York at Binghamton, 1994) is on the history of labor and ecology in the Loíza region in Puerto Rico. The author wishes to thank Amílcar Tirado Avilés and the editorial committee for its interest and collaboration.

The boundaries of Puerto Rican culture, which is best described as both colonial and migrant, are themselves ambiguous and far-flung.[10] But it is a national culture nonetheless, and it demonstrates broad coherences and patterns that would be senseless to ignore. Indeed, in recent years, even statehood supporters have recognized that Puerto Rico is culturally a nation.[11] What the nationalists may have greater difficulty in recognizing is that, like all national cultures, Puerto Rican culture is heterogeneous and has many variations—race and culture, spatial, class, gender, age, and others—that are demonstrated not only by individuals and groups, but across contexts and situations. These variations, one of which can be characterized by culture, range from subtle fissures to virtual social warfare.

Thus culture is formed by the discernible, changing patterns of thinking and acting of a group.[12] It is through culture that a group gains awareness of itself and others, of its potential as a group and as individuals. There is no need to equate culture strictly with a national culture, let alone with any given institutions or structures. Culture exists at all levels in multiple forms; however, these forms mingle and connect. Determining the connections between the ephemeral and particular (known as "practices") and the general and longer-term (known as "patterns," "contexts," "spaces," and "social relations") keeps historians busy and perplexed.

Specific historical conditions, mediated by cultural and political currents and projects of particular groups, and premised on inclusion and exclusion, alliance and hegemony, shape the historical field of national culture. Broader levels of definition are linked integrally to the national center as evidenced in such terms as: "Caribbean," "African-American," "Latin American," etc.[13] National culture is protean and problematic, but then what isn't? Complexity does not mean we need to rule out all coherence and all pattern, but that we should look more closely. Perhaps it will be useful, in this regard, to consider the cultural and political projects of *cultura negroide* and *antillanismo*—the two major AfroPuerto Rican movements in the twentieth century—as permeable cultural and sociohistorical practices, spaces and contexts.

■ *Cultura negroide*

Partly due to centuries of interaction, cultural contexts in Puerto Rico in are less like keystones than like unstable gases. Concepts such as syncretism, transculturation, and creolization seek to grasp that dynamism. Attempts to isolate, within Puerto Rican culture, a bedrock of *hispanidad*[14] are as futile as those that would elaborate a Taíno nation or an African essence. However, AfroPuerto Rican culture has been especially prone to treatment as a discrete though subordinate field; and this was done earliest in the paradigm of *cultura negroide* (or *afro-negroide*), a name that I employ somewhat arbitrarily to designate the first epoch of public AfroPuerto Rican cultural expression in this century.

The term "*cultura negroide*" is evidently loaded. "*Cultura*" by itself throws up fences, whereas "*negroide*" focuses attention too narrowly on color.[15] Moreover, the "*-oide*" ending infuses *negroide* with a sense of artificiality and inferiority, the nearest equivalent occurs in science fiction, when a writer addressed the difference between being "human" and being "humanoid." But the term "*cultura negroide*," and especially *poesía negroide*, was current in Puerto Rico already in the 1930s.[16] As in other representations of "Africanism" in the Americas in the first half of the twentieth century,[17] including the thrust of *Négritude* and Haitian *Indigénisme*, Puerto Rico's *cultura negroide* sought in Puerto Rico relatively "pure," "African" patterns and traits surviving among people of African descent, though perhaps the larger frame of reference was not Africa but something closer: blackness, *lo negroide*, and geographically, an impressionistic Caribbean. Blackness, whatever it was or deemed to be, was at the root of lo *negroide*; the exclusively African, rather than Indian or folk-European pedigree of many traits, in particular the determination of their specific origins and meaning in given zones within the continent tended to require further research.

It was in literature, and especially in poetry, that *cultura negroide* attained its most explicit articulation. The two leading poets are Luis Palés Matos and Fortunato Vizcarrondo. Both men wrote most of their *negroide* poetry in the 1920s and 1930s, Palés was the earlier of the two to publish. Both authors, I should note, might have taken issue with the terms *"cultura"* and *"negroide":* Palés used the additives *"afro-antillana"* and *"antillana"* to describe his poetry at a time when the term *"afrocubanismo"* was current in Cuba. Yet the work of Palés, even more than Vizcarrondo, is at the center of popular definitions of *poesía negroide*. Palés' poetry is full of onomatopoeic plays on word sounds, e.g., of Caribbean and African geography, and of AfroPuerto Rican words. Most of Vizcarrondo's poetry, on the other hand, fully depend on AfroPuerto Rican speech.

Beside Palés Matos and Vizcarrondo, there are some thirty other poets who wrote in the *negroide* vein, or on AfroPuerto Rican themes, in the 1920s-1960s (Palés, to be sure, is among the very earliest in Latin America as a whole). For most well-known Puerto Rican poets, it became fashionable to have at least one or two *negroide* pieces. Then again, there were also other black poets such as Victorio Llanos Allende, who like Vizcarrondo was also from Carolina. His poem *"La Negra Cora"* is *negroide* not in speech, but definitely in content:

> *Batiendo su cuerpo entero*
> *al compás de la tambora*
> *se mueve la negra Cora*
> *con un vaivén sandunguero.*[18]

The main *negroide* traits include sensuality *(sandunguería, sabrosura)*, indeed a heightened experience and deployment of all the senses, directly corresponding to a deemphasis on the rational, and an appeal to the "primitive"; festiveness *(bachata)* to the point of self-conscious primitiveness; sensual and fluid body movement; upbeat music and rhythm, especially on hand drums; enchantment with the coastal landscape; idealization of the traditional, rustic lifestyle of the *negros de la costa*.

In Palés Matos' 1926 poem *"Pueblo Negro"* (originally titled *"Africa")*, and one of his earliest "black" poems, he offers a compelling image of a village reminiscent of Medianía:

> *Esta noche me obsede la remota*
> *visión de un pueblo negro...*
> *—Mussumba, Tombuctú, Farafangana—*
> *es un pueblo de sueño,*
> *tumbado allá en mis brumas interiores*
> *a la sombra de claros cocoteros....*
>
> *Allá entre las palmeras*
> *está tendido el pueblo...*
> *Mussumba, Tombuctú, Farafangana*
> *Caserío irreal de paz y sueño.*[19]

Cultura negroide is also significant for its celebration of black and sometimes mulatto beauty,[20] though often caricaturing "primitive" sensuality. Its cultural representations raise issues of race, gender, and class that require closer discussion, as it was women, and especially black women from the working classes, who were deemed to be most erotic, and whose persona was entirely eroticized.[21]

Finally, there is also in *cultura negroide* social and political comment from a democratic perspective, made with deft irony and razor-sharp imagery. In Vizcarrondo's poetry there is a series of eighteen such poems. By far the best known of these is *"¿Y tu agüela a'onde ejtá?"* The current of social and political comment, almost entirely absent from Palés Matos' work, was important in *poesía negroide*. It was as well as one of the key currents of in Puerto Rican socially aware poetry as a whole. Partly because Palés did not practice that subgenre, it is not usually seen as part and parcel of the definition of *cultura negroide*, or as a social manifesto of far broader import.[22]

In the explicitly racist conceptions of the period, it is important to note, there were only certain fields of expression open to *negroide* poetry; even though a "black" poet like

Vizcarrondo could write "white" poetry—this is, after all Puerto Rico—the literary canons demanded that the themes of one and another genre remain distinct. The call for a *poesía mulata* made by Palés, as in Cuba by Guillén, attains in this light a fuller iconoclastic connotation.

In a preface to the second edition of Vizcarrondo's *Dinga y mandinga*, of all places, we find a brazen distinction between "white" and "black" poetry. "White" poetry is classically spiritual, "black" poetry a coarse portrayal of the *costumbres de negros*, defunct or nearly so. And black poetry—"and this happens in every poem of the *negroide* genre that I know, by different authors"—is not "inspired in beauty in any of its manifestations."[23] In this reading, *negroide* poetry is mindless and heartless, purely physical, indeed metabolic.

> [I]n this class of poetry nothing is found that speaks to the mind or the heart in its whispers, but here is much in its awkward *[desarticulada]* cadence that, upon being felt by a good part of the mestizo population of those countries, accelerates the circulation of their blood, transmits activity to their nervous system and puts their muscles in movement [etc.][24]

And this is a "positive" assessment of Vizcarrondo's poetry. Martínez Acosta has such a "high" opinion of Vizcarrondo that he urges him to abandon "black" poetry altogether, in order to attain, as a "white" poet, true beauty, pure art, and genuine success.[25] For *negroide* poetry was destined to become but a "painful historical memory" of the uphill struggles of blacks during and after slavery.

In music and dance, there was more freedom for black and mulatto artistic expression, though there was no shortage of critics denouncing "vulgarity" and "lewdness." José A. Balseiro, for instance, the Puerto Rican literary scholar most recognized and honored abroad, wrote that the *bomba* had been born in Ponce "among whores."[26] In any event, in music and dance lo *afro-puertorriqueño* gained a preeminence, and more genuine expression, that it was denied in literature. While the musical boundaries of *cultura negroide* are subject to debate when viewed as a broad cultural movement or epoch, clearly the *negroide* in the early twentieth century broke with the boundaries imposed on it in slave times as "black music," and indirectly spawned the *plena*—simultaneously, of course, as music and dance—which also developed in the early years of the century.

The *plena* also expressed a more critical understanding of social class and everyday life than did poesía *negroide*. From the time of its origins in Ponce, the working-class currents that shaped the *plena* were evident, during a period of intense internal migration and social transformation.

> The emergence of the *plena* coincided with the consolidation of the Puerto Rican working class; it accompanied and lent idiosyncratic musical expression to that historical process [...] Many of the best-known *plenas*, from the earliest times, tell of strikes, working conditions and events of working-class life; they give voice, usually in sharp ironic tones and imagery, to the experience of working people in all its aspects (Flores 1993: 89).

The *plena* reached commercial success with Canario (Manuel Jiménez) in the 1930s, both in Puerto Rico and in New York, as Puerto Rican music.[27] Rafael Hernández, a mulatto, also wrote a number of "afro" pieces, both *plenas* and rumbas. César Concepción, also a mulatto, led the best known big band that featured the *plena*. These were, in a sense, the mulatto and musical dimensions of *cultura negroide*.[28]

Indeed, several of Vizcarrondo's poems were musicalized as *plenas*, especially the anthemic "¿Y tu agüela a'onde ejtá?." This poem is, significantly, Vizcarrondo's strongest social comment; hence it was especially congenial to the *plena* tradition, forming a natural point for *plena* and *poesía negroide* to intersect. The subject, racial identity vs. family loyalties, was fundamental:.

The title *"¿Y tu agüela a'onde ejtá?"* became a universal refrain in Puerto Rico. Even in 1996, albeit in a contradictory discursive setting (among other things, because it is voiced by a white comedian in blackface), *"¿Y tu agüela a'onde ejtá?"* was a standard line in a top-rated Puerto Rican television show (as we have said, one line from that poem, *"El que no tiene dinga, tiene mandinga,"* is among the best-known Puerto Rican proverbs).[29] Characteristically, it is not generally known in Puerto Rico that this song was originally a poem, or that its author was Vizcarrondo. In a sense, Vizcarrondo this achieved what poets envy: a condition of anonymity.[30] The genius of Canario, Rafael Hernández and Pedro Flores in the 1930's, and in the 1950s and the 1960s of Rafael Cortijo and Ismael Rivera, can be better appreciated in light of the crosscurrents of *afropuertorriqueñismo* as a whole; but I can only suggest the point here.

Cuisine—the sense of taste, metaphorized as *el sabor*—is also crucial in *cultura negroide*, as in Puerto Rican culture generally. And cuisine is an integral part of a selective, bucolic view of the coastal life of *los negros*. Eating AfroPuerto Rican food in the rustic restaurants of Loíza Aldea complete with straw huts *(bohíos)* and coconut-shell open hearths *(burenes, fogones)* is representative of a country existence. This was increasingly common through the 1930s and 1940s, when going for a drive "in the country" outside San Juan became popular. *Loíza Aldea* could also be a discreet place to pursue an affair.

Then since the 1970s the pursuit of *comida negroide*, as it were—or *comida típica* as it is more frequently called—continued more massively in the legendary roadside *friquitines* (kiosks) of the "wild" littoral of Piñones between San Juan and Loíza, which itself was regarded as a large-scale lovers' lane. Eating "typical" fare at a rustic, not very clean wooden kiosk made of assorted planks, the food fried in a large cauldron heated by burning coconut husks and firewood and washed down with coconut water (which the *loiceños* used to discard) became an act of affirmation of difference, of culture and identity.

Land crabs, which were scarcer and more expensive, lost in gastronomical importance to the simpler fritters, which continued to be made in Piñones with the traditional crops and catch of the region, even if some ingredients were increasingly brought from afar: evidence of a "constructed" localism, to a degree. The fare is both of islandwide currency *(bacalaítos, alcapurrias, salmorejo de jueyes, casabe)* or more strictly of Loíza *(empanadas, tortillas*, not to forget *caña* [bootleg rum] of which Loíza has long been the island capital.[31] Vizcarrondo captured the gustatory dimensions of *cultura negroide* in one of the verses of his classic *"Loíza Aldea"* (1942):

> *Salve, pueblo de pajuílej,*
> *De jicácoj y pejcao,*
> *De juéyej y de casábej,*
> *De tottíyaj y rosiao.*[32]

Similarly, and in another poem titled *"Loíza Aldea,"* Carmelina Vizcarrondo wrote *"Loíza, negra en casabes/en tortillas y en hechizos"* ("Loíza, black in cassava/in tortillas and sorceries").[33] Seafood such as conch *(carrucho)* and octopus were also in demand in *Loíza* and *Piñones*, and the dishes went well with the territory, for they were well regarded for their supposedly mild aphrodisiac effects. Not surprisingly, the urban-folk terms for a secret lover is *chillo* and *chilla*, a well-esteemed fish in seafood restaurants (the term is also a pun on "hurry," as in *chillar gomas*, or *"¡Chíllalas!"*

Indeed, the gastronomy of *cultura negroide*, enmeshed with the wider gastronomy of the coast and the sea, is close to the nitty-gritty of contemporary Puerto Rican national identity, at least in its more festive and erotic definitions. Like popular music and sport, food is a space where *los negros* took over or were constrained (or rather, as José Luis González reminds us, where they held their own). It is equally one of the strongest, and literally gut-level continuities of *cultura negroide* right to the present.

Despite the considerable gains that the perspective of *cultura negroide* represented, it tended to racialize AfroPuerto Rican culture, robbing it of its historical depth and complexity (of which almost little was known, or studied). To Palés, who was the leading thinker and poet of *cultura negroide*, AfroPuerto Rican culture always remained "the other."

Palés separated *lo negro* from the Puerto Rican. He segregated him at the very moment in which he saw him "mixed" with "us." He denied *lo negro* by pretending, as he said, that he "lives physically and spiritually with us." He rose above the predominant prejudice of the time by conceiving a culturally mulatto Puerto Rico, but as a product of his milieu, he remained subject to the prejudices of his contemporaries.[34]

It is little wonder that in literature, *cultura negroide* remained virtually confined to poetry. Typically, *poesía negroide* was written, with greater or lesser fidelity, in an Afro–Puerto Rican speech (*lengua bozal*), whose authenticity, longevity, and African lineage remains in dispute.[35] Zenón, for one, entirely rejects the existence of a *lengua negra* in Puerto Rico and he even questions significant modes of pronunciation in heavily black areas such as Loíza. At the same time, he criticizes those who would minimize or deny the existence of a substantial number of "*afronegroide*" words.[36] With regard to language, the complexity and difficulty of Zenón's position is again evident: on the one hand, he rejects the racist isolation of AfroPuerto Rican cultural contexts; on the other hand, he affirms their existence and creativity against those who would negate them.

The great declaimer of *poesía negroide*, Juan Boria, a black schoolteacher from Dorado,[37] attracted large audiences from the 1950s to the 1980s with the poetry of Palés and Vizcarrondo. Boria became something of a curator of *cultura negroide: el Faraón de la poesía negroide* or of *el verso negro*. For some, the entire AfroPuerto Rican literary tradition was confined to the poems recited by this one man (though in the 1960s and 1970s, the black *declamadora*, singer and dancer Sylvia del Villard achieved greater recognition among younger, now *antillanista* audiences. Boria had the foresight, and the sense of tradition, to pass the mantle some years before his death to a declaimer in his twenties, Julio Axel Landrón.

Cultura negroide also spatialized *lo afropuertorriqueño* in ways that connect with the notion of cultural context but which reify this notion. In *cultura negroide*, the town of Loíza—"Loíza Aldea" as it came to be called in this century—became the symbol and practically the only recognized locus of AfroPuerto Rican culture. "*Allá en Loíza es que están los negros*," *cultura negroide* seemed to say. Anthropologists agreed: noting the existence of "significant concentrations of persons of prevailingly negroid phenotype" in Loíza, Mintz identified proportion of blacks as the greatest in Puerto Rico—at more than 50 percent.[38]

Lo negroide in Loíza was crowned by the *annual fiestas de Santiago*, the best-known and most closely studied single aspect of AfroPuerto Rican culture.[39] The tradition of such salience in Loíza and Puerto Rico generally that it migrated to New York, where they are a major event in the Puerto Rican community.

■ *Antillanismo*

The terms "*antillanismo*" and "*afroantillanismo*" have been far longer in use in Puerto Rico than might seem, and at least since Palés Matos used them in 1932.[40] But these terms are more aptly used to denominate the intellectual and artistic currents that succeeded *cultura negroide* in the 1960s. Expressed in literature, salsa music, historiography, drama and elsewhere, *antillanismo* tends to distance itself from *cultura negroide*, but rarely explicitly; it is actually quite close to *cultura negroide* in spirit. *Antillanismo* has been far more influential than *cultura negroide*, and has been a prevailing cultural influence among Puerto Rican intellectuals and artists of the younger generations over the last two decades: it is as close to a Zeitgeist as we may come in contemporary Puerto Rico. Moreover, *antillanismo* has largely defined the discussion on AfroPuerto Rican culture and history over the last two decades.

Proponents of *antillanismo* offer little in the way of definition, perhaps because *antillanismo* itself prefers movement, rhythm, and sensuousness. Some important tenets of *antillanismo* come from Palés himself, in the interview and exchanges that took place in 1932, where he coined the term *antillanismo*. Strikingly, however, in his poetry exoticism and "otherness" of *lo negroide* prevail. Even in Palés' broad-ranging prose approaches, as seen above, *lo negro* has been equated with a "primitive nature."[41]

Crucially, however, *antillanismo* no longer views black culture in Puerto Rico as essentially distinct, but as a—or the—major component of Puerto Rican national culture—its hardest edge, as it were. This approach, which can be seen as "integrationist" but is in fact far more than that, coexists uneasily with *antillanismo* in a sense that the African dimension remains distinct, and with the result that it is an unending source of exoticism.

In regard to *cultura negroide*, *antillanismo* enriches perspectives on AfroPuerto Rican culture in interesting ways: *Antillanismo* authors have been exceedingly prolific, with an enormous number of works especially in music and literature, specifically short stories and novels. Poetry does not have in *antillanismo* the prominence that it gained in *cultura negroide*, and *antillanismo* in good measure has simply incorporated that legacy. The late Sylvia del Villard, the great black *declamadora* and dancer who made blackness a profound part of the protest culture of the late 1960s and 1970s and who was a major force behind the rise of *antillanismo*, performed, like Juan Boria, the poems of Palés and Vizcarrondo.[42] Younger poets who are probably the major poetic figures of *antillanismo*, such as Ana Irma Rivera Lassén and Juan de Matta García (who calls his poetry *"negrista"*),[43] have been prominent in other fields or remain underrecognized as poets in Puerto Rico.

The Puerto Rican community in the U.S., especially through salsa music, was extremely important in the development of *antillanismo*, to an even greater degree than was the case of the *plena* in the 1920s and 1930s. The early music of Willie Colón which explicitly demonstrated an African accent in such songs as *"Che Che Colé,"* and *"Ghana'é,"* sung in modified *negroide* beat by Héctor Lavoe of Ponce and New York, became lasting anthems for a generation of Puerto Ricans. In *"Che Che Colé,"* Lavoe sang: *"Vamos todos a bailar/este ritmo africano"*; in *"Ghana'é,"* references to Africa were evident in the title itself. These songs, and others of the early and mid-1970s (e.g. Cuban Celia Cruz's *"Químbara"*; Rubén Blades/Willie Colón's *"Canto Abacuá"*), stand out as remarkable tributes and bridges to Palés Matos himself, complete with fanciful "African" names and sound plays. Musically, the relationship between salsa rhythms and the *plena* rhythms of Cortijo, Ismael Rivera, and Tite Curet Alonso remains problematic.

Antillanismo holds Africa more explicitly, if still too vaguely and romantically, in its frame of reference. The African dimensions presented tend to be artificially bounded, pushed toward an exotic, colorful niche almost indistinguishable from the earlier *cultura negroide* approach. We are not confronted with the African presence as a dimension constitutive of a heterogeneous Puerto Rican social culture as a whole. Indeed, as Jean Besson writes: [T]he emergence of an Afro-Caribbean history has been delayed not only through the Eurocentric approach to the region's past, but also by a preoccupation with the passive retention of Africanisms.[44] One of the most interesting exceptions, in which Africa has a more concrete and critical meaning, is *"Colobó"* (1970), sung by Ismael Rivera and exactly contemporary with Willie Colón's more "African" songs:

> *Tierra adentro en Colobó*
> *el ambiente es noble y sano*
> *aquí vibra en emoción*
> *el tambor ritmo africano*
>
> *Bajo el frondoso palmar*
> *hay tranquilidad sin par*
> *Aunque digan que hay atraso*
> *Colobó es para gozar.*[45]

At the same time, and to its credit, *antillanismo* also fixed its sights squarely on "mulatto culture," *la mulatez*, as a vital component. *Antillanismo*, writes the Peruvian literary critic Julio Ortega, focuses on "the world of the mulatto and the black."[46]

The AfroPuerto Rican tradition—for instance, the *fiestas de Santiago*—is now viewed as being, at least in part, more historically as an expression of cultural and political resistance, connected to traditions of slave resistance and *cimarronaje*.[47]

Beyond the discreet or playful sensuality of *cultura negroide*, *antillanismo* aims for sensuality, indeed eroticism. As in *cultura negroide*, the depiction of women, and of male-female relations are central to *antillanismo's* expression. In the music of Ismael Rivera, and in addition to the tender love songs such as *"Sale el sol,"* we find others that describe men's violence against women *("Si te cojo")*, and still others *("Pa lo que tú le das")* where the man is rebuked for abusing the woman and for "giving" her only rice and beans and *"palo, puño y bofetá"* ("club, fist and slaps").[48] *Antillanismo* is more explicitly historical than *cultura negroide*. When Ana Lydia Vega writes of *historicidio* as the historical near-obsession of the writers of her generation, she is most specifically referring to the *antillanista* writers.[49] The major manifesto of *antillanismo*, *País de cuatro pisos*, is more historical than literary in character.

Historians have welcomed the work of Rodríguez Juliá, the leading *antillanista* literary figure (see below). Fernando Picó recently wrote a brief appraisal of Rodríguez Juliá's work, entitled "Edgardo, give us more books" (*"Edgardo, danos más libros"*), where he praised Rodríguez Juliá's talent for "listening and recording the voices of the past and present" and urged him to continue publishing new works. Vega, probably the most accomplished and innovative *antillanista* writer, recently wrote a historical novel set in a slave plantation in the island's southeast coast, suggestively titled *Falsas crónicas del Sur*.[50] *Antillanismo* has broader spatial parameters than *cultura negroide*. For the latter, the relevant space was strictly Loíza Aldea, with some reference to Guayama (Palés birthplace); few other images were offered. *Antillanismo* not only set forth Puerto Rico's coast in general as the relevant space; it also identified an counter-space, the highlands *(altura)* as the rival of the coast. The *altura*, since 1910 the heartland of Puerto Rican cultural nationalism, was now viewed by *antillanismo* as a conservative, white, overbearing pseudo-redoubt of Puerto Rican national culture. Puerto Rico's coastal dimension, the *antillanistas* insisted, needs reevaluation over and above the *altura* as a vital historical and cultural space.[51] Finally, *antillanismo* has identified more closely with the Caribbean region than has *cultura negroide*. While other Caribbean islands, like parts of Africa, appear rather fleetingly in the poetry of Palés, now Puerto Rican *antillanistas* are setting short stories and novels in other Caribbean islands, with an overriding focus on those island's African dimensions.

Locally, for *antillanismo* perhaps the main icon is no longer the Loíza Aldea of *cultura negroide*, but rather Piñones. Piñones is also in Loíza, but it is more rural and is at the same time closer to San Juan. Medianía, or at least the areas of Medianía that are more accessible to outsiders, is perhaps too urban, too evidently poor, and decidedly unbucolic in terms of the current ecological *mentalité*. Piñones, however—always San Juan's favorite "lovers' lane"—has "wild" beaches hard by the coastal highway and thus readily available to our automobile culture.[52] The area consists of old communities, large *cocales*, fritter stands *(friquitines, negocitos, kioskos)* and large unbuilt space close to San Juan.[53] The struggles of its communities against eviction, and later against hotel and residential construction, are also part of the area's allure of independence.

A 1991 essay by Rodríguez Juliá, *"Piñones. Una crónica"* locates Piñones in contemporary Puerto Rico.[54] This essay, which chronicles a drive through Piñones, attempts to evoke a sense of place and of memory. Rodríguez Juliá is also mindful of changes in the Piñones landscape, especially in terms of restaurants and food stands that lent the area its particular mood and character. Yet the chronicle remains quite oblivious to the *piñoneros* themselves (except, on one occasion, as African characters straight out of *negroide* poetry). In all, Piñones here seems to remain a passive stage for outsiders' jaunts and reveries, with little more than a recent past.

Another, and perhaps more representative, text on Piñones is by Coqui Santaliz, a well-known journalist and writer. The article, titled *"Divina herencia en Vacía Talega"* (Divine Heritage in Vacía Talega), begins:

> *Oh Piñones, who does not have you in some nook of memories robbed from the impositions of time. Ah, Piñones-Vacía Talega, without time* (sin tiempo). *An* alcapurria *(crabmeat fritter) crossing the distances of the city. Our Afro-Caribbean* [afroantillana] *heritage in each maroon look of dignity* [en cada mirada cimarrona de dignidad]. *An idealized world*

that we thought would never end. The enclosed beach coves [pocitas] of my childhood; the little roads of interminable holes of that beach that was indeed ours. For everyone a spot [...] Always a hideaway to escape metropolitically [metropolitanamente] *from the pollution of body and soul.*[55]

There are evident continuities between *cultura negroide's* Loíza Aldea and the Loíza and Piñones of *antillanismo*. In both, there is a reaffirmation of an AfroPuerto Rican space as a "hard-core" Puerto Rican space. Luis Rafael Sánchez's bittersweet story of emigration *"La guagua aérea"* (The air bus) comes to mind. One of the passengers on a San Juan—New York flight remarks, in a moving evocation of Piñones (...and Cortijo):

I cannot live in Puerto Rico because there's no life for me there, so I'll bring it with me bit by bit; in this trip, four crabs from Vacía Talega, in the trip before, a fighting cock, in my next, all of Cortijo's records.[56]

Other Puerto Rican emigrants did not carry crabs in their suitcases, but perhaps went even further, renaming the old and spirited Puerto Rican community in the Lower East Side Loisaida and celebrating the *fiestas de Santiago*. Whatever the real changes in the Loíza coast, it remains a forceful presence in the Puerto Rican imagination.

Yet this vital identity at once AfroPuerto Rican and Puerto Rican remains entangled in *antillanismo*, and in contemporary Puerto Rican culture in general, with an iconization that suggests a backyard "Orientalism"[57] imposed on the AfroPuerto Rican heritage. Perhaps the iconization is cognizant of the specificity of that tradition, but it is rather self-centered all the same.

■ *Zenón, González, Rodríguez Juliá, Ferré*

A more specific discussion of four leading authors in writing in the *antillanista* vein may further clarity my argument. In 1974, Isabelo Zenón published the first (and more important) volume of his pathbreaking *Narciso descubre su trasero*,[58] the leading critique of racism in Puerto Rican culture, particularly in literature and language. Zenón stressed not only the denial of the *puertorriqueñidad* of Puerto Ricans of color but also the denial by black and mulatto Puerto Ricans of *lo negro*. The distance between *negro* and *africano* in *Narciso* seems, however, immense, almost unbridgeable.[59] The absence of a sustained claim to a radical AfroPuerto Rican distinctiveness is precisely what places Narciso outside *cultura negroide*, and Zenón virtually denounces *cultura negroide* at several points in his book.

However, in its insistence on the integral belonging of AfroPuerto Rican culture in Puerto Rican culture, Zenón established a key theme of *antillanismo*. Zenón viewed Puerto Rican culture as tripartite composed of Taíno, African and Spanish influences.[60] The boundaries between the three components are strictly phenotypical; Zenón's message is that all are responsible for forming Puerto Rican culture. (Zenón's advocacy of Puerto Rican independence and his allegiance to an embattled Puerto Rican national culture go far to explain this perspective.[61])

Zenón did not tackle in *Narciso* the vexing question of an AfroPuerto Rican cultural context and was quick to label *cultura negroide* as racist. His investigation of the nexus between Africa and Puerto Rico, e.g., the differences and connections between *africano* and *negro* or on the cultural roots of Puerto Rican folk religious practices such as *santiguo* or *espirituao*, are literally self-effacing.

Zenón takes up the matter of the *africano* versus the *negro* only in a footnote. There he relies largely on the authority of Roger Bastide, who himself appeals to specialists on the anglophone Caribbean. The quotes from Bastide are left without comment.[62] In becoming *negro*, according to Bastide, the *africano* disappeared: slavery was too brutal and long-lasting. Bastide and Zenón do not take note of the historical particularities of Puerto Rico and the hispanophone Caribbean, where slavery was truly strong only in some regions, during some decades of the nineteenth century. In other regions, an old, creole, peasant, free blackmulatto-white population contextualized slavery in ways very different from the anglophone

Caribbean. Thus Zenón's cryptic comment that the contribution of el negro to Puerto Rican culture is far vaster than that of *el africano*, and that the contributions of *el negro* have been essentially a matter not of groups, but of individuals, strikes me as simplistic. So does Zenón's tacit endorsement of Bastide's comment that *los negros* have "no affective attachment to the land" and that the joint ownership of "family land" was strictly a response to the plantation system.[63]

Zenón's perspective on "black" religious culture is more complex. He offers a long quote from Puerto Rican historian Salvador Brau, in whose writing *santiguo* virtually becomes a Galician tradition. Zenón also suggests that black spiritualists *(espiritiaos)* were common and authoritative simply because people trusted and feared them more.[64] Zenón is especially concerned to counter racist dismissals of supposedly "black" practices.[65] However, Zenón equally recognizes that it is also racist to dismiss the African cultural legacy in Puerto Rico as irrelevant. Thus he concludes that more reflection on this matter is necessary.[66] His conclusion underscores the existence of an important tension in Puerto Rican culture, specifically in his discussion of AfroPuerto Rican culture. In *Narciso*, *lo afropuertorriqueño* approaches, but still at a distance, crucial referents of AfroPuerto Rican/Puerto Rican historical experience: social group, territory, cosmogony, and history.

Zenón has not written about the *antillanismo* that flourished in the later 1970s and 1980s, a trend that sprang in part from *Narciso* itself. But one might surmise important areas of disagreement, beginning with the point of contact between *antillanismo* and *cultura negroide*. Perhaps this partly explains Zenón's relative silence after *Narciso* and the shift in his work, interestingly, toward gender.[67]

A second major work of *antillanismo* is a historical-cultural essay, José Luis González's *El país de cuatro pisos* (1980).[68] González, who had originally criticized Zenón's book as simplistic, by 1980 provoked debates at least as strong as those unleashed by *Narciso* six years before. González broke both with Zenón's tripartite cultural and racial schema to argue that Puerto Rican culture and history has been fundamentally African and Afro-Caribbean since the sixteenth century. Indeed, González argued, the first and presumably "truest" Puerto Rican were black, indeed "African." The structure of González's argument, though not the conclusions, have interesting parallels in M.G. Smith's "plural society" model.[69]

However, González's essay was read as a devastating attack on hispanophilia and its class correlate, the collapsed Puerto Rican national bourgeoisie. It is a sign of the intellectual tone of Puerto Rico that the specific implications of *País de cuatro pisos* for the discussion of AfroPuerto Rican culture went largely unheeded. *País de cuatro pisos* remained a major point of reference through the renewed hispanophilia of the late 1980s and the *Quinto Centenario*. But little is gained merely with renovated icons, even if they are neatly categorized as "black" and "mulatto," *antillano* or *afroantillano*.

The most ambitious and influential *antillanista* author in Puerto Rico today is Edgardo Rodríguez Juliá. He was already a recognized writer when he published his first widely read work on a AfroPuerto Rican theme, *El entierro de Cortijo* (1983*). El entierro* is about the mass wake and burial in 1983 of Rafael Cortijo, the *plena* musician who was probably Puerto Rico's greatest percussionist and band leader in this century.

In *El entierro*, Rodríguez Juliá reproduces photographic detail actual and historical images of Cortijo's Cangrejos (Santurce) milieu, which historically has been closely linked with Loíza. A sense of the deep historicity and wide-ranging ramifications of AfroPuerto Rican culture permeates the work; the tone is reminiscent of the best of Melville Herskovits, in his insistence on the vitality—however transformed—of the African heritage in the Americas.[70] Rodríguez Juliá, however, brings the locale full speed into an urban-present-with-a past, and the work is far more open to contradiction, including class contradiction, than Herskovits' efforts.

Moreover, Rodríguez Juliá dispenses with the scholarly "objectivity" of a Herskovits, since in exploring "black" identity Rodríguez Juliá recognized he was probing deep into his own. Nonetheless, the ethnographic spirit—for better and for worse—is fully with Rodríguez Juliá as he makes his way through the crowd in Cortijo's burial, where the writer captures a myriad of social types expressive of contemporary Puerto Rican popular identity: "To define is easy, but how difficult it is to describe!"[71] After *El entierro*, Rodríguez Juliá published a historical novel set in the 1790s about a maroon utopia in the mangrove country outside San Juan, entitled *La noche oscura del Niño Avilés* (1985).

While Rodríguez Juliá's genuine interest in history, and its connections with contemporary reality, has broken new ground in Puerto Rican literature, his approaches to AfroPuerto Rican history does not sufficiently register complexity and ambiguity. Rodríguez Juliá too quickly accepts stark dichotomies—highlands vs. coast, black-mulatto vs. *jíbaro*, peasant vs. proletarian, rural vs. urban—for Puerto Rican history, sharply distinct worlds populated since the nineteenth century by white highland peasants and black coastal proletarians. More generally, Rodríguez Juliá casts AfroPuerto Ricans as slaves, rebels, or maroons.

Perhaps this is why Rodríguez Juliá ultimately despairs of the possibilities even of his own field of literature: in order to attain a critical, historical understanding, he avers, writers must turn outside their field and to music. He perceives the intent of *antillanismo* to be "clear in music, more than in literature." While literature provides "sketches" at best, music offers "truly the chronicle of those new values, of those new ways of seeing reality."[72] This is perhaps why he was at his best in his first widely known work, the brief chronicle *El entierro de Cortijo* (1983).

New values or old? In her recently published *House on the Lagooon*, Rosario Ferré vindicates the role of literature with a summa of sorts of the *antillanista* literary tradition; it is a masterful achievement that may signal the dusk of that canon.[73] In a steady stream of writings since the 1970s, Ferré has interwoven ethnic-racial conflict with two dimensions that had been eclipsed in *antillanismo* especially in the works of Zenón and González: class and gender. Much of her work is "an extended evocation of a black, popular Puerto Rican culture."[74] In *House on the Lagoooon* an additional conflict is explicitly developed: between literature, here personified by the female protagonist, who writes the novel, and power, represented by the domineering husband. Hence the clash of *géneros*, both biological and intellectual.

But instead of "the world of *plena* culture" that appears elsewhere in her work,[75] *House on the Lagoon* is governed by the clash of two telluric worlds—Africa and Spain—which are both seen as permanent essences. Angolan sorcerers and *conquistadores* from Extremadura battle it out in a metaphoric space that combines González's architectural metaphor—the house—with Rodríguez Juliá's mangrove geography—the lagoon. Unlike other *antillanista* works, here *antillanismo* has fully seen, and depicts the enemy…and it is Spain.

In *House on the Lagoon*, Ferré narrates the rise and decline of a Spanish and Spanish–Puerto Rican mercantile dynasty, the Mendizabals, in a history intertwined with that of the black servant family (surnamed Avilés, like Rodríguez Juliá's hero) that lives in the basement of the house on the lagoon. The adversaries are clearly Spain and Africa, with a more specific, historical Puerto Rican culture not quite present: as in *País de cuatro pisos*, a generalized black Africa is the surrogate for Puerto Rican popular culture. Ferré expresses *lo africano* with a purity that mimics the exoticism that has afflicted *antillanismo* and *cultura negroide*.

Ferré's nearly *palesiano* exoticism is especially sustained in her depiction of the African religious culture of Petra Avilés and her family, a devotion that the author exclusively on the cult of Eleggua. As depicted in *House*, the Avilés' belief in Eleggua is a piece of an intense and unperturbed *africanía*, which perhaps corresponds to the last wave of slave imports to Puerto Rico in the nineteenth century, and which concentrated on the south coast. And Petra Avilés indeed comes from Guayama, in the south coast (and Palés birthplace).

But in regions whose inhabitants descend from an older population, say, from slaves brought in during the sixteenth to eighteenth centuries, including the zone of Cangrejos-Piñones where the novel is set, matters are different. Though this topic needs much more research, it is probable that in the latter zone, as elsewhere in San Juan's peripheral "black belt" (see below), the popular religious culture is based on a more diffuse and more creolized *espiritismo*, with marked African and perhaps Taíno legacies. Ferré addresses AfroPuerto Rican folk religion with a schematism that echoes, again, *"País de cuatro pisos": lo africano* is the first "story" and *lo español* and, to a lesser degree, other European "presences" are the second "story."

At times the novel seems to present a Puerto Rico for beginners, a new age postcard with heavy-handed (but colorful and exotic) "African" features. Ferré's second story is strikingly more "Castillian" than González's. We see little cultural creativity beyond the description of a specifically Puerto Rican historical milieu. The novel sheds some light, but not very much, on more specifically Puerto Rican forms of racism.

In the work of Zenón, González, Rodríguez Juliá and Ferré, there has been an immensely important development of an AfroPuerto Rican point of view on Puerto Rican history and culture. Truly, the literary *Generación del Ochenta* that these writers, and others such as Vega and Arcadio Díaz Quiñones, have shaped, and that in fact extends from the 1960s to the present, has revolutionized the transformed the heritage of the previously central *Generación del Treinta* active a half-century earlier. In the U.S. and in the anglophone Caribbean, parallel developments have taken place in terms of African-American culture over the last three decades, perhaps with particular vitality and influence in the social sciences. In Puerto Rico, in a process that has deep roots, this evolution has unfolded with special vigor in literature. Puerto Rican social science, including history, has a lot of catching up to do.

For African-American scholarship in social science and history has moved far beyond Bastide, M.G. Smith, Clarke, and Herskovits—important referents, explicit or not, for the Puerto Rican authors—in the years since *Narciso*, and even as *País de cuatro pisos*, *El entierro de Cortijo*, *Niño Avilés*, and *House on the Lagoon* were being written. The quest for a reified, contextless (or context-free) understanding of "African survival" has been abandoned, as has its radical opposite, namely, the argument that the slaves' "Africanness" was wiped out.

A more promising quest for nonstatic "grammatical principles" of West African culture, coupled with detailed attention to history and cultural innovation, shapes much of the intellectual agenda.[76] Thus the uniform emphasis on the plantation as the overall organizing "total institution" of Caribbean social life—and which weighs heavily in Antonio Benítez Rojo's *The Repeating Island*[77]—has yielded ground to the heterogeneous historical processes, including diverse peasant modes of life, in the different Caribbean territories. This has had profound consequences for the ways in which the West African heritage has been retained and transformed.

The distance we have traveled from *cultura negroide* is clear: the African dimension is no longer an exotic, subordinate "other," but a distinct, central, constitutive component of Puerto Rican culture. Juan Flores' commentary on González's *País de cuatro pisos* is applicable, on the whole, to all three authors. In their work, he writes, "the recovery of the African root was given full analytical articulation, and where the facile equation of Puerto Rican cultural identity with the syncretic fusion of Spanish-plus-Taíno-plus African components is finally exploded.... It is the culture of black slaves and their descendants that eventually surfaces as the mainstay of the general culture of society, especially at the popular level."[78]

Despite its immense critical importance, the *antillanista* perspective remains cramped on several counts: first, as Flores notes, there is the unilateral emphasis on ethnic and racial typing and the indifference to social class dimensions. Indeed, *antillanismo* collapses race and culture and class, considerably complicating any understanding of race and culture and leading straight into facile romanticism. There is also a perceptible impatience in much of *antillanismo*, which is fundamentally literary in scope, vis-á-vis history, including historical research and rethinking, as well as with regard to critical social science approaches. Third, one senses in *antillanismo* an ultimate failure to see Puerto Rico in the Caribbean context and beyond: despite flourishes of Caribbean reference, the frame of mind remains decidedly insularist.

The superficial and reified aspects of *antillanismo* do not exist in isolation, and need to be viewed in light of the preceding tradition of *cultura negroide*. Indeed, in important ways, *antillanismo* is a retooled and more imaginative *cultura negroide*—certainly more historical and more political and certainly more wide-ranging than *cultura negroide*, but still too close to the latter. In its historical vision, *antillanismo* seems still to lack the conceptual approaches and the historical understanding needed to reappraise Puerto Rican popular culture in the thick of its social relations. Like *cultura negroide*, *antillanismo* tends to focus too exclusively on the experience of "blacks," who are constructed rather abstractly as a stable, phenotypically-defined group that has remained basically homogeneous throughout.

Negroidismo stressed festive aspects, while *antillanismo* pointed at least as much to historical racism and oppression and to cultural aggression. Both approaches thus neglected the experience of a large and very diverse population of blacks and mulattos during the era of slavery and afterward. Accordingly, historical studies in the *antillanista* vein tended to seek the black experience either under slavery and immediately after emancipation, or in the history of San Juan and other coastal cities during the nineteenth and twentieth centuries. These are important fields: but almost nothing has been said about the agrarian experiences of AfroPuerto Ricans two or three generations out of slavery in the first decades of the twentieth century.

In sum, much of Puerto Rico's social history has been absent from all sides of the discussions on AfroPuerto Rican culture. To a large extent, neglect of the sociohistorical dimensions of culture has also marked Afro-Caribbean studies generally (but see Olwig 1985; Besson 1979, 1984a, 1984b, 1988; Carnegie 1990; Berléant-Schiller 1977, 1978; Besson and Momsen 1987; Lowenthal 1979).

■ *Conclusion: Rethinking AfroPuerto Rican culture*
Cultura negroide was the first broad cultural current to focus on the specific cultural expression of Puerto Rican blacks and mulattos. *Cultura negroide* was an important step forward insofar as it pointed to the specificity of AfroPuerto Rican culture, for it made aspects of AfroPuerto Rican culture better known and in some ways dignified the island's African legacy. However, *cultura negroide* constructed AfroPuerto Rican culture Eurocentrically, as unique, primitive, erotic, and irrational.[79]

Antillanismo began in 1960s in conjunction with the protest culture and a renewed independence and labor movement, took *cultura negroide* forward. *Antillanismo* strongly developed themes already in *cultura negroide*, if not necessarily in Palés Matos' poetry; primarily a denunciation of racism in particular and of social injustice in general. The poetry of Vizcarrondo is an especially important, albeit neglected, bridge between *cultura negroide* and *antillanismo* in this regard. The broad Caribbean scope of *antillanismo* and the turn toward Africa are clearly indebted to Palés.

In other ways, *antillanismo* moved ahead—of special importance are its broad social critique, strong antiracism, alertness to mulatto culture and to hybridity, openness to class dimensions, a systematic interest in social history, a more explicit sense of Africa, and a sense of the interaction between the different artistic and scholarly components that make it up. Crucially, *antillanismo* views the AfroPuerto Rican presence not as a distinct essence, but as a major component of Puerto Rican national culture. These directions begin to break with the premises of *antillanismo* itself.

Yet the dominant currents of *antillanista* cultural expression, even in its most recent and impressive creations, continue to harbor strong continuities with *cultura negroide* and a tendency merely to hallow refurbished *negroide* icons: eroticism and primitiveness still seem to carry the day. One senses that there are many possibilities beyond *antillanismo* that would do more than stand in the shadow of, or invert the presuppositions behind, both *antillanismo* and *cultura negroide*.

To approach these possibilities, I can do no better than to turn once again to poetry. For poetry is ahead of other literary genres—let alone the human sciences—on this score. There is in several younger poets an interesting urge to move beyond *cultura negroide* and *antillanismo*: Ana Irma Rivera Lassén in the early 1970s, when *antillanismo* was in full bloom, and more recently Juan de Matta García. In seminal poems, both hark back critically to Palés' *"Pueblo Negro."* Rivera Lassén reads the black village's "languor" quite differently from Palés:

> *Negro,*
> *Negra,*
> *hermanos de la piel y el dolor,*
> > *hoy quiero romper los recuerdos*
> *del pueblo que duerme*
> *entre las palmeras*
> > *con rumor de canto monorítmico*
> *en el viento.*[80]

Less explicitly, de Matta García in *"Pueblo mío"* sees another, far broader *pueblo*, a word that means both town and people in Spanish. A *pueblo* is not just *negro*, as in Palés' poem, but one that is both black and white. De Matta also plays with Palés image of the night, in the lines that open the last poem of his remarkable collection *Prietuscos y tarcualitos*:

> *Negro y blanco. Pueblo mío*
> *mi pueblo puertorriqueño*
> *llevas la noche por fuera*
> *o, siendo blanco, por dentro…*[81]

With more dazzle and fire, Tato Laviera rejects a hallowed, hollowed Loíza Aldea (as well as the *negroide* Palesian literary tradition) masks strewn in the junkers of pop culture along other domesticated folk icons (Latino "La Bamba," African "Pata Pata").

> *ay baramba bamba*
> *suma acaba*
> *quimbombo de salsa*
> *la rumba matamba*
> *ñam ñam yo no soy*
> *de la masucamba*
> *papiri pata pata*
> *loíza musaraña.*[82]

And the poet Mayra Santos views the distancing from the *negroide* tradition as necessary to break the bounds of a "narrow social choreography and psychology" of blackness in Puerto Rico. She remembers trying to find in Puerto Rican literature those:

Voices that escaped the narrow social choreography and psychology that characterizes the proper representation of blackness in social space. Other black characters, not Tembandumba de la Quimbamba, not Chianita Gobernadora, not (with all my respect) the black men performed by Juan Boria or the African women given into motion by Silvia del Villard.

I wanted to find an artistic configuration for race other than the dark seductress, the joker/trickster figure, or the living representation of tradition and ancestry.[83]

For a cultural expression that had its greatest strength in poetry, it was perhaps to be expected that the most stimulating critiques of *cultura negroide* and *antillanismo* have come from the ranks of the poets. And from that poetry, and from the viewpoints offered by contemporary social science and historiography, I have attempted to reapproach the *"Pueblo Negro"* par excellence, Loíza: the historical heartland of *cultura negroide* and *antillanismo*.

In line with *negroide* and *antillanista* perspectives, the Loíza litoral and other locales around Puerto Rico (principally Guayama) are usually viewed as homogeneously black and, at least historically, isolated. From such an isolating perspective, Palés, Vizcarrondo and other poets, as well as various songwriters, have written superb verse on Loíza or Loíza-like milieus. While riddled with false conceptions, Eurocentrism, and even racism, these literary approaches are not wholly arbitrary construction, but rather incorporate important historical and cultural dimensions of the Loíza litoral and point to the distinctiveness of this zone in ways that we need to bear in mind. These approaches, of course, also speak volumes about the ways in which Loíza—and AfroPuerto Rican culture generally—has been perceived by the authors and their social milieus.

But the poetry of Palés and Vizcarrondo does not tell—and probably could not tell—the whole story. Palés and Vizcarrondo, like Ricardo Alegría in his own work on the *fiestas de Santiago*, resorted to explanations based largely on "isolation." The work of the young critical poets, who focus perhaps too narrowly on general issues of racial and class oppression, also cast aside the important historical issues that the *negroide* writers touched on. We need to look closely not only at phenotypical race, or at a culture directly inferred from race, but at culture actively entwined with social relations.

Another part of the story would locate the Loíza litoral and other areas where AfroPuerto Ricans were especially concentrated in the context of larger, historical, and quite hybrid wholes. This entails looking closely at a history of specific local ecologies, labor processes, and social relations, to the extent that the archival and oral sources allow. We need to look closely at the various social groups that shaped and were shaped by AfroPuerto Rican tradition. We need, in short, a more concrete and historical sense of *afropuertorriqueña* culture.

In this effort, AfroPuerto Rican cultural studies also need to explore works far beyond Puerto Rico where similar issues are being raised, including the wealth of work on Afro-Caribbean and African-American culture in general. Indifference to U.S. African-American culture is especially glaring, while Africa remains virtually unknown. Of course, the problem has been reciprocal: Afro-Caribbean and African-American studies have displayed remarkable ignorance of Puerto Rico's specific social history. In historical analysis, it seems as if we are forced to choose between being classified as yet another Sugar Island peopled by slave masses and being evicted from the Caribbean region.

Among Puerto Ricans, the racialization of cultural discussion has blocked discussion of AfroPuerto Rican history and culture. A necessary affirmation of human universality, perhaps because made abstractly, has proved cooptable through the parading of disembodied folklore that "all" can share equally. Cultures are all the same, that is to say Eurocentrics, and the problem has been considered merely one of unjustified distinctions between skin color. Yet specific cultural identities, including complex national identities, are precisely the strongest expression of more universal fields of humanity—indeed, they are those fields.

Moreover, race and culture are not the only relevant dimensions; we cannot say that they are more fundamental. Concurrent, competing identities, often denied and suppressed, exist in terms of gender, sexual preference, class, ideology, nation, generation, and many other dimensions of personal and social experience that are quite impossible to conjoin neatly. All these identities are typically both multiple and overlapping. Both *cultura negroide* and *antillanismo* recognized this multiplicity, even if to an extent that seems insufficient today.

So-called "multiculturalism" in the U.S., whose Puerto Rican variants attempt to appropriate and coopt *cultura negroide* (especially) and *antillanismo*, falls far short as well: its selective sense of identities is precarious, its purism with regard to different "ethnic" traditions is disingenuous, and its artistic expression is bland. And above all, the assumption made by advocates of multiculturalism that some sort of mainstream Anglo-American (or, for that matter, "[Hispano-] Puerto Rican") identity is above the fray, beyond complexity and contradiction, is absurd.

People make the various identities that they live their own and shape an active humanity—that is, a history—by thought and action. Bringing these dimensions together in historical analysis, to understand the motivations and possible directions of human action is a challenge that we can hardly hope to meet fully; however, we can probably do better if both the specificity and universality, the identity and multiplicity of social life are held in dialectic tension.

Of course, a striking instance of this movement is the story that I have only sketched here: our own complex and very historical trajectory over the last eight decades, as Puerto Ricans, from *cultura negroide* to *antillanismo*, to a sense of possibilities beyond. As the history of these intellectual movements becomes that of the social groups and historical contexts that drove them forward, the concepts and perspectives of those movements gain in depth and meaning, and our own direction becomes perhaps more distinct. ■

ENDNOTES

1. The major defense of "racial democracy" in Puerto Rico remains Tomás Blanco 1942 essay, *El prejuicio racial en Puerto Rico.* Río Piedras, Ediciones Huracán, 1985 (with an introductory study by Arcadio Díaz-Quiñones). The more significant analyses of racism in Puerto Rico are Isabelo Zenón, *Narciso descubre su trasero,* 2 vols.. Río Piedras, Editorial Furidi, 1974–75; Martín Sagrera, *Racismo y política en Puerto Rico: la desintegración.* Río Piedras, Editorial Edil, 1973; and Eduardo Seda Bonilla, "Dos modelos de relaciones raciales: Estados Unidos y América Latina," *Revista de Ciencias Sociales,* 12, 4, 1968, pp. 569–98. For a general approach from the perspective of the diaspora, with some affinities with "racial democracy" arguments, see Clara Rodríguez's discussion of Puerto Rican as a "rainbow people" in *Puerto Ricans: Born in the U.S.A.* Boston, Unwyn Hyman, 1989.
2. Arcadio Díaz-Quiñones, *La memoria rota.* Río Piedras, Ediciones Huracán, 1993, p. 59.
3. "Sedoso o áspero"; Isabelo Zenón, Prologue to Juan de Matta García, *Prietuscos y tarcualitos. Poemas negristas y otros poemas.* Arecibo, Editores GarAndú, 1991, p. iii.
4. Visiting U.S. researchers, especially in the 1940's-1950's, became enchanted with Puerto Rico's "racial democracy": in time, however, most came to know better. See, e.g. Sidney Mintz, "The role of Puerto Rico in modern social science," *Revista/Review Interamericana,* 8, 1, 1978, pp. 7–16.
5. Isar Pilar Godreau, "Where is race in this gumbo: semantics in Puerto Rico race and color talk." Paper delivered before the 1995 Meeting of the American Anthropological Association, Washington, D.C.. In Puerto Rico, even the more common racial terms present large difficulties. Defining who is negro or *prieto* ("black"), *blanco* ("white"), *de color* ("of color"), *moreno* ("dark"), *jabao* ("yellow"), *trigueño* ("light-dark"), *cano* ("blond"; partly from "americano"?) or *colorao* ("reddish white"), *jincho* (very light skinned, to the point of a sickly appearance), *mulato,* etc. is daunting, and even more so in translation. The direct, polar terms of *blanco* (white) and *negro* (black) are the least frequently used. The categories and variants themselves clamor for closer attention.
6. See Lola Aponte, "Para inventarse el Caribe: la construcción fenotípica en las Antillas hispanófonas," *Bordes,* 2, 1995, pp. 5–14.
7. "AfroPuerto Rican" follows the Spanish term, which carries neither hyphen nor slash: *afropuertorriqueño,* and usefully softens or problematizes boundaries. To be sure, *afropuertorriqueños* not universally accepted in Puerto Rico; *afroantillano* is much more frequently used, especially to refer to music and *dance, and* less often to poetry where the term *"poesía negroide"* remains current.
8. "He who is not African on one side, is on the other." The phrase plays with the words *dinga* and *mandinga,* both of which refer to African peoples: the Mandé or Mandingos of the Western Sudan, and the Dinkas further east. But the phrase has a further connotation, using the sense that was given to the term *mandinga* in the Spanish colonial era, as "the devil." Thus, this further translation might read: "He who does not have Africa in him, has the devil."
9. And contrary to the views of, for instance, the Julian Steward team in the 1940's, in Puerto Rico there is one culture, a complex and conflictive national culture, not a jumble of "subcultures." See Steward et al., *The People of Puerto Rico,* Champaign-Urbana, University of Illinois Press, 1956. See also Mintz, "Puerto Rico: an Essay in the Definition of a National Culture," in U.S.-Puerto Rico Status Commission, *Status of Puerto Rico. Selected background studies prepared for the U.S.-Puerto Rico Status Commission on the Status of Puerto Rico,* Washington, D.C., U.S. Government Printing Office, 1966, pp. 339–434. In this major essay, whose location in Mintz's overall work has never been assessed, the heterogeneity of Puerto Rican culture and its links to other cultures are seen as fatal to its claims for "nationalness.".. while comparable traits in U.S. and West European "national cultures" are not discussed.
10. Juan Flores, "Living borders/Buscando America: Languages of Latino Self-Formation" (with George Yúdice). In Flores, *Divided Borders: Essays on Puerto Rican Identity.* Houston, Arte

Público Press, 1994, pp. 199–224.
11. Thus the Executive Director of the Institute of Puerto Rican Culture under the current pro-statehood New Progressive Party Administration, Luis Díaz, has stated that "culturally" and "sociologically," Puerto Rico is a nation. , Díaz stated that Gov. Pedro Rosselló's controversial remarks (in January 1996) to the effect that Puerto Rico is not a nation simply recognized Puerto Rico's lack of political sovereignty. *El Nuevo Día,* March 31, 1996, p. 16. See Juan M. García Passalacqua, "Neonationalist tide rises in Puerto Rico," *The San Juan Star,* June 2, 1996, p. 25.
12. The term "practices" is often invoked in the definition of culture and it is certainly useful in directing our attention to the material acts of social life. The "context" inherent in the concept of "cultural context" is constituted, in large measure, by the practices themselves. This is no abstract exogenous structure that defines its contents and suppresses human agency. People's thoughts, however, and above all the patterns of those thoughts would seem as important as their practices: thought viewed not as free-floating form/"representations," but in dialectical relationship to substance/practice.
13. On the relationship and conflict between Puerto Rico's "Latin American" and "Caribbean" identities, see Juan A. Giusti Cordero, "Puerto Rico entre los pueblos antillanos y latinoamericanos. Algunos problemas de método," *Plural,* 4, 1–2, 1985, pp. 177–95.
14. *"Hispanismo"* has a long and complex history in Puerto Rico that far transcends the field of literature, and which has interesting reworkings in the diaspora. This history should be of interest to specialists in Caribbean, U.S. or Latin American cultural studies, but has rarely drawn their sustained attention. U.S. researchers would find much that is illuminating for understanding the history, in their own country, of anglophilia (the opposite, of course, is also true).
15. Thus *"negroide"* suggests something that is black, but is not even really, deeply black; that would be (too) African. *"Negroide"* also implies something that is perhaps even "abnormally," "pathologically" black. Partly as a result of this, *"lo negroide"* was tacitly expected to spawn no more than minor, "local color" literature. The term *"negrista,"* which is used especially with regard to poetry, is preferable but does not necessarily go beyond color.
16. In *"Pueblo Negro,"* Palés' enamourment with sound even led him beyond the African mainland and beyond the zones of the Atlantic slave trade: for the town of Farafangana is in the Malagasy Republic, on its Indian Ocean coast: an area that is historically more Malay than black African. Luis Palés Matos, *Tuntún de pasa y grifería.* Edición de Mercedes López-Baralt. Río Piedras, Editorial Universitaria, 1993, p. 111. See also, by Palés, "Kalahari," ibid., pp. 116–18.

    With Palés, we are far from the historical Africa and Caribbean of his contemporary Arturo Alfonso Schomburg, the great Puerto Rican researcher on the history of Africa and the African diaspora. Schomburg had no relationship that I am aware of with either Luis Palés Matos or Vizcarrondo, despite his marked interest in poetry. Schomburg did however correspond with several persons in Puerto Rico and remained interested in Afro-Puerto Rican history until the end of his life. See Victoria Ortiz, "Arturo A. Schomburg: a Biographical Essay," *in* The *Legacy of Arturo A. Schomburg,* New York: Schomburg Center for Research in Black Culture, 1986, pp. 65, 83.
17. See Melville Herskovits, "The ahistorical approach to Afroamerican studies: a critique," *American Anthropologist,* 62, 4, 1960, pp. 559–68.
18. Jorge Luis Morales, ed., *Poesía afroantillana y negrista,* Río Piedras, Editorial Universitaria, 1981, p. 68.
19. Palés Matos, *Tuntún de pasa y grifería,* pp. 111–113.
20. See, on the beauty of a mulatto woman, Vizcarrondo's "La mulata," in Fortunato Vizcarrondo, *Dinga y mandinga (Poemas).* San Juan, Instituto de Cultura Puertorriqueña, 1976, pp. 56–58.
21. See, for instance, Palés Matos' "Majestad negra" and Vizcarrondo's "¡Qué negrota!," in Palés Matos, *Tuntún de pasa y grifería,* pp. 114–15, and Vizcarrondo, *Dinga y mandinga,* pp. 46–47. See Arcadio Díaz Quiñones, *El almuerzo en la hierba,* Río Piedras, Ediciones Huracán, 1982, for an enthusiastic antillanista appraisal of Palés, and the critique of Díaz Quiñones' analysis by Gerald Guinness in his "Here and elsewhere, I. Luis Palés Matos"; in Guinness, *Here and elsewhere. Essays on Caribbean Literature.* Río Piedras, Editorial de la Universidad de Puerto Rico, 1993, pp. 1–41.
22. See Victorio Llanos, "Como pintan a los negros," in Morales, *Poesía afroantillana y negrista,* p. 73. "Por bien que parezca un negro/ lo pintan siempre deforme/creyendo que en el pellejo/ conlleva una ofensa enorme."
23. C. Martínez Acosta, Excerpt from a book review of the first edition of *Dinga y mandinga*

24. (1942), included as an introduction to the book. *Dinga y mandinga* p. xxv.
25. Vizcarrondo, *Dinga y mandinga,* p. xxi.
26. Ibid.
27. Quoted in Zenón, *Narciso,* p. 297; parallel comments have often been made about jazz and the tango. All quotes to *Narciso* are to the first volume.
28. Flores, *Divided Borders,* p. 89; see also Ruth Glasser, *My Music is My Flag: Puerto Rican Musicians and Their New York Communities, 1917-1940.* Berkley:University of California Press, 1995.
29. "The real roots of the plena, as is universally acknowledged, are in the bomba; all the early pleneros [...] were originally bomberos, and the most basic features of the plena derive directly or indirectly from bomba." Flores, *Divided Borders,* p. 88.
30. One parallel refrain to "El que no tiene dinga, tiene mandinga" in the anglophone Caribbean is "Go home and look at your grandmother." Eric Williams, *The Negro in the Caribbean,* New York:Haskell House, 1991.
31. "¿Y tu agüela a'onde ejtá?" was originally interpreted by Ruth Fernández, the first major mulatto commercial female singer in Puerto Rico. She was the first artist of color, for instance, to sing (in 1940) at the Condado Vanderbilt, then the major tourist hotel.
32. Caña is also called lágrimas de mangle ("tears of the mangrove"), alluding to its frequent fabrication site: the mangrove forest, which offered both seclusion and firewood.
33. Vizcarrondo, *Dinga y mandinga,* p. 8.
34. Carmelina Vizcarrondo, "Loíza Aldea," in Morales, *Poesía afroantillana y negrista,* p. 121. Carmelina Vizcarrondo belonged to the same former slaveowning family of Carolina where Fortunato's surname originated.
35. Zenón, *Narciso,* p. 47. See De Matta García's poem, "El Antipalés," in *Prietuscos y tarcualitos,* pp. 6–7.
36. See Manuel Alvarez Nazario, *El elemento afronegroide en el español de Puerto Rico.* Río Piedras, Editorial Universitaria, 1956.
37. Zenón, *Narciso,* p. 209.
38. Dorado, about as far west of San Juan as Loíza is eastward, is a coastal municipality with a heavily black population and a historical ecology of mangroves, marshes, savannahs, coconut groves, etc. much like Loíza.
39. Mintz, "An Essay in the Definition." p. 219. It is perhaps remarkable that Mintz did not carry out research in an AfroPuerto Rican zone, despite his early expertise in Puerto Rican culture and society (1940's-early 1960s) and his subsequent specialization (since the late sixties) in Afro-Caribbean and Afro-American culture.
40. The masked *vejigantes* (costumed, raucous "devils") of Loíza's patron-saint feasts of Santiago the Apostle (St. James) became the best known—and perhaps most overworked—icon of *cultura negroide,* and *vejigante* masks have been the object of innumerable graphic works. Santiago is akin to the Yoruba deity Ogún, though it is improbable that many Yoruba settled in Loíza. The vejigante coconut-shell masks of Loíza "became a prominent feature of the artistic generation of the 1950's and went on to become a symbol of Puerto Rican culture" (Benítez 1992: 109).
41. See Angela Negrón Muñoz, "Hablando con Don Luis Palés Matos," a 1932 interview reproduced in José I. De Diego Padró, *Luis Palés Matos y su trasmundo poético.* Río Piedras: Ediciones Puerto, 1973, and accompanying texts.
42. The one poem where Palés perhaps comes closest to breaking with lo negroide is in his *later* "Mulata-Antilla" (1949), in *Tuntún de pasa y grifería,* pp. 193–95; but still the distance that remained to be traveled remained large.
43. Del Villard did not—and probably for good reason—escape criticism from Zenón, who considered her negritud to be overly exotic and somewhat contrived, not unlike Juan Boria. This muffled internal debate among Afro-Puerto Rican artists and intellectuals has not received the attention it deserves, perhaps partly because these artists and intellectuals have not been especially keen on promoting a more public debate.
44. De Matta García, *Prietuscos y tarcualitos.*
45. Jean Besson, "Family land as a model for Martha Brae's New History," in Charles V. Carnegie, ed., *Afro-Caribbean Villages in Historical Perspective.* Kingston, African-Caribbean Institute of Jamaica, 1987, p. 125.
46. Colobó is a barrio of Loíza, in Medianía some kilometers east of Piñones across the Río Grande, but like Piñones on the Loíza litoral. "Colobó" was sung by Ismael Rivera, of Cortijo y su Combo in the 1950's and later with his own groups.
47. "El mundo de lo mulato y negro." Julio Ortega, *Reapropiaciones. Cultura y nueva escritura en*

Puerto Rico. Río Piedras, Editorial de la Universidad de Puerto Rico, 1991, p. 29.
47. David Ungerleider, "Loíza: más allá del folclore," in Lydia Milagros González, ed., *La tercera raíz. Presencia africana en Puerto Rico.* San Juan, Centro de Estudios de la Realidad Puertorriqueña [CEREP] and Institute of Puerto Rican Culture, 1992.
48. Both "Sale el sol" and "Si te cojo" are anthologized in "Ismael Rivera Oro," Tico Records cassette 4XT-JMTS-1433 (1979). "Pa lo que tú le das" is featured in "Cortijo y su Conjunto invites you to dance (Los invita a bailar)," Tropical TRLP 5098. On Ismael Rivera, see Rafael Figueroa Hernández, *Ismael Rivera: el Sonero Mayor,* San Juan, Instituto de Cultura Puertorriqueña, 1993.
49. Ana Lydia Vega et al., *Historia y literatura.* San Juan: Editorial Postdata, 1995.
50. Vega, *Falsas crónicas del sur.* Río Piedras, Editorial de la Universidad de Puerto Rico, 1991.
51. Literary critic Julio Ortega has noted: "[I]n Puerto Rico there has been a movement away from privileging the jíbaro peasant to more recently privileging the figure of the black, vindicated and toned variously [matizado] as *black* [prieto], `red' [grifo] and *mulatto.*" Ortega, *Reapropiaciones,* p. 29.
52. Never mind that the Piñones sand dunes were devastated in the 1940's by sand extraction...most of its the beaches look wild today.
53. A typically enraptured journalistic text: "When visiting Piñones, one cannot but stop in one of the hundreds of food stands on the highway, bringing the visitor the best of the island's hearth [lo mejor del fogón isleño]. A visit to Piñones becomes, thus, a different experience, not only for its culinary pleasures, but also because as we go along new landscapes come into view and reveal byways that transform the ride into a voyage of discovery." María Teresa Morón, "Un paseo por Piñones," *El Reportero,* January 29, 1986, p. 18. The estimate of "hundreds" of food stands is a gross exaggeration. See also "Playa, fritura y sol en Piñones. Fin de semana de antojos `criollos'" ("Beach, fritters and sun in Piñones. A weekend of `creole' delights"), by Félix Jiménez, *El Nuevo Día,* April 10, 1985, p. A third piece, again of a culinary nature, reads: "The wooden shacks line the stretch of Piñones beach that fronts the tropical pines and mangroves. Their names are as colorful as their peeling paint [...] The air is smoked from wood fires that cook bacalaítos (codfish fritters) in sizzling lard." "The essence of a good bacalaíto," *The San Juan Star,* November 9, 1994, p. 25.
54. Edgardo Rodríguez Juliá, "Piñones. Una crónica." *El Nuevo Día, Revista Domingo,* September 22, 1991, 4–9.
55. *Puerto Rico Ilustrado/El Mundo,* May 1, 1988, 12–13.
56. "The flying bus," trans. Elpidio García-Díaz, in *Images and Identities: The Puerto Ricans in Two World Contexts,* New Brunswick, Transaction, 1987), p. 22.
57. Not wholly unlike Europeans who acknowledged the "greatness" of Oriental civilizations, Puerto Ricans who primarily identify themselves with a Hispanic heritage are also drawn to negroide music, poetry or graphics arts. However, "the essential relationship [is seen] to be one between a strong and a weak partner." Edward Said, *Orientalism.* New York:Pantheon Books, 1978, p. 40. Cultura negroide is typically disembodied folklore, subject to the same misperceptions as other such phenomenona in folklore in general (frozen quality, ahistoric, asocial, etc.) as of specifically Afro-American ones (preoccupation with African survivals or innocuous African-European "syncretism," etc.). The rather eerie, enigmatic impression produced by the three-pointed coconut masks of Loíza's vejigantes, when pulled out of their festive context, perhaps captures the perception of lo negroide in AfroPuerto Rican culture.
58. The immediate impact of *Narciso* was a veritable bomba. Zenón's polemical work played no small part in the crisis of the Ateneo Puertorriqueño, Puerto Rico's oldest and most venerable cultural institution. Juan Angel Silén, *La generación de escritores de 1970 en Puerto Rico* (1950-1976), Rio Piedras, Editorial Cultural, 1977.
59. Zenón, *Narciso,* pp. 45–6.
60. Zenón called his tripartite scheme of Puerto Rican culture "trinitarian.".. with inevitably religious undertones of veracity and authority?
61. Why are so many of the most defenders of negritud in Puerto Rico supporters of independence, while others (if probably a smaller and less conspicuous group) as strongly in favor of statehood, or commonwealth? How do the discourses of negritud shape and become shaped by political status preferences? This is a Puerto Rican "twist" to the discussion of black culture that needs to be considered seriously, and which only partially resembles the longstanding U.S. debate between black separatism and integration, as analyzed by Harold Cruse and most recently by Cornel West in *Race Matters,* Boston, Beacon Press, 1993. See Godreau, "Where is race in this gumbo."
62. Bastide liberally incorporates conclusions of Edith Clarke and M.G. Smith. The anglophone

Caribbean—at least as grasped by Smith and Clarke—had an almost radically different historical experience vis a vis the Hispanic territories in terms of the comprehensiveness, continuity and strength of plantation slavery vis–á–vis heterogeneous form of peasant social relations.
63. The quote from Roger Bastide appears in Zenón, *Narciso,* p. 45, and originated in his *Las Américas Negras: Las civilizaciones africanas en el Nuevo Mundo.* Madrid:Alianza Editorial, 1969.
64. Zenón, *Narciso,* p. 215.
65. Zenón underscores his point with a poem by Vizcarrondo, "El santiguo." To him, this poem is analogous to the positions he is criticizing. *Narciso,* pp. 212–14.
66. Zenón, *Narciso,* p. 205.
67. After *Narciso,* which was his master's thesis for the University of Puerto Rico, Zenón wrote his doctoral dissertation on women in the writings of Federico García Lorca. Zenón's turn toward gender issues has an interesting parallel in Ana Irma Rivera Lassén (see below), who shifted from Afro-Puerto Rican poetry in the early 1970's to a leading role in the Puerto Rican feminist movement. Both Zenón and Rivera Lassén continue involved with issues of race and culture and stress the connections between these issues and gender.
68. The earlier *Conversación con José Luis González,* published just after *Narciso* and its own storm of debate, anticipated many of the themes of (the even more controversial) next work by González. Río Piedras, Ediciones Huracán, 1980.
69. M. G. Smith, "A framework for Caribbean studies," in *The plural society in the British West Indies.* Berkeley: University of California Press, 1965.
70. Herskovits, "The ahistorical approach."
71. One of the most provocative "ethnographic" commentaries in *El entierro de Cortijo* concerned Afro-Puerto Rican surnames from the San Juan-Cangrejos-Loíza region: Verdejo, Cortijos, París, Romero, Pizarro, etc.
72. Juan G. Gelpí underlines the continuities of Rodríguez Juliá's later contemporary chronicles with his earlier writings, where he pursued a monolithic national identity. See Gelpí, *Paternalismo y literatura en Puerto Rico.* Río Piedras, Editorial de la Universidad de Puerto Rico, 1993, pp. 45–60.
73. Ortega, *Reapropiaciones,* p. 144. Poetry, of course, may have its own view of this.
74. See Giusti, "De Pandora a Elegguá: una lectura histórica de Rosario Ferré, The House on the Lagoon," forthcoming in *Historia y Sociedad* (Puerto Rico), 7, 1994–5.
75. Flores, *Divided Borders,* p. 101. See, among Ferré's earliest work, "Maquinolandera" in *Papeles de Pandora.* "Maquinolandera" borrows the title of an early song by Cortijo y su Combo, sung by Ismael Rivera.
76. Sidney Mintz and Richard Price, *An Anthropological Approach to the Afro-American Past: a Caribbean Perspective.* Philadelphia, Institute for the Study of Human Issues, 1976; reissued as *The Birth of Afro-American Culture. An Anthropological Perspective.* Boston, Beacon Press, 1992; Henry Louis Gates, *The Signifying Monkey: A Theory of Afro-American Literary Criticism.* New York:Oxford University Press, 1988. Important recent work includes Paul Gilroy, *The Black Atlantic. Modernity and Double Consciousness.* Cambridge, Harvard University Press, 1993; John Thornton, *Africa and Africans in the Making of the Atlantic World, 1400–1680.* Cambridge, Cambridge University Press, 1992; Joseph E. Holloway, ed., *Africanisms in American Culture.* Bloomington, Indiana University Press, 1990; Sandra T. Barnes, ed., *Africa's Ogun: Old World and New.* Bloomington, Indiana University Press, 1989. See also Robert Farris Thompson, *Flash of the Spirit. African and Afro-American Art & Philosophy.* New York, Vintage, 1984; and Lawrence W. Levine, *Black Culture and Black Consciousness: Afro-American Folk Thought from Slavery to Freedom.* New York, Oxford University Press, 1977.
77. Antonio Benítez Rojo, *La isla que se repite.* Hanover, N.H., Ediciones del Norte, 1989.
78. Flores, *Divided Borders,* pp. 63–4.
79. In general, coastal barrios and coastal municipios in the eastern portion of Puerto Rico have been estimated to have high percentages of blacks: Salinas and Carolina (more than 40 percent) and Guayama and Humacao (more than 30 percent). Both Mintz and Manuel Alvarez Nazario link these high percentages to African slave imports and sugar plantation production. Yet areas where plantation slavery were most important, such as Ponce and Mayagüez, do not figure among the highest percentages; and as we shall see, plantation production was, historically, far less important in Loíza than might be surmised. The large number of free black and maroon squatters in the entire San Juan periphery, the fertility of the sandy loams of the Loiza litoral, the disuasion of insect pests and malaria, and the Loiza litoral's exposure to attacks by Caribs until the seventeenth century, all seem to have been more significant than

plantation slavery itself in shaping the durable numerical preponderance of Afro-Puerto Ricans in Loíza.

80. In Spanish, *pueblo* has the double sense of town or village and of "the people"; it seems a deliberate reference to Palés' classic "Pueblo Negro." The Spanish word *monorítmico* might be translated sardonically-but quite literally, as "monkey-rhythmical." And in the closing line of the poem, Lassén plays with the phrase *pueblo negro* and writes (again, seemingly in direct reference to "Pueblo negro"): "we are driven by the vision of a new pueblo" ("nos obsede la visión de un pueblo nuevo").
81. De Matta García 1991: 95.
82. Tato Laviera, el moreno puertorriqueño (a three-way warning poem) (1979). These lines are mostly untranslatable; see Flores, *Divided Borders,* pp. 157-181. "Loiza Musaraña" means something like "Loiza pipedream."
83. "Tembandumba de la Quimbamba" is the fanciful name given by Palés Matos to the sensual, majestic black woman who is the central character of his poem "Majestad Negra" (Palés Matos 1992, pp.114-115). "Chianita Gobernadora" was the only unwittingly smart central character—in blackface—of a highly succesful political satire show in the 1960's-1970's.

HÉCTOR MÉNDEZ CARATINI
PORTFOLIO

Viva Santiago, fotografía de Héctor Méndez Caratini ©

Héctor Méndez-Caratini was born in San Juan, Puerto Rico, in 1949. He attended Boston University, the University of Puerto Rico and the Centro de Estudios Avanzados de Puerto Rico y El Caribe, San Juan, Puerto Rico. He studied photography at the Germain School of Photography in New York City and attended photography and video workshops at the Center for Creative Photography, Arizona; The Visual Studies Workshop, NY; Harvard University's CLL, Mass.; and in México City with recognized masters of photography. He is a founding member and past president of the Asociación Fotográfica de Puerto Rico, Inc. and of the Consejo Puertorriqueño de Fotografía, Inc., both pioneering organizations that promote the development of photography as an art medium. For the past 17 years, Méndez-Caratini has been an ophthalmic photographer specializing in stereoscopic retina photographs for the national medical research studies at the University of Puerto Rico. The photographs included in this volume of *CENTRO* are of the *Fiestas de Santiago Apostol* in Loiza, Puerto Rico. © 1996 Héctor Méndez-Caratini

■ *Vejigante de Loiza,* fotografía de Héctor Méndez Caratini ©

■ *Toque de Bomba*, fotografía de Héctor Méndez Caratini ©

■ *Máscaras de Caballero, Loiza*, fotografía de Héctor Méndez Caratini ©

Negar lo negro sería gazmoñería:
Luis Palés Matos, Margot Arce, and the Black Poetry Debate

MAGALI ROY FEQUIERE

> The novelty resides in the fact that the discourse on "savages" is... a discourse in which an explicit political power presumes the authority of a specific knowledge and vice versa. Colonialism becomes its project and can be thought as a duplication and fulfillment of the power of Western discourses on the human varieties.
>
> V. Y. Mudimbe, *The Invention of Africa*

I first started thinking about Luis Palés Matos' poetry when I was a student at the University of Puerto Rico in the mid-1970s. We had just read his Afro-Antillean poems for an introductory literature course, and a good friend and I continued the discussion after class. My friend and I agreed that Palés' poems were beautifully written, seductively musical, and astonishing in their refashioning of the word. The poems even interpellated our subjectivity— we were two young mulattas who felt represented in and courted by the verses of "Mulata Antilla."[1] Yet, as a reader with a burgeoning political consciousness, I felt uneasy. I was dimly aware that if at one level the poems celebrated blackness, they also mocked or trivialized it.

It was around that time that I read Isabelo Zenón Cruz's path breaking book *Narciso descubre su trasero: el negro en la cultura puertorriqueña.*[2] His study was causing a tremendous stir among students and intellectuals. For my part, I had never read anything like it, and his argument forever changed the way I would view Puerto Rican literature and culture. Zenón's thesis, that Puerto Ricans of African descent had been excluded from the discourses of the nation, national culture, and national literature, was applauded by many. Others were stunned, even angry Zenón so eloquently and boldly placed racism in to the forefront of intellectual debate. However, even the skeptics were unable to dismiss the enormity of the issues elevated in by Zenón's work.

Two decades later, *Narciso descubre su trasero* continues to challenge Puerto Rican thinkers and intellectuals. The controversy spawned by the book parallels the debate on Palés Matos' "black verses" in many significant ways. Both authors question the racist assumptions held by many within the intelligentsia, and propose a reassessment of the historical legacy of Afro-Puerto Ricans to national culture. Zenón's intervention, though, signals a radical departure from the discourse exemplified by Palés. As a *puertorriqueño negro*, his critical perspective does not admit the mediation of Creole intellectuals to speak his truth. My own work on the racial and gender underpinnings of the discourse of national identity endeavors to answer Zenón's call to specifically engage blackness as an intellectual and cultural issue. Together with others who have been stimulated by his valiant example, I remain deeply indebted to the dialogue he initiated.

■ *Forjemos, pues, una poesía antillana*

The publication of Luis Palés Matos' "black verses" caused a stir in the literary and intellectual environment of the 1930s. Palés Matos' call for the creation of an Antillean poetry that would better reflect the racially mixed character of Puerto Rican culture provoked reactions as varied as outrage, derision, fear, and applause in different sectors of the reading public.[3] Palés, in a famous interview with Angela Negrón Muñoz, stated that the creation of a literature with an Antillean character was a necessity at this historical juncture. "Poeta que se abstrae de su genuino elemento," according to Palés, "so pretensa inspiración de universalidad y trascendentalismo, es pez fuera del agua, y sólo realizará una poesía académica para uso de los intelectuales."[4] Moreover, Palés saw the Caribbean's black heritage as crucial. As he saw it, the cultural and social existence of the Spanish Caribbean was based on the transculturation of Spanish and African cultures into a new cultural entity. It is because of this socio cultural reality that a truly Caribbean poetry needed to engage the black element. "Me refiero al negro," he told his interviewer, stressing that blacks were an important racial nucleus "que con nosotros se ha mezclado noblemente y que por lo fecundo, lo fuerte y lo vivo de su naturaleza ha impreso rasgos inconfundibles en nuestra psicología, dándole precisamente su verdadero carácter antillano."[5] For Palés, the new black poetry was not a mere poetic "ism." It was a cultural imperative. We can infer that where in Europe the "black vogue" was a fashionable appropriation, in the Caribbean, for Palés, the "black vogue" had an immediate cultural referent. Puerto Rican popular culture was the product of racial mixing:

> *No conozco, pues, un solo rasgo colectivo de nuestro pueblo que no ostente la huella de esa deliciosa mezcla de la cual arranca su tono verdadero el carácter antillano. Negarlo sería gazmoñería. Esta es nuestra realidad y sobre ella, debemos edificar una cultura autóctona y representativa con nobleza, con orgullo y con plena satisfacción de nosotros mismos.*[6]

In essence, Palés called for a recognition of an accomplished fact in Puerto Rican national culture. In his interview, it is clear that he referred to the national popular subject: "las manifestaciones de nuestra vida popular." And where others had seen Puerto Rico's black heritage as a weakness, he saw a source of strength and vitality.

The novelty and true meaning of Palés's call to the intelligentsia can be pieced together by looking at the responses of his peers—members of the group called Generación del Treinta—to his provocative criticism of the *criollo* lack of vision.[7] The response was immediate and unequivocal. J. I. de Diego Padró's "Antillanismo, criollismo, negroidismo"[8] was published a week following the poet's interview. In that article, Palés' avant-garde confrere saw absolutely no need to consider Puerto Rico's black heritage, since blacks had

---

MAGALI ROY FEQUIERE is assistant professor of Women's Studies at Knox College in Galesburg, Illinois, where she teaches Caribbean literature and feminist theory. She is currently completing a book entitled *Women, Creole Identity and Intellectual Life in Early Twentieth Century Puerto Rico*. The author would like to thank Susan M. Dever for her help with this essay. ■ Luis Palés Matos

no culture that in any way approximated the sophistication of Euro-American cultural achievements. For de Diego Padró,

> *En la confrontación y barajamiento de estas dos culturas, una superior y otra inferior, fue debilitándose como es natural, y perdiendo contenidos autóctonos la cultura negra. Hasta que el negro asimiló y adoptó a las mil maravillas la cultura que nos llegó de Occidente.*[9]

Spanish descendants have not changed, even though the tropics might have slightly affected their liver and physical features. De Diego Padró reiterated that *"el quantum de la población coexistente en las Antillas, pese a la diversidad de color y origen, es de estructura psicológica y de cultura eminentemente europeas."*[10] His discussion centered mainly on theories of cultural transmission and survival. In short, as a *criollo*, de Diego Padró championed the colonialist's perspective without ever mentioning it by name. What was missing in his discourse was a discussion of colonialism's effects on culture.

Palés responded to the attacks with the essay "Hacia una poesía antillana" in which he expanded on his earlier interview. He reaffirmed that both the Spaniard and the African had changed through intermixing of race and culture. In the Spanish Caribbean, sustained Palés, it was the mulatto who was the true representative of the majority of the population. It was *"el nuevo tipo del mulato,"* towards whom, *"se ha desplazado el acento vital de las tres islas."* Extending his reply to De Diego Padró, Palés advances his view that there was no such thing as the purely "universal" in art and culture. *"El inefable limbo utópico de extensión ideal ilimitada que llamamos cultura universal"* is a chimerical pursuit in and of itself, he argued. *"Y el artista que acuciado por un falaz objetivo de universalismo, desdeña su genuino elemento y se dispara en vuelo hacia esas zonas de miraje, se pierde irremediablemente en un caos de palabras, de conceptos y de imágenes horros de toda significacción humana."*[11] Palés completed his essay with a reiteration of his original call to the Caribbean poets of Puerto Rico: *"Forjemos, pues, una poesía antillana."*

In the same issue of the newspaper, another hostile reaction was printed in conjunction with Palés' response. The title of Luis Antonio Miranda's retort captured the essence of his position: *"El llamado arte negro no tiene vinculación con Puerto Rico."*[12] In this piece, Miranda absolutely negated the existence of a Spanish Caribbean culture or racial type: *"No existe un tipo antillano como no existe una cultura antillana."* Instead, he asserted, *"el antillano está definido a perfección en el tipo ibérico continental."*[13] Nothing in Puerto Rican popular culture had African origins, ran Miranda's delusory ethnocentrism. He emphasized, *"En nuestra isla no hay mezcla alguna de culturas, a excepción del exotismo que nos ha llegado del norte* [U. S. cultural imperialism]."[14]

Miranda was clearly horrified by the thought that black "primitivism" might be found anywhere in Puerto Rico. Black poetry would be a "throwback" in Puerto Rico's race toward civilization: *"Tal arte, que es un positivo salto atrás, no tiene vinculación con nuestra isla."*[15] Miranda's cultural paranoia stemmed from the classic Creole "whitening" project itself which harbored the always present danger of the throwback. Following the logic of racial purification through the "whitening of the race," he believed that Puerto Rican culture would eventually rid itself of all traces of black parentage.

Months later, Palés was defended by his brother Vicente with "Sobre una poesía antillana," to which G. Miranda Archilla responded in February of 1933 with "La broma de una poesía prieta en Puerto Rico."[16] The controversy was far from over when the young critic Margot Arce, recently returned form doctoral studies in Spain, entered the debate. After the publication of her first essay on the subject, she would in turn find herself in the midst of a disagreement with Tomás Blanco, one of Palés' main supporters.

The questions raised by Palés' "black verses" were unsettling for the Generación del Treinta's white *criollos,* who had a vested interest in maintaining virtual racial segregation. European racial doctrines, which placed whites at the zenith of human evolution and blacks at the bottom, enjoyed wide acceptance among the Puerto Rican literate classes. The literate elite implicitly nodded to these racist doctrines to intellectually justify their racism and their race based privileges. Essayist Antonio Pedreira's *Insularismo*, published in 1934, is a case in point. As a cultural leader, he proposed that race-mixing had in fact retarded the development of Puerto Rico as a nation. Pedreira's appeal to Puerto Rico's youth was clearly directed to Puerto Rico's *criollos*, not to blacks or mulattos.

■ *Negros Teóricos: Margot Arce's Contribution to the Debate*

I will now analyze Margot Arce's contribution to the exegesis of Palés' "black verses." For all Palés stated intent to include Puerto Rico's black heritage in the debate over the racial basis of Puerto Rican national culture, his *negrista* project failed to be truly inclusive of Afro-Puerto Rican experience at a number of critical levels. Palés is highly selective in his rendition of the black experience in Puerto Rico and the Caribbean. Moreover, such inclusion is impossible given the very terms upon which the inclusion is predicated. Alienation of black historical participation from the national patrimony is a fundamental assumption of the writings of the "black poetry" debate. *Lo negro* by definition is relegated to the realm of the senses or of primitive difference, and the participants of the debate tacitly agree to a reduction of blackness to those elements that can be safely consumed by a Creole audience. Slavery, black survival, and resistance are erased from both the poetry and the debate. In so doing, Creole participation in a history of enslavement and discrimination is effaced or transformed into a blackness devoid of true human dimension. *Lo negro* will surface only when made palatable to the Creole's self-image. Within this contex, Margot Arce's essays on Palés' *negrista* poetry can be seen as supportive to some extent of his project, but they also position people of African descent outside the realm of *lo puertorriqueño*.

We must place Margot Arce's "Los poemas negros de Luis Palés Matos" in the context of a heated controversy regarding the meaning of these poems and the meaning of the term "black poetry."[17] At the time of the debate, the poems had only appeared in journals and newspapers. The publication of *Tuntún de pasa y grifería* would not occur until 1937. Arce entered the debate as one of the defenders of Palés and remained throughout the years an important agent in the poetry's canonization. Even though she was a staunch supporter of Palés, her views remained biased. It is interesting to note that more than forty years after Palés' work first surfaced, Arce remained silent about her role in the debate. Her famous prologue to the 1978 editions of the poet's works for the Ayacucho publishing house situated her outside the controversy, as an objective voice.

"Black poetry," or *poesía negrista* in the Puerto Rican context, is poetry that is only thematically "black." It is not poetry written by black people. Thus, the oft-repeated phrase *"el tema del negro y de lo negro"* are ambiguous signifiers whose very ambiguity is endemic to the so-called "black poetry" project. Like the white abolitionists seventy years earlier, most readers and critics of this poetry firmly believed that a white writer could write poetry that would "interpret and penetrate the black soul." Margot Arce's view was no exception. Her privileged position and her acceptance by the literary elite sanctioned her tendentious interpretation of the meaning of black culture for many decades. An examination of her commentary, delivered in 1933 at the University of Puerto Rico, will detail how this critic, "interpreted and penetrated the black soul."

Even in the sexist environment of the 1930s, Arce's intervention in the black poetry debate could not be ignored by her male peers. Her assessment of the poems were the subject of a public talk in 1933 at the university published some months later, in 1934, in a well-known local daily.[18] In 1950 this talk would be reprinted as part of a collection of her essays entitled *Impresiones: notas puertorriqueñas*.[19] By this time her reputation in academia was firmly established.

The revisions that Arce made to the original version of her essay are worth noting. In the original version, the first two paragraphs allude to the then contemporary polemic over the poems in the press. There she states her understanding of poetry as closed and self-referential. *"Todo poema es un mundo cerrado y suficiente,"* Arce cautions, *"que se justifica a sí mismo y que está más allá de la retórica y de la lógica."*[20] In the 1950 revision of her 1933 commentary published in *Impresiones*, she updated her readers. Arce opens by recognizing Palés as a noted figure and notes that the international diffusion of his poetry stands as testimony to its artistic merit. Seventeen years after her first analysis she revises her understanding of island history by deleting her previous references to the political reference to 1898 as *"año trágico y decisivo"* mentioned in the original. Also deleted is the reference to Puerto Rico's limited cultural environment.

Were these exclusions meant to distance Arce the "objective" literary critic from Margot Arce the advocate of independence for Puerto Rico? Very possibly. Any reference to the year of the U. S. invasion of the Island might have harmed her credibility as an authoritative critic in the repressive political climate surrounding intellectual discourse in the 1950s.

For Arce, Palés' "black verses" represent one of the poet's greatest achievements. Her commentary traces his development from his provincial Guayama origins, his early verses, and readings to the appearance of his first "black poem" in 1926, "Pueblo negro."[21] Her analysis addresses the complexity and technical mastery of Palés' poems, praising his work for having achieved "a truly universal stature" by virtue of the poet's position within the modernist discourse on blackness. In her view, Palés' universal appeal resulted from his association with European trends. She remarks that

> *Si no tuvieran otro valor, los poemas de Palés valdrían por el solo hecho de haber incorporado a la poesía puertorriqueña un tema de actualidad de interés casi universal. La gente moderna se ha preocupado por la música, la escultura y los mitos de los africanos hasta incorporarlos a las manifestaciones artísticas de la cultura.*[22]

Arce includes Palés and herself among the *"gente moderna,"* whom she normalizes in this essay as modern, civilized, white people. She writes, *"Es probable que estemos viviendo uno de esos acercamientos teóricos a la naturaleza por oposición a lo civilizado . . . ."*[23] Arce thus constructs a binary opposition between nature—*"lo africano"*—and that which is civilized—*"lo europeo."* The approach sets up a clear dichotomy between the modern as white and the primitive as black. In the rewriting of the essay for *Impresiones*, she deletes her references of Pablo Picasso and jazz music as expressions of the preoccupation of modern people with the culture of Africans. The negritude vogue is long over by 1950, and nascent anticolonial struggles around the world no longer allow whites the freedom to indulge in superficial fascinations with "the black primitive."

Key to Arce's analysis is the thesis that Palés' black themes have—above all else—a literary genesis. She substantiates this contention by underscoring the poet's familiarity with the works of Blaise Cendrars, Frobenius, and Langston Hughes. She also points out the influence that the rhythms of black popular dances had on Palés' poetry. She forwards a third notion, with somewhat less enthusiasm, that Palés was also inspired by the Island's fairly large black and mulatto population. But how did Puerto Rico's blacks inspire the poet? As Arce sees it, while Palés specifically incorporates the rhythms of Puerto Rican black music to his poetry, he does not make use of other black Puerto Rican cultural manifestations.[24] In Palés' work, the relationship of "black poetry" to a Puerto Rican socio historical referent is limited, as the critic sees it: *"Mas del negro puertorriqueño, [Palés] ha incorporado a su poesía únicamente el ritmo de sus danzas populares."*[25] Furthermore, Arce asserts that the blacks in Palés' poems are not Puerto Rican at all. She writes that the black

> *es un negro exótico: el de la jungla africana, el ñáñigo de Cuba, o el negro supersticioso y hechicero de la selva de Haiti. Es un negro teórico, hipotético, abstracto, que Palés no ha visto y que ha creado con datos de procedencia literaria.*[26]

This statement provoked a public outcry, which forced Arce to retract some of her views in a second article entitled "Más sobre los poemas de Luis Palés Matos."[27] But even in her retraction, as I will discuss elsewhere, Arce remained unconcerned with the status of referents in Palés' literary representations.[28] She was much more interested in separating Puerto Rico from the purported backwardness and savagery associated with Afro-Caribbean religious practices. She responded to these criticisms of her 1933 commentary by adding in the *Impresiones* version of "Los poemas negros" that the black theme in Palés has a social as well as a literary genesis. As we saw in her first essay, she did not point to any immediate

Puerto Rican social referent for this poetry. As we shall see, it would be much easier and more desirable to see a "truthful" representation of the *Antillas negras* in Haiti.

Consistent in all her essays is Arce's belief that Palés, with poems such as "Elegía del duque de la mermelada" and "Lagarto verde," had masterfully exposed the "true nature" of the Europeanized Haitian elite. As she wrote in her 1933 commentaries:

La superstición ancestral y primitiva es más poderosa que el refinamiento postizo de los salones. El condesito de la limonada puede portarse versallescamente, mas una sola palabra bastaría para desnudarle de los artificios de la etiqueta y despertarle los viejos resabios de sus parientes de la selva.[29]

By 1950 she softens her stance a bit. No longer does she see as a given that Hatians are primitives; instead, she says that the poem represents this as such, *"aparece como más poderosa que el refinamiento postizo de los salones."*[30]

Ethnic essences were not new to Arce; the concept was fundamental to her style of criticism. Her analysis invariably presupposes the existence of racial essences or characteristics proper to every racial grouping. In 1930, before any of these essays were published, she had written a commentary on ethnic-nationalist essences entitled *"El carácter español."* No doubt she followed in the footsteps of the Spanish Generation of '98, whose copious literature on the Spanish "spirit and character" aligned Castillian culture solely with white European culture, thus negating the influence of non-white Peninsular peoples.[31] Arce accepted and unwittingly proceeded to illustrate the assumption that Europeans were racially superior in the Puerto Rican environment.

For Arce, Palés' poetry literally captures and renders the "spirit of the black race," which his superior vantage point converted into poetic "truth." But what is the "truth" that this poetry reveals? To answer this question, Arce compared the Cubans Nicolás Guillén and Emilio Ballagas with Palés Matos. Since poetry, by elite definition, is the domain of cultured, literate Europeans, popular or subaltern artists cannot produce poetry. Arce distances Palés' art from that of Nicolás Guillén and Emilio Ballagas, whom she regards as cultivating a less cultured poetry:

Luis Palés Matos es un poeta culto, mejor dicho culterano. El artificio de su poesía se manifiesta en el cuidado verdaderamente gongorino que dedica a la parte formal y metafórica. Se aparta de los modos poéticos populares; interpreta lo negro como un blanco civilizado y escéptico. Se diferencia así esencialmente de Nicolás Guillén y Emilio Ballagas.[32]

Ultimately, in this reading, Palés' capital achievement lies in the formal aspects of his "black poetry," which remind her in their technical virtuosity of the work of Gongora.[33]

Palés' well-publicized statement on the role of peoples of African descent in Caribbean culture are viewed with skepticism by Arce. *"Los antillanos no somos hispánicos puros,"* Palés had said in the interview for *El Mundo*, *"somos españoles con maneras de mulato y alma de negro; el factor negro actúa en la cultura antillana como aislador o como agente precipitante."*[34] Note that, even for Palés, Puerto Ricans are still Spanish with a twist. The "black factor" provided Puerto Ricans with a measure of exoticized difference.

Palés Matos believed, as did his generation, that races had innate characteristics. He also thought that culture was a product of race:

Las características del negro, tamizadas en el mulato, influyen en las manifestaciones de nuestra vida popular; en la música con la plena, el son y el mariyandá, y con el cuatro, el tambor y el güiro, instrumentos musicales de la murga mulata, influyen en las manifestaciones de nuestra música popular y en la política, con la pasión, la elasticidad y el verbosismo.[35]

Here Palés carefully stresses that those mulatto and black "characteristics" are present in the popular culture of the Island. He does not include the literary elite in this statement, for it is clear that they are not part of *"nuestra vida popular."* This puts the elite in a quandary, for any successful aristocracy has to project its class interests as representing those of the majority of the people. At the same time, the majority has to identify—in some measure—with the interests of the ruling elite. As critics like Arcadio Díaz Quiñones have discussed, acceptance of Puerto Rico's mixed-race heritage was a necessary political strategy embraced by intellectuals like Tomás Blanco and the populist alliance of the Partido Popular Democrático.[36] Palés' detractors within the elite were not willing to consider his ultimately mild propositions.[37] My criticism of Palés' reduction of the black experience to a mere cultural catalyst does not diminish the significance of his bold stance, in the racist cultural context of the 1930s, regarding Puerto Rican's debt to an African Motherland.

By insisting that black culture is fundamental to a truly Antillean poetry, Palés rejected the hispanophilia and negrophobia of the Generación del Treinta. Arce can consequently commit herself only in part to Palés' project. In the 1934 essay, she conceded that the black presence was a differentiating element of Caribbean culture, writes, *"Por lo menos no podemos negar que el negro es un ingrediente diferenciador."* But she would delete this statement for her 1950 version. Moreover, in the earlier essay, she was very reluctant to envision the profound cultural implications of Palés' project. At that stage, she had cautiously called for a more thorough study of the black presence in Puerto Rico. *"Sería preciso un poco más de investigación minuciosa para asegurarlo,"* she wrote. Yet by 1950, this statement is also omitted. In 1933, Arce was emphatic in her denial of the idea that black culture was the culture that gave Puerto Rico its Caribbean character. She claimed that *"parece un tanto arriesgado afirmar que [la influencia negra] sea . . . caracterizante."*[38] In her view and the view of most members of the Generación del Treinta, the characterizing influence is Spanish culture and "race." Much is at stake in this denial of black presence, history, and culture in Puerto Rico. The reality of hundreds of years of race-mixing and transculturation cannot be easily reconciled with the ideology of ethnic essentialism espoused by Arce's brand of cultural nationalism. If Puerto Ricans are transplanted Spaniards, who are all these people of innumerable skin colors who live on the Island? Better not to acknowledge those troublesome *"manifestaciones de nuestra vida popular"* such as music, family structure, humor, cuisine, pronunciation, even the very maligned African custom of sitting *"ñangotao"* style or the whitening imperative present in the accepted rule of *"adelantar la raza."* Better not to acknowledge the Creole elite's role in the enforcement of racial prejudice and light-skin privilege amongst its ranks and in its ethos.

One of the most important revisions Arce made in her essay refers to the question of the point of view presented in the poems. She appeals to a discourse of objectivity to talk about what is designated as "other." Her claim is that Palés, because he is a white man of culture, is able to objectively view and be critical of black cultural "lack." Is it that Palés is a white explorer in a "dark continent" of black difference? Arce ascribes to the poet what amounts to imperial or imperialistic eyes.[39] In 1933 she had written:

> *Los temas son: descripciones de pueblos y de costumbres negros, evocaciones de la mitología africana, ritos y supersticiones mágicas, visiones de paisaje y de geografía negra, sátira de la aristocracia de Haití y contrastes humorísticos entre la cultura del blanco y la del negro. Al tratar estos temas, Palés se coloca en un punto de vista objetivo e interpreta lo negro con cierta condescendencia complacida y escéptica de hombre blanco que duda de todo, hasta de su propia cultura.*[40]

But the later version reads: *"Al tratar estos temas, Palés se coloca en un punto de vista subjetivo e interpreta lo negro con cierta condescendencia complacida y escéptica de hombre blanco que duda de todo, hasta de su propia cultura."*[41] Where first Arce had wanted to see objectivity, she later saw a subjective interpretation of the themes of Tuntún.

Arce also modifies her judgment on the rhythm of the poetry: *"El efecto de insistencia y monotonía se obtiene por medio de la construcción o composición simétrica del poema."* Previously she had seen monotony; now she sees variation: *"El efecto de insistencia y de variación se obtiene por medio de la construcción o composición simétrica del poema, como se advierte en Danza negra y Bombo."*[42] She clearly had misunderstood the wealth of Afro-Caribbean rhythm, a misconception she corrects in the latter version. The same is true of her statements on African and Afro-Caribbean dance. Deleted in 1950 are her remarks on dance as the quintessential form of expression for "primitive"—she means black—people. She had written in 1933, *"La interpretación del alma negra es acabada porque la danza es a mi juicio, la más trascendental voluntad de expresión de todo pueblo primitivo."*[43] These disparaging assessments are excised from the 1950 version.

Some of the more problematic implications of how Palés' "black verses" have been used are exemplified in Arce's claim that a white, "cultured" writer is a privileged interpreter of the "black soul." For whom, we ask? For a white audience, for a black audience, or for a "universal" audience? In her comments in Impresiones she stands fast to her claim that of Palés' poetry is to be seen as universal. Let's return again to Arce's comparisons between the black poet and the white poet who write about the black experience. A universal vantage point, *"desde arriba"* and *"en blanco,"* is, for Arce, superior to that of Guillén: *"pero su [Palés's] interpretación por objetiva y distanciada logra mayor agudeza."*[44]

Why does Arce insist on the superiority of Palés' "objective vantage point?" What is at stake when Arce stresses that Palés is a white man in contrast to the black Nicolás Guillén for example? Arce had said, *"No es en manera alguna un poeta popular; es un blanco civilizado que interpreta lo negro con buen humor y una pizca de ironía."*[45] Guillén and Ballagas *"ven al negro desde abajo, desde dentro y en negro."*[46] Palés, in contrast, is able to see blacks "humorously." Unfortunately, the joke is at the expense of black people, and Arce is laughing with Palés at what they perceive as the stupidity or naiveté of black people. Even by 1950 she reiterates that Palés, *"Se aparta de los poetas populares; interpreta lo negro como un blanco civilizado y escéptico."*[47] Still, in this later version, she persists in keeping the slanderous remarks about blacks as uncivilized and credulous beings. Arce concludes her essay with a profession of faith in the superiority of art over historical reality. Palés' poetic renditions of the black character are deemed superior to the reality of the historical black experience. With Palés' creation, as Arce would have it, *"se cumple el axioma de que la realidad poética supera siempre a la histórica realidad cotidiana."*[48] Ultimately, Arce inflates the role of literature and proposes that it can act as a substitute for history. ■

ENDNOTES

1. Published in 1937, this is one of Pales' most anthologized poems.
2. Isabelo Zenón Cruz, *Narciso descubre su trasero: el negro en la cultura puertorriqueña* (Humacao: Ediciones Furidí, 1974-1975) two volumes.
3. Pales Matos, *El Mundo* interview, 13 Nov. (1932), given to Angela Negrón Muñoz, "Hablando con Don Luis Palés Matos." A reprint of this text can be found in Margot Arce's edition of *Luis Palés Matos: poesía completa* (Caracas: Biblioteca Ayacucho, 1978), 213-218.
4. Palés Matos, interview, *El Mundo* 13 November (1932), unpaginated.
5. Palés Matos, (1932).
6. Palés Matos, (1932).
7. As an intellectual formation, the *Generación del Treinta* advocated a rethinking of Puerto Rican culture within the narrow parameters of a Spanish/Creole-based cultural nationalism.
8. de Diego Padró, "Antillanismo, criollismo, negroidismo," *El Mundo* 19 Nov. (1932).
9. For additional information on his position, see also de Diego Padró's "Tropicalismo, occidentalismo, sentido de la cultura," *El Mundo* 18 Dec. (1932) Unpaginated. Reprinted in J. I. De Diego Padró, *Luis Palés Matos y su trasmundo poético* (Río Piedras: Ediciones Puerto, 1973) 109-121.
10. de Diego Padró, "Antillanismo, criollismo, negroidismo," *El Mundo* 19 Nov. (1932).
11. de Diego Padró, (1932).
12. Luis Palés Matos, "Hacia una poesía antillana," *El Mundo* 26 Nov. (1932).
13. Luis Antonio Miranda, "El llamado arte negro no tiene vinculación con Puerto Rico," *El Mundo* 26 Nov. (1932).
14. Miranda, (1932).
15. Miranda, (1932).
16. Miranda, (1932). Emphasis in the original.
17. See Margot Arce's introductory essay to the Ayachucho edition of Palés' poems cited above.
18. It is customary for Puerto Rican literary criticism to stress that a number of Palés' black poems predates Nicolás Guillén's *negrismo*. It is of little value for my arguments to engage in a discussion regarding who first wrote about this notion. A more important project would be to compare the anxiety at the base of the *negrista* projects of both *criollo* Cubans and *criollo* Puerto Ricans. What is the level and quality of influence that the Cubans might have exerted on the Puerto Rican scene in the 1930s? A Cuban writer like Juan Marinello was very well known in Puerto Rico. But, by the same token, it is not clear that other Cuban writers like Carpentier had an audience in Puerto Rico before the Cuban Revolution.
19. Margot Arce, *El Mundo,* 21 Jan. (1934). Unpaginated.
20. Margot Arce, *Impresiones: notas puertorriqueñas* (San Juan: Editorial Yaurel, 1950).
21. Arce, "Los poemas negros," *El Mundo* 21 Jan. (1934).
22. "Pueblo de negros," an earlier composition in prose, reflects a more negative attitude toward blacks.
23. Arce, (1934).
24. Arce, (1934).
25. Even Palés' vision of the black experience is narrow. Palés says nothing of the history of black resistance to racism and oppression, nothing of black people's humanity.
26. Arce, (1934).
27. Arce, (1934).
28. This essay was reprinted under the title "Rectificaciones" for the 1950 edition.
29. I discuss these questions more fully in Race, Gender, and the Generación del Treinta, Toward a Deciphering of Puerto Rican National Identity Discourse. Diss. Stanford University, 1993.
30. Arce, (1934). Emphasis added.
31. Arce, *Impresiones*, 46. Emphasis added.
32. Arce had studied in Spain at the time when these concepts, developed by Unamuno, Ortega y Gasset, and others, enjoyed great acceptance. We must not forget that Ortega was the com-

mentator and presenter of German philosophy and metaphysics through his *Revista de Occidente*.
33 Arce, (1934). The statements are identical in both versions. Ballagas was also a white man, but his poems imitated a black popular voice.
34 One of the constants of Arce's critical style is this criticism by analogy.
35 Palés, interview, (1932).
36 Palés, interview, (1932). Emphasis added.
37 See Arcadio Díaz Quiñones' introductory essay, "Tomás Blanco: racismo, historia y esclavitud," *El prejuico racial en Puerto Rico* (Río Piedras: Ediciones Huracán, 1985).
38 For a more detailed discussion, see R*ace, Gender, and the Generación del Treinta*.
39 Arce, (1934).
40 I borrow this phrase from Mary Louise Pratt's book on the discourse of white imperialist explorations, *Imperial Eyes: Travel Writing and Transculturation* (London: Routledge, 1992).
41 Arce, (1934). Emphasis added.
42 Arce, *Impresiones,* 48. Emphasis added.
43 Arce, *Impresiones,* 49.
44 Arce, (1934).
45 Arce, *Impresiones,* 51. Emphasis added.
46 Arce, (1934).
47 Arce, *Impresiones*, 50.
48 Arce, (1934) and *Impresiones*, 50-51. This statement is identical in both versions. Emphasis added.

REFERENCES

Arce de Vázquez, Margot. *Impresiones: notas puertorriqueñas* . San Juan: Editorial Yaurel, 1950.
"Los poemas negros de Luis Palés Matos," *El Mundo* 21 Jan. (1934). Unpaginated.
de Diego Padró, J. I. "Antillanismo, criollismo, negroidismo." El Mundo 19 Nov. 1932. Unpaginated.
—"Tropicalismo, occidentalismo, sentido de la cultura," *El Mundo* 18 Dec. (1932) Unpaginated. Reprinted in de Diego Padró, J. I. *Luis Palés Matos y su trasmundo poético*. Río Piedras: Ediciones Puerto, 1973. 109–121.
Díaz Quiñones, Arcadio. Introduction. "Tomás Blanco: racismo, historia y esclavitud." By Tomás Blanco. *El prejuicio racial en Puerto Rico* . Río Piedras: Ediciones Huracán, 1985.
Miranda, Luis Antonio. "El llamado arte negro no tiene vinculación con Puerto Rico," *El Mundo* 26 Nov. (1932). Unpaginated.
Negrón Muñoz, Angela. "Hablando con don Luis Palés Matos." *El Mundo* 13 Nov. (1932). Unpaginated.
Palés Matos, Luis. *Luis Palés Matos: poesía completa*. Ed. Margot Arce de Vázquez. Caracas: Biblioteca Ayacucho, 1978.
—"Hacia una poesía antillana." *El Mundo* 26 Nov. (1932). Unpaginated.
Pratt, Mary Louise. *Imperial Eyes: Travel Writing and Transculturation*. London: Routledge, 1992.
Roy-Fequiere, Magali. Race, Gender, and the Generación del Treinta: Toward a Deciphering of Puerto Rican National Identity Discourse. Diss. Stanford University, 1993.
Zenón Cruz, Isabelo. *Narciso descubre su trasero: el negro en la cultura puertorriqueña.* 2 vols. Humacao: Ediciones Furidí, 1974–1975.

Afro-Puerto Rican Radicalism in the United States

WINSTON JAMES

They were both black and Puerto Rican, both in their youth burned with the fire of Puerto Rican nationalism, both migrated to the United States as young men, and both settled, lived and died in New York City. Yet Arturo Schomburg (1874–1938) and Jesús Colón (1901–1974) are seldom mentioned in the same breath. Each is known, it is fair to say, by a different set of people, with different political and intellectual interests; they made different friendships and associations, and were driven, eventually, by different passions. It is true that Schomburg and Colón were of different generations, but that hardly accounts for the striking difference in their political evolution, and in the perception and remembrance of them. The fact is that, despite similar points of political origin, they followed radically divergent political paths, were absorbed by different objectives, and had dissimilar destinations. Schomburg died an ardent Pan-Africanist, with definite black nationalist sympathies wedded to the struggles and aspirations of Afro-America. Colón died a socialist and Puerto Rican nationalist, with no time for black nationalism. How do we account for the marked difference in the political trajectory of these two men? How does one explain their political evolution against the historical background of the Hispanic Caribbean and the Puerto Rican society from which they both came? How did America and the articulation of race in American society conditioned their political evolution? These are some of the key questions I hope to address in this essay.

One thing is clear from the outset: Arturo Schomburg, not Jesús Colón, was the Puerto Rican political aberration. For one of the most

Reflections on the Political Trajectories of Arturo Schomburg and Jesús Colón

striking patterns that emerges from the examination of the Caribbean experience in the United States in the first half of the century is that among black radicals from the Hispanic Caribbean there was relative indifference, if not aversion, to black nationalism. Such a position contrasted sharply with a noticeable attraction to an unhyphenated socialism. Arturo Schomburg's sympathy for black nationalism, his profound interest and pioneering work in the history of peoples of African descent, was not shared by his black Puerto Rican compatriots in New York City in the 1920s and 1930s. And Schomburg's anomalous situation cannot be explained without understanding the specificity of race in the Hispanic, as well as in the non-Hispanic, Caribbean. Puerto Rico could not have produced a Marcus Garvey, the Jamaican-born founder of the black nationalist Universal Negro Improvement Association, and Jamaica, by the same token, could not have produced a Jesús Colón. Differences in the ways that race operated hold the key to explaining this pattern. There is thus a need to outline and analyze, if only briefly, these important but rarely examined intra-Caribbean differences that, it should be noted, carry over into the diaspora in America. And as will be argued, Schomburg's peculiar political evolution cannot be accounted for outside of these intra-Caribbean variations.

Up to about 1800 the Hispanic Caribbean islands were colonies in which a comparatively large number of Europeans decided to live, or ended up living, on a permanent basis. In comparison to the northern European colonies, landholdings were small, even though the land-population ratio was large. After the center of gravity of Spanish America shifted to the gold and silver riches of Mexico and Peru in the early sixteenth century, the islands became relatively underexploited. Their links to the expanding capitalist world economy were not as strong as it was to be for the Caribbean colonies that Britain, France, and Holland acquired in the seventeenth century. In the wake of the exploits of Córtes and Pizarro, the islands' population declined as their inhabitants rushed to partake in the new-found riches of the mainland. *"Dios me lleve al Perú,"* they cried in Puerto Rico. The stampede was so great that the Spanish authorities feared the entire departure of the European population of the islands, thus jeopardizing their hold on them. To obviate this danger, the Council of the Indies issued decrees in the 1520s and 1530s prohibiting the unauthorized emigration from the islands. The penalty for illegal departure was death and the confiscation of property.[1] Subsistence farming and ranching became the mainstay of the islands. Cuba, Puerto Rico, and Santo Domingo, from the earliest days of settlement had African slaves, but the percentage of the black population that was free was consistently higher than that which obtained in the non-Hispanic colonies of the New World.

With capitalism far more developed than in Spain, over the centuries Britain, France, and Holland had the economic and political infrastructure to exploit their Caribbean possessions far more systematically and intensively than Spain ever did. Apart from its economically inhibiting feudal system, Spain was spoiled by the great wealth extracted from the mainland in the form of precious metals. The islands, previously the center of Spanish colonial attention in the New World, were, by the mid-sixteenth century, of minor, if any, intrinsic value to Spain, functioning as handmaidens to the mainland colonies—as re-fueling stations and garrisons, aiding the protection of convoys on their way to Spain laden with American gold and silver.

Havana's early colonial history is instructive. Significantly, Havana flourished in the late sixteenth century only after the French burned it down in 1555, and it finally dawned on the Spanish that Cuba, and Havana in particular, had to be held in order to service and safeguard the traffic with the mineral-rich American mainland. Cuba was strategically located, and on its defense depended the defense of Spain's New World. Havana's sheltered and expansive natural harbor had to be defended, not for the security and well-being of Cuba's inhabitants per se, but for its vital role in Spain's maritime trade. Accordingly, garrisons were established in Havana, providing for a resident armed force, fluctuating in number between four hundred and a thousand men. Fortifications were built, protecting the city from Spain's envious rivals. After the 1560s, to minimize the plunder of pirates, Spain's trans-Atlantic shipping sailed under the escort of an armed convoy. The system known as the *flota*, consolidated Spain's maritime traffic into two annual fleets to the Americas. On the return to Europe, both *flotas* put in at Havana, preparatory to the long and dangerous journey across the Atlantic, protected by a fleet of armed galleons. For centuries to come, Cuba depended on Mexican money to subsidize the military and administrative expenses of the island. The Mexican *situados*, which was received by other islands apart from Cuba, would continue into the nineteenth century, clearly indicating the subordinate and auxiliary position of the islands to the mainland.

WINSTON JAMES teaches history at Columbia University. His previous publications include *Inside Babylon: The Caribbean Diaspora in Britain* (London and New York: Verso, 1993), which he edited with Clive Harris. His next book is *Holding Aloft the Banner of Ethiopia: Caribbean Radicalism in America, 1900–1932*, which will be published by Verso in the fall of 1996. The author would like to thank the *CENTRO* editorial board and in particular Blanca Vázquez, Roberto Rodríguez, and Juan Flores for their comments on an earlier version of this essay. Solsirée del Moral assisted with the research and offered comments for which the author is grateful. Over the last few years, he has benefited from the very helpful conversations with Juan Flores, Agustín Laó, Palmira Ríos, and Miriam Jiménez about the history of Puerto Rico, the peculiarities of the black experience on the island and the world of Arturo Schomburg and Jesús Colón.

Havana's population grew, and grew well out of proportion to the rest of the island. The extensive construction of houses and forts stimulated economic growth. The *flotas* brought four to five thousand additional people to Havana for weeks at a time, twice a year. Many had come from the mainland with newly acquired fortunes, eager to have a good time before their forty-five day voyage home. They required entertainment, lodgings, and food. The silver and gold triggered inflation as it stimulated economic growth. Havana quickly acquired the reputation of being the most expensive place in the Indies. It was also during the sixteenth century that Havana became infamous for its gamblers, merchants, vendors, deserters, con-men, thieves, and prostitutes—a reputation that a revolution finally broke four centuries later.

Havana's prosperity rippled through western Cuba. Farmers, cattle breeders, and artisans benefited. But Havana's success was directly connected to the demise of the eastern end of the island. Santiago de Cuba, Cuba's colonial capital established in 1515, languished in the south east as the *flotas* and their riches came and went on the north coast of the island, touching land only in Havana. By 1553, the Council of the Indies ordered the governor of the island to transfer his residence from Santiago de Cuba to Havana. In 1594 Havana was officially designated a city *(ciudad)*, no longer a mere town *(villa)*. Thirteen years later, in 1607, the colonial authorities officially declared Havana the capital of Cuba, the seat of the governor and captain-general—formally acknowledging what had long been a fact.

By 1608, Havana was home to more than half the island's 20,000 inhabitants. Eastern Cuba languished, envious of Havana's contrived and rapid preeminence, resentful of the Spanish colonial yoke. Hardly defended by the colonial authorities, eastern Cuba was easy prey to French, British, and Dutch attackers: Santiago and Bayamo were attacked by the French in 1603, and again in 1628 and 1633; in 1652 the French took over Baracoa and attacked Remedios. The English sacked Santiago in 1662, and in 1665 the French busied themselves with destroying Sancti Spíritus. Henry Morgan sacked Puerto Príncipe in 1668, and John Springer plunder the town of Trinidad in 1675. Four years later Puerto Príncipe was attacked again.

Inadequately supplied by Spain, easterners were, nevertheless, forbidden from trading with foreigners. The citizens of Santiago, Bayamo, Baracoa, and other eastern towns ignored Spanish mercantile law and traded with Dutch, British and French merchants along the coast, developing a vibrant system of smuggling. The Spanish authorities attempted to clamp down on the flagrant violation of their laws, but through a series of spectacular revolts between 1602 and 1607, they learned to turn a blind eye and to leave the locals to their own devices and thriving contraband trade.

Through such historical experience, Havana, and to a great extent western Cuba as a whole, came to be regarded as Spanish colonial possessions, the stronghold of colonial authority. Eastern Cuba, especially Oriente province, in contrast, is often perceived as de facto, Cuban, even when Spain was the nominal possessor of the island.[2]

Outside of Havana and western Cuba, from the mid-sixteenth to the eighteenth century, Spain's insular possessions languished, the region turning in upon itself and into a colonial backwater; they lacked the gold and silver that held Spain's attention on the mainland. It was in this context of relative neglect that the northern European powers were able, by the early seventeenth century, to pluck away, one by one, a number of islands from the Spanish imperial body politic.

Spain's imperial malaise and neglect of the islands—as well as its effective abandonment of eastern Cuba in the late sixteenth century—provided local opportunity for those who lived in them. For one thing, imperial nonchalance provided a level of de facto autonomy for the inhabitants that they otherwise would not have enjoyed. The development of a substantial (relative to the slave population), black peasantry in the sixteenth right up to the eighteenth century cannot be explained outside of this wider context. It was also such circumstances that facilitated the growth and reproduction of a large (compared to the slave population), white, small-holding, settler population in the Spanish islands. Along with these developments, there occurred a level of interaction between the black and white population that was prolonged and unparalleled in the New World.

By the late eighteenth century, however, the noisy march of European capitalism had disturbed the rustic somnolence of the Spanish Caribbean. Starting with Cuba, the slave trade dramatically expanded, gigantic plantations were laid out and established, and the smallholding peasantry found it increasingly difficult to maintain its cherished independence. For the enslaved Africans, the acquisition of manumission became more difficult as their labor became more valuable. In short, Spain's Caribbean possessions became progressively more like the northern European colonies as sugar became the crop of choice.

The metamorphosis of the Spanish Caribbean rapidly accelerated after revolution broke out in Saint Domingue, the richest sugar colony in the New World, in 1791. The Haitian slaves punched a massive hole in the world sugar market. Almost 80,000 tons of sugar were produced on the eve of revolution in 1791. But, with the destruction wrought by a devastating war and with a new and fiercely independent peasantry shunning the diabolical plantation system, Haiti produced only 8 tons of sugar in 1836.[3] The *hacendados* in the islands, like their counterparts elsewhere, took advantage of this unprecedented and unique opportunity. And so the sugar revolution, which first broke out in the British possessions in the seventeenth century, belatedly took hold of the Hispanic territories, spreading from Cuba in the middle of the eighteenth, moving to Puerto Rico and on to the Dominican Republic in the nineteenth and early twentieth century.[4] But even during the nineteenth century, during the din and turmoil of King Sugar ascending his throne, dripping with the blood of Africans, the Hispanic territories displayed distinct characteristics vis-à-vis the non-Hispanic areas, carried over from their classic, and relatively prolonged, settler period. And these characteristics, as will be demonstrated later, included the place of race and color in their social structure.

The dissimilar political economy that shaped the two areas of the Caribbean profoundly affected their demographic and ethnic patterns which, in turn, significantly influenced the articulation of race and color. In this respect, one key difference is that whites made up a much larger proportion of the population of the Hispanic Caribbean relative to the proportion found in the non-Hispanic Caribbean. It is true that racial definitions of "white" tend to be more elastic in the Hispanic compared to the non-Hispanic Caribbean, but, even by the most restrictive criteria, the Hispanic areas of the archipelago have always had a relatively high proportion of white people among their inhabitants. Thus, while the Hispanic Caribbean, with the exception of the Dominican Republic, had, for instance in the nineteenth century, approximately half of its population designated as "white," the non-Hispanic Caribbean, typically, had less than 10 percent so defined.[5]

Prior to the abolition of slavery, the Hispanic Caribbean had a proportionately larger free non-white population compared to that in the non-Hispanic territories. The rate of manumission was much higher in the former area. Thus, on the eve of abolition in 1834, less than twelve out of every hundred non-white Jamaicans, and only seven out of a hundred non-white Barbadians, were free; all the others were enslaved. By contrast, almost sixty per cent of non-white Cubans were free in 1880, six years before abolition, and ninety per cent of their Puerto Rican counterparts were free by the time of abolition in 1873 (see Table I, below.) This distribution of black freedom in the archipelago was not an aberration of the nineteenth century. It was a secular trend. In 1773 less than one percent (0.7 percent), of black and mulatto Barbadians were free, 534 out of 69,082. Their Jamaican counterparts hardly fared better, 2.3 percent being legally free, 4,500 out of 197,300, in 1775. In the same year, 41 percent of non-white Cubans (30,847 out of 75,180), and a stunning 82.2 percent of their Puerto Rican brothers and sisters were free.[6] Why the massive differential between British and Spanish territories? As a number of scholars have argued, this was largely due to the relative economic backwardness of the Spanish possessions and of Spain itself, and was rather less a product, as some had previously suggested, of supposedly benign cultural characteristics of Spanish colonialism in the region. After all, as sugar became king in the nineteenth-century, it was in Cuba, under the same Catholic Spanish colonial rule, that the rate and ease with which the slaves acquired their manumission diminished, while the slave trade dramatically expanded. Unable to mobilize the resources to import anywhere near as many African slaves as they claimed they needed, the Puerto Rican *hacendados* in the nineteenth century, in a desperate bid to solve the labor "scarcity" problem, subordinated

TABLE 1

Slave and Free Non-White Population in Nineteenth-Century Americas

Colony/Nation (Year)	Slave	Free Non-White	Percentage Non-White Free
Cuba (1880)	199,885	267,547	57.4
Puerto Rico (1872)	31,635	251,709	88.8
Barbados (1833/34)	82,807	6,584	7.4
Jamaica (1834)	310,000	42,000	11.9
United States (1860)	3,953,760	488,070	11.0
United States (Southern states) 1860	3,953,696	261,918	6.2
Brazil (1872)	1,510,806	4,245,428	73.7

peasants and workers, black and white alike, to the rule of capital through extraordinarily coercive legislation.[7]

Sources: Cuba: Kenneth F. Kiple, *Blacks in Colonial Cuba, 1774–899* (Gainesville: University Presses of Florida, 1976), p. 70; Puerto Rico: Luis M. Díaz Soler, *Historia de la Esclavitud Negra en Puerto Rico*, 3rd. ed. (Río Piedras: Editorial Universitaria, Universidad de Puerto Rico 1981), p. 256; Barbados: Jerome S. Handler, *The Unappropriated People: Freedmen in the Slave Society of Barbados* (Baltimore: Johns Hopkins University Press 1974), pp. 18–19; Jamaica: Gad Heuman, *Between Black and White: Race, Politics, and the Free Coloreds in Jamaica, 1792–1865* (Oxford: Clio Press, 1981), p. 7; United States: Ira Berlin, *Slaves Without Masters: The Free Negro in the Antebellum South* (New York: Pantheon, 1974), pp. 136–137, 396–397; Brazil: Herbert Klein, "Nineteenth-Century Brazil," in David W. Cohen and Jack P. Greene, eds., *Neither Slave Nor Free: The Freedmen of African Descent in the Slave Societies of the New World* (Baltimore: Johns Hopkins University Press, 1972), p. 314.

The black and white peasantry underwent some of the same travails in the Hispanic Caribbean. Reflecting upon the draconian labor laws passed in Puerto Rico in the mid-nineteenth century, Sidney Mintz rightly noted the "color-blindness of the planter class" when it came to coercing labor to work on the *haciendas*.[8] Adversity often bonded the oppressed, joining black and white together. Because of these historical patterns, blackness was therefore not as profoundly associated with subordination in the Hispanic as it was in the non-Hispanic areas of the archipelago.[9] The occupational distance between the black and mulatto in the Hispanic Caribbean was less than it was in the non-Hispanic Caribbean.

In 1872, the year before abolition, it was estimated that 35 percent of Puerto Rican slaves were mulatto or mestizo; indeed, 1.5 percent were described as "white." In 1832, two years before abolition, 14 percent of Barbadian and 10 percent of Jamaican slaves were colored; none was designated as "white."[10]

The distinct pattern of interaction between black and white contributed to the growth of a relatively large colored population in the Hispanic compared to that in the non-Hispanic Caribbean.[11] The sexual relations between black and white in the Hispanic Caribbean, and Puerto Rico in particular, were less marked by the profound imbalance of power that characterized such relations in the non-Hispanic Caribbean, especially in Jamaica and St. Domingue. While in Puerto Rico such cross-racial relations were often established between black and white workers and peasants, in Jamaica and St. Domingue they were generally ones between white masters or overseers and female slaves in their charge. In any case, the offspring of such unions were regarded as neither "black" nor "white"—they were a category *sui generis*. (This kind of formulation would come into sharp conflict with the fundamentally binary—"black"/"white"—distribution of the racialized population in the United States.)

The high level of interaction between black and white peasants and workers, and the many points at which their interests and fortunes converge, help to explain another outstanding feature of Hispanic Caribbean society: the high level of black mobilization and enthusiasm for nationalist projects. It is no accident that Oriente Province, the most eastern province of Cuba, was the place that the support for the Ten Years War and the independence struggle against Spain was greatest. Both the 1868 and 1895 insurrections began there. Oriente had a large black and colored free population who had exceptionally good access to land through ownership, rent or squatting. The small peasantry predominated there, black and white, with remarkably similar land tenure patterns. "Oriente was a place of parity and proportion, of equity and equality," said Louis Pérez, describing the turn of the century milieu. The language is hyperbolic, but there is much truth to it. It is in this environment that the encroachment of the Spanish government and the local *peninsulares* provoked joint revolt.[12] The free people of color (black and mixed-race) in Puerto Rico enjoyed even greater access to the land than did their counterparts in nineteenth-century Cuba. In 1860, six years before the revolt in the north-western town of Lares, they made up over 35 percent of the peasant farmers, 34 percent of proprietors and over 36 percent of the artisans of the island; the free colored population was estimated to make up 46 percent of Puerto Rico's free population at the time.[13]

From *el grito de Lares*, Puerto Rico's nationalist insurrection in 1868, through the Ten Years War and Cuba's war of independence of the 1890s, right up to the victory of the Fidelistas in 1959, black people have not only been present, but have been prominent and distinguished fighters in the anti-colonial struggle. In Cuba's war against Spain, almost half of the fighters were black. Antonio Maceo, Cuba's "bronze titan" and his brother José fell on the field of battle, as did countless other black Cubans. The sacrifices of war not only strengthen the bonds of fellowship between black and white patriots, it also reinforced the claims of citizenship and belonging.[14] And even when the white ruling class, such as that in Cuba in the aftermath of independence, tighten the screws on black people, this should not be read as simply reflective of white popular opinion and behavior.[15] In Puerto Rico, Ramón Emeterio Betances (1827–1898), a mulatto, is, as José Luis González put it, "recognized by all supporters of Puerto Rican independence as the Father of the Nation."[16] Arturo Schomburg and Jesús Colón were only two of a long and distinguished line of black or "colored" Puerto Rican nationalists: from Francisco Gonzalo "Pachín" Marín, Sotero Figueroa, Pedro Albizu Campos, right down to Felipe Luciano, Chairman of the Young Lords (migrant Puerto Rico's equivalent of the Black Panthers) in the early 1970s.

The British, French, Dutch and Danish Caribbean had no equivalent of the popular cross-racial nationalism that developed in Puerto Rico and Cuba in the nineteenth and early twentieth century. The white creole minority was too small and fearful of the black masses to break with London, Paris, Amsterdam or Copenhagen. The mulatto elite often harbored nationalist yearnings, at times hating the metropole, especially its arrogant

European-born agents. But their contempt for and fear of the African masses was more powerful than any desire they may have had to sever links with the mother country. The masses, for their part, despised the mulattos, the white creoles as well as the European-born whites. Moreover, they always viewed the metropolitan center, and the monarchy in particular, as bulwarks against the tyranny of officialdom and the tender mercies of the local oligarchy who vigorously opposed their emancipation. In short, unlike the black and white *criollos* in the Spanish Caribbean—and for that matter, on the continent—no one was sufficiently desperate, or hated the colonial center enough to make a bid for independence, nor did they feel themselves powerful enough to succeed in such a venture. Britain and Spain in the nineteenth century were by no means military, political or economic equivalents.

At a number of levels, then, the Hispanic Caribbean, because of its historical and cultural experience, displays distinct differences with the non-Hispanic Caribbean in the perception and operation of race and color.

But throughout the Caribbean, Hispanic and non-Hispanic, there existed—nationalist collaboration notwithstanding—a hierarchy of race and color where the "whiter" and "lighter" are generally located at the top of the social pyramid, with the "darker" at the bottom. Caribbean societies were and are characterized, to a greater or lesser degree, by what the late Gordon Lewis has aptly dubbed a "multi-layered pigmentocracy."[17] Despite this general pattern, individual "black" people could be found relatively high up the socio-economic ladder. And although after emancipation insidious practices of discrimination occurred, especially in the professions and in the colonial administration of the northern European possessions, no discriminatory legislation, explicitly based upon race, sat on the statute books of the islands.[18] Social class, which overlapped considerably with race and color, was the primary mechanism of overt social stratification and ordering. It is true though that in the Hispanic Caribbean, and in Puerto Rico in particular, the degree of overlapping between race and class was not as exact as it was in the British and French territories. Thus in nineteenth and early twentieth century Puerto Rico, considerable collaboration between members of the working class and their organizations took place across racial lines. This was especially so among the *tabaqueros* and artisans, many of whom were black and colored. The United States Resident Commissioner, Henry Carroll, with evident surprise, reported at the turn of the century that of the eleven working class representatives who testified before him, nine were black, and all except one, could read and write, and all were decently clothed.[19]

It is for these reasons that black Puerto Ricans, compared to Caribbean migrants from the non-Hispanic areas of the region, entered the United States with relatively low "race" or black consciousness. They seldom articulated their demands on the basis of race. They were not used to being mobilized on the basis of their blackness or their race, but on the basis of their class. And while racism in early twentieth-century America heightened the race consciousness of black migrants, in general, black Puerto Ricans responded differently. The characteristic behavior of this group of migrants has historically been to close ranks with fellow "Spanish" compatriots—"black" and "white" together—distinguishing themselves, deliberately or otherwise, from those classified as "Negroes" in the United States. Writing in 1925 of the black migrants from the Caribbean, the Jamaican radical and journalist W. A. Domingo observed that the "Spanish element has but little contact with the English-speaking majority. For the most part they keep to themselves and follow in the main certain occupational lines." Wallace Thurman, the African American critic and novelist, made the same observation a few years later, using almost identical words to those used by Domingo: "The Spanish Negro…stays to himself and has little traffic with the other racial groups in his environment."[20] From time to time, noted a sociologist in the 1930s, "one may see a very dark Negro who will be speaking Spanish more loudly than the rest. They say he does not wish to be mistaken for an American Negro. All are Latins." In *Harlem: Negro Metropolis*, his 1940 study, Claude McKay noted that the African American in Harlem "cannot comprehend the brown Puerto Rican rejecting the appellation 'Negro,' and preferring to remain Puerto Rican. He is resentful of what he considers to be the superior attitude of the Negroid Puerto Rican."[21]

There was an almost complete absence of involvement of this group of diaspora Africans in black nationalist politics during the heady days of the First World War and early 1920s. It is not insignificant that the Universal Negro Improvement Association (UNIA) branches in Cuba, Costa Rica, Panama, and elsewhere in Latin America were constituted with few exceptions of migrant workers from the non-Hispanic Caribbean and especially those from Jamaica. And in Cuba, where the UNIA had its largest organized contingent outside of the United States—no less than 52 branches at its peak—the Afro-Cubans would sometimes attend the meetings of the Garveyites, but seldom joined the organization. It was a similar pattern throughout the Isthmus, where the Anglophone and Francophone Caribbean migrant workers and their descendants in Panama, Costa Rica, Nicaragua, Honduras and Guatemala accounted for virtually the entire membership of the UNIA in the region.[22] Although a Nicaraguan, Maymie Leona Turpeau De Mena (known affectionately as Madame De Mena within UNIA circles), was one of the movement's most famous, distinguished, selfless and admired members in the late twenties and early thirties—she became the International Organizer of the UNIA in 1929—Garveyites of Afro-Latino origin were thin on the ground in the Caribbean, rarer still in Central America, and virtually nonexistent in the United States.[23] Small wonder then, that the delegates to UNIA Conventions from Cuba had surnames like Collins, Cunning, and Taite; from Guatemala, Bourne; from Panama, Reid; from Santo Domingo, Van Putten. Going by his name, one would be inclined to think that Elie García was Hispanic, but he was in fact Haitian.[24] Domingo was the name of a Jamaican, the first editor of Garvey's newspaper, *The Negro World*. Although Carlos Cooks (1913–1966), an important figure among Harlem's black nationalists from the 1930s to the 1960s, was born in the Dominican Republic, he was brought up in an English-speaking community of British Caribbean migrant laborers on the island. Both his parents, James Henry Cooks and Alice Cooks, had earlier migrated from neighboring St. Martin. They were staunch Garveyites, as many of these migrants were in the 1920s. As a child, young Carlos' father and uncle took him with them to UNIA meetings. Cooks came to the United States in 1929.[25] Carlos Moore, the most outspoken and controversial black nationalist critic of some of the policies of postrevolutionary Cuba, was born in Oriente of British Caribbean parents (his father was Barbadian; his mother, Jamaican), within a milieu of English-speaking migrants who worked on Cuba's sugar plantations.[26]

Thus, Arturo Schomburg, who migrated to New York in 1891, was, against such a background and pattern, conspicuous in Harlem in the 1920s for being a black Puerto Rican who actively supported and identified with black nationalist aspirations, and with the struggles of African Americans.[27] His life's project, was, in the vocabulary of the time, "the vindication of the Negro race." It was a counter struggle against racist ideology, characteristically entailing the assiduous documentation—in practice, at enormous personal cost—of the achievements of people of African descent, past and present, around the world. Schomburg dedicated himself to this lifelong struggle when, as a schoolboy in Puerto Rico, one of his teachers had told him that black people had no history, no heroes, no great moments. This cruel racist propaganda, inflicted on him as a child, appeared to have been the primary source of the fuel that drove his lifelong quest. But the fact that he belonged to a youth club in which the study of history was a key element also contributed to his mission. For in this club, "there was a tendency among the whites and near-whites to point with more pride to the achievements of their white ancestors, than the blacks seemed able to their ancestors." Young Schomburg noted this and decided to study up on the achievements of black Puerto Ricans, so that when his white associates began to tell of what history white Puerto Ricans had made, "he could talk equally as freely of the history black Puerto Ricans had made." According to Schomburg a kind of "historic rivalry" developed between the members of the club, and he found his researches extending to the Virgin Islands, Haiti, San Domingo, Cuba and the other islands of the Caribbean. When he came to the United States, he pursued his hobby more systematically and extensively and began to collect books on black people, their experience and, most notably, their achievements across space and time.[28]

J. A. Rogers, a personal friend of Schomburg's, noted that with a family to support and with his "continual outlay for books," Schomburg was often "financially pinched."[29] But Schomburg's passionate collecting of books, prints, manuscripts, and paintings by and related to Africans would continue to the end of his life.[30] And in 1926 the Carnegie Corporation bought his collection of "over 10,000 books, manuscripts, newspapers, prints, and other materials"[31] allegedly, at a fifth of its intrinsic value for the New York Public Library. The collection, accumulated by Schomburg over a period of thirty-five years, would form the nucleus of what became the Schomburg Center for Research in Black Culture, based at the branch library at the corner of 135th Street and Lenox Avenue in Harlem. Alain Locke, the distinguished Howard University philosopher and close friend of Schomburg's, rightly noted that the price "patriotically" set by Schomburg for his collection "represented a figure so far below the market value of the collection that the transaction must be seen as a joint benefaction of the collector" and not the gift of the Carnegie Foundation solely.[32] With reference to the $10,000 paid for the collection, Schomburg himself explained his action:

> That sum is hardly what the books cost me. Some of those books are actually priceless, and cost a great deal of money. Others, not so rare, cost less. But the whole amount hardly gives me back the money I spent to get them. My time, labor, etc., go free, and I give them gladly. I am proud to be able to do something that may mean inspiration for the youth of my race. I would have gladly given the books outright had I not felt, in a way it would be unfair to the public, for, as a gift they might not have been deeply appreciated as they are by having cost something. Those who know what they cost, naturally feel there must be some real value attached to them.[33]

In a 1925 essay, Schomburg gave an indication of his project, its rationale, and some of its results. "The American Negro must," he proclaimed,

> remake his past in order to make his future. Though it is orthodox to think of America as the one country where it is unnecessary to have a past, what is a luxury for the nation as a whole becomes a prime necessity for the Negro. For him, a group tradition must supply compensation for persecution, and pride of race is the antidote for prejudice. History must restore what slavery took away, for it is the social damage of slavery that the present generation must repair and offset. So, among the rising democratic millions, we find the Negro thinking more collectively and more retrospectively than the rest, and apt out of the very pressure of the present, to become the most enthusiastic antiquary of all.
>
> Vindicating evidence of individual achievement have as a matter of fact been gathered and treasured for over a century....But this sort of thing was on the whole pathetically over-corrective, ridiculously over-laudatory; it was apologetics turned into biography....There is the definite desire and determination to have a history well documented, widely-known at least within racial circles, and administered as a stimulation and inspiring tradition for the coming generations.... [T]he remote racial origins of the Negro, far from being what the race and the world have been given to understand, offer a record of creditable group achievement when scientifically and impartially viewed, and more important still, that they are of vital general interest because of their bearing upon the beginnings and early development of human culture.[34]

Jesús Colón (1901–1974), Schomburg's compatriot, arrived in New York in 1918. A committed socialist before he left Puerto Rico, he became involved in the struggles of Puerto Rican and Cuban cigarmakers—*tabaqueros*—in New York, was a member of the Socialist Party (and later, a Communist Party member), and fighter for Puerto Rican independence. From all the evidence, a charming, urbane and sensitive man, Colón was remarkably untouched by black nationalism. Schomburg's interest in black history and politics and his apparent drift away from the Puerto Rican struggle remained a mystery to Colón right up to the end of his life: "[S]omething happened whereby Arturo shifted his interest away from the Puerto Rican liberation movement and put all his energy into the [black] movement."[35] Schomburg's behavior evidently raised eyebrows in the Puerto Rican community in New York. According to Bernardo Vega, another of his compatriots, when Schomburg moved "up to the neighborhood where North American Blacks lived," quite a few Puerto Ricans who knew him thought that he was "trying to deny his distant homeland."[36]

Vega might not have been as mystified as Colón was by Schomburg's behavior, but he nevertheless found it somewhat bizarre. In his discussion of Schomburg, he set up, no doubt unconsciously, an insidious and disturbing binary opposition between being "black" and being "Puerto Rican." Despite himself, the feeling is imparted that by having been interested in the African experience in the Americas, Schomburg had somehow diminished, if not deserted completely, his Puerto Ricanness. Significantly, Vega never described Colón—who was several shades darker than Schomburg—as "black," but Schomburg is so described. Colón was Puerto Rican, while Schomburg became black; Schomburg, apparently, could not have been black and Puerto Rican at the same time—Vega, at any rate, found it difficult to think of Schomburg as black *and* Puerto Rican. In what is, nonetheless, a generous and moving tribute to Schomburg, Vega concludes: "He came here as an emigrant and bequeathed a wealth of accomplishments to our countrymen [Puerto Ricans] and to North American blacks. What a magnificent example of solidarity among all oppressed peoples!"[37] Schomburg, undoubtedly, would have appreciated this warm tribute, especially from an esteemed and distinguished compatriot as Bernardo Vega. But I am inclined to believe that, as a fervent Pan-Africanist, Arturo Schomburg would prefer that his work be seen as an act of self-help, rather than one of solidarity. And this is so because he counted himself as a member of Africa's scattered children who also happened to have been born in Puerto Rico. Like his mentor, John Edward Bruce, he regarded oppressed people of African descent as belonging to one family. Schomburg used the first-person plural "We" when talking of people of African descent.[38] Clearly, this dimension of Schomburg's thinking and political loyalties fell outside Bernado Vega's purview. That he found Schomburg so difficult to classify and conceptualize is not entirely Vega's fault; Schomburg was one of a rare breed of Puerto Ricans, if not a species of one.

The key to the singularity of Schomburg as a Puerto Rican black nationalist lies in his background. He was unusual in five important respects. First, Arturo's mother, Mary Joseph, was an *extranjera*, not a Puerto Rican. She was a black migrant worker from St. Croix, in the Virgin Islands, with strong family ties not only to St. Croix but also to the Danish-controlled sister island of St. Thomas. Second, Arturo's father was the son of a German immigrant and a Puerto Rican woman. Some sources claim, inaccurately, that Arturo's father was himself a German immigrant from Hamburg.[39] In any case, his father's side of the family not only had strong foreign connections, it also had strong northern European, non-Iberian roots; such a background was hardly typical of nineteenth century Puerto Rican society. Schomburg, whose parents were unmarried, had little contact with his father. According to his son, Schomburg senior was a merchant who was born in Mayaguez, on the western end of the island. From the questionnaire that Schomburg answered in the 1930s for a study of the black family, it is evident that he knew very little about his father's side compared to his mother's side of his family.[40] Indeed, according to his biographer there is no evidence that Schomburg's father "recognized him as his son or supported either child or mother. Nothing suggests that Arturo was raised as an heir of the Schomburg family, a name well known in Puerto Rico."[41]

Third, because of his parents' estrangement, Arturo was brought up by his mother and was thus substantially influenced by the culture of his mother's native land, the Virgin Islands. Moreover, fourth, Arturo during his boyhood spent time probably several years in the Virgin Islands, where he apparently lived with his mother's relatives and claimed to have attended St. Thomas College, a secondary school. There is, however, no record to corroborate his claim of having gone to St. Thomas College. Significantly, Schomburg—

who was especially fond of his maternal grandfather, Nicholas Joseph, a butcher—clearly enjoyed life among his relatives and friends on St. Croix and St. Thomas. And evidently, he imbibed the culture of the Virgin Islands. Indeed, on the basis of reading Schomburg's work on the Islands, the Secretary of the St. Thomas Public Library, thought that Arturo was a native Virgin Islander. "Your mention of your boyhood days here carries a ring only possible with a son of the soil," he told Schomburg.[42] Fifth, unlike many Puerto Ricans and indeed, Hispanic Caribbeans at the time, Arturo Schomburg was not a Catholic, nominally or otherwise, but an Episcopalian; he adopted the religion of his mother and his maternal grandparents. All of his own children were brought up in the Protestant Episcopal Church. Schomburg, in marked contrast to the Puerto Rican and Cuban *tabaqueros* who migrated to the United States around the same time that he did, was profoundly religious. As discussed later, the *tabaqueros* were renowned for their atheistic and freethinking ways, linked to their political radicalism. It is possible that Schomburg may have grown more religious as he got older, but what is clear is that he harbored a deep religious faith, which came from his mother's side of the family. In his published writings as well as in his letters, he often referred to the Bible and make religious allusions; the Bible was, evidently, one of the many books he knew very well. In a 1932 letter, he told a close friend:

> I have a number of Communist friends who are often trying to make me deny the existence of a God, but instead of keeping silent I just turn loose after their method of reasoning and give them Hell. I say for instance, the feeling that there is a God is living within me[;] it was in my mother before me and I noticed it in my grand mother when in her olden days and could sca[r]cely see call her daughter to read some passage she wanted to hear once more. It is needless for you to try and change me, no more than change the table of multiplication as it was taught to me.[43]

Two months later, in February 1933, Schomburg gathered up his hat and coat and stormed out of a Brooklyn meeting at which he was the guest speaker. He left the platform because T. R. Poston, the chairman, a radical African-American journalist, interjected his strong disagreement with Schomburg's assessment of Abraham Lincoln's position on the race question. Lincoln was "a man without prejudice," Schomburg was reported to have said. Poston disagreed, saying that if it had been left up to Lincoln, "it is more than probable we would still be slaves." Praise is due, Poston said, to people like William Lloyd Garrison, "in preference to Lincoln who only freed us to win the war." Schomburg was wrong about Lincoln—who, incidentally, he had always had a soft spot for—and Poston was more right than wrong. Several members of the audience, one newspaper reported, were "incensed" at the "uncalled for remark of the chairman." Apparently, Poston had not been asked to comment on Schomburg's hour-long speech and was, therefore, discourteous in commenting at all, let alone criticizing the speaker—and before an audience of four hundred. Poston had clearly exceeded his brief as chair of the meeting. Schomburg was, understandably, angry with Poston. And it was understandable, too, that he walked out of the meeting. But Schomburg took his leave in an uncharacteristically deplorable and undignified manner, for he left the meeting declaring, one report says, that "he would have no more to say to his Communist friend."[44]

A year earlier, in a vivid portrait of Harlem street-life, Schomburg dismissed a black Communist street-corner orator as "just a sound artist." The man has never been to Russia, Schomburg said, but "waxes eloquent on Lenin and the Five Years Plan, however," Schomburg continued, "were he to have to eke out an existence[,] we believe [he] would fall from grace, a volunteer to a subject he knows nothing whatever."[45]

It is not clear where Schomburg's anti-Communism of the 1930s came from. But it appears that at least one source of his growing opposition was the ideological clash between his religious worldview and what he perceived as the atheistic outlook of the Communist Party. The extent to which Schomburg's religious belief contributed to his alienation from the Puerto Rican and Cuban revolutionary nationalists at the turn of the century is by no means clear, but it might have played a role. Certainly, if, as he claimed, his religiosity was as unchanging as the laws of mathematics, then he would have been uncomfortable all along with his comrades in Las Dos Antillas, militant rationalists and free-thinkers that they were. One similar, contemporaneous Afro-Cuban group in Tampa, Florida, made no secret of their views. Formed in 1900, they called themselves La Sociedad de Libre Pensadores de Martí-Maceo.[46] But as we will see, Schomburg's negative attitude toward the Communist Party of the United States and growing profession of religious faith did not make him a conservative.

Asked, in the questionnaire mentioned earlier, who influenced him the most, Schomburg replied that it was his mother. He evidently loved and idealized her. She represented the "painstaking and faithful ideals of womanhood." To her son, Mary Joseph was "a loving mother of high and pure ideal."[47]

In short, though he was born in Puerto Rico and, apparently, spent most of his childhood there, Arturo Schomburg was substantially shaped by the culture of the non-Hispanic and Anglophone Caribbean.[48] Schomburg, astonishingly, discouraged his children from learning Spanish.[49] Although he worked for years with Pura Belpré, a black Puerto Rican librarian, he never, reported one writer, spoke to her about their "shared heritage and mother tongue."[50] But, on reflection, given the evidence of Schomburg's formation, it is not surprising. For, Schomburg had a dual heritage and mother tongue—one Hispanic, the other non-Hispanic. And it now appears that the non-Hispanic heritage was equally as strong as, if not stronger than, the Hispanic one. For most of his life he used the Anglicized version of his first name, although he increasingly returned to Arturo toward the end of his life. Less than a year before he died, in one of his most despairing letters, brought on by his daily exposure to black Harlem's desperate plight during the Depression, Schomburg wrote to his close friend and confidante, the African-American journalist, Wendell P. Dabney: "You request me to practice moderation. I am sick and tired of the conditions that I see every night in Harlem. I am still dreaming," he confessed, "of going to the Virgin Islands and spending the remainder of my life in the calm and solicitude that can only be had in such a restful place."[51] There is no mention of Puerto Rico in the letter, let alone its consideration by Schomburg as a final resting place. After he broke with the Cuban and Puerto Rican nationalists around 1898, Schomburg maintained no close friendships within the Puerto Rican community. In marked contrast, he established, broadened and cultivated his closest friendships not only among African Americans, but also among fellow Afro-Caribbean migrants from the English-speaking Caribbean, including Hubert Harrison and Casper Holstein from the Virgin Islands.

Given such a background and orientation, it comes as no surprise that Schomburg's political trajectory in the United States bore remarkable similarity to that of Caribbean migrants from the non-Hispanic areas of the archipelago. But his disillusion with Cuban and Puerto Rican exile nationalist politics in America at the turn of the century,[52] his painful experiences of Jim Crow segregation when he visited his children in the South, his membership and leading role in a black masonic lodge, his working in a job that was isolated from other Puerto Ricans, his befriending and being profoundly influenced by leading black nationalists of the day, especially John E. Bruce and Hubert Harrison, all contributed to the direction in which Schomburg's politics and worldview developed.

We should never forget, however, that Schomburg chose to withdraw from Puerto Rican and Cuban nationalist politics, chose to marry African-American women, chose to expend his energies on developing the black Prince Hall Lodge, chose the close association with black nationalists such as Bruce and Harrison, chose to live in the black San Juan Hill district of Manhattan at the turn of the century and, later, black Harlem, rather than live in one of New York's Puerto Rican neighborhoods. All of these choices become comprehensible only in the context of his formation before migrating to the United States. This is not to say that his early biography *determined* the pattern of his choices, but that it *predisposed* him to make the choices he made. After all, his immediate contemporaries and black Hispanic friends in New York, such as Rafael Serra (Cuba) and Sotero Figueroa (Puerto Rico) made different choices and followed a different, more orthodox, path.[53] Schomburg's close friend, Claude McKay, noted that in appearance, Schomburg was like "an Andalusian gypsy, olive-complexioned and curly-haired, and he might easily have become merged in that considerable class of foreigners who exist on the fringe of the white world." But Schomburg, observed McKay, "*chose* to identify himself with the Aframerican (sic) group."[54] Thus, to view Schomburg's political evolution in the United States as simply the product of his generational location and circumstances is to ignore the clear and concrete choices that he made in his life.

Schomburg's accomplishments, especially given his limited educational background, verged on the miraculous. He was in fact, despite his pretensions to the contrary, an autodidact. He was in 1892, co-founder and Secretary of Las Dos Antillas, a society of Cuban and Puerto Rican revolutionary nationalists, inspired by José Martí. He served as its Secretary up to 1896. Schomburg was struck by the double blow of Martí's and Antonio Maceo's death in combat in 1895 and 1896, respectively, during Cuba's war against Spain. His fellow *afroborinqueño*, the revolutionary poet "Pachín" Marín, also fell in Cuba's war of independence. The United States declared war against Spain in February 1898, and by July of the same year Spain had surrendered, ceding the Philippines and Guam, along with Cuba and Puerto Rico, to the Americans. The Puerto Rican and Cuban revolutionaries in New York quarreled among themselves, disagreeing on how to respond to the new and unforeseen circumstances. The Puerto Rican section of the Cuban Revolutionary Party dissolved itself in 1898. With a combination of disgust and disillusion, Schomburg ended his direct and deep involvement in Puerto Rican and Cuban nationalist politics, turning his attention almost exclusively to Afro-America.

Schomburg's subsequent positions and pronouncements on Puerto Rican independence, which admittedly are still in need of a thorough charting, were contradictory—at least apparently so—inconstant, confused and certainly confusing. But to claim, as one writer does, that toward the end of his life Schomburg "advocated statehood for Puerto Rico," is, on the basis of the evidence offered, to misrepresent him.[55] In fact what Schomburg said, in the very letter used to adduce such a conclusion, was this: "*If* the majority of the [Puerto Rican] people are of the opinion they should seek membership in the American Union, I am for it."[56] Schomburg, whose letter was in response to American objections to Puerto Rican migration to the mainland, pointed out that had President McKinley acceded in 1898 to the petition of the Puerto Rican Revolutionary Party for a plebiscite on independence, Puerto Ricans would perhaps have less need to migrate to the United States. Schomburg, in the 1930s, might very well have advocated statehood for Puerto Rico—who knows?—but I have seen no evidence, nor has anyone presented any evidence so far to suggest that he did. And in the absence of such evidence it ought not to be claimed that he did.

In 1892, Schomburg had joined El Sol de Cuba, a lodge made up of Cuban and Puerto Rican freemasons in New York. By 1911 he was Master of the lodge. In the same year he changed the name to the Prince Hall Lodge, in honor of the founder of black freemasonry in America. In 1775, Hall, a black abolitionist, believed to have been born in Barbados, established the first black lodge in America, African Lodge No. 1, in Boston, Massachusetts, where he was a leader of the black community. By the time Schomburg became its master, El Sol de Cuba, had changed considerably in its composition since its founding in 1881. African Americans and English-speaking Afro-Caribbeans constituted the overwhelming majority of its members. According to Harry Williamson, a former deputy grand master and historian of the lodge, after the Spanish-American war the lodge's membership began to "dwindle." It was in this context of declining Hispanic Caribbean participation that Schomburg played an important role in recruiting new members. In 1918, Schomburg was promoted to Grand Secretary to the Grand Lodge of the State of New York, a position he held until 1926.[57]

Schomburg also played an important role in the formation of the Negro Society for Historical Research. In 1911, he co-founded and served as the secretary-treasurer of the society, with his close friend and mentor, John E. Bruce, as its president. On the recommendation of Bruce, Schomburg became a member of the prestigious American Negro Academy, founded by Alexander Crummell in 1897 to wage intellectual and ideological war against white supremacy and racist propaganda. In 1920, only six years after he had joined, Schomburg became its president. But despite his making important scholarly contributions to the work of the Academy, the institution withered under Schomburg's superintendence. The Academy began its decline before Schomburg became its president, but his living in New York while the organization had its base in Washington, D. C., did not help matters. Schomburg over-stretched himself and was inattentive to the day-to-day business of the Academy. It foundered in 1928.[58]

Schomburg's forte was collecting and research, and it was in those areas that he excelled. As McKay delicately put it, he was not "typically literary." And his private taste in books was "inclined to the esoterically erotic." But, said McKay, Schomburg possessed "a bloodhound's nose in tracing any literary item about Negroes. He could not discourse like a scholar, but he could delve deep and bring up nuggets for a scholar which had baffled discovery."[59] The praise that Schomburg received from *cognoscenti*, such as that from his close friend, Dr. John Wesley Cromwell, former president of the American Negro Academy, was expansive. In the aftermath of Schomburg's successful search for some rare publications of Benjamin Banneker, the brilliant black mathematician and astronomer, Cromwell wrote:

> How can I adequately express to you my indebtedness for your rescue of Banneker from the seclusion in which he has been for one hundred and twenty years. Think of it, biographers, bibliophiles, enthusiastic devotees—Latrobe, Bishop Daniel A. Payne, the Banneker Institute, the noble army of admirers, and what-not, have all absolutely failed to cast down their buckets where they were and secure the refreshing waters you have drawn up! You are entitled to more than a vote of thanks for this one act. There can be no disputing the authenticity of the facsimile of a contemporaneous publication.[60]

Schomburg was not a fluent writer, in either English or Spanish.[61] Though his writing often had passages of real eloquence, it lacked the ease and grace with which his compatriot Jesús Colón wrote both languages.[62] But what Schomburg lacked in expression he more than made up for in knowledge. Schomburg is often celebrated as a bibliophile, but he was much more than a bibliophile, outstanding though he was in that area of activity: Schomburg was also an outstanding scholar, even if he could not discourse with the same facility of most scholars, he operated on the basis of the most taxing criteria of intellectual rigor. He was a restless truth-seeker. What he hated most about much of European and Euro-American historiography was its lies, its pernicious lies, especially against people of African descent. The truth never frightened him. "Truth should prevail whether we like it or not," he told a young scholar.[63] And through his legendary patience and stamina in the quest for truth, he developed an arguably unrivalled fount of knowledge about people of African descent and their experience over time and space. Celebrated black intellectuals such as W. E. B. DuBois, Hubert Harrison, James Weldon Johnson, Alain Locke, J. A. Rogers, and Carter G. Woodson have not only drawn upon Schomburg's unequalled collection of books, prints, paintings, and manuscripts, they have also drawn upon Schomburg's extraordinary knowledge and sure-footed intellectual guidance, which he freely gave. More often than not, Schomburg's contribution was inadequately acknowledged, or unacknowledged altogether, by his more formally educated and credentialed black contemporaries. Alain Locke admitted that Schomburg was the "silent co-author" of many volumes on black history and culture. But Locke said this after Schomburg was dead and buried—and in a manuscript that to this day remains unpublished.[64] As he grew older, Schomburg increasingly resented the ingratitude, and sometimes downright intellectual dishonesty, of some of those whom he helped. He sometimes complained too much, but there was substance to his complaint. "First chance you have at a Library get hold of J. W. Johnson's *Black Manhattan*," he wrote a friend in 1934,

> examine the following material, inside the cover is a copy of the Brooklyn Handicap, picture of Ira Aldridge, a collection of Ira Aldridge photostat play-bills [—] since the original were consumed by fire at Wilberforce [University], the only collection ex[t]ant is in the Schomburg Coll.[—] the picture of Frederick Douglass[;] hours

spent with the author to select which one he should use. Help him to find exact knowledge that Ira Aldridge was born in N[ew] Y[ork]. That Milburn did originate the melody of "Listen to the Mocking Bird"[,] etc. Then turn to the Preface and see for yourself the passive way this "great American" thanks his fellow man. It is a scream! I mean he thanks the collection and mentions my name for having collected play bills, no personal reference of a man's thought. It is hell, how some men do things. But the Good Lord has kept me this long for some purpose or other.[65]

James Weldon Johnson was not the only black intellectual to be privately censured by Schomburg in this manner. Du Bois, Alain Locke, and especially Carter G. Woodson were similarly criticized.[66] Despite the enormous assistance that Schomburg provided in the preparation and illustration of Woodson's 1922 book, *The Negro in Our History*, nowhere does Woodson acknowledge Schomburg's help. In the course of a carefully executed and damning review published in the *Negro World*, Schomburg made indirect reference to the fact that Woodson did not acknowledge the help provided. "A charitable appreciation for those who helped Dr. Woodson with rare prints, engravings, etc., would not have in any way harmed him in the preface," said Schomburg. "It is one of the few books lacking this feature of long-established custom."[67] A decade later, Schomburg told his friend Boddy, "Woodson is all for himself, he held a meeting of his society [the Association for the Study of Negro Life and History] here in N[ew] Y[ork] and never mentioned one word of the [Schomburg] collection. I know why. You might as well know of it," suggested Schomburg. "I made a report to the American Negro Academy for the publication of a Journal, a committee was appointed made up [of] [Arthur U.] Craig, Woodson and myself. Six months later Woodson came out with his *Journal of Negro History*. That's why he is afraid of me, and treats me with deference. 'Forgive them Father.'"[68] Schomburg grew quite bitter about what he perceived as the opportunism of many black intellectuals. Six weeks before his untimely death, in a letter to a close friend, he wrote:

I notice that since I am not giving out sources of material to these impecunious writers there is a scarcity of books written by Negroes on the market. Many of them have been annoying me for information and I have closed my mouth tighter than a clam. Not even the loving glances of beautiful damsels will make me fall from the pedestal that I have put my information. I have come to the conclusion that lots of them are like a bunch of vultures on the limb of a tree waiting to pounce down on some information that they can offer a publisher.[69]

If Schomburg did indeed clam up, it was not long enough for any of his contemporaries to have noticed. For, one of the most recurring descriptions of Schomburg by his contemporaries, albeit after his death, is the generosity with which he shared his knowledge. This sharing of knowledge came from a profound dual obligation that Schomburg felt he had to black people: on the one hand, an obligation to those who have gone before, remembering their struggle, dreams and accomplishment; and, on the other, an obligation to the next generation, the young, to reinforce and buttress them in a hostile social environment that professes their "racial" inferiority and often denies their very humanity, the humanity of people of African descent. Schomburg's project is often misconstrued. He was far less interested in persuading white people of black people's humanity and accomplishment than in convincing black people themselves of their own worth and historical stature as members of the human family. Schomburg tried to blast to pieces the centuries-old, granite accretion of black self-doubt and enforced amnesia, and sought the cultivation of a self-confident and historically informed people with the capacity to fight, precisely because they feel that they deserve better. He believed that, for people of African descent, being self-confident in the world and being historically informed went together. It is impossible for a black person to be at ease with him or herself in the world while believing the lies of Europe about black inferiority, African historylessness and lack of accomplishment.

These beliefs and ideas formed the driving force behind Schomburg's extraordinary and strenuous counter-hegemonic exertions.

But Schomburg's concern with the black past was not entirely pragmatic and instrumental. Schomburg had a profound and enduring respect for those who had gone before, their pain and anguish, their dreams and aspirations, their humiliation and accomplishment. Toussaint Louverture, Jean Jacques Dessalines, Henri Christophe and the Haitian revolutionaries would be hard pressed to find a more reverent rembrancer than Arturo Schomburg. And he remembered not just the black high and mighty; his imagination traveled with the humble black slave. Schomburg also had a warm and human interest in the young and had a profound impact upon those who encountered him at the 135th Street Library in Harlem. And beyond the more widely acknowledged help and encouragement he provided for the young writers and artists of the Harlem Renaissance, Schomburg had a deep interest in the education of children. Kenneth B. Clark, the distinguished black psychologist, is one of many who could testify about Schomburg and his relation with the young. Clark, who grew up in the center of Harlem, recalled meeting Schomburg when he was about twelve years old.

> On one of my trips to the library, I decided that I was going to go upstairs to the third floor, that forbidden and mysterious area reserved for adults. As I climbed the last flight, I felt the excitement of an interloper. I was prepared for the risk of a polite or more direct rejection. When I entered the room, a large man, whom I later came to know as Arthur Schomburg, got up from his desk and came over to me and smiled. He didn't ask me what I wanted. He merely put one arm around my shoulder and assumed that I was interested in books. On that first day of meeting Schomburg, I knew I had met a friend. He didn't ask me whether my mother was poor. He never told me to improve myself. Her accepted me as a human being and through this acceptance helped me to share his love of, and his excitement in, the world of books.[70]

Schomburg, forever concerned with group survival, became more worried about the prospects for black people in the United States as he grew older. Even though he at times expressed great faith in Franklin D. Roosevelt and the New Deal, Schomburg remained pessimistic. Less than a year before he died he made a bleak prophecy: "I am becoming very doubtful of the Negro finding a place for himself in the next quarter of a century. I believe that the forces that are working in this nation against radicalism and syndicalism are going to convert their forces like pincers and crush our group. We will either be relegated to the level of the sidewalk or back to Africa in the spirit of the philosophy of Marcus Garvey."[71]

Schomburg was a strong supporter of Marcus Garvey, but he never believed in the idea of a return to Africa. The fact that in all seriousness, albeit in momentary despair, that he contemplated such an idea showed the darkness and desperation that invaded Schomburg's thoughts toward the end of his life. But Schomburg's attitude toward Garvey, and by extension, toward black nationalism requires elaboration here. These are in fact some of the most underexplored issues surrounding Schomburg's life and politics, yet some of the most crucial to elucidating his politics.

It is somewhat misleading to claim, as one author does, that Schomburg was a Garvey "disciple."[72] Schomburg had more than ample opportunity to join the UNIA, but never did. Having said that, however, Schomburg's support of Garvey was very strong, even passionate, and remarkably enduring.

It appears that from his very earliest encounter with Garvey, Schomburg's rebel heart began to sing. Never a conservative, Schomburg admired Garvey's audacity, his lionheartedness. Schomburg's closest friends reacted in a similar manner to the emergence of Garvey and the UNIA. After initial hesitation, John Edward Bruce, Schomburg's spiritual father, threw in his lot with Garvey, became an official, a columnist of the *Negro World*, and one of the UNIA's leading intellectuals and staunchest defenders up to his death in 1924, aged 68. William Ferris, like Bruce, a leading member of the American Negro Academy, became at an even earlier stage than Bruce a fervent supporter of Garvey and an official of the UNIA, editing the organizations newspaper through its most crucial years. (George Schuyler, who hated Garvey, said that Ferris, a graduate of both Yale and Harvard, provided the best philosophical defense of Garveyism that he had ever heard.)[73] Dr. John Wesley Cromwell, a former president of the American Negro Academy, and a very close friend of Schomburg's was also a strong supporter of the UNIA. Schomburg shared some of his innermost thoughts about Garvey and the UNIA with Cromwell, who lived in Washington, D. C.

Schomburg evidently attended the 1919 UNIA convention in New York. He reported to Cromwell that "our friend" Ferris delivered a very inspiring address that "shook the timbers of the ceiling" of Liberty Hall. Garvey, he said, "stood out prominently as a man of principle who will be heard a great deal in the days to come for his peculiar and inspiring character….I believe," continued Schomburg, "Garvey will give a good account of his stewardship and his name will go down in history for fidelity and integrity in the Negro's cause for righteousness."[74]

In another letter, Schomburg could hardly contain himself. "The *Negro World* is going over the top this week[,] 10 pages! I am mailing you a copy with an article on Garvey." He expressed his delight with the proposed naming of the first three ships of the Black Star Line, incorporated by the UNIA, after Frederick Douglass, Phillis Wheatley, and Booker T. Washington. He hoped the next ship will be named after another African American hero, Paul Cuffee. "The 'Black Star line'," Schomburg exclaimed, "is going to increase its capital from $500,000 to $10,000,000! then there will be an unusual howl from the doubters. Garvey is the man!"[75] In yet another letter to Cromwell, clearly written in a state of excitement, immediately after acknowledging receipt of Cromwell's letter, Schomburg declared: "Garvey Veni, Vidi, Vici—I think our leaders have gone to the woods none at hand to answer Garvey."[76]

Schomburg wrote for the *Negro World*, translated letters for Garvey, sided with Garvey in his disputes with Du Bois, spoke to UNIA branches up to as late as the mid-1930s, well after Garvey's and the UNIA's star had fallen. If Schomburg had doubts about aspects of Garvey's program, he did not, apparently, express them publicly until the 1930s, well after Garvey had left the American scene. And even then, Schomburg never condemned Garvey. In a 1935 newspaper article in which he discussed Garvey, his strongest criticism of the man was Garvey's claim to "control four hundred million followers." Garvey's positive contribution was what attracted Schomburg:

> We cannot forget Marcus Garvey who for several years gave us much inspiration in trying to awaken the dormant mind of our people and in doing so, aroused the ire of his enemies. However, leaving out of the question the right or wrong of his doctrines, we must admire his indomitable courage when he not only talked but got his [1920] convention that held sway for 30 days to appoint a commission to cross the Atlantic ocean and journey to Geneva, where they presented [to the League of Nations] their message in the most exacting manner with diplomatic requirements and the amenities of the day.[77]

A year later, in an implied rebuke of Garvey, Schomburg wrote that "men who battled in and out of season for the American colored people to remain here in the land of their birth rather than to run across the sea [to Africa] chasing rainbows, served posterity best, and now merit our everlasting thanksgiving."[78] Despite this remark (which was explicitly aimed at John B. Russwurn, who left America in disgust for Liberia in the 1830s), Garvey had a special place in Schomburg's heart. In 1935, reflecting on the Italian invasion of Ethiopia and the ensuing crisis within the League of Nations, Schomburg's thoughts turned to Garvey. Referring to him as "Chief Garvey," Schomburg wrote:

> We may excoriate Marcus Garvey for his titles of nobility but even today, he is nearer the seat of the League of Nations than any of his opponents who are here still lingering with us, self appease after crumbs from the masters [sic] table. They

lack his element of courage, his dignity in prison and his steadfast will in the adversity of the day knowing that Ethiopia shall yet rule.[79]

Schomburg remembered Garvey better than Garvey remembered him—yet Garvey did not forget Schomburg. In exile in London, Garvey received news of Schomburg's untimely death. In an editorial entitled, "Passing of A Great Man," published in his magazine, *The Black Man*, Garvey said that they met "once or twice" and that he could not claim any particular friendship with Schomburg, but the two men "shared the mutual friendship of others." Garvey said it was difficult to find anyone more interesting than Arthur Schomburg.

In sixty-four years of life he wrapped up in himself the highest ambition of usefulness to his race. He in New York particularly, engaged himself in the intellectual details that would ultimately help the Negro to establish his status among other races of the world. He was not known from many platforms, but every platform scholar and every man of intellectual count in America knew that Arthur Schomburg lived and that his work was a living testimony to a man who was devoted to a worthy cause....It is a pity that the race has lost such a useful man at such a time.[80]

Although the Great Depression and its disproportionately harsh impact upon Afro-America got him down, to the very end, Schomburg never gave up and remained an activist. During the 1930s he traveled to Washington on a delegation from Harlem in support of the "Scottsboro Boys," the nine black boys and young men wrongfully accused of raping two white women and condemned to death in Alabama; he actively supported Claude McKay and the right for black people to organize on their own in the Negro Writers' Guild; he supported the "Don't Buy Where You Can't Work" campaign in Harlem and went on a delegation to Blumstein's store, the focus of much of the protest, seeking the employment of black people in other than menial jobs; he protested the Italian invasion of Ethiopia and corresponded with Roosevelt over his government's policy on the issue; he sided with Republican Spain against Franco's fascists.

He had an extraordinarily sturdy constitution—"the body and energy of a powerful Spanish bull," claimed McKay[81]—that undergirded his relentless activity on behalf of "the race." But on June 10, 1938, following complications caused by a tooth infection, Schomburg suddenly died—simultaneously shocking and saddening his friends. He was sixty-four. "I have done my mite," he modestly wrote in a 1934 letter, to "lift up the Negro to a better appreciation of his worth."[82]

In general, Jesús Colón had different dreams and nightmares and moved in different circles to Schomburg. His world was not that of *los negros Americanos*, nor was his preoccupation the fate of Afro-America. Colón had remained faithful to the world of the *tabaqueros*—in whose midst he was born—and faithful to the struggles of the Puerto Rican migrant community (especially in Brooklyn and in *El Barrio* in East Harlem), and faithful to Puerto Rican nationalism and international socialism.

Colón was born in 1901, in the dignified working class world of Puerto Rico's tobacco growers and cigarmakers in Cayey.[83] One of his earliest childhood memories is of hearing through his window at about ten every morning a clear, strong voice coming from the big cigar factory at the back of his house. He later discovered that the voice was that of *el lector*, the reader, who read to the one hundred and fifty cigarmakers as they bent over their desks, silently rolling tobacco leaves into neat cigars. "The workers," he reported, "paid fifteen to twenty-five cents per week each to the reader. In the morning, the reader used to read daily paper and some working class weeklies or monthlies that were published or received from abroad. In the afternoon he would read from a novel by Zola, Balzac, Hugo, or from a book by Kropotkin, Malatesta or Karl Marx. Famous speeches like Castelar's or Spanish classical novels like Cervantes' *Don Quixote* were also read aloud by '*El Lector*.'"[84] The cigarmakers were among the most literate and most highly educated groups of workers in Puerto Rico.

Interestingly, because of the tradition of *la lectura*, illiteracy was substantially uncoupled from ignorance. Even though some of the cigarmakers were unable to read and write, they were nonetheless highly informed and educated persons. "So you were amazed," reported Colón, "by the phenomenon of cigarmakers who hardly knew how to read and write, discussing books like Zola's *Germinal*, Balzac's *Pere Goriot*, or Kropotkin's *Fields, Factories and Workshops*, during the mild Puerto Rican evenings in the public square."[85]

By the time Colón was born, the expansion of capitalism into tobacco processing was well under way. The independent cigarmaker was being transformed from an artisan into a proletarian, along the lines of the one hundred and fifty that worked in the "big factory" at the back of Colón's house in Cayey. The erosion of their autonomy and the ineluctable compromising of their craft by the logic of capital, mass production, and its accompanying labor process aroused the opposition of the tobacco workers. Coming out of a political culture that respected the dignity of labor, that had nurtured a tradition of *parejería*—disrespect for hierarchy and pride of self—that placed great value upon education and the cultivation of the mind, a culture that had been informed by the most progressive, scientific, rationalist ideas afloat in the world, the artisans and especially the *tabaqueros*, were in the vanguard of political and social dissent in Puerto Rico.[86] Spurred on by the pressures of capitalist amalgamation and aggregation, the *tabaqueros* embraced, even more passionately, revolutionary socialist and anarcho-syndicalist ideas. Adversely affected, especially after the American conquest of their land in 1898, by rapid economic and social changes, the cigarmakers became one of the most class conscious and combative sections of the Puerto Rican working class. It was they who spearheaded the founding of the Puerto Rican Socialist Party in 1915. And significantly, the party was founded in Bernardo Vega's and Jesús Colón's birthplace, the town of Cayey, in the heart of Puerto Rico's tobacco country. Colón, who was only fourteen, joined the Socialist Party that very year.[87] Colón, then, grew up in an environment of radical and socially conscious workers.

As a schoolboy at the Central Grammar School in San Juan, he was bright, had an early passion for writing, was respected by his fellow students, and evidently possessed qualities of leadership. His three-paragraph letter expressing the condolences of his class, his teacher and the principal over the death of the mother of one of his classmates was deemed the best by his teacher and the principal, of the forty submitted by his class of eighth-graders, and his was the one sent to the bereaved family. Another one of Colón's classmates told their American History teacher that her textbook was missing from her desk. When no one admitted to having seen or taken the missing book, the teacher, a Mr. Whole from Montana, imposed a fine of ten cents per student on the entire class. "Everybody shall bring ten cents tomorrow," he commanded, "otherwise he or she will not be allowed to come into my class."

The students were outraged and the following morning they resolved not to pay. His classmates elected Colón chairman of a committee of three to present their demands to the principal. The students, *en bloc*, boycotted Mr. Whole's class. And from the square where they gathered, they watched Mr. Whole through the window to see what his next move would be when they did not turn up to class. Tired of waiting for the students, the teacher went to the principal's office. Colón presented the students' case and finished by saying "very emphatically that the class refused to come in until Mr. Whole rescinded the ten cent order." Mr. Whole backed down. Not only was this Colón's first strike, it was a successful one.[88]

Around the age of sixteen, Colón was elected by the whole student body of his school, to the editorship of the school magazine, *¡Adelante! [Forward!]*.

It was in connection with *¡Adelante!* that Colón revealed a crucial event in his political formation. While his school was being rebuilt in 1917, classrooms were temporarily located in makeshift wooden barracks elsewhere in the city. The students dubbed the new quarters "Barracones," which were located in a working class district called Puerto de Tierra, near the docks in San Juan.

During a dock workers' strike, the workers, their wives, and supporters held a demonstration to publicize their cause. Parades and public demonstrations had been outlawed by the authorities during the strike period. Jesús Colón and some four hundred students were enjoying their after-lunch break when the parade of striking dock workers was passing. Distracted by the noise, the students rushed to look, sticking their heads in the slats in the fence for a better view. As they watched the parade of workers and their wives marching down the street, they noticed about a dozen mounted policemen armed with carbines coming from the opposite direction. Undeterred, the marchers continued, "with slogans and union banners flying." Over forty years after the incident, Colón could still remember clearly what happened:

> As the mounted police saw the parade formation coming towards them, they lined up on their large, strong horses, into an impassable fortress from one side of the street to the other. There was a moment of suspense and indecision on the part of the workers—it might have been fifteen seconds or more. To us boys and girls, with our heads between the fence slats, these seconds of hesitancy were like an eternity. At last, taking two steps forward, one of the strikers holding a banner began to march forward and sang at the same time: *Arriba los pobres del mundo/De pie los esclavos sin pan.*[89]
>
> He continued marching with head up toward the mounted police. The rest of the strikers with their wives and their sisters followed after him.
>
> The one in charge of the mounted platoon gave a signal, so imperceptible that nobody seemed to notice. The police moved as if by a spring, moving their carbines to their shoulders and taking aim. It was done rapidly, but coolly, calmly, dispassionately. It seems to me as if I can see them right now. Another almost imperceptible signal and all of them shot at the same time. The worker with the banner was the first to fall pierced by the police bullets.

Colón noticed a "strange thing" happening. Instead of intimidating the marchers, the shooting stiffened their resolve and "incensed them to a fury." The strikers and their supporters continued marching forward until "strikers, horses, women, children and police were in a whirling mass of fighting humanity." Women stabbed the underbelly of the police horses with long hat pins, causing them to dislodge their riders into the melee. "The strikers kept on pushing, singing and fighting the police," said Colón. One of the policemen managed to mount his horse and sped off to summon reinforcement. As the street cleared—the marchers realizing that the police had gone for help—six strikers, "making a human stretcher of their hands and arms woven together, took the body of their dead companion away."

Despite the principal's frenetic ringing of the school bell, calling the children back to class, Colón's and the other young heads of Central Grammar School looked heedlessly out onto the street, horrified and spellbound as if riveted to the slats in the fence.

A sixteen-year-old who witnessed the event reported it for *¡Adelante!* In his article, entitled "Honest Struggle of Our Parents," he lamented: "Our dear fathers struggle for bread but they fall vanquished, covered with blood." He grew up to become the President of the Puerto Rican Confederation of Labor. "Nothing," said Colón, "in those schoolrooms of old Barracones has taught me as much as that encounter between the workers and the police that eventful day."[90]

Within a year of the incident, Colón, empty handed, walked up the gangway from San Juan dock onto the "S.S. Carolina" and stowed away to New York City. In his new abode, he continued what he had begun in his native Puerto Rico: he expanded his education, earning against the odds his high school diploma by attending night school in Brooklyn, and attended St. John's University for two years; he sustained and deepened his love affair with books, sparked by the *tabaqueros* in Cayey; he worked at the craft of writing and wrote for the working class and radical publications in New York and Puerto Rico; he became one of the most important organic intellectuals of exiled Puerto Rico: it is not for nothing that he called one of his newspaper columns *Lo Que El Pueblo Me Dice [What the People Tell Me].*[91] For some sixteen years he wrote columns for the Communist press in America, rolling with the punches as the party and its press declined and dwindled. Starting with *The Daily Worker* in 1955, becoming a contributing editor of the magazine *Mainstream*, to *The Worker* (which was no longer daily) from 1958 to 1968, Colón ended his journalistic career with the *Daily World*, from 1968 to 1971, and died three years later.

Colón founded and led numerous cultural and political organizations among the Hispanic population. Included among these were the Alianza Obrera Puertorriqueña, Ateneo Obrero Hispano, Sociedad Fraternal Cervantes, the latter being the Spanish-speaking section of the International Workers Order. A multi-ethnic and multi-racial order, the IWO was founded in 1930 by members of the Communist Party and Jewish radicals. It dedicated itself to providing workers with insurance and other services. It played an active role in the formation of the Congress of Industrial Organizations and campaigned for the unemployed during the Depression years. By 1947, the IWO had almost 190,000 members. Colón by this time was in charge of thirty Spanish and Portuguese-speaking lodges affiliated to the IWO throughout the United States.[92] Colón joined the Communist Party in 1933—having, apparently years earlier, left the Socialist Party—and remained a loyal Party member up to his death forty years later. Between 1953 and 1968, he made three unsuccessful bids for public office in the New York State Assembly and New York City Council, the last for City Controller on the Communist Party ticket. Like many other radicals at the time, Colon was hauled up in front of the House Un-American Activities Committee; unlike many others, he was remarkably unfrightened by the McCarthyites. He was, instead, outraged by them. As his testimony shows, he was courageous and combative, dubbing the witchunters "the Un-Americans," symbolically turning the tables on his persecutors. A man of almost sixty at the time, he apparently escaped unpunished by the authorities.[93] The Cuban Revolution and the guerrilla movements in Latin America fueled his political ardor and optimism and brought him cheer during the autumn of his life.

Through the course of his life, Colón maintained an unusually straight political line of march: he was and remained an active socialist and an *independentista* from his early youth to the end of his days.

Given his background and experience, it is not surprising that Colón was a class man, not a race man, exercised more by issues of class than of ethnicity and race. Thus, of the two, the enigmatic and anomalous figure, is not Jesús Colón, the Puerto Rican black socialist, but Arturo Schomburg, the Puerto Rican with strong black nationalist sympathies. *Schomburg*, and not Colón, is the Puerto Rican aberration.

Thus, it is more extraneously than by its actual contents that one discovers that the author of the beautifully written, charming, generous, and wise—I have weighed my adjectives carefully—document, *A Puerto Rican in New York and Other Sketches*, was indeed black. The Puerto Ricans' "American hero," Colón accurately wrote in 1961, "was and still is Vito Marcantonio," the remarkable Italian-American radical Congressman from East Harlem who represented the district, almost without break, from 1934 to 1950.[94] While Schomburg bursting with excitement over the Black Star Line proclaimed: "Garvey is the man!" and that "Garvey, *veni, vidi, vici*," nowhere in Colón's writing do the words Marcus Garvey appear. Never once in his more than four hundred pieces of writings is the acronym UNIA to be seen; neither man nor organization was praised or condemned by Colón. It was as if Garvey had never lived and the Universal Negro Improvement Association had never been born. Arriving in New York in 1918 and living in the city right up to his death in 1974, it would have been impossible, even though he lived most of the time in Brooklyn, for Colón not to have heard of Garvey and the UNIA.[95] He clearly had no interest in either.

Significantly, the Civil Rights Movement of the late 1950s and 1960s roused Colón to reflect—publicly and more explicitly—about race and racism in the United States, in his native Puerto Rico and elsewhere. It was as if the movement, triggered by the arrest of Rosa Parks in December 1955, had given him permission to remember painful experiences, hitherto repressed, and had endowed him with the right to speak out more openly about racial oppression. "Little Things are Big" and "Hiawatha into Spanish," two of his most skillfully executed sketches, are at once under-stated and searing indictments of racism. They were both written during the heat of the Civil Rights Movement in 1956. It was also in 1956 that Colón first mentions Schomburg in writing, describing him as "a great Negro

Puerto Rican," and "a great figure in the life of the 19th century Puerto Rican in New York."[96] In the following year, Colón encouraged his Puerto Rican compatriots to march on Washington on the Pilgrimage of Prayer, organized by A. Philip Randolph and the civil rights leadership. Colón attended the march, was deeply moved by it, and told his readers about the event. "Phrase Heard in a Bus," published in 1957, like "Hiawatha into Spanish," recalled incidents of racism that he had experienced and bottled up for forty years. The school desegregation struggles in Little Rock, Arkansas, also commanded a column in 1957.[97]

Colón, it should be said, did discuss, if only infrequently, racism in his writings of an earlier period. But the language he mobilized was that of anti-fascism rather than that of anti-racism. The analysis was unsatisfactory and crude. In fact, it is fair to say that although his understanding of the phenomenon of racism improved significantly over time, Colón, even in the 1950s and 1960s, never adequately came to grips with the complexity and embeddedness of racism in American society. This failure was not entirely Colón's; it was also that of the Communist Party of the United States, to which he belonged. Like the Communist Party, he never saw racism as anything other than the direct result of ruling class manipulation, and an expression of false consciousness on the part of white workers. And so in 1943 he perceived the Ku Klux Klan as "the Trojan horse of nazifascism [*nazifascismo*]" in America.[98] Even in the 1950s and 1960s his conception of racism never went much beyond describing the phenomenon as imperialist and capitalist "poison." In his discussion of the crisis at Central High School in Little Rock in 1957, Colón no less than three times in seven short paragraphs used poison as a noun or a verb to capture the phenomenon of racism. "We should not forget, looking at the gains," he declared, "that the basic admission that Negroes ought to have the same rights and privileges as anybody else is not yet recognized flatly and in life without any ifs or buts, by the majority of the white population that has been poisoned for years by those capitalist interests who thrive and profit by this policy of divide and conquer. We progressives," he continued, "of all races, have been as yet unable to win the wide masses of the white people, especially in the South, from this poison of Chauvinism that keeps the working class and the people in general weak and divided." Writing in the organ of the Communist Party of the United States, he told his comrades that they cannot "exorcise chauvinism from people by ridiculing, insulting, howling and calling them ignorant. By this method of insult and innuendo all that we can achieve is to alienate those who are just getting rid of the capitalist poison."[99]

Having conceptualized racism in such a manner, Colón, not surprisingly, was overly optimistic as to the extent to which socialists could provide the antidote. Education and exemplary deeds on the part of "progressives" was the remedy. Accordingly, he applauded and encouraged every act of class solidarity and human decency that countered racism. He was right to have done so, but he overestimated the effects of his civilized cheerleading and encouragement in the pages of *The Daily Worker* and *The Worker*.[100] Colón was never comfortable when it came to talking about race. It is interesting that his column on the "The Negro in Puerto Rican History" was requested by his readers, not a subject he himself chose to write on. And although he had promised to write the following week on "The Negro in Puerto Rico Today," Colón's essay on the subject appeared, not a week, but four columns and over a month later.[101] In the interim he wrote on "Soviet Exhibition in Havana," and other good things, which he apparently thought were more worthy subjects.

Colón was at home talking class politics, the Cuban revolution, the Puerto Rican struggle and American imperialism in Latin America. He was out of his depth when it came to the madness of race in America. It was as if his mind was too cultivated and civilized, his instincts too decent, generous and human for him to have plumbed the depths of American racism. And he squared the circle of his analysis by crudely, and repeatedly, reducing race to class, and racism to bourgeois conspiracy—hence the notion of racism as capitalist poison.[102]

But the emphasis of class and nationality over race by Colón and other Puerto Ricans in New York has substantially been a reflection of the greater salience of the former, class, compared to race within Puerto Rican society itself. And the discrimination that they experience as a group—partly on linguistic and cultural grounds—in the United States reinforces the salience of class and nationality.[103] The Spanish language itself cemented the bonds of national and ethnic identification over more narrowly racial identification. Indeed, Spanish has become so emblematic of Puerto Rican identity that, as Samuel Betances noted, "one cannot separate a Puerto Rican identity from the Spanish language."[104] It also provided the nexus to a wider Latin American cultural identity and transnationality. For, Puerto Ricans in New York City in the early part of the century, as Sánchez-Korrol observes, "read Spanish language newspapers; saw Mexican and Argentinean films; listened to Spanish radio stations; formed associations which promoted Spanish language and culture; danced and listened to Latin music."[105]

The Catholic religion provided a similar force of cohesion, though a far less powerful one than the Spanish language, among the Puerto Ricans, which transcended race and color.[106] This is not to say that racism and colorism did not exist within the community. It did and does. Even Colón, that most sanguine of Puerto Rican voices, acknowledged its existence.[107] What the centripetal and shepherding power of a common language and a common religion does in a hostile environment is to act as a countervailing force against the centrifuge of race, color, and difference within the group. Powerful though they were, the centripetal forces could not hold everyone. Bernardo Vega reported that when he arrived in 1916 there were "quite a few black *paisanos* [compatriots]" especially in East Harlem, between 99th and 106th streets. But some of them, including Schomburg, Augustín Vázquez, and Isidro Manzano, "later moved up to the black North American neighborhood," that is, black Harlem proper. Vega, unfortunately, does not explain why this movement took place, nor does he give us the proportion of the black Puerto Ricans who moved in this way. The most we get from his account is that "some" did.[108] And we learn nothing about Vázquez and Manzano apart from the bare facts of nationality and color as they marched up to Harlem and out of the pages of history, unrecovered to this day.

A Puerto Rican scholar recently wrote that, "Puerto Ricans were White and Black; Puerto Ricans were neither White nor Black. From the Puerto Rican perspective, Puerto Ricans were more than White or Black."[109] Memorable though the formulation may be, it elegantly obfuscates more than it reveals about the actual relation between dark-skinned and light-skinned Puerto Ricans at home and abroad.[110] Matters were and are far more complex than such a simplistic rendering would lead one to believe. Not only was there racism and colorism, the commitment to non-racist behavior and anti-racism was not evenly spread among the Puerto Rican migrants either. The *tabaqueros* were, apparently and not implausibly, the most committed, and the light-skinned Puerto Rican middle class, the least so.[111] Indeed, one *tabaquero* migrant who came to New York in 1913, went so far as to tell Bernardo Vega, that "when it came to the so-called better-off people, some of them were even more prejudiced than the Americans."[112] Vega reported that from the earliest years of migration anti–Puerto Rican prejudice pushed some members of the community, "the better-off ones in particular," to try passing for "Spaniards" so as to minimize the prejudice against themselves. "There were even those who went so far as to remain silent in public. They made sure never to read Spanish newspapers in the subway or to teach Spanish to their children. That's right, that's what they did, I know it for a fact," reported Vega. He contrasted this behavior with that of the working class Puerto Ricans, in whose community "Spanish was always spoken, and on the train we read our papers for all to see. The workers," he said, "were not afraid of being called 'spiks'. They did not deny their origin. Quite the contrary: they struggled because they knew that they were Puerto Ricans and, in a broader sense, Hispanic."[113]

The power of the forces against group cohesion should not be underestimated. Vega tells of the horrendous persecution of his uncle's family in 1900. Antonio Vega's white neighbors on East 88th Street tolerated his presence but drew the line at his having black visitors (Antonio's swarthy compatriots) to his apartment. One Sunday afternoon, nine men called, unexpectedly, upon Antonio Vega. Looking serious, they all refused to sit down and did not even bother to take their hats off. "We come on behalf of the tenants of this building," said one of them. "We bear no ill feeling toward anybody, but this is a white neighborhood," he declared, contradicting himself. "We have noticed that you frequently have Negroes coming to your house. People around here don't like that. We do hope that in the future you will be more careful about who you invite to your house." When Antonio tried to object, the spokesman closed him down: "See here, we have not come to discuss the matter. If you wish to keep up such friendships, then you should just move out!" Bernardo Vega reported that his uncle tried to speak again, but the visitors "promptly turned on their heels and were gone. And from that day on, not a word was exchanged with the neighbors." That did not mean that the neighbors were not heard from. Soon after the delegation, they went into action:

> Someone picked up a baby carriage that Antonio's wife had left in the hall and threw it into the street. Next a bunch of kids broke it in pieces, with all the neighbors watching. And the next day the wheels of the broken carriage were at the front door of the apartment. The day after that someone threw a rock through the front window, and a few days later they found the hallway in front of their door covered with feces. As if that was not enough, the family's mail was stolen and their gas was shut off.

Life became "unbearable" in the Vega's nice apartment. Ignoring the behavior of the neighbors, a strategy initially adopted, became impracticable as the harassment escalated. The family had no where to turn:

> Calling the police was useless. When they lodged a formal complaint about the disappearance of their mail, the authorities promised to investigate but never even took the trouble to visit the building. The superintendent was part of the scheme, as was the agent who managed the building. Pressure built up all around them to move out!

But one of Antonio Vega's daughters, Vasylisa, valiantly resisted the pressure, insisting that the family not submit to the racists. She followed her own counsel. "One night she hid, waiting to catch by surprise whoever it was that was throwing filth on their doorsteps. It was a woman; she jumped up, grabbed her by the hair, and smeared the feces in her face. The scuffle woke up all the tenants, who were outraged." The entire family was arrested that night. Morris Hillquit, the socialist leader, bailed them out and later served as the family's lawyer. But Vasylisa was convicted and, for the same crime, lost her job with the Board of Education because of what they called her "improper conduct." Vanquished, Antonio Vega and his family moved from East 88th Street.[114]

Thus, the pressure on light-skinned Puerto Ricans to reject their dark-skinned compatriots in exchange for a quiet life, to behave badly—to behave like the *Yanquis*, "ugly Americans," as Colón would put it—was at times enormous. (Of course, quite a number of these white Puerto Ricans behaved like "ugly Americans" back home in the island—they needed no encouragement.) But since the Vasylisas of this world are a precious few, it is only natural that some Puerto Ricans would yield to the powerful forces of bigotry. In more homogeneous Puerto Rican communities like *El Barrio*, group cohesion across racial lines were better maintained.[115] Speaking of the consolidation of this area of East Harlem as a Puerto Rican community, Bernardo Vega remarked that "through this entire area, life was very much like it was back home. Following the example set by the *tabaqueros*, whites and blacks lived together in harmony."[116] Even allowing for Vega's touching partiality for the *tabaqueros*—a sentiment that runs through the entirety of his *Memoirs*—the strength of Puerto Rican cohesion along national and class lines, in contrast to racial division, is well documented, undeniable and remarkable. McKay, looking in from the outside, was struck by the interaction between the "white and the yellow and the brown Puerto Ricans," who he thought, "insouciantly mingle on equal terms."[117]

The cross-racial cohesion, which varied in strength over time, among working class Puerto Ricans at home and in exile, combined with a relatively low race consciousness, and a comparatively high level of educational attainment and class consciousness made it easier for them to work with white people in radical organizations such as the Socialist and

Communist Parties in the United States. African Caribbeans in general—but in particular those from the Hispanic territories—because of their experience in the Caribbean were, clearly, not as prone to view white people with the degree of distrust and suspicion that African Americans were. We are relatively familiar with the names of Caribbeans such as Hubert Harrison, Wilfred Domingo, Cyril Briggs and Otto Huiswoud in discussions of black radicalism in early twentieth century America. Yet Jesús Colón, as early as 1918—the very year he arrived in the United States—was not only a member of the Socialist Party, but was a member of the first committee within the Party to be made up of Puerto Ricans.[118] As a Jamaican sociologist observed, Afro-Caribbeans, compared to Afro-Americans, are "less fearful of whites and also have less hatred of them."[119]

Given his background and experience, it is perfectly rational and understandable that Colón adopted the political positions that he did. His was the trajectory of the radical Puerto Rican who happened to be black. Schomburg, through background, circumstances and choice, evolved in a different direction. He embraced African Americans with as much intensity as Colón lovingly clinged to his exiled Puerto Rico. Schomburg became a Pan-Africanist and worked vigorously to vindicate his disinherited and maligned race. He is remembered and revered by African Americans primarily for his most conspicuous, monumental and vibrant legacy, the Schomburg Center for the Study of Black Culture, at the New York Public Library in Harlem. And no history of the Harlem Renaissance is complete without the recognition of Schomburg's enormous contribution to that cultural and political flowering. In general, those who know about Schomburg know nothing of Colón. Colón is remembered by Puerto Rican New York, its radical intelligentsia and activists. Arturo Schomburg is hardly known in this, Colón's, world. And when known, he is hardly seen as a member of the Puerto Rican community, even on the minimal basis of descent. He is given over, as it were, to Afro-America, in which he sought his political and intellectual home. The very images that survive of the two men reinforce this reading of their near-counterpointing political lives. Here is a photograph of Schomburg at a reception for the Liberian President-elect; there is Colón at the *Pueblos Hispanos* annual dinner. Here is Schomburg with his black brothers of the Prince Hall lodge; there is Colón with the comrades of the Sociedad Fraternal Cervantes over which he presides. Schomburg writes for the *Negro World;* Colón for *Pueblos Hispanos*.

But it is time we dissipate the mutual ignorance of and indifference toward Colón and Schomburg by their respective intellectual and political followers and celebrants. Black nationalist, Pan-Africanist, socialist and Puerto Rican nationalists would benefit from engagement with the work and example of both Colón and Schomburg, for they have much to teach us. Such an engagement would be in the spirit of the two men. One thing that these two striving and distinguished *afroborinqueños* had in common was a passionate love for books and the knowledge they contained along with the emancipatory power of truth and knowledge. (They were children of the Enlightenment, steeped in its rationalist worldview and optimism, which, incidentally, is not as bad as postmodernists would lead us to believe.) Schomburg and Colón should be recognized by all progressive people, especially those of African descent, for the enormous exertion they made, in their own way, trying to make a better and more decent world for all of us to live in—regardless of race, color and class. We should cherish their memory, their effort, and their rich legacy; they deserve nothing less. ■

ENDNOTES

1. James Dietz, *The Economic History of Puerto Rico: Institutional Change and Capitalist Development* (Princeton: Princeton University Press,1986), pp. 6–7; Eric Williams, ed., *Documents of West Indian History, 1492–1655* (Port of Spain: PNM Publishing Company 1963) pp. 38–40; Louis A. Pérez, *Cuba: Between Reform and Revolution*, 2nd ed. (New York: Oxford University Press, 1995), pp. 31–34; Franklin W. Knight, *The Caribbean: The Genesis of a Fragmented Nationalism* 2nd ed. (New York: Oxford University Press 1990), p. 40; Arturo Morales Carrión, *Puerto Rico: A Political and Cultural History,* (New York: W. W. Norton, 1983), Chap. 2; Fernando Picó, *Historia General de Puerto Rico,* 5th Ed. (Río Piedras: Edición Huracán 1990) pp. 72–97.

2. The foregoing discussion of Havana and Cuba has drawn upon Knight, *Caribbean,* pp. 44–46, and especially upon the excellent analysis of Pérez, *Cuba,* pp. 34–48; see also John Robert McNeill, *Atlantic Empires of France and Spain: Louisbourg and Havana, 1700–1763* (Chapel Hill: University of North Carolina Press, 1985), esp. pp. 85–92, 97–104; Alan J. Kuethe, "Guns, Subsidies, and Commercial Privilege: Some Historical Factors in the Emergence of the Cuban National Character, 1763–1815," *Cuban Studies,* No.16, 1986; idem., "Havana in the Eighteenth Century," in Franklin W. Knight and Peggy K. Liss, eds., *Atlantic Port Cities: Economy, Culture, and Society in the Atlantic World, 1650–1850* (Knoxville: University of Tennessee Press 1991).

3. Production statistic from Knight, *Caribbean,* Table 3, p. 365.

4. For a good overview of this process see, Manuel Moreno Fraginals, Frank Moya Pons, and Stanley Engerman, eds., *Between Slavery and Free Labor: The Spanish-Speaking Caribbean in the Nineteenth Century* (Baltimore: Johns Hopkins University Press 1985); the classic analysis of the transition in Cuba is provided by Manuel Moreno Fraginals, *El ingenio: El complejo económico social cubano del azúcar.* Tomo 1, 1760–1860 (Havana: UNESCO, 1964); but also see Franklin Knight, *Slave Society in Cuba During the Nineteenth Century,* (Madison: University of Wisconsin Press, 1970), and Rebecca Scott, *Slave Emancipation in Cuba: The Transition to Free Labor, 1860–1899* (Princeton: Princeton University Press, 1985). Sidney Mintz, *Caribbean Transformation* (Chicago: Aldine Publishing Co., 1974), Gordon Lewis, *Puerto Rico: Freedom and Power in the Caribbean,* (New York: Monthly Review Press,1963), Francisco A. Scarano, *Sugar and Slavery in Puerto Rico: The Plantation Economy of Ponce, 1800–1850* (Madison: University of Wisconsin Press, 1984), and James L. Dietz, *Economic History of Puerto Rico* provide valuable accounts of the transition in Puerto Rico. Harry Hoetink, *The Dominican People, 1850–1900 : Notes for a Historical Sociology,* (Baltimore: Johns Hopkins University Press, 1982) provides a good account of the transition in the Dominican Republic.

5. See Knight, *Caribbean,* Table 4, pp. 366–367, for a statistical overview of the ethnic composition of the islands during the early nineteenth century. Ethnic composition and identity formation in the Dominican Republic were, of course, over-determined by the latter's troubled relation with Haiti. See Harry Hoetink, "The Dominican Republic in the Nineteenth Century: Some Notes on Stratification, Immigration, and Race," in *Magnus Mörner,* ed., *Race and Class in Latin America* (New York: Columbia University Press, 1970); idem., *The Dominican People*; Frank Moya Pons, "The Land Question in Haiti and Santo Domingo: The Sociopolitical Context of the Transition from Slavery to Free Labor, 1801–1843," in Fraginals, et al., eds., *Between Slavery and Free Labor.*

6. Jerome Handler, *The Unappropriated People: Freedmen in the Slave Society of Barbados* (Baltimore: Johns Hopkins University Press, 1974), p. 18; Douglas Hall, "Jamaica," in David Cohen and Jack Greene, eds., *Neither Slave Nor Free: The Freedmen of African Descent in the Slave Societies of the New World* (Baltimore: Johns Hopkins University Press 1974), p. 194; Kenneth Kiple, *Blacks in Colonial Cuba, 1774–1899* (Gainesville: University Presses of Florida 1976), p. 3; Luis M. Diaz Soler, *Historia de La Esclavitud Negra en Puerto Rico* (Rio Piedras: Universidad de Puerto Rico 1981), p. 94. The distribution of slaves and freemen in the French, Danish, and Dutch Caribbean was similar to that of Barbados and Jamaica; see articles by Léo Elisabeth, Gwendolyn Midlo Hall, and H. Hoetink in Cohen and Greene, op. cit.; and Neville Hall, *Slave Society in the Danish*

West Indies: St. Thomas, St. John and St. Croix, (Kingston: University of the West Indies Press, 1992), p. 5.

7. See Knight, *Slave Society;* Rebecca Scott, *Slave Emancipation in Cuba*; Mintz, *Caribbean Transformations*, esp. pp. 82–94; Dietz, *Economic History*, pp. 34–53; Francisco Scarano has shown that between 1812 and 1828, while the free population in Puerto Rico's sugar growing districts of Mayaguez, Ponce and Guayama increased by an average of 62 percent, the slave population grew by 296 percent; the rate of surplus extraction intensified, the treatment of slaves deteriorated as sugar boomed: Scarano, *Sugar and Slavery in Puerto Rico*, pp. 25–34.

8. Mintz, *Caribbean Transformations*, p. 94.

9. See the excellent essay on the subject by Harry Hoetink, "`Race' and Color in the Caribbean," in Sidney Mintz and Sally Price, eds., *Caribbean Contours,* (Baltimore: Johns Hopkins University Press 1985); and also the very sharp observations of Gordon Lewis in relation to Puerto Rico, in his *Puerto Rico,* esp. pp. 281–288, as well as those of Mintz, *Caribbean Transformations*, pp. 55–58 and 126–130.

10. Benjamín Nistal-Moret, "Problems in the Social Structure of Slavery in Puerto Rico During the Process of Abolition, 1872," in Fraginals et al., eds., *Between Slavery,* pp. 146–147; B. W. Higman, *Slave Populations of the British Caribbean, 1807–1834* (Baltimore: The Johns Hopkins University Press 1984), p. 116; idem., *Slave Population and Economy in Jamaica, 1807–1834* (Cambridge: Cambridge University Press 1976), p. 142.

11. For an overview of the position of this category of people within the Americas during slavery, see David Cohen and Jack Greene, eds., *Neither Slave Nor Free*.

12. Louis Pérez, "Politics, Peasants, and People of Color: The 1912 `Race War' in Cuba Reconsidered," *Hispanic American Historical Review,* Vol. 66, No.3, February 1986, p. 512; Robert B. Hoernel provides a very thorough analysis of late nineteenth and early twentieth-century Oriente in his "Sugar and Social Change in Oriente, Cuba, 1898–1946," *Journal of Latin American Studies,* Vol. 8, Pt. 2, November 1976; see also, Lisandro Pérez, "Iron Mining and Socio-Demographic Change in Eastern Cuba, 1884–1940," *Journal of Latin American Studies,* Vol. 14, Pt. 2, November 1982; Rebecca Scott, *Slave Emancipation*, esp. pp. 256–259; Ada Ferrer, "Social Aspects of Cuban Nationalism: Race, Slavery, and the Guerra Chiquita, 1879–1880," *Cuban Studies*, No.21, 1991; Karen Robert, "Slavery and Freedom in the Ten Years' War, Cuba, 1868–1878," *Slavery and Abolition,* Vol. 13, No.3, December 1992; Aline Helg, *Our Rightful Share: The Afro-Cuban Struggle for Equality, 1886–1912* (Chapel Hill: University of North Carolina Press, 1995.)

13. Diaz Soler, *Historia de la Esclavitud,* p. 256; Olga Jiménez de Wagenheim, *Puerto Rico's Revolt for Independence: El Grito de Lares* (1985; Princeton and New York: Markus Wiener Publishing 1993), p. 22. Strangely, Jiménez de Wagenheim claims that in 1860, "more than half of the peasant farmers, artisans, and proprietors" were members of the free colored population, but the evidence she points to, quoted above, does not sustain her assertion; see Jiménez de Wagenheim, pp. 21–22. José Luis González thinks that black Puerto Ricans, even during the period of slavery, had a greater attachment to the island than the whites, many of whom were in fact foreigners. Francisco Scarano forcefully brings out the role of foreigners in Puerto Rico's sugar industry in the nineteenth century. See José Luis González, *Puerto Rico: The Four-Storeyed Country and Other Essays* (1980; Princeton: Markus Wiener Publishing, 1993), pp. 9–13; Scarano, *Sugar and Slavery in Puerto Rico,* esp. Chap. 4. In both Cuba and Puerto Rico the discriminatory policies of the Spanish toward creoles and especially toward black creoles, helped to trigger and sustain black participation in the revolts.

14. Patricia Weiss Fagen, "Antonio Maceo: Heroes, History, and Historiography," Latin American Research Review, Vol. xi, No.3, 1976; Philip Foner, *Antonio Maceo: The "Bronze Titan" of Cuba's Struggle for Independence* (New York: Monthly Review Press, 1977); Donna M. Wolf, "The Cuban Gente de Color and the Independence Movement, 1879–1895," *Revista / Review Interamericana,* Vol. 5, Fall 1975; Aline Helg, *Our Rightful Share*.

15. This is a point that is very effectively made by Pérez in his revisionist analysis of the so-called *la guerra de razas* of 1912 in Oriente province; see Pérez, "Politics, Peasants";

Helg, in her valuable book, tends to understate the level of cross-racial collaboration in Cuban history.
16. José Luis González, *Puerto Rico: The Four-Storeyed Nation,* p. 128.
17. Gordon Lewis, "Race Relations in Britain: A View From the Caribbean," *Race Today*, Vol. 1, No.3, July 1969, p. 80; idem., *Main Currents in Caribbean Thought: The Historical Evolution of the Caribbean in its Ideological Aspects, 1492–1900* (Baltimore: Johns Hopkins University Press,1983), p. 9.
18. It is worth noting though that the *Cedula de Gracias* that was granted to Puerto Rico in 1815 gave free black immigrants to the island half the amount of land that it granted to free whites, three instead of six acres. Indeed, the free black immigrant was allocated the same amount of land that a white immigrant would be granted for each slave he brought to the island. Dietz, *Economic History of Puerto Rico,* p. 21. In Cuba, a battery of explicitly anti-discriminatory legislation was passed in the 1880s and 1890s, thanks largely to the vigorous agitation of the people of color. Hugh Thomas, *Cuba, or the Pursuit of Freedom* (London: Eyre & Spottiswoode 1971), p. 293; Wolf, "The Cuban Gente de Color," pp. 407–408.
19. Lewis, *Puerto Rico,* p. 282.
20. W. A. Domingo, "Gift of the Black Tropics," in Alain Locke, ed., *The New Negro: An Interpretation* (New York: Albert and Charles Boni Inc, 1925), p. 342; Wallace Thurman, *Negro Life in New York's Harlem* (Girard, Kansas: Haldeman-Julius Company 1928), p. 17.
21. Ira Reid, *The Negro Immigrant: His Background, Characteristics and Social Adjustment, 1899–1937* (New York: Columbia University Press, 1939), p. 101; Claude McKay, *Harlem: Negro Metropolis* (New York: E. P. Dutton & Co.,1940), p. 136.
22. See Tony Martin, *Race First: The Ideological and Organizational Struggles of Marcus Garvey and the Universal Negro Improvement Association* (Westport, Conn.: Greenwood Press, 1976), esp. pp. 49–51; Martin claims, not implausibly, that the Cuban UNIA was "largely Jamaican in composition," (p. 50). See also Rupert Lewis, *Marcus Garvey: Anti-Colonial Champion* (London: Karia Press 1987), pp. 99–123; Bernardo García Dominguez, "Garvey and Cuba," in Rupert Lewis and Patrick Bryan, eds., *Garvey: His Work and Impact* (Kingston: Institute of Social and Economic Research, University of the West Indies, 1988); Amy Jacques Garvey, *Garvey and Garveyism,* (New York: Macmillan 1970). For more on the pattern of migration within and beyond the Caribbean, see Franklin Knight, "Jamaican Migrants and the Cuban Sugar Industry, 1900–1934," in Manuel Moreno Fraginals, et al., eds., op. cit.; Velma Newton, *The Silver Men: West Indian Labor Migration to Panama, 1850–1914,* (Kingston: Institute of Social and Economic Studies, UWI, 1984); Bonham Richardson, *Panama Money in Barbados, 1900–1920,* (Knoxville: University of Tennessee Press, 1985); and B. Richardson, "Caribbean Migrations, 1838–1985," in F. Knight and C. Palmer, eds., *The Modern Caribbean,* (Chapel Hill: University of North Carolina, 1989). See also the special double issue "Ethnicity, Class and the State in Central America," of *Cimarrón* (Vol. II, Nos. 1–2, Spring/Summer 1989).
23. The Afro-Panamanian (non-Caribbean) mother of Maida Springer Kemp, the political activist and trade unionist, was one of the few Afro-Latina Garveyites. For more on Maida Springer Kemp see, "Maida Springer Kemp," in Ruth Edmonds Hill, ed., *The Black Women Oral History Project*, Vol. 7, (Westport: Meckler Publishing, 1991), pp. 39–145, and Yevette Richards, "'My Passionate Feeling About Africa': Maida Springer-Kemp and the American Labor Movement,'" (Ph. D. diss. Yale University 1994). For De Mena's background see Robert Hill, ed., *The Marcus Garvey and Universal Negro Improvement Association Papers,* (hereafter referred to as the *Garvey Papers),* Vol. vi, (Berkeley: University of California Press 1986), pp. 117–118 n. 1; cf. Jeannette Smith-Irvin, *Marcus Garvey's Footsoldiers of the Universal Negro Improvement Association* (Trenton: Africa World Press, 1989), pp. 59–63.
24. Garvey Papers, Vol. iii, p. 789, and Vol. ii, p. 120 n.1.
25. See Robert Harris, Nyota Harris, Grandassa Harris, eds. *Carlos Cooks and Black Nationalism: From Garvey to Malcolm* (Dover, Mass: The Majority Press, 1992).

26. Conversations with Carlos Moore, March 1996, Kingston Jamaica. Moore's most widely known work on Cuba is *Castro, the Blacks and Africa* (Los Angeles: Center for Afro-American Studies, University of California, Los Angeles, 1989).

27. Elinor Des Verney Sinnette, went so far as to claim that Schomburg was a Garvey "disciple", but this, I believe, despite Schomburg's undoubted enthusiasm for the UNIA (but which he never joined) is an overstatement. See Sinnette, *Arthur Alfonso Schomburg: Black Bibliophile and Collector A Biography,* (New York: New York Public Library and Wayne State University Press 1989), p. 123. The Puerto Rican population in the United States had dramatically increased from 1,513 in 1910 to 11,811 in 1920 with 62.3 percent of the total living in New York City in 1920. By 1930 the total Puerto Rican population in America had reached 52,774; some claimed it was as high as 200,000, but this is more than likely an overestimation. In any case, the overwhelming majority of the migrants lived in New York City. See Manuel Maldonado-Dennis, *The Emigration Dialectic: Puerto Rico and the USA,* (New York: International Publishers, 1980), Table 1, p. 131, and History Task Force, *Centro de Estudios* Puertorriqueños, *Labor Migration Under Capitalism: The Puerto Rican Experience* (New York: Monthly Review Press, 1979), pp. 223–225, who both use the lower estimates, and Virginia E. Sánchez-Korrol, *From Colonia to Community: The History of Puerto Ricans in New York City* (Westport: Greenwood Press, 1983), pp. 58–66, who leans toward the higher figures while admitting the "debatable" nature of all the estimates. The enumeration of the Puerto Rican migrant community in the United States was complicated by the political status of the migrants.

28. Floyd J. Calvin, "Race Colleges Need Chair in Negro History—A. A. Schomburg," *Pittsburgh Courier,* March 5, 1927. Both Ortiz and Sinnette, Schomburg's biographers, incorrectly deduced that this information was first divulged by Schomburg to the black Cuban writer, Gustavo E. Urrutia, during Schomburg's visit to Cuba in the winter of 1933. In fact, Urrutia's article did not come from a direct interview with Schomburg, it is, almost in its entirety, a direct translation of Calvin's article that had been published six and a half years before Schomburg visited Cuba. See Gustavo E. Urrutia, "Schomburg," *Diario de La Marina,* November 2, 1933; Victoria Ortiz, "Arthur A. Schomburg: A Biographical Essay," in The Schomburg Center for Research in Black Culture, *The Legacy of Arthur Alfonso Schomburg: A Celebration of the Past, A Vision for the Future* (New York: Schomburg Center for Research in Black Culture, 1986), pp. 18–117 (published in Spanish and English). See pp. 21–23 for reference to Urrutia's article; Sinnette, pp. 13–14.

29. J. A. Rogers, "Arthur A. Schomburg: 'The Sherlock Holmes of Negro History' (1874–1938)," in Rogers, *World's Great Men of Color,* Vol. ii (New York: Macmillan Publishing Company, 1972), p. 452.

30. For more on this most remarkable man, see Calvin, "Race Colleges"; Simon Williamson, "History of the Life and Work of Arthur Alonzo [sic] Schomburg," July 18, 1938, unpublished ms., reel 10, Arthur A. Schomburg Papers; Claude McKay, *Harlem: Negro Metropolis,* op. cit., pp. 139–142; J. A. Rogers, "Schomburg is the Detective of History," Norfolk Journal and Guide, July 5, 1930; idem., *World's Great Men of Color,* Vol. ii, pp. 449–453; Jean Blackwell Hutson, "The Schomburg Collection," in John Henrik Clarke, ed. *Harlem: A Community in Transition* (New York: Citadel Press, 1969), pp. 205–209; Ernest Kaiser, "Schomburg, Arthur Alfonso," in Rayford Logan and Michael Winston, eds., *Dictionary of American Negro Biography* (New York: W. W. Norton and Co., 1982), pp. 546–548; Victoria Ortiz, "Arthur A. Schomburg: A Biographical Essay"; Elinor Des Verney Sinnette, *Arthur Alfonso Schomburg;* Flor Piñeiro de Rivera, ed., *Arthur Alfonso Schomburg: A Puerto Rican Quest for His Black Heritage* (San Juan: *Centro de Estudios* Avanzados de Puerto Rico y el Caribe, 1989), pp. 17–50.

31. Howard Dodson, "Introduction," Schomburg Center for Research in Black Culture, *The Legacy of Arthur Alfonso Schomburg: A Celebration of the Past, A Vision for the Future* (New York: Schomburg Center, 1986), p. 7.

32. Alain Locke, "In Memoriam: Arthur Alfonso Schomburg, 1874–1938," foreword to Arthur Schomburg, "Negro History in Outline" (Bronze Booklet No.8). Alain Locke Papers, Moorland-Spingarn Research Center, Howard University. The Bronze Booklet series was edited by Locke. Booklet No.8 was never published.

33. Floyd J. Calvin, "Race Colleges Need Chair in Negro History."

34. Arthur A. Schomburg, "The Negro Digs Up His Past," in Alain Locke, ed., *The New Negro,* op. cit., pp. 231–232.
35. Colón cited from interview in Elinor Des Verney Sinnette, *Schomburg,* p. 23; the second pair of parentheses is Sinnette's. The interview with Colón was conducted on 27 June 1973 and he died in May 1974. Colón did write a nice, though passionless, little sketch of Schomburg in the early 1960s, "Arthur Schomburg and Negro History." It was written for Negro History Week and published in *The Worker,* February 11, 1962. Claude McKay, a very close friend of Schomburg, observed that intellectually the latter was proud of his Spanish heritage and fond of Puerto Rico. Yet, Schomburg, he wrote, "cultivated no social contact with Harlem's Puerto Ricans." McKay, who had a keen eye for such matters, also noted that Schomburg was thrice married, "each time to an American Negro woman, and he reared 7 children." McKay, *Harlem: Negro Metropolis,* p. 142.
36. César Andreu Iglesias, ed., *Memoirs of Bernardo Vega: A Contribution to the History of the Puerto Rican Community in New York* (New York: Monthly Review Press 1984), p. 195.
37. Iglesias, pp. 66 and 195–196.
38. For the most accessible source of Bruce's views, see Peter Gilbert, ed., *The Selected Writings of John Edward Bruce: Militant Black Journalist* (New York: Arno Press 1971); see for instance, p. 143, where Bruce talks about black people of African descent belonging to "branch[es] of the Hamatic (sic) family the wide world over." Some of Schomburg's own writings are brought together in Flor Piñeiro de Rivera, ed., *Arthur Alfonso Schomburg: A Puerto Rican Quest for His Black Heritage* (San Juan: Centro de Estudios Avanzados de Puerto Rico y el Caribe, 1989). Schomburg's relation with Bruce is traced in Sinnette's *Schomburg.* Curiously, although it carries a portrait of Bruce signed by himself and addressed to "My dear friend A. A. Schomburg," there is no mention of Bruce's relation with Schomburg in the text of the Schomburg Center's own biographical portrait, Victoria Ortiz, "Arthur A. Schomburg."
39. For a good evaluation of the evidence concerning Schomburg's parents see Ortiz, pp. 19–25, and Sinnette, pp. 7–9.
40. The questionnaire was filled out in the 1930s for E. Franklin Frazier's study, *The Negro Family in the United States* (Chicago: University of Chicago Press, 1939); Schomburg's completed questionnaire is among Frazier's papers: "A Study of the Negro Family," questionnaire No.2597, E. Franklin Frazier Papers, Moorland Spingarn Research Center, Howard University.
41. Sinnette, p. 14.
42. Alton Adams to Arthur Schomburg, February 1, 1927; reel 1, Arthur Schomburg Papers. Sinnette, pp. 14–17; see also Ortiz, pp. 23–25.
43. Schomburg to [Dr. J. M.] Boddy, December 15, 1932; reel 7, Schomburg Papers.
44. *New York Age,* February 18, 1933.
45. Schomburg, "Harlem Echoes," *The Union,* June 30, 1932.
46. Gary R. Mormino and George E. Pozzetta, *The Immigrant World of Ybor City: Italians and Their Latin Neighbors in Tampa, 1885–1985* (Urbana: University of Illinois Press, 1987), pp. 186–187.
47. "A Study of the Negro Family," questionnaire No.2579.
48. The hegemonic culture in the Danish Virgin Islands from the eighteenth century to 1917, when the islands were sold to the United States, was British. The Danes constituted a small minority of the planters on all three islands, the lingua franca was English–Creole based (even though there was considerable Dutch influence in St. Thomas in the eighteenth century), the newspapers were overwhelmingly published in English, and when the authorities decided to educate the slaves the language of instruction was English. Neville Hall reported that a Danish writer in 1840, noting the presence of European "foreigners" in the Virgin Islands, lamented the fact that St. Croix had never been colonized by his countrymen and had never been Danish "except in the narrowly political sense. If all it took to be Danish was the flag and the judicial system, then St. Croix was Danish. But colonization implied more than territorial claim and a body of laws." Neville

Hall, "Empire Without Dominion: The Danish West Indies, 1671–1848," in idem., *Slave Society in the Danish West Indies,* pp. 18–19; see also Hall, "Education for Slaves in the Danish Virgin Islands, 1732–1846," in Ruby Hope King, ed., *Education in the Caribbean: Historical Perspectives* (Kingston: Faculty of Education, University of the West Indies, 1987).

49. Sinnette, *Schomburg,* p. 166; Ortiz, "Arthur A. Schomburg," p. 99.
50. Ortiz, "Arthur A. Schomburg," p. 99.
51. Schomburg to Dabney, August 19, 1937; reel 7, Schomburg Papers.
52. See Ortiz, "Arthur A. Schomburg," pp. 25–35, and Sinnette,*Schomburg,* pp. 20–23.
53. The role of Rafael Serra and Sotero Figueroa in Cuban and Puerto Rican nationalist exile politics are discussed, albeit *en passant,* in Iglesias, ed., *Memoirs,* and in Gerald Poyo, *"With All, and for the Good of All": The Emergence of Popular Nationalism in the Cuban Communities of the United States, 1848–1898* (Durham, NC: Duke University Press, 1989); and Isabelo Zenon Cruz, *Narciso Descubre su Trasero: El Negro en la Cultura Puertorriqueña,* tomo 1, 2nd ed., (Humacao, Puerto Rico: Editorial Furidi, 1983), pp. 149–150; Donna M. Wolf, "The Cuban *Gente de Color* and the Independence Movement, 1879–1895," *Revista/Review Interamericana,* Vol. 5, Fall 1975, pp. 418–419; Serra's politics after his return to Cuba in 1902 are discussed in Helg, *Our Rightful Share,* pp. 133–136; see also "Sotereo Figueroa," (reel 11, Schomburg Papers); this is an English translation of an obituary apparently published in a Havana magazine, *La Discusion,* Oct. 10, 1923 (Figueroa died on Oct. 5, 1923). The translation was made by Figueroa's son, Pace Figueroa; it was not accompanied by the Spanish original.
54. McKay, *Harlem,* p. 140, emphasis added; McKay wrongly attributed this choice on the part of Schomburg to his "African blood," but, as we have seen, there was more to it than that.
55. Victoria Ortiz, "Arthur A. Schomburg," p. 39.
56. Schomburg to the *New York Herald Tribune,* April 24, 1935, emphasis added. The letter was never published.
57. Williamson, a close friend of Schomburg's, evaluated the latter's work as a freemason in "Arthur A. Schomburg: The Freemason", [March 13, 1941], reel 5, The Harry A. Williamson Papers, Schomburg Center.
58. See Alfred Moss, Jr., *The American Negro Academy: Voice of the Talented Tenth* (Baton Rouge: Louisiana State University Press, 1981), which is harsh in its criticism of Schomburg's presidency and more than a bit nativistic in tone; see esp. pp. 221–222.
59. McKay, *Harlem,* p. 141.
60. Cromwell to Schomburg, July 17, 1928, cited in J. A. Rogers, "Schomburg is the Detective of History," *Norfolk Journal and Guide,* July 5, 1930; this article, with minor changes, formed the profile of Schomburg later published in Rogers' *World's Great Men of Color.*
61. Miriam Jiménez first brought to my attention problems in Schomburg's written Spanish.
62. Much of Schomburg's published work in English went through substantial editing before entering the public domain. Sinnette registers this fact but barely discusses it. Her claim that Schomburg's written Spanish was "impeccable" is, at best, debatable. Sinnete, p. 13.
63. Schomburg to Ira De A. Reid, July 18, 1935; reel 8, Schomburg Papers.
64. Locke, "In Memoriam: Arthur Alfonso Schomburg," p. 1, of unpaginated script.
65. Schomburg to Boddy, New Year's Day 1934; reel 7, Schomburg Papers.
66. See, for instance, Schomburg to J. M. Boddy, December 15, 1932, and New Year's Day 1934; Schomburg to "My Dear Nestor" [Wendell P. Dabney], undated.
67. Schomburg in *Negro World,* November 4, 1922; reprinted in Theodore G. Vincent, ed., *Voices of a Black Nation: Political Journalism in the Harlem Renaissance* (San Francisco: Ramparts Press, 1973), pp. 340–341. A week after Schomburg's review, Bruce also complained in the pages of the *Negro World* about Woodson's behavior. According to Bruce, Woodson had promised to acknowledge photographs provided by the Negro Society for Historical Research (founded and led by Bruce and Schomburg), but never did; Tony

Martin, *The Pan-African Connection: From Slavery To Garvey and Beyond* (Cambridge, Mass.: Schenkman Publishing Company, 1983), p. 104, citing *Negro World* of November 11, 1922.

68. Schomburg to Boddy, December 15, 1932; reel 7, Schomburg Papers. As early as 1916, Schomburg complained to Bruce about Woodson "stealing our thunder." [Tony Martin, *Race First: The Ideological and Organizational Struggles of Marcus Garvey and the Universal Negro Improvement Association* (Westport, Conn.: Greenwood Press, 1976), p. 83.] It was only after a closer reading of Schomburg's voluminous correspondence that I came to understand more fully what McKay—a man who knew Schomburg well—meant when he said that Schomburg was "full of wonderful love and admiration and hate, positively liking his friends and positively disliking his foes." (McKay, Harlem, p. 142.) The love came through Schomburg's published work, but the hate hardly showed. "He strangely combined a simple, disarming exterior and obscure inner complexes," observed McKay, shrewdly. (Ibid.)
69. Schomburg to W. P. Dabney, April 29, 1938.
70. Cited in Flor Piñeiro de Rivera, *Arthur Schomburg*, pp. 42–44.
71. Schomburg to Dabney, August 19, 1937.
72. Sinnette, *Schomburg*, p. 123.
73. George Schuyler, *Black and Conservative: The Autobiography of George S. Schuyler* (New Rochelle: Arlington House), p. 144.
74. Schomburg to Cromwell, July 28, 1919; John Wesley Cromwell Family Papers, Moorland-Spingarn Research Center, Howard University.
75. Schomburg to Cromwell, undated, [Summer? 1920?]; Cromwell Papers.
76. Schomburg to Cromwell, August 4, 1921; Cromwell Papers.
77. Arturo A. Schomburg, "Neroes in the League of Nations," *New York Age*, September 14, 1936.
78. Schomburg, "Our Pioneers," *New York Amsterdam News*, September 19, 1936.
79. Schomburg, "Neroes in the League of Nations."
80. *The Black Man*, July 1938, pp. 1–2.
81. McKay, *Harlem*, p. 142.
82. Schomburg to Boddy, New Year's Day, 1934; reel 7, Schomburg Papers.
83. See Jesús Colón, *A Puerto Rican in New York and Other Sketches*, (New York: Masses and Mainstream, 1961) and the foreword by Juan Flores to the 1982 edition (published in New York by International Publishers). More details on Colón's life and work are provided by his close friend, compatriot, and comrade Bernardo Vega (César Andreu Iglesias, ed., op. cit.); the Jesús Colón Papers, *Centro de Estudios Puertorriqueños*, Hunter College, City University of New York; and by Edna Acosta-Belén and Virginia Sánchez Korrol, in their introduction, "The World of Jesús Colón," to Jesús Colón, *The Way it Was and Other Writings* (Houston: Arte Público 1993).
84. Colón, "A Voice Through the Window," in *A Puerto Rican in New York*, p. 11.
85. See Angel Quintero-Rivera's sparkling essay, "Socialist and Cigarmaker: Artisans' Proletarianization in the Making of the Puerto Rican Working Class," *Latin American Perspectives*, Vol. x, Nos. 2 and 3, Spring and Summer 1983, p. 27; Colón, ibid., p. 11; Bernardo Vega discusses the transfer of this political culture to New York: Iglesias, *Memoirs*, Ch. 4. See also Louis Pérez, "Reminiscences of a Lector: Cuban Cigar Makers in Tampa," *Florida Historical Quarterly*, April 1975; Gerald Poyo, "With All, and for the Good of All"; Patricia Cooper, *Once a Cigar Maker: Men, Women, and Work Culture in American Cigar Factories, 1900–1919* (Urbana: University of Illinois Press, 1987), p. 66. The practice of reading while the cigarmakers roll began in Cuba in the 1860s, spread to Puerto Rico soon after and traveled with Cuban *tabaqueros* to Tampa, Florida, in the nineteenth century.
86. Angel Quintero-Rivera has a fine discussion of this culture and the corrosive processes undermining the artisans at the turn of the century; see his "Socialist and Cigarmaker"; also see Dietz, *Economic History*, pp. 85, 116–118.
87. Acosta-Belén and Korrol, "The World," p. 22; Iglesias, p. xvii and Ch. 1.

88. Colón, "My First Literary Venture," and "My First Strike," both in *A Puerto Rican.*
89. Lyrics from a Spanish version of *The Internationale.*
90. Colón, "The Way to Learn," in *A Puerto Rican,* pp. 17–21.
91. In *Pueblos Hispanos,* between 1943 and 1944.
92. There is no biography of Colón, but see the helpful biographical sketch in *Centro de Estudios Puertorriqueños,* Hunter College, *The Jesús Colón Papers: Finding Aid* (1991), pp. 6–7; see also Acosta-Belén and Korrol, "The World of Jesús Colón," pp. 22–25; Roger Keeran, "The International Workers Order and the Origins of the CIO," Labor History, Vol. 30, No.3, Summer 1989; Roberto P. Rodríguez-Morazzani, "Linking a Fractured Past: The World of the Puerto Rican Old Left," *CENTRO: Journal of the Center for Puerto Rican Studies,* Vol. vii, No.1, Spring 1995, p. 24.
93. See Colón, "I Appear Before the Un-Americans," *The Worker,* November 29, 1959; idem., "The Un-Americans and the Americans," *The Worker,* December 6, 1959; and "Statement by Jesús Colón to the Walter Committee on Un-American Activities," reprinted in Colón, *The Way it Was and Other Writings,* pp. 100–102.
94. Colón, op. cit., p. 200; for more on the relationship between Puerto Ricans and Marcantonio, see Salvatore John LaGumina, *Vito Marcantonio: The People's Politician,* (Dubuque, Iowa: Kendall/Hunt Publishing Co., 1969), esp. Chap. vii, Iglesias, ed., op. cit., pp. 183–190; Felix Ojeda Reyes, *Vito Marcantonio y Puerto Rico: Por Los Trabajadores y Por la Nacion,* (Río Piedras: Ediciones Huracán, 1978) esp. pp. 9–55; idem., "Vito Marcantonio and Puerto Rican Independence," *Centro de Estudios Puertorriqueños Bulletin,* Spring 1992; Virginia E. Sánchez Korrol, *From Colonia to Community,* pp. 187–194; Jeff Kisseloff, *You Must Remember This: An Oral History of Manhattan from the 1890s to World War II* (New York: Schocken Books, 1989), pp. 337–380; Gerald Meyer, *Vito Marcantonio: Radical Politician, 1902–1954,* (Albany, New York: State University Press of New York, 1989); idem., "Marcantonio and El Barrio," *Centro de Estudios Puertorriqueños Bulletin,* Spring 1992, which is drawn from Meyer's book.
95. Although Colón in his American sojourn lived mainly in Brooklyn, he also lived in Harlem for some time during the First World War and perhaps after. He in fact revealed in more than one of his autobiographical sketches that he, his brother and later the rest of his family, including his mother and father, lived at 143rd Street between Lenox and Seventh Avenue. This was very much the heart of black Harlem at the time. Indeed, Colón wrote that "In those days the few Puerto Ricans around lived in the heart of the Negro neighborhood together with the Negro people in the same buildings; many times as roomers in their homes." This is an exaggeration. (On the basis of the manuscript census for 1925 Sánchez Korrol concluded that "the incidence of blacks and Puerto Ricans sharing buildings was limited" and less frequent than Puerto Ricans sharing with Jews, Italians, Russians, and Irish. There is no reason to believe that there would have been more black and Puerto Rican sharing of space a few years earlier.) It is true, however, that some black Puerto Ricans in the early years did live in the way described by Colón. The point, however, is this: Colón lived in Harlem at a time that the Garvey movement could not have been missed. See Colón, "How to Rent an Apartment Without Money" and "The Day My Father Got Lost," both in *A Puerto Rican in New York,* pp. 43–45, and 46–48; Sánchez Korrol, p. 59.
96. Colón, "Little Things are Big," *Daily Worker,* June 27, 1956; "Hiawatha Into Spanish," *Daily Worker,* November 13, 1956; "The Library Looks at the Puerto Rican," *Daily Worker,* March 5, 1956; these were later included in *A Puerto Rican in New York.*
97. Colón, "Pilgrimage of Prayer," "I Went to School on Friday in Washington, D. C.," "Phrase Heard in a Bus," "Little Rock," published in The *Daily Worker,* May 14, 1957; May 21, 1957; July 2, 1957; October 8, 1957, respectively.
98. Colón, "Los Otros Estados Unidos," *Pueblos Hispanos,* April 10, 1943, p. 3. It is significant that Colón wrongly referred to the Ku Klux Klan as the "Klux Klux Klan," not once, but twice in this article.
99. Colón, "Little Rock," *Daily Worker,* October 8, 1957; also see *The Worker,* July 12, 1959, where Colón refers to "ugly Americans contaminated with the imperialist poison of race superiority." A decade earlier, he complained that the popular media, such as the *Daily*

News and the *Daily Mirror* were, every day, poisoning the minds of his fellow Puerto Ricans against the Negro [*envenan la mente todos los días contra el negro*] and others: "El Prejuicio y la Independencia," *Liberación,* June 19, 1946, p. 7.

100. See especially, Colón, "Is Language a Barrier?," *Daily Worker,* January 30, 1956; also see, idem., "Pilgrimage of Prayer;" "Little Rock;" "Marching in the Snow," *Daily Worker,* March 2, 1958; "As I See it From Here," *The Worker,* Sept. 7, 1958; "The Powell Campaign," *The Worker,* Sept. 14, 1958; "The Question of Voting for Your Own Kind," *The Worker,* Oct. 5 and 12, 1958.

101. "The Negro in Puerto Rican History," and "The Negro in Puerto Rico Today," *The Worker,* February 7, 1960, and March 13, 1960, respectively.

102. I am at a loss to adequately explain how Colón, a man of undoubted decency and integrity, could tolerate the moral stench of the Communist Party through Stalin's purges of the 1930s; through the Hitler Stalin Pact of 1939; the murder of Trotsky by a self-confessed assassin doing Stalin's work in 1940; through Khrushchev's chilling revelations about Stalin in his "secret speech" in 1956; through the invasion of Hungary in 1956; and through Moscow's military suppression of the Prague Spring in 1968. At each of those turning points along the bumpy road of twentieth century official Communism, the world Communist movement, including the CPUSA, lost members, but not Comrade Colón, who died in 1974, clinging to the Party.

103. Oscar Handlin, *The Newcomers: Negroes and Puerto Ricans in a Changing Metropolis* (Cambridge, Mass.: Harvard University Press, 1959), pp. 59–60. Colón in his newspaper columns meticulously documented these acts of anti-Puerto Rican discrimination and the responses to them. See in particular, "A Judge in New Jersey," and "Because He Spoke in Spanish," *Daily Worker,* January 16, 1956, and April 9, 1957, respectively; and idem., "Ten to 30 Years—For 2 Cigarettes," and "Racism in Glendale and Ridgewood," *The Worker,* November 16, 1958, and July 5, 1959, respectively.

104. Samuel Betances, "African-Americans and Hispanics/Latinos: Eliminating Barriers to Coalition Building," *Latino Studies Journal,* Vol. 6, No.1, January 1995, p. 15.

105. Sánchez Korrol, *From Colonia to Community,* p. 70.

106. It is almost certain that the *tabaqueros* and their families made up the majority of the Puerto Rican community in New York up to the 1930s. (Iglesias, p. 98; Sanchez Korrol, p. 137; Angelo Falcón, "A History of Puerto Rican Politics in New York City: 1860s to 1945," in James Jennings and Monte Rivera, eds., *Puerto Rican Politics in Urban America* [Westport: Greenwood Press 1984], p. 23). And as they were renown as radicals and freethinkers, the church would have had negligible influence over the life of the community in the early years. In 1917 Hubert Harrison reflected despondently upon how few black freethinkers there were in America. His spirits soared, however, when his survey endearingly noted that "The Cuban and Porto Rican cigar-makers are notorious Infidels, due to their acquaintance with the bigotry, ignorance and immorality of the Catholic priesthood in their native island." (Hubert Harrison, *The Negro and the Nation* [New York: Cosmo-Advocate Publishing Co., 1917] p. 46.) The evidence from Key West and Tampa, Florida, is that the *tabaqueros* there, too, had no time for religion and, least of all Catholicism. Indeed, they were described as "openly antagonistic" toward the Church. Thus, up to 1939, only 100 out of the 12,372 Cubans living in Ybor City (Tampa), were members of the Catholic Church — 0.8 per cent of the population. (DeWight R. Middleton, "The Organization of Ethnicity in Tampa," *Ethnic Groups,* Vol. 3, December 1981, pp. 293–94); Mormino and Pozzetta, pp. 210–223. For more on this, see Jay P. Dolan and Jaime R. Vidal, eds., *Puerto Rican and Cuban Catholics in the U. S., 1900–1965* (Indiana: University of Notre Dame Press, 1994). (The book in fact comprises two excellent monograph-length essays: Jaime R. Vidal, "Citizens Yet Strangers: The Puerto Rican Experience," pp. 11–143, and Lisandro Pérez, "Cuban Catholics in the United States," pp. 147–208.) For the Puerto Rican and Cuban background to this popular anti-clericalism see Quintero Rivera, pp. 26–28; R. del Romeral (Ramón Romero Rosa) "The Social Question and Puerto Rico: A Friendly Call to Intellectuals," in Angel Quintero Rivera, ed., *Workers' Struggle in Puerto Rico: A Documentary History* (New York: Monthly Review Press, 1976), pp. 22–25; Gordon Lewis, *Puerto Rico: Freedom and Power in the Caribbean* (New York: Monthly Review Press, 1963), pp. 271–280; Sidney Mintz, *Worker in*

the Cane: A Puerto Rican Life History (New York: W. W. Norton, 1974), pp. 36 and 96; and Vidal, esp. pp. 11–25; Lisandro Pérez, pp. 147–157; for a wider but brief Latin American overview, see Leslie Bethell, "A Note on the Church and the Independence of Latin America," in Leslie Bethell, ed., *The Independence of Latin America* (Cambridge: Cambridge University Press, 1987), pp. 227–232.

107. See, for example, Jesús Colón, "El Prejuicio y la Independencia," *Liberación,* June 19, 1946; idem., "The Negro in Puerto Rico Today," *The Worker,* March 13, 1960; and "Angels in My Hometown Church," in *The Way It Was,* pp. 53–54.

108. Iglesias, p. 12.

109. Clara Rodríguez, *Puerto Ricans, Born in the U. S. A.* (Boulder: Westview Press, 1991), p. 51.

110. See Samuel Betances' classic essay, "The Prejudice of Having No Prejudice in Puerto Rico," Parts I and II, *The Rican,* Winter 1972 and Spring 1973; also see José Luis González, *Puerto Rico;* and Angela Jorge, "The Black Puerto Rican Woman in Contemporary American Society," in Edna Acosta-Belén, ed., *The Puerto Rican Woman: Perspectives on Culture, History, and Society,* 2nd ed. (New York: Praeger, 1986); and Roberto Santiago, ed., *Boricuas: Influential Puerto Rican Writings* (New York: Ballantine Books, 1995).

111. The *tabaqueros* in Florida had the same non-racist reputation, especially in the nineteenth century. The mixture of shades boggled the racist Southern mind. See Durward Long, "The Making of Modern Tampa: A City of the New South, 1885–1911," *The Florida Historical Quarterly,* Vol. xlix, No.4, April 1971, p. 342; Middleton, "The Organization of Ethnicity," pp. 289–290; Susan Greenbaum, "Afro-Cubans in Exile: Tampa, Florida, 1886–1984," *Cuban Studies/Estudios Cubanos,* Vol. 15, No.1, Winter 1985, pp. 60–61; Poyo, *"With All and For the Good of All,"* Chap. 5.

112. Iglesias, *Memoirs,* pp. 105–106. As we have seen, Colón acknowledges the existence of racism within the Puerto Rican community, but his discussion is flawed by his overstating of the *Yanqui* genesis of the phenomenon.

113. Iglesias, p. 97; Colón also complained about those who try to pass for Mexican, Chileans, Costa Ricans and other nationalities. Colon, "El Prejuicio y la Independencia," *Liberación,* 19 June 1946, p. 7.

114. Iglesias, pp. 85–86.

115. The fact that *El Barrio* was located in a relatively liberal, Northern state is not insignificant. For among the Cubans in Florida, as the pressures of Jim Crow increased at the end of the nineteenth century, so did the tendency for separation along color and racial lines. See Long, "The Making of Modern Tampa," p. 342; Middleton, "The Organization of Ethnicity," pp. 289–290, 295; Greenbaum, "Afro-Cubans," pp. 59–65; Poyo, *"With All and For the Good of All,"* Chap. 5.

116. Iglesias, p. 151.

117. McKay, *Harlem,* p. 136.

118. Iglesias, ed., op. cit., p. 112.

119. Dennis Forsythe, "West Indian Radicalism Abroad" (Ph. D. diss., McGill University 1973), p. 126, n. 28.

JOSE SANTIAGO

OLD★TIME
CHRISTOBEL TORRIENTI
BLACK STARS

OLD★TIME
JOSE MENDEZ
BLACK STARS

OLD★TIME
MARTIN DIHIGO
BLACK STARS

TETELO VARGAS

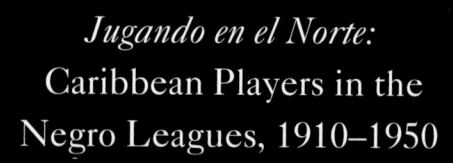

Jugando en el Norte:
Caribbean Players in the
Negro Leagues, 1910–1950

ADRIAN BURGOS JR.

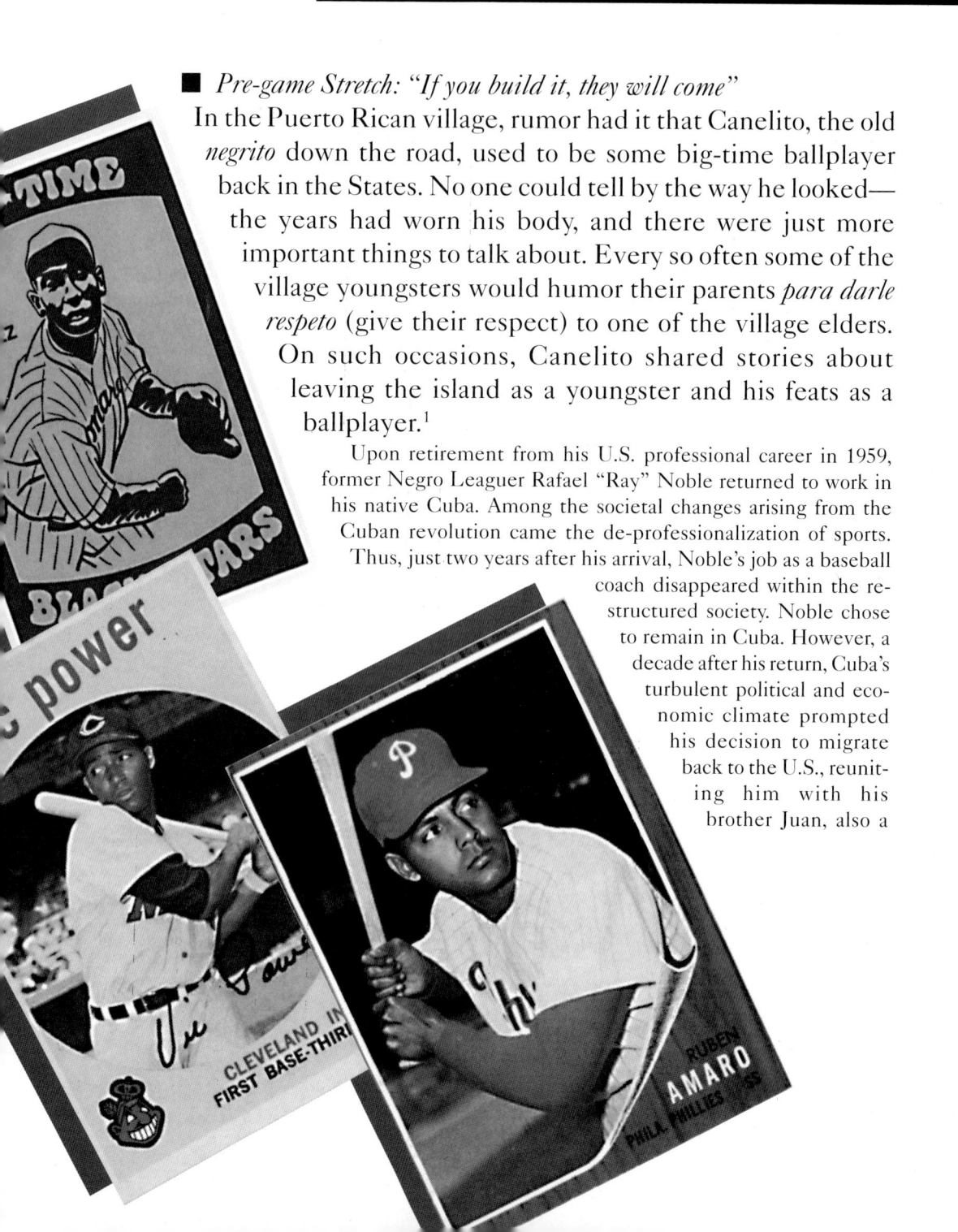

■ *Pre-game Stretch: "If you build it, they will come"*

In the Puerto Rican village, rumor had it that Canelito, the old *negrito* down the road, used to be some big-time ballplayer back in the States. No one could tell by the way he looked—the years had worn his body, and there were just more important things to talk about. Every so often some of the village youngsters would humor their parents *para darle respeto* (give their respect) to one of the village elders. On such occasions, Canelito shared stories about leaving the island as a youngster and his feats as a ballplayer.[1]

Upon retirement from his U.S. professional career in 1959, former Negro Leaguer Rafael "Ray" Noble returned to work in his native Cuba. Among the societal changes arising from the Cuban revolution came the de-professionalization of sports. Thus, just two years after his arrival, Noble's job as a baseball coach disappeared within the re-structured society. Noble chose to remain in Cuba. However, a decade after his return, Cuba's turbulent political and economic climate prompted his decision to migrate back to the U.S., reuniting him with his brother Juan, also a former Negro League player. Proudly gripping a bat commemorating the New York Giants' 1951 World Series triumph, Noble stated that he had only recently received the bat from his daughter in Cuba. Pointing out the bat's many nicks and scratches from the hands of his grandson, Noble commented *"Si ese niño supiera con que jugaba"* (If that little boy only realized with what he played)."[2]

Canelito and Noble may not be representative of all Afro-Caribbean[3] ball players who came to the U.S. pursuing professional careers, but juxtaposing their stories with other ball players relate the parallels that their lives have taken as members of the African Diaspora.[4] Specifically, the experiences of these players speak to the challenges Caribbean migrants faced in their movements throughout the Americas. More than a geographically situated location, the Americas encapsulate the sites where their identities were shaped through their movement between and among the various countries. Within this world, the choice of economic livelihood these men pursued took into account multiple factors: the player's resource base-including networks, regional economies, and political conditions at home and abroad. Professional baseball gave them the opportunity to leave "home" and continue in another part of this world, permitting these ball players to carry with them information and experience gained along their travels.

This paper seeks to illuminate Caribbean ball players experience of "race" as migrants within the Americas. Based on findings from archival research and oral interviews, I submit that as members within the trans-American community these ball players experienced race in a situational and relational manner.[5] Plainly stated, the social experience of race is contingental, locational, and referential. Additionally, racial constructs were permeable and negotiable; for through their everyday activities and formation of trans-Atlantic community, these men challenged the effectiveness of their assigned race.[6] Therefore, the internalization of race as an idea enabled them at different moments to act in specific, informed ways to procure services, goods, or rights.

■ *Strangers in the Outfield*

Mirroring U.S. societal conditions and race relations heading into the twentieth century, members of various racial/ethnic communities created institutions to meet the needs of those excluded from the white mainstream. Starting in the late nineteenth century, the imposition of a color line by white professional ball players and league management coalesced efforts by African Americans to form their own professional leagues. Various "Negro Leagues" developed from this effort. In 1920, former ballplayer turned entrepreneur Andrew "Rube" Foster pooled financial resources from a conglomeration of black and white businessmen to create the most successful and viable Negro League.[7] The League's demise began in 1947 with the Brooklyn Dodgers signing of Jackie Robinson. In the ensuing decades, major league baseball's (MLB) integrationist project began to disempower the mark of race at the institutional level.

Actually, notions of "race" and the "color line" had already been problematic tools of exclusion since Caribbean ball players participated on either side of the racial fault line. Nonetheless, histories produced on either baseball institution have been presented in duotones (black and white) disregarding the gradations of color and cultures arising from the African Diaspora in the Atlantic World. This present work focuses on Caribbean participants in the Negro Leagues, the world in which they lived, and their understandings of race. Complicating baseball's historical representation, this treatment engages important aspects of the player's social world: baseball's transmission into the Hispanic Caribbean, the images of North America the game represented, his arrival into North America as part of political generations,[8] and the game's adoption by working class people.

ADRIAN BURGOS JR. is a third-year doctoral student at the University of Michigan, specializing in Caribbean and American History. This article is part of a dissertation examining Latinos as members of overlapping diasporas and the formation of a Latino identity in the U.S. through their participation in North American professional baseball.

■ *Vintage baseball card collection courtesy of Dean Carlos Hortas, Arts and Humanities, Hunter College*

Caribbean participation in the Negro Leagues dates back to the first decade of the twentieth century. In actuality, allusions to Cubans among Negro League teams were made as early as the 1880s as U.S. born African-American ball players manipulated Cuban identity. The Cuban Giants, a team wholly comprised of African Americans, were primary performers in this regard, speaking gibberish "Spanish" while on the field and referring to each other by Spanish names. Other teams also played on this racial ambiguity, usurping the Cuban name to draw the interest of fans desiring to watch the foreigners play.[9]

That Negro League teams toyed with racial identity before the twentieth century demonstrated a racial awareness. They identified a Cuban type that one could imitate. By the late 1870s, the game was fully ensconced in Cuba, resulting in the country's first professional team, Almendares, and development and nurturance of a local talent pool.[10] Concurrent with this process, increasing numbers of Cubans secured jobs with U.S. professional teams. Cuban players soon discovered the power of baseball's racial fault line. Subsequently, Caribbean ball players wandered to their side of this racial divide: major league baseball for those could "pass" and the Negro Leagues for all others.

I am not suggesting that Caribbean players became "racialized" (i.e., became black) after they arrived in the U.S. Rather, that early in the twentieth century the U.S. paradigm on "race" and color had to adapt to the influx of these ball players who, although having what many considered "black" phenotypic features, maintained a different language and culture that pigeonholed them as living in a state between black and something else. Migration within the Caribbean and to the U.S. also complicated racial assignment. These circuits of movement have destabilized static notions of national and "racial" identity of these Caribbean countries, as well as reiterated the relational aspect of race.[11]

Through their experience in the States, Caribbean players directly encountered U.S. racial perceptions. At first, the view developed that this encounter forced a decision upon them to either assimilate into the white mainstream culture or be relegated to a subservient position within North American society. This issue of deciding between becoming white or black (in U.S. racial terms) proved troublesome for those who insisted on maintaining their identity.[12] Critical race theory, however, has progressed. Current theoretical concepts such as "racial formation" and "multipositionality" explicate the processes leading to the formation of "new" identities.[13] The utility of these newly constructed identities-such as Latino or Asian American-lay in their ability to allow an individual to perceive, for example, Puerto Ricans as Latinos and not privileging the black and white paradigm.

■ *The Problem of Racial Assignment in a Period of Segregation*
As mentioned above, indicative of race's ambiguity, as well as its fluidity, a small number of Caribbean players played in the Major Leagues and the Negro Leagues prior to Jackie Robinson's 1947 arrival.[14] Two members of this group were Hiram Bithorn and Sal "Chico" Hernández, battery mates for the Chicago Cubs during the 1942 and '43 seasons. Bithorn, a Puerto Rican, worked as a starting pitcher, but never played in the Negro Leagues. The Cuban-born Hernández, on the other hand, caught for the Cubs during these two seasons, and two years later in 1945 reappeared playing for the Indianapolis Clowns in the Negro League.[15]

Recently, one of the game's historians argued that perhaps Bithorn should receive credit for being the "pioneer of baseball's integration," stating that "perhaps the greatest difference between Jackie Robinson and Bithorn . . . was the "color" of their linguistic inflections, the distinctive rhythms of their speech patterns."[16] Such an argument privileges a North American paradigmatic view of race and color, for although many in the U.S. were "suspicious" of Bithorn's racial ancestry (he was of Spanish and Danish descent), within the confines of his native Puerto Rico, he was viewed as a *blanco* (white). Moreover, in 1938, when the Puerto Rican Professional Winter League launched its inaugural campaign (1938), some of the league officials questioned Bithorn's Puerto Rican identity. Consequently, Bithorn began his initial season as a *refuerzo* and not as a *nativo*.[17]

The case of Roberto Vargas also relates the difficulty of racial ascription. Although Vargas was "a light-complexioned Puerto Rican [he] was considered black," this perception excluded him from major league baseball until Robinson broke the color barrier.[18] In this manner, many Latinos suffered exclusion from Major League Baseball and its minor leagues, their identity being marked by "racial" perception and suspicion of their heritage. The confrontation between U.S. racial perceptions and the introduction of "foreigners" eventually led to a reformulation of racial constructs, in this instance, resulting in the incorporation of African descendants from the Hispanic Caribbean.

Prior to Bithorn and Olmo's arrival, all the Caribbean players that had played in the Majors during the twentieth century were Cubans. Two of the first, Rafael Almeida and Armando Marsans, had to be presented as "Castillian" by the Cincinnati press in order to temper possible player and fan reaction.[19] This became the language by which Caribbean players were referred to so as not to offend North American racial sensibilities. Later, as more Cubans joined the Majors, all "Latins" were grouped together as Cuban. The press treatment of Luis Rodríguez Olmo's identity, in 1942 the second Puerto Rican in the major leagues is instructive in this regard.

Olmo, a native-born Puerto Rican born in 1919, signed with a U.S. minor league club in 1940. As Olmo began to venture into the North American baseball world, the press had difficulty in categorizing him. This issue is clearly demonstrated in a 1940 letter to *The Sporting News* by Olmo's brother. Written in response to an earlier item that told of a contract sent to "Roberto [sic] Olmo, 21-year-old Cuban outfielder," being returned, Olmo's brother wrote:

> His correct name is Luis Rodríguez Olmo, but he is known as Luis Olmo, and he is a Puerto Rican, a proud American citizen.
>
> No doubt the contract was not received by my brother because it was incorrectly addressed. So far his name has been given out correctly only once, when you published the reserve lists. Later he was called Lewis Elmo and now as Roberto Olmo. Some confusion with Spanish names.[20]

This letter is telling in a number of ways, among them is the manner it illuminates the press's difficulty and also how Olmo and his brother perceived themselves.

As racial beings shaped in their native lands, many Caribbean players saw race as an idea that could be manipulated. In turn, they developed new social practices in the attempt to maneuver through race as an idea for their own gain. Seasonal movement within the Americas compounded their experiences and reinforced the relational aspect of race. During their careers, conversations on racial issues provided a forum for Caribbean players to share their understandings of race with African Americans. These and other types of conversations formed the networks of mutual exchange that helped to make their lives within the Americas more bearable.

Political relations between the U.S. and a player's country of origin influenced the geographical pattern of Caribbean arrivals to the Negro Leagues. In light of US-Cuban cultural ties, and baseball's early introduction there, the majority of Caribbean ball players in the Negro Leagues were Cuban. Political conditions in the Dominican Republic also contributed to the players' national distribution.

Sharing the island of Hispaniola, and containing a significant population with "visible" African ancestry, on several occasions the Dominican Republic and Haiti's political histories have intertwined.[21] In a way similar to how Cuban racial ideology garnered popular support during the Race War of 1912,[22] concerns about race, Haiti's proximity in this case, affected the Dominican Republic's Creole elite thought and influenced their actions. In the 1930s, General Rafael Trujillo consolidated his power and control. Promoting *Hispanidad*, a Dominican identity that stressed Spanish heritage and disassociated itself from African ancestry, Trujillo initiated a State campaign against those noticeably black. Crossing over into Haiti along the mountainous region separating the two nations, the Rio Massacre resulted in the death of more than 25,000 black "Haitians."[23] The Dominican state's coding of blacks as "Haitians" and the disassociation with being "Haitian" —that is, having African ancestry partly explained the absence of Dominicans in the Negro Leagues.[24]

One of the first generation of Dominican Major League players, Felipe Alou wrote about the (non-)issue of race while growing up in during the 1930s:

> There was never any talk concerning race problems or race inequality. Furthermore, my mother is a Caucasian, the daughter of a Spaniard who migrated to the Dominican Republic. My father is a Negro, the grandson of a slave who had most likely been imported from Africa to work on the farms.[25]

In his autobiography, Alou reflected "when Latins came to America to play baseball they are often shocked by the racial issue and by its scope...For the [American] Negro the situation is ever present. For the Latin it is far away."[26]

■ *The Batting Order*

In 1905, Tinti Molina's Cuban Stars became the first Cuban team to tour the U.S.. Fifteen years later, with the formation of the Negro National League, Molina's squad formally joined the Negro Leagues.[27] Two of the subjects for this investigation, José Méndez and Cristobel Torriente had their initial Stateside professional experience while members of this team. Though both exhibited superb talent on the field, Torriente generated the most enduring remembrances.

The powerful Torriente's on-field success during a Cuban winter league game spun off myths that earned him the sobriquet "The Black Babe Ruth." Discussing "The Cuban Strongboy," two of Torriente's contemporaries stated the following:

> No wonder the New York Giants were scouting him. Since he was a relatively light-colored Cuban ("Indian color," said Kansas City pitcher Chet Brewer; the same complexion as Babe Ruth said Cardona), he might have passed and gone onto to stardom in the big leagues, but his hair gave him away.[28]

Torriente's case is just one of many where phenotypical markers served as justification for exclusion from major league baseball.

No matter how powerful their swing, fleet their steps, or light their complexions, Caribbean ball players could not escape U.S. racial stereotyping. The image of the virile "African" or black man became a prevalent topic or trope during the late nineteenth and twentieth centuries. Black men were described as beasts, rapists, and fiends. To neuter them the media emphasized the entertainment talents of African Americans.

In accord with this racial ideology, on-field success in competition with whites could be interpreted as a direct assault on white supremacy and the white male's position within American society. Thus, in the twentieth century's first decade, after several Major League clubs incurred diminishing returns against Cuban teams during their winter tours, American League President Ban Johnson decreed a ban: "We want no makeshift club calling themselves the Athletics to go to Cuba to be beaten by colored teams."[29] This ban eliminated a site where masculinity could be contested athletically, on a professional level, between men from the different "racial" groups. Other sites of leisure also saw calls for prohibition of interracial competition. In the U.S., African-American boxer Jack Johnson's defeat in 1910 of the white Jim Jeffries for boxing's heavyweight championship also led to cries for such a prohibition.

In terms of race ideology, the negroization of Caribbean ball players by white and black daily newspapers in the U.S. and their strict use of the dichromatic type-either black or white-underscored cultural difference. In turn, specific cultural practices or behaviors as well as linguistic communication were interpreted on U.S. racial terms. Therefore, Torriente's wearing of a bandanna while playing was interpreted as a flamboyant gesture, and a player's inability to communicate in English associated him with African Americans—neither could speak proper English. This association is especially apparent in newspaper accounts when they provided phonetic transcription of interviews conducted with African American and Caribbean players. These portrayals demonstrated how Caribbean players were negatively portrayed as exotic, inarticulate, and/or as flamboyant.[30]

José de la Caridad Méndez also left his mark on North American professional baseball. Like Torriente, Méndez's talent drew the New York Giants' attention. Illustrating the club's seriousness in their pursuit of Méndez, John McGraw's wife-McGraw being the team's manager-reflected:

> Without mincing words, John bemoaned the failure of baseball himself included, to cast aside custom or unwritten law, or whatever it was, and sign the a player on ability alone, regardless of race or color." But the Giants trained in Texas, she explained and McGraw understood the significance and severity of segregation laws. At no time did he wish to offend the ordinance of people who lived by them 365 days of the year. Thus he settled for players who were undeniably Cuban.[31]

This passage relates the wide expanse that U.S. race ideology traversed as well as its effect. Mrs. McGraw's words expressed concern about possibly subverting racial practice in Texas by bringing Méndez. Probing deeper into her statement about settling for "players who were undeniably Cuban," one becomes aware that her statement advanced a particular association of Cuban with whiteness and/or Spanish ancestry. Clearly blackness did not fit their definition of Cuban for how else can one explain the exclusion of the native-born Méndez from being "undeniably Cuban." Even so, throughout his twenty-year Major League career, Cuban pitcher Adolfo Luque, who passed whatever litmus employed for Caribbean talent, faced "press and fan treatment later associated with Negro ball players."[32]

Tragically, both Torriente and Méndez suffered early deaths. In 1938, Torriente died in poverty, the consequence of his alcoholism at the age of 43. Recalling Torriente's bouts with alcohol, a former teammate, Alejandro Crespo, described Torriente's deteriorating state:

> Instead of going back to Cuba to manage, he stayed in Chicago and made his own booze,' recalled one teammate. The winter was cold, and he drank, drank, drank. His face swelled up from the booze. At spring training he couldn't hardly stand up in the batter's box without falling. He was in such bad condition, no team wanted him.[33]

Torriente did not lack support or friends. Rodolfo Fernández remembered that in 1935, while playing for the New York Cubans, Martin Dihigo, the team's manager, convinced team owner Pompez to bring Torriente back to New York City. Dihigo put Torriente up in a Harlem apartment, and thereafter he, along with others, visited Torriente periodically to check on his condition.[34]

Méndez, on the other hand, died of tuberculosis a couple of years after managing the Kansas City Monarchs to consecutive pennants in 1923 and 1924. Chet Brewer, reflected on his manager: "He spoke English pretty well. Some words would tie him up, but he spoke well enough. He was a shrewd manager and really a good teacher of baseball."[35] The fact that the Monarchs hired Méndez to manage their club, signified not only his managerial ability, but also his capacity to communicate with his ball players.

Interestingly, rumor of Méndez's death once circulated throughout the black press. In the first half of July 1913, the *Chicago Defender* reported:

> Méndez is missed but the greatest black twirler that ever held the sphere will probably pitch no more. He has gone too far back. The great white way has found another victim for its follies.[36]

It took the *Chicago Defender* until February of the following year to print a retraction: "Contrary to the news that has been circulated throughout the U.S., Méndez, the great pitcher, is living and pitching great ball. He is with the Havana team."[37] This episode not only illustrates the press's difficulty keeping abreast of Caribbean ball players, it also conveys the barrier that language presented to not only Caribbean players but also to the U.S. press. Moreover, the *Defender's* announcement of Méndez's death documents the existence of a network for disseminating information; for though incorrect, the rumor received enough transmission for publication in the widest circulating black newspaper.

■ *Rain Delay*

Several sources helped to frame this discussion. Evelyn Brooks Higginbotham's insights in "The Metalanguage of Race," affirmed the development of race as a (meta-) language through which societal members engage in conversation.[38] Acknowledging race's role within contestation of power and privilege, Higginbotham outlined the manner historians may draw from this conversation:

> [W]e must expose the role of race as a metalanguage by calling attention to its powerful, all-encompassing effect on the construction and representation of other social and power relations, namely, gender, class, and sexuality. . . [and] recognize race as providing sites of dialogic exchange and contestation, since race has constituted a discursive toll for both oppression and liberation.[39]

Higginbotham's formulation gave this study the capacity to incorporate different geographic locales because their twentieth-century political history and the dynamics of trans-Atlantic slavery have already produced a dialogue on race. Thus, terms such as black, *Negro*, mulatto, *pardo*, *blanco*, and white have specific meanings in the different countries. And although there were distinct national discourses on race that established meaning to these terms, the overall effect of racial constructs on those within these conversations speak towards a larger discussion.

Ball players' movement and resettlement within the Americas promoted the re-articulation and formulation of racial constructs. Yet, this did not occur only within one realm of society. While the State engaged in this conversation through its formal legislative enactments and institutionalized practices, individuals developed pro-active and/or re-active strategies towards these constructions, either pressing for expansion of rights and privileges on the one hand, or seeking to maintain their hegemony, on the other.[40]

In the U.S., part of the twentieth century historiographical dialogue on race has debated two modes: race as an idea and/or race as ideology.[41] As an idea that "marks difference," race can either unite a group or make distinctions between groups of individuals. Within the Negro League ball players' community, race functioned as an idea through which they acknowledged a shared ancestry arising from the African Diaspora. This does not mean that Afro-Caribbean ball players lost markers of their ethnic identity. As players' memory and periodical accounts gave witness, at times ethnic difference secured for Afro-Caribbean ball players services forbidden to "blacks."

The second mode of race is ideology. The ideological operation of race is revealed in a process whereby "those in power are able to subdivide the overall population into social groupings "races" for self-serving purposes."[42] Within the baseball profession, the ideological manifestation of race is seen in major league baseball's color line which segregated professional ball players from the late nineteenth century through 1947. Furthermore, major league segregation led to the creation of racial institutions. In this instance, Negro League baseball, as an institution, organized itself on and around racial categories and racial inequality. Thus, its material existence fulfilled specific racial needs, resulting in a space where African Americans and Latinos could both enjoy sport, and, perhaps more importantly, contribute employment opportunities and financial capital to local black economies in the United States.[43]

To gain a more coherent understanding of how Caribbean ball players arrived in the U.S. as racial beings, the trans-Atlantic world, as a conceptual tool, provides the site where an individual's identity undergoes the process of being figured, disfigured, and reformulated. Unlike current major league players, Negro Leaguers often played throughout the calendar year. After the regular season's completion, the more talented Negro League players signed to play winter league ball in a Caribbean country, November through February. These circulatory, seasonal movements framed the ball players' working lives, their understanding of race, and their participation within the greater process of "racial formation" in the U.S.[44]

The career choices these ball players made corresponded, to some degree, with their family backgrounds. Ball players from economically poor families often lacked access to training and/or education that would give them the capacity for social mobility. Reflecting back, Rodolfo Fernández recalled that lack of educational attainment or facilities sometimes gave a poor young man "hardly no other choice" but to pursue baseball as a career.[45] A ball player's success may complicate how he confronted race. Defining class in relational terms, a ballplayer securing a bigger contract can either be elevated into a different socioeconomic class within his community or assigned racial group, or be reminded of his working-class roots through fulfillment of family economic obligations.

■ *Baseball's Caribbean Diaspora*

Starting in the mid-nineteenth century, baseball took on a diasporic dimension throughout the Caribbean basin. In these countries, baseball developed a local following that attached their own meaning and purpose to the game. Thus, although some may perceive the game as a cultural import with U.S. imperialist overtones, the game's arrival and spread throughout reveals otherwise. In the Caribbean, Cubans became the primary movers of baseball, serving as "ambassadors" of the game and transporting the sport wherever they laid down to rest.[46]

Dating back to the mid-1860s, baseball functioned as an instrument of resistance within the Cuban independence struggle against Spain. In 1895, the colonial Spanish regime banned baseball as subversive. More significant than a form of leisure, for Cubans "Baseball has long served to give expression to Cuban nationality, both as a means to nationhood and as a metaphor for nation."[47] Consequently, baseball acquired specific meaning: "Cubans discerned that baseball could create a national community out of racially mixed and socially diverse fans, thereby suggesting the possibility of consensus around which to pursue nationhood."[48]

The game's diasporas became a common cultural point of reference that later allowed Caribbean players to envision themselves as a group. Adding further foundation, continued violent struggles against colonial Spain caused many Cubans to flee the island, settling in Puerto Rico and the Dominican Republic. This Cuban migration led to the game's further spread and blurred national identities since many migrants never returned.[49]

The attempt to formulate new constructions of national identity and end racist practices were two outcomes of the different Caribbean independence movements seeking to break Spain's colonial hold. In the twentieth century, when Afro-Caribbean ball players arrived in the U.S., they were able to perceive themselves as a group due to the colonial and postcolonial discourses that shaped their racial identity. These discourses gave specific meanings to "race" dependent on the particular nation's discourse.

In the Cuban case, although baseball developed as a space where a "racially mixed" and "socially diverse" population could pursue nation, Cuban politics of race suggested that there remained resistance towards such an ideal. Orestes "Minnie" Miñoso's recollection of his Cuban childhood relates the use of sport as a racially marked institution. Miñoso's autobiography revealed subtle forms of racist practices. Addressing time spent in Havana at the inception of his baseball career, Miñoso encountered privatized use of sport at the Vedado Tennis club. Thinking back on the club, and attempting to prove that Cuba did not represent a racial paradise, Miñoso wrote,

> It was a status symbol to belong to this Club. It was here tournaments were held to select the best amateur teams in Cuba, where I longed to one day play in the Amateur Cuban Series, . . . Many great Cuban stars went to the big leagues from the team represented here; . . . The status-conscious Vedado Tennis Club, alas, remained closed to me and many other Cubans, ball players and non-ball players, because they excluded blacks from membership.[50]

That the Vedado Tennis Club, where Cuban national teams were selected, excluded blacks, who formed a significant part of the Cuban population, appeared contradictory to Miñoso. Especially in the context of Cuban national identity, the delineation between rights and privilege based on color had little room within the articulation of a nonracial national identity. On the other hand, whites who implemented this exclusivity made it part of their hegemony, and as such, the sporting field continued as a site of contestation.

Which club a Caribbean player joined depended on his skills and the time period. During years the Negro Leagues operated, most Caribbean players performed on teams primarily composed of Cubans. Beginning with Molina's club in 1920, the Cuban Stars provided Caribbean talent with their initial Negro League experience. Prior to 1920, only exceptionally talented ball players such as Torriente and Méndez played for other ballclubs. In 1935, Pompez's Cuban Stars joined the Negro National League as the New York Cubans; the National League's revised formation created more jobs for Negro Leaguers as new franchises gained "major league" status.[51]

United States involvement in World War II effort contributed to the rising number of Caribbean talent in the Negro Leagues, as more African Americans either voluntarily joined or were drafted for military service or opted for jobs within the defense industry. Several teams like the Baltimore Elite Giants, the Indianapolis Clowns, and the Birmingham Black Barons-restocked their club rosters by signing Caribbean players. However, these were not "replacement" players. Much to the contrary, these clubs took advantage of talent they knew existed through their player's participation in Caribbean winter leagues.

■ *Game's Over, Now What: Forming Networks, Making Friends*

Formation of a community between Caribbean and African American Negro League players solely premised on race is quite tenuous and can become easily jeopardized. Inclusion of Afro-Caribbean players from three countries partly demonstrates the elusiveness of such a community. Yet race as a metalanguage in the trans-Atlantic world remains pivotal; wherever Caribbean ball players lived, the possibility existed that it could become a site of "dialogic exchange and contestation."[52] The formation of networks that did not privilege a rigid racial or cultural boundary enabled these men to confound the effectiveness of U.S. race ideology. These ball players empowered themselves through their networks, which allowed them to make informed and calculated decisions within the Americas, thereby avoiding certain pitfalls and creating alternate means.

When Rodolfo Fernández and his Cuban Stars teammates departed Cuba for the first time in 1932 and arrived in New York, things were already in order. Once in New York City, the twenty-one year old Fernández started to acclimate to his newfound surroundings. Fortunately, the Cuban Stars arranged his housing in Harlem, convenient to Spanish Harlem (Barrio Latino) and the Cuban Stars' "home" field, the Polo Grounds. Looking back on his first encounter with the North, Fernández spoke about the changes that he has seen in Harlem and the Barrio Latino:

> Considering the change it was to leave your own country and to find yourself in such a large place, and it is not as it is now, where a Latino arrives and wherever you go one can hear people talking in Spanish, at that time that did not occur. Although we did have the Barrio Latino-which had movie theaters, newspapers, it had everything, it still was quite difficult because there really were not many Latinos around during that time. Eventually, living here became like a routine.[53]

Far from the familiar spaces of Guanabacoa (Havana Province), Fernandez's quick ability to adapt to life in New York so that it soon became "a routine," partly arose from preparations made by team owner Pompez. These arrangements made, Fernández did not have to go "apartment-hopping" in an unfamiliar town. Rather, as he recalled,

> At that time, we lived in family-houses. One family would rent out two rooms, and another family would rent one room out; because that was a really difficult time period. We paid three dollars a week rent. But the ball players were not the only

ones who were earning very little money, those with the jobs here, many of them were only making seven or eight dollars a week.[54]

During the thirties, the Depression resounded throughout the Americas. Mostly, an arrangement of mutual convenience, housing arrangements made for the ball players exemplified two things: desperate economic conditions, and the establishment of networks. At twenty-five years old, Rafael Noble decided to pursue his professional career in the U.S. and joined the New York Cubans. As usual, Pompez handled housing arrangements.

Pompez's arrangements with independently owned family houses spanned several decades and revealed a multicultural network within the Harlem community. Playing with the Cubans from 1945 to 1948, the first family Noble lived with was Jamaican, and as he remembered, African-American homes constituted the majority of host families.[55] Thus, Pompez's ball players were situated into Harlem in a manner that led to development of connections within the African-American community.

Adjustment to life in the U.S. took on different forms depending on the individual and circumstance. In New York City, the existence of a Barrio Latino within Harlem eased the transition for those ball players on the Cuban Stars and the New York Cubans. For these men, living in a black community facilitated their ability to envision a common past and mutual interests. The Caribbean ball players' everyday experiences (living in Harlem and traveling throughout the country) quickened awareness of their assigned race, and provided them with a group (African Americans) with whom to share their collective experience. Sharing information—on popular spots, "shady" characters, and employment opportunities—throughout their careers, Caribbean and African American Negro Leaguers built a lasting network drawing from these experiences and continuing beyond retirement from professional baseball.

■ *Baseball as Skilled Contract Labor*

In 1946, entering his third year with the Indianapolis Clowns, Armando Vasquez's contract paid him $250 a month. Considering the constant travel and the few days off for Negro Leaguers, calculating this salary over a thirty- day work period, Vasquez's daily earnings stood at $8.33 a day.[56] Taking into account that the Negro League season lasted eight months from March to October this daily wage held. However, extending the salary over an entire year—a six-day work week and a two-week paid vacation—this daily wage fell to $6.67. Thus, for many Negro Leaguers it was necessary to play ball throughout the year or work an off-season job to maintain their standard of living. For Caribbean players, local pressures to play winter ball and its consideration as a "honor, especially for their hometown" resulted in their making substantially less than their counterparts.

The issues of economics and racial climate within a player's employment decision-making figured central in the case of Perucho Cepeda. A native Puerto Rican born in San Juan in 1905, Cepeda and his son Orlando represent Puerto Rico's greatest father-son tandem. Both are enshrined in the Island's Hall of Fame. Pursued many times by Negro League teams, especially by Pompez, the elder Cepeda never left the Caribbean.

Able to gain stable employment with a local city government in Puerto Rico, Cepeda enjoyed the security of a year-round job that allowed him to work and play professional ball. This flexibility placed Cepeda in a special category of Afro-Caribbean ball players. Remembering the winter league scene, Rodolfo Fernández remarked:

> I had the fortune to know outside the American ball players, many of the good Latino ball players: Coímbre, Tetelo Vargas, Peruchin [Orlando] and his father, Perucho with whom I played with on the 1937 Ciudad Trujillo team. But his father never came to the United States because at that time we really did not make a lot of money. And then, if somebody had a really good job, he did not leave it to play baseball, because he could play every Sunday. . .Those people, they did not live off baseball. In Cuba, there were some really good ball players that were recruited (offered contracts) to play in the United States, but they would not accept the

offers because they had jobs that paid more than professional ball. At that time, professional was in name only, it is not like today.[57]

The differential in players' winter league salaries partly arose from team quotas on the number of U.S.-born players *(refuerzos)*. Therefore, winter leagues teams aggressively pursued the best available talent. Plainly stated, the winter leagues became an African American players' market.[58] In his autobiography, Negro Leaguer Wilmer Fields, veteran of more than ten Caribbean and Latin American campaigns, reiterated the importance for African-American players to secure a winter league position:

> But I can see why other ball players would press the owners for more money: they didn't have employment during the winter months in Latin American countries. Not everyone could make it down there, and you better believe if you didn't produce you didn't last long.[59]

What Fields's passage failed to illuminate is the pivotal role Caribbean players took within this push for winter employment. Many times, up-and-coming players entered the winter months without jobs and relied on Caribbean teammates or managers to serve as their agents. This relationship worked for Joe Black. A young pitcher with the Baltimore Elite Giants, toward the end of the 1950 season, Black asked "Rudy" Fernández to keep him in mind. Sure enough, after a tournament in Venezuela, Fernández, now a manager, brought his team back to Cuba and became aware of a position that was available on another team, and Black gained winter employment.[60]

Fernández's experience attested to the fact some friendships formed during the Negro Leagues continued to serve as a link to the past as well as affirming the bonds between Caribbean ball players and the African American community. Visiting with Armando Vásquez, he shared old photo albums with pictures of him and his fellow ball players—both Caribbean and African American—at various functions and social gatherings. Citing the particular occasions, an especially important gathering in Vasquez's opinion was the annual reunion games in Union City, New Jersey.[61] Held for more than ten years, these games featured retired Cuban, some Puerto Ricans, and ball players from Negro League and major league baseball. These reunions often brought out big stars of the Cuban entertainment community such as the *gran salsera* Celia Cruz. Historically speaking, these reunion games served as a ritualistic space for the affirmation of the community's Cuban, and Latino, identity.

Despite major league baseball's color line, which separated members of the Caribbean community, these ball players still maintained contact across the racial divide. It was not, however, a simple endeavor. Many Negro League teams rented major league stadiums and scheduled their home games when Major League teams were on the road. For example, the New York Cubans shared the Polo Grounds with the New York Giants, which meant that these ball players rarely had a chance to interact. On the other hand, since the Dodgers resided in Brooklyn, this gave players on either side of the color line opportunity to meet. Fernández explained how he kept in contact with Adolfo Luque and Miguel Angel Gonzalez, two Cubans who enjoyed long major league careers, during the season:

> When I first arrived to the United States Luque played with the New York Giants and Miguel Angel played with the Cardinals. During that time they only played day games, and after the games Luque would come from the Polo Grounds and come to visit "La dulceria de Simon," a Cuban candy maker who had a place on Lenox and 114th street, and then stop in to visit. . . . He [Miguel] would come many times during the afternoon right here to the Barrio. One day I went out to Ebbets Field, waited around after the game because Miguel Angel had told me to wait for him after the game, and afterwards we took the subway and talked. Consequently, I saw him several times because I had recommended him several black ball players for his Club Havana.[62]

While Caribbean players worked at maintaining friendships and national identity, they also undertook another project. Through their daily interactions, Afro-Caribbean players cultivated a better understanding of the peculiar behavior and responses inherent to U.S. racial ideology. Though most could not speak the language at first—I refer here to both English and the metalanguage of race in U.S. terms—they observed and learned ways to negotiate race. So, for example, after his first year often ordering the same meal since he spoke very little English, Armando Vásquez plotted a strategy that put him in position to get what he wanted, food.

Drawing on these experiences, Vásquez noted "in certain places I had the good fortune that since I did not know the language, [when] I would arrive at restaurants where they would not serve black people, and I would arrive speaking in Spanish and they would serve me."[63] On recognition that Spanish served as a marker of difference, so that he became transformed in the eyes of the person serving—from black to something different—Vásquez made sure to speak only in Spanish when he arrived at restaurants. This realization soon worked to the entire team's benefit, becoming part of the team's arsenal. Attempting to offset racial perceptions, teams sometimes drafted an Afro-Caribbean player to order food at known spots where "blacks" were denied services.

■ *Were They Really Here? Reflections*

For some Afro-Caribbean ball players, racial conditions in the U.S. provoked serious concerns. In the cases of major league all-stars Luis Tiant Jr. and Orlando Cepeda, their fathers had already encountered the societal path dictated by U.S. racial ideology. In 1975, after being denied exit visas from Cuba for two decades, Luis "Lefty" Tiant Sr. returned to the U.S. Still sporting the skinny legs on his almost frail physique, Tiant tossed the opening pitch at a Red Soxs' game, then settled in to watch his son, Luis Jr., pitch for the first time since the Cuban revolution. Afterwards, reporters asked "Lefty" Tiant whether he had encouraged his son to play baseball. The elder Tiant, veteran of more than ten seasons with the New York Cubans, reflecting on those years and the separation from his son, responded "I didn't want Luis to pitch . . . I didn't want him to come to America. I didn't want him to be persecuted and spit on and treated like garbage like I was."[64]

Orlando Cepeda's father, "Perucho," made the conscious decision to avoid the U.S. scene entirely. Cepeda's employment status played a major part in his decision, but in his choice he also recognized the racial climate in the States. In 1941, Pompez came closest to getting Cepeda to play in the U.S., even listing him on the Cubans' roster. Orlando Cepeda remembered his father's career and rationale for never venturing North:

> Never, though he was asked time and again, would he play a game of baseball in the United States. How could a man be as great a ballplayer as my father and not want to accept the fine offers he received from the States?
>
> ...I can remember him bringing Satchel Paige and Josh Gibson, the greatest pitcher and the greatest catcher who ever lived, to our house in Ponce, and I can remember them telling me what a great player my father was.
>
> But there was discrimination against Puerto Rican ball players in the United States, and my father would not play there. Even in the final years of his life, when he still was playing ball and the discrimination (so they told him) had disappeared, he would not set foot in the States.[65]

Similar to "Lefty" Tiant, racial conditions appeared so harmful and alienating that Cepeda simply refused to head north. Informed by African-American Negro Leaguers, Cepeda did not fantasize about life in the States. Rather, information he received indicated it was not worth leaving his job and family to pursue his professional career in the States.

Approaching the end of their ballplaying careers, a number of concerns enter their minds. Along with the fear of embarrassing themselves by becoming a "hanger-on," transition to everyday life effected these men in varying ways. For the majority of Negro Leaguers, "retirement" meant reentering the black community as workers. This transition was eased by the networks they had developed during their career. Thus, many of the jobs they obtained resulted from their network of kin, friends, and community contacts. During the mid-1940s, some ball players took advantage of U.S. wartime economic expansion which opened jobs previously forbidden to women and blacks. Yet, although employment opportunities increased, the type of employment available to them imparted their position within American society.

After their professional days, employment opportunities for Negro Leaguers conveyed how race continued to influence their economic lives. More specifically, it reflected American society's overall structure. The manner in which these men obtained their jobs disclosed ethnic links and usage of informal networks. In example, following his last season in Mexico, Vásquez returned to New York City and began work at a Bronx toy factory arranged through a friend. After his 11-year professional playing career, Fernández managed several years in the Caribbean. Yet, when he finally chose to settle down, his connections brought his return to New York. Like the community network Pompez employed to house his players, the network of friends these men relied on as connections demonstrated how the networks continued to fulfill their needs after their professional careers.

■ *Post-Game Wrap-Up*

This project does not propose to naturalize or essentialize difference among people of the African diaspora in the Americas; rather, it acknowledges that these ball players came to the United States as racial beings and endeavors to demonstrate the manner that they maneuvered through race as an idea. This idea functioned to unite the Afro-Caribbean and African American ball players through the notion of a shared, common historical past. Moreover, in their encounter with U.S. racial ideology, these ball players empowered themselves through the development of strategies, often carried out through networks, that disrupted racial constructs. Understanding that phenotypical features often formed an individual's perception of race, the strategies they employed manipulated these perceptions to extract services denied to "blacks."

The sum of these experiences for Afro-Caribbean ball players does not represent evasion from their assigned racial group—for example, "a mulatto escape hatch" whereby they gained whiteness.[66] Much to the contrary, Caribbean ball players on either side of the color line were subjected to racialized treatment. Yet, despite living in the U.S. for more than four decades, the ball players interviewed held strongly to their national identity and continued to understand "race" as supplemental in the construction of an individual's identity, although not in the totality of an individual's social and racial interactions. Thus, they still referred to U.S.-born individuals as *"Americanos"* in the first instance and reverted to phenotypical distinctions *"blanco"* or *"negro"* to explicate differential treatment.

These ball players' experiences testify to the permeability of race. This study rooted in their everyday activities, provides a purview into the world of those who did not fit neatly into the dominant racial paradigm in the U.S.—they were neither "black" nor "white" as so defined in U.S. racial terms. Racial assignment divided Caribbean ball players onto either side of the existing racial fault line. However, their everyday behaviors demonstrate that they did not sit idly, but rather negotiated racial constructs and manipulated "difference" to better their daily lives. ■

The list of acknowledgments of those who lent support to this paper is endless. Yet, failure "de dar respeto" would be a great offense. In this vein, I would like to acknowledge Rodolfo Fernández, Armando Vásquez, Rafael Noble, Melvin Duncan and Chester Gray for sharing part of their life experiences. Also, thanks to Dick Clark who placed me in contact with the aforementioned; the National Baseball Hall of Fame Library and Archives' staff, especially Scot Mondore, Tim Wiles and Greg Harris; John McKiernan Gonzales, Doris Dixon and Wilson Valentín helped me edit and think out loud, and Dolly Túa, who assisted in the translation of Spanish articles and lent emotional stability throughout. Finally, my professors from the African Diaspora seminar, Earl Lewis and Fred Cooper, and members of CENTRO's editorial board, who shared their scholarly advice in this paper's development.

ENDNOTES

1. Jesus Sanabria, a Puerto Rican graduate student from the Island, shared this childhood memory of Canelito. He could not recall Canelito's proper name but stated that he was quiet and unassuming within the village's social life. That this student only remembered this man by his nickname Canelito, a derivative of the Spanish word for cinnamon and reflective of his skin color, speaks to the construction of identity and race in public memory.

2. Personal Interview with Rafael Noble, February 24, 1995, Brooklyn, New York. During his pro career, Noble enjoyed a unique trifecta, playing on championship teams in the Caribbean World Series (Cuba, 1956), Negro League World Series (New York Cubans, 1947), and Major League Baseball (Giants, 1951). Note all interviews conducted in Spanish were translated into English by Adrian Burgos.

3. In the context of this study, Afro-Caribbean reflects the countries from which these ball players originate Cuba, Puerto Rico, and the Dominican Republic. However, I will often use Caribbean which includes Afro-Caribbean because it is often difficult to distinguish the two in terms of "race" and acknowledge the manner that these men subverted the efficacy of these categories to better their economic and social lives.

4. For a work that discusses issues of the African Diaspora, in this instance relating to a trans-Atlantic British-Caribbean circuit, see Paul Gilroy, *The Black Atlantic: Modernity and Double Consciousness* (Cambridge, Massachusetts: Harvard University Press, 1993).

5. For the purpose of this study, a community may be defined as an aggregate group of individuals who recognize or acknowledge some commonalty (an idea, ancestry, or geographic location) and organize themselves within a set of boundaries; moreover, individuals and/or forces, both internal and external, undertake the dynamic processes of negotiation and contestation that complicate the limits and result in the fluidity of such boundaries.

6. The application of everydayness to writing social history is wonderfully explicated in Thomas Holt's "Marking: Race, Race-Making, and the Writing of History," American Historical Review 100 (February 1995): 1–20. Vital to this project is Holt's assertion that in everydayness, "race is reproduced via the marking of the racial Other and that racist ideas and practices are naturalized, made self-evident, and thus seemingly beyond audible change. It is at this level that race is reproduced long after its original historical stimulus-the slave trade and slavery-have faded. It is at this level that seemingly rational and ordinary folks commit irrational and extraordinary acts," p. 7.

7. Although the Negro Leagues have enjoyed a revival of sorts, the literature produced still lacks a complex, substantial treatment of Caribbean participants. Surely, language difference presented an obstacle for many investigations; however, during their careers Caribbean and African American ball players dealt with this challenge. This present article is part of a larger project that attempts to historicize the participation of Caribbean players in North American professional baseball, looking at issues of race and identity formation, especially as related through the memory of those involved. The seminal text on the Negro League is Robert Peterson, *Only the Ball Was White* (New York: Oxford University Press, 1970). Also see Donn Rogosinn, *Invisible Men* (New York: Athenum, 1983). Peterson dedicated chapter eight to Rube Foster and the organization of the Negro National League, pp. 103–115. On Major League Baseball's integration see Peterson's chapter fourteen "Emancipation Proclamation", p. 183–205; and Jules Tygiel, *Baseball's Greatest Experiment* (New York: Oxford University Press, 1983). For general reference on the Negro League teams and players, see James Riley, The Biographical Encyclopedia of the Negro Baseball Leagues (New York: Carroll & Graf Publishers, 1994). (Hereafter cited as The Biographical Encyclopedia).

8. It is important to understand the lives of these individuals as being influenced by as well as helping to shape the politics of the community. As professional ball players, they had the opportunity to travel throughout the Americas, and transmit information of a social, cultural, and political nature. And, as argued throughout this paper, baseball was definitely part of the Latino community's cultural milieu in the U.S. and the various Caribbean countries. For a discussion that focuses on how understanding political generations influence the shape of a group's politics, see Roberto Rodriguez-Morazzani, "Puerto Rican Political Generations in New York: Pioneros, Young Turks, and Radicals," *Boletín del Centro de Estudios Puertorriqueños* vol. IV, no. 1 (Winter 91–92): 96–116.

9. Archival materials at the National Baseball Hall of Fame Library & Archive (hereafter NBHFLA), include the Ashland Collection that contains the indexed research notes of Robert Peterson. Gleaning from a May 20, 1909 article in the New York Age, Peterson listed the Cuban Giants roster: it contained no ballplayer with a Hispanic surname. On the other hand, the Cuban Stars roster contained only Hispanic surnames. See also Peterson *Only the Ball Was White,* p. 36; and Rob Ruck's *The Sandlot Seasons: Sport in Black Pittsburgh* (Westport, CT: Meckler Publishing, 1993), p. 66.

10. Written in 1949, Ildefonso Ortega's article "Historia Del Club Almendares" stated that Almendares' Club founder, Doctor Carlos Zaldo, picked up the game while studying at Fordham University and formed the club upon his return to Cuba. Negro League Folder, "Magazine 'Fotos' from Puerto Rico," Ashland Collection, NBHFLA. The first known professional Cuban ballplayer in the U.S., Esteban Bellán, played on the Troy Haymakers (NY) in 1871, having already played for Rose Hill College while studying at Fordham. See Daniel C. Frio and Marc Onigman, "'Good Field, No Hit': The Image of Latin American Baseball Players in the American Press, 1871–1946," Revista/Review Interamericana (1979): 199–208. In their study, Frio and Onigman focused on a select number of Latin American-born ball players as a distinct group and investigate the development of the "Good Field, No Hit" image. They noted that their approach sought to avoid "inherent methodological dangers involved in trying to classify players using only last names as criteria." However, the manner that race helped to construct the media's perception of these ball players remained outside their analysis. For more on Esteban Bellán, see Esteban Bellán Biographical File, NBHFLA. For a nuanced discussion of baseball's early period in Cuba and its development, see Louis A. Pérez Jr., "Between Baseball and Bullfighting: The Quest for Nationality in Cuba, 1868–1898," The Journal of American History (September 1994): 493–517.

11. For example, due to constant migration from the Dominican Republic to Puerto Rico, and other Caribbean islands to a lesser extent, nation is also losing its effectiveness as foundational in how we understand identity. Consider the following concerns: Is identity bound by geography? If so, how do we begin to explain the maintenance of Puerto Rican identity by those living stateside and their children reared on the mainland? And what of children born in Puerto Rico to Dominican parents, especially those without American citizenship: are they Puerto Rican? Dominican? American?

12. For one of the first scholarly treatments of this concern, see Clara Rodríguez, "Puerto Ricans: Between Black and White," New York Affairs 1:4 (1973): 97–101.

13. Michael Omi and Howard Winant theorized the concept of "racial formation" citing its origins in the US Civil Rights Movement and the nation's subsequent racial politics. Concisely, they defined racial formation as "the sociohistorical process by which racial categories are created, inhabited, transformed, and destroyed." Omi and Winant, *Racial Formations in the United States* (Philadelphia: Temple University Press, 1991), p. 55. On multipositionality, see Earl Lewis, "Invoking Concepts, Problematizing Identities," Labor History 34 (Spring/Summer1993): 292–308.

14. For a work that attempts to deal with Latinos as a distinct group ('race') in baseball, but fails to delve into race as a social construction thereby leading to misguided conclusions, see Peter Bjarkmann's *Baseball with a Latin Beat* (Jefferson, NC: McFarland Company, 1994). Bjarkmann cites Cuban Jose Acosta and Jack Calvo as the only two Caribbean players to play in both the Major League and Negro League circuits. At this point in my research, I have located ten.

15. Bithorn's Major League career spanned seven seasons; however, Bithorn served two of these years in the US Navy. After Hernandez played for the Cubs during these two seasons, he also played in Mexico before joining the Clowns. Personal Interview with Armando Vasquez; New York, NY: February 20, 1995. Interview. For more on the careers of Bithorn and Hernandez, see Hiram Bithorn Biographical File, NBHFLA; and Salvador "Chico" Hernandez Biographical File, NBHFLA.

16. Bjarkmann, *Baseball With a Latin Beat*, p. 194.

17. Each club was permitted to have a limited number (usually three or four) of refuerzos, this category being players who were not native-born Puerto Ricans. Eventually, "NuyoRicans," that is Puerto Ricans born in New York, were considered native players and were not counted against a team's allotment of refuerzos. Conversations with Luis Alvelo (Caguas, Puerto Rico, June 1995). Alvelo is a native Puerto Rican baseball historian, member of SABR's Negro League

Committee, and possesses one of the widest personal collections of material on Puerto Rico's Winter Leagues. I am much indebted for his assistance.

18. Riley, *The Biographical Encyclopedia,* p. 801. Vargas later played for the Milwaukee Braves in 1955, seven years after he began his career in the Negro League.

19. See Daniel C. Frio and Marc Onigman, "'Good Field, No Hit',"passim.

20. Newspaper clipping, "Olmo a Puerto Rican," The Sporting News (April 18, 1940) in Luis Rodriguez Olmo Biographical File, NBHFLA.

21. For a discussion of the processes whereby phenotype becomes normalized within different societies, see Peter Wade, "'Race', Nature and Culture," Man 28: 17–34.

22. For a discussion of the Race War of 1912, see Aline Helg, *Our Rightful Share: The Afro-Cuban Struggle for Equality, 1886–1912* (Chapel Hill: University of North Carolina Press, 1995).

23. Ruck, *The Tropic of Baseball*, p. 52–53. On Hispanidad see Pedro L. San Miguel, "Discurso racial e identidad nacional en la Republica Dominicana," Op. Cit. 7 (1992): 68–120.

24. Another possible reason contributing to the absence of Dominican talent, the Dominican Republic operated its own summer league from 1930 to 1937 in competition with the Negro League. Ironically, the drive for excellence produced both the strongest team composed of Negro League talent, Ciudad Trujillo, and helped to bankrupt the league due to Trujillo's exorbitant spending on player contracts. After this seven-year summer league experiment, the Dominican league returned to a winter schedule.

25. Felipe Alou and Herman Weiskopf, *Felipe Alou…My Life and Baseball* (Waco, TX: Word Books, 1967), p. 29.

26. Ibid., p. 103.

27. Starting in 1923, two teams operated under the name Cuban Stars: Molina's team, referred to as Cuban Stars West, remained in the Negro National League, while Alejandro Pompez's Cuban Stars formally joined the Eastern Colored League and designated Cuban Stars East. Todd Bolton, "Beisbol Behind the Veil: Latin Americans in the Negro Leagues," Ragtyme Sports (December 1994), p. 23.

28. John Holway, *Blackball Stars* (Westport, CT: Meckler Publishing, 1988), p. 126. Torriente's playing career spanned three decades from the 1900s to the 1930s, and included stints with the Chicago American Giants, Cuban Stars, and Detroit Stars.

29. The Detroit Tigers toured Cuba during the winter of 1909 and 1910; in the latter year, Ty Cobb refused to travel south with the team to play against Cuban teams. Michael M. Oleksak and Mary Adams Oleksak, *Beisbol: Latin Americans and the Grand Old Game* (Grand Rapids, MI: Masters Press, 1991), p. 20–22.

30. Writing that a ballplayer said "I'm hokay" instead of "I'm okay" is one example of such a 'phonetic' translation. For a discussion of language in the Puerto Rican experience in New York, see Juan Flores, John Attinasi, and Pedro Pedraza, "Puerto Rican Language and Culture in New York City" Caribbean Life in New York City (New York: Center of Migration Studies of New York, 1987): 221–234.

31. Holway, Blackball Stars, p. 56. Drawing from John McGraw's quote that "Méndez would be worth $50,000 'if' he was white" in the Chicago Defender, Robert Peterson commented "It is a funny proposition, but at that John McGraw knows a player and he tried to play [Charlie] Grant at second base but was blocked by Cap Anson of Chicago, who succeeded in barring the dark face out of the major leagues." Research Notes etc. "Possibly from R. Peterson," Ashland Collection, NBHFLA. The Defender article is from August 1912.

32. Frio and Onigman, "Good Field, No Hit," p. 203.

33. Bak, Turkey Stearnes and the Detroit Stars, p. 133–4.

34. Personal Interview with Fernández, February 22, 1995, New York, NY. Riley, *The Biographical Encyclopedia,* p. 788. This is not the only instance when the Caribbean community pooled their resources to return a ballplayer to his native land. Riley reported that this also occurred for Puerto Rican Tomas Quiñones in the 1970s. Ibid., p. 646.

35. Holway, *Blackball Stars,* p. 58. For a history of the Monarchs, see Janet Bruce, *Kansas City Monarchs* (Lawrence: University Press of Kansas, 1985).

36. Research Notes etc. "Possibly from R. Peterson," Ashland Collection, NBHFLA.

37. Ibid.

38. Evelyn Brooks Higginbotham, "The Metalanguage of Race," Signs: Journal of Women in Culture and Society 17 (1992) : 251–274.

39. Ibid., p. 252.

40. This draws heavily from Omi and Winant's reading of Gramsci's concept of hegemony, which they state may be understood as "the conditions necessary, in any given society, for the achievement and consolidation of rule... Although rule can be obtained by force, it cannot be secured and maintained, especially in modern society, without the element of consent... [Moreover], in order to consolidate their hegemony, ruling groups must elaborate and maintain a popular system of ideas and practices-through education, the media, religion, folk wisdom, etc.-which he called 'common sense.' It is through this production and its adherence to this 'common sense,' this ideology (in the broadest sense of the term), that a society gives its consent to the way in which it is ruled." Michael Omi and Howard Winant, Racial Formations in the United States (Philadelphia: Temple University Press, 1991), p. 66–67.

41. Earl Lewis, "Race, the State, and Social Construction" forthcoming in Stanley I. Kutler ed. Encyclopedia of the United States in the Twentieth Century (New York: Simon and Schuster, 1995): 1–89. For another reading of US race ideology, see Barbara Jeanne Fields, "Slavery, Race and Ideology in the United States of America" New Left Review, 181 (1990): 95–118.

42. Lewis, "Race, the State, and Social Construction," p. 2–3.

43. For an in-depth discussion of the race and its material existence, see Eduardo Bonilla-Silva, "Rethinking Racism: Towards a Structural Interpretation," CRSO Working Paper # 526 (October 1994).

44. Omi and Winant laid out this process in Chapter 4, "Racial Formation" pp. 53-76. Concisely, they defined racial formation as "the sociohistorical process by which racial categories are created, inhabited, transformed, and destroyed." Racial Formations in the United States, p. 55

45. Both Fernández and Vásquez stated that they began training in carpentry, but that it was difficult to secure such training in Cuba; sometimes connections had to be employed in order to secure such training. As Fernández remembered, "During that time period [the Depression years in Cuba] families would have one son learn carpentry, the other tailoring, and another to be a barber. You see for Latinos, it was not like here if you're a carpenter that is all you are; and if you are a plumber that is all you do. In the Latin countries, they had to learn all different skills."

46. This perception of Cubans as ambassadors arose from a conversation with a Mexican semi-professional ballplayer who, during the 1940s, played against and saw many Negro Leaguers in Mexico City. Phone interview with Señor Martinez, December 10, 1994. For a study on the origins of baseball in Yúcatan, see Gilbert Joseph, "Forging the Regional Pastime: Baseball and Class in Yúcatan," Joseph Arbena ed. *Sport and Society in Latin America: Diffusions, Dependency, and the Rise of Mass Culture* (Westport, CT: Meckler Publishing, 1988): 29–61.

47. Pérez, "Between Baseball and Bullfighting," p. 494. Addressing those who may question the use of sport as a mode of resistance, Louis Pérez argues: "[A]lthough any given sport may arrive in a country loaded with moral codes and normative imperatives, the meaning and use assigned to those imported values respond to a wide range of local social constructions and political needs. A sport can serve as an instrument of empire and a means of social control, but in another place and at a different time, it can readily serve as a source of liberation and a means of nationality." Ibid., p. 494. Trinidadian C.L.R. James advanced a similar argument in Trinidad's use of cricket in their struggle against the colonial Great Britain *in Beyond a Boundary* (Durham, NC: Duke University Press, 1994). See also Frank E. Manning, "Celebrating Cricket: Symbolic Construction of Caribbean Politics," American Ethnologist 8 (August 1981): 616–632.

48. Pérez, "Between Baseball and Bullfighting," p. 509.

49. Pérez covered the game's spread in the 1890s on pages 514–17 of "Between Baseball and Bullfighting." Rob Ruck discussed Cubans that fled the island for the Dominican Republic in his chapter "Apostles of Baseball" in *The Tropic of Baseball* (Westport, CT: Meckler Publishing, 1991), pp. 1–16.

50. Orestes "Minnie" Miñoso with Fernando Fernandez and Bob Kleinfelder, *Extra Innings: My Life in Baseball* (Chicago: Regnery Gateway, 1983), p. 21.

51. Todd Bolton, "Pompez' Greatest Aggregation: The 1935 New York Cubans," unpublished paper, p. 1.

52. Higginbotham, "Metalanguage of Race," p. 252.

53. Fernández Interview. For a literary study that looks at life in El Barrio (Latino) retold in Puerto Rican autobiographies, see Eugene Mohr, *The Nuyorican Experience* (Westport, CT: Greenwood Press, 1982). Among autobiographies that describe this experience are Piri Thomas, *Down These Mean Streets* (New York: Alfred P. Knopf, 1967); and Edward Rivera, *Family Installments: Memories of Growing Up Hispanic* (New York: William Morrow and Company, 1982).

54. Ibid. Focusing on the Detroit Stars, Richard Bak provided a similar picture based on the information he collected through oral interview and periodical accounts. Bak stated, "Ball players encountered little trouble finding a place to park their pillow. The clubs usually found them a bachelor apartment a short trolley ride from the park, or else introduced them to a family thrilled to have a ballplayer under their roof. As a rule, a player's salary and status allowed him to live in the more fashionable, less congested section of black Detroit." Bak, *Turkey Stearnes and the Detroit Stars,* p. 126.

55. Noble Interview. When Pompez began to secure housing arrangements for his ball players remains to be documented, but its importance is that it dates the establishment of networks between Caribbean (Latinos) and African Americans within the Harlem community.

56. During the interview with Vásquez, he showed me this contract that he has maintained in his possession, (February 21, 1995). In comparison, during that year, major league baseball's yearly minimum salary stood at $5,000 ($625 per month); and the mean salary averaged $11,294 (approximately $1,400 per month). "Average Player Tops $891,000," New York Times, April 10, 1991.

57. Fernández Interview.

58. Although white players went south to for Caribbean winter ball, I say an "African American player's market" because of the substantial difference in salaries between the major leagues and Negro Leagues. Thus, not only were African Americans a "hot" commodity, they also personally enjoyed the capacity to earn substantially higher monthly salaries than during their regular seaon monthly.

59. Wilmer Fields, *My Life in the Negro Leagues: An Autobiography by Wilmer Fields*, (Westport, CT: Meckler Publishing, 1992), p. 24.

60. Black went on to impress the team's manager, Brooklyn Dodgers second basemen Billy Herman, who contacted the Dodgers front office, leading to their signing of Black. Fernandez Interview.

61. A public television channel from Milwaukee, WMVS, filmed part of their documentary "Jonron: A Look at Baseball's Immortal Latinos" (1983) during one of these reunion games. Among those in attendance were Minnie Miñoso, Armando Vázquez, Rubén Amaro, Manuel "Cocaina" García and Adrian Zabala. This documentary is part of the Film, and Recorded Sound Collection, NBHFLA. Vázquez showed me a picture of Celia Cruz who had come to the game. Vázquez Interview. Fernández added that other Negro League and Major League ball players, non-Cuban, would also participate at times. In particular, he recalled visits by José "Pantalones" Santiago (Puerto Rican), Victor Pellot y Power (Puerto Rican), Roberto Avila (Mexican), and Sam Jethroe (African American).

62. Fernandez Interview. Interestingly, before his twenty-year major league career, Adolfo Luque played on two Negro League teams, the Cuban Stars (1912) and Long Branch Cubans (1913).

63. Vásquez Interview. Pedro Formenthal offers a similar response. Extremely troubled by the racial climate in the U.S., Formenthal preferred playing in Latin American countries; while playing for

the Memphis Red Sox, Formenthal "demonstrated his disdain for the prevailing social conditions by using Cuban passport to dine at a white restaurant in Dallas, Texas." Riley, The Biographical Encyclopedia, p. 289.

64. Luis Tiant Jr. Biographical File, NBHFLA.

65. Orlando Cepeda with Charles Einstein, *My Ups and Downs in Baseball* (NY: G. P. Putnam's Sons, 1968), pp. 26–27. The elder Cepeda died at an early age, forty-nine years old. His nickname Perucho means the Bull in Spanish. The information about Pompez's recruitment is from Riley, *The Biographical Encyclopedia,* p. 162.

66. Carl Degler proposed this concept of "mulatto escape hatch" when discussing Brazil's racial history in *Neither Black Nor White: Slavery and Race Relations in Brazil and the United States* (New York: MacMillan Company, 1971).

PRIMARY SOURCES

Collections

Ashland Collection: National Baseball Hall of Fame Library & Archive, Cooperstown, NY.

Research Notes, etc., "Possibly from Robert Peterson," Ashland Collection.

• Player Files:

Francisco "Pancho" Coímbre File. Luis "Canena" Marquez File.

Martin Dihigo File. Luis "Lefty" Tiant Sr. File.

National Baseball Hall of Fame Library & Archive Biographical Collection.

• Biographical Files:

Hiram Bithorn File. Luis Rodriguez Olmo File.

Minnie Minoso File. Luis Tiant Jr. File.

• Negro League Box.

Spanish Articles on the Negro Leagues File.

Negro League Newspaper Clippings, 1930–1960 File.

Negro League Newspaper Clippings, 1990 to Present File.

•Film and Video, "Recorded Sound Collection."

"Jonron: A Look at Baseball Immortal Latinos" 1983 documentary, WMVS, Milwaukee.

Interviews

Personal interview with Rodolfo Fernández. New York, NY: February 22,1995.

Personal interview with Rafael "Ray" Noble. Brooklyn, NY: February 24, 1995.

Personal interview with Armando Vázquez. New York, NY: February 20, 1995.

REFERENCES

Alou, Felipe and Herman Weiskopf, Felipe Alou . . . *My Life and Baseball*. Waco, TX: Word Books, 1967.

Cepeda, Orlando with Charles Einstein. *My Ups and Downs in Baseball*. New York. G. P. Putnam's Sons, 1968.

Fields, Wilmer with John Holway. *My Life in The Negro Leagues*. Westport, CT: Meckler Books, 1992.

Holway, John B. *Blackball Star: Negro League Pioneers*. Westport, CT: Meckler Publishing, 1988.

—. *Black Diamonds*. Westport, CT: Meckler Publishing, 1989.

Miñoso, Orestes "Minnie" with Fernando Fernandez and Bob Kleinfelder. *Extra Innings: My Life in Baseball*. Chicago: Regnery Gateway, 1983.

Minoso, Minnie with Herb Fagen. *Just Call Me Minnie: My Six Decades in Baseball*.Champaign, IL: Sagamore Publishing, 1994.

Rosa, Wilfredo. "Francisco Coimbre, gloria del béisbol de Puerto Rico," El Boricua: Organo Oficial de la Federacion de Pueblos de Puerto Rico, no. 2 (December 1993): 24.

Unsigned. "Average Player Tops $891,000," New York Times (April 10, 1991).

Secondary Sources on Baseball and Sport

Arbena, Joseph, ed. *Sport and Society in Latin America: Diffusion, Dependency, and the Rise of Mass Culture*. New York: Greenwood Press, 1988.

Bak, Richard. Turkey Stearnes and the Detroit Stars: *The Negro Leagues in Detroit 1919–1933*. Detroit, MI: Wayne State University Press, 1994.

Bolton, Todd. "Beisbol Behind the Veil: Latin Americans in the Negro Leagues," Ragtyme Sports (December 1994): 23–25.

—. "Pompez' Greatest Aggregation: The 1935 New York Cubans," unpublished paper.

Bjarkmann, Peter. *Baseball with a Latin Beat*. Jefferson, NC: McFarland Company, 1994.

Frio, Daniel C. and Marc Onigman. "'Good Field, No Hit': The Image of Latin American Baseball Players in the American Press, 1876–1946," Revista/Review Interamericana (1979): 199–208.

Pérez, Louis A. "Between Baseball and Bullfighting: The Quest for Nationality in Cuba, 1868–1898," *The Journal of American History* (September 1994): 493–517.

Oleksak, Michael M., and Mary Adams Oleksak. *Beísbol: Latin Americans and the Grand Old Game*. Grand Rapids, MI: Masters Press, 1991.

Onigman, Marc and Daniel Frio. "Baseball Triumphs of Latin Players Obscured by Ethnic Slurs, Jokes," *The Washington Post* (March 5, 1978).

Peterson, Robert. *Only the Ball Was White*. New York: Oxford University Press, 1992.

Riley, James A. *The Biographical Encyclopedia of the Negro Baseball Leagues*. New York: Carroll & Graf Publishers, 1994.

—. *Dandy, Day, and the Devil*. Cocoa Beach, FL: TK Publishers, 1987.

Ruck, Rob. *The Tropic of Baseball*. Westport, CT: Meckler Publishing, 1991.

Tygiel, Jules. *Baseball's Greatest Experiment*. New York: Oxford University Press, 1983.

Van Hyning, Thomas. *Puerto Rico's Winter League: A History of Major League Baseball's Launching Pad*. Jefferson, NC: McFarland & Co., 1995.

Sources on Race and Identity in the Transatlantic World

Bonilla-Silva, Eduardo. "Rethinking Racism: Towards a Structural Interpretation," CRSO Working Paper # 526 (October 1994).

Degler, Carl. *Neither Black Nor White: Slavery and Race Relations in Brazil and the United States*. New York: MacMillan Company, 1971.

Fields, Barbara Jeanne. "Slavery, Race and Ideology in the United States of America." New Left Review 181 (1990): 95–118.

Flores, Juan. *Divided Borders: Essays on Puerto Rican Identity*. Houston: Arte Público Press, 1993.

González, José Luis. Puerto Rico: *The Four Storeyed Country*, trans. Gerald Guinness. New York: Markus Wiener Publishing, 1993.

Helg, Aline. *Our Rightful Share: The Afro-Cuban Struggle for Equality, 1886–1912*. Chapel Hill: University of North Carolina Press, 1995.

Higginbotham, Evelyn Brooks. "The Metalanguage of Race," *Signs: Journal of Women in Culture and Society* 17, no. 2 (Winter 1992): 251–274.

Holt, Thomas. "Marking: Race, Race-Making, and the Writing of History," *The Journal of American History* 100, (February 1995): 1–20.

Lewis, Earl. "Race, the State and Social Construction." forthcoming in *Encyclopedia of the United States in the Twentieth Century.* New York: Simon and Schuster, 1995.

Mohr, Eugene. *The Nuyorican Experience*. Westport, CT: Greenwood Press, 1982.

Omi, Michael and Howard Winant, *Racial Formations in the United States*. Philadelphia: Temple University Press, 1991.

Padilla, Félix. *Latino Ethnic Consciousness: Puerto Ricans and Mexicans in Chicago*. South Bend, IN: University of Notre Dame Press, 1985.

Rodríguez, Clara. "Puerto Ricans: Between Black and White," *New York Affairs* 1, no. 4 (1973): 92–101.

Rodríguez-Morazzani, Roberto, "Puerto Rican Political Generations in New York: Pioneros, Young Turks, and Radicals," *CENTRO,* Vol. IV, no. 1 (Winter 91–92): 96–116.

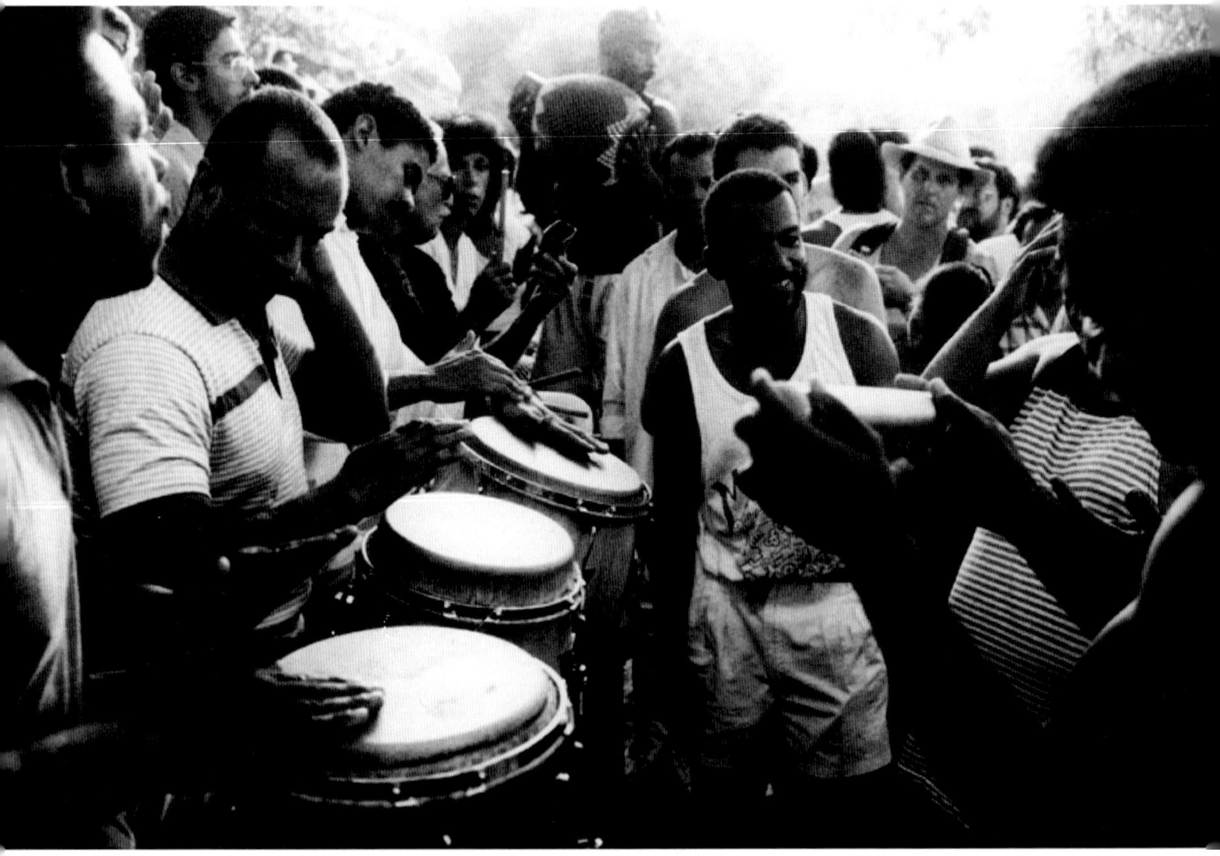

Beyond the Rainbow:
Mapping the Discourse on Puerto Ricans and "Race"

ROBERTO P. RODRIGUEZ-MORAZZANI

Prefabricated Negroes are sketched on sheets of paper and superimposed upon the Negro community; then when somebody thrusts his head through the page and yells, 'watch out there, Jack, there're people living under here,' they are shocked and indignant.

Ralph Ellison[1]

Over the past three decades there has emerged a body of writing, relatively small when compared with that addressing other issues, which attempts to explore the question of "race" as it pertains to Puerto Ricans. What follows is a preliminary critical analysis of some of the more significant statements on Puerto Ricans and racial identity for this period.[2] It is intended to engage two general theoretical pursuits. The first consists of analyzing the history of *racial formation*, that is, the transformation over time of what counts as "race," the obtaining of racial membership, and the overarching material and discursive forces that produce these effects and meanings. The second concern focuses on racial subjectification and subjection: how social agents are defined or define themselves as racial subjects, and what sort of social subjection this entails both for the racially formed *(racialized)* and racially forming *(racializing)* producers.

"Race" is understood here as a socially constructed category with no basis in empirical sciences such as biology. Yet, it should be stated that "race," while socially constructed and constituting an ontologically empty and metaphysical concept, is real in so far as identities are constituted based on "race" as an *ontologically grounded* category. Hence, the paradox of "race" as a social construct and as something that has real, indeed monstrous, effects. For while "race" might be a fiction, it is a fiction that informs and organizes the actions of people and the structures of power. For this reason it is important to historicize and deconstruct the racial discourses on which notions of "race" are maintained. In this connection it is also important to point out that the concept of "race" is not universal, not even in Western history. In fact, the concept of "race" can be traced historically.[3]

Such concerns replace the problems of empirical testing of racial attitudes, which had guided much earlier thinking and aptitudes with analyses of the body of discourse concerning Puerto Ricans and "race"/racism. They seek to surmount the irresolvable difficulties of objectively measuring an attitude measurement by means of analyzing the discourse about racially constituted bodies and subjects. Here discourse serves as an analytical category connected to the production of material practices. These displacements also mark a shift in the rules of analytic engagement, from the passive distance of objective social science to active commitment in resisting the particular racisms of given historical moments. The

---

ROBERTO P. RODRIGUEZ-MORAZZANI is director of research in history at the Centro de Estudios Puertorriqueños, Hunter College and a member of the *CENTRO* Editorial Board. This article has been edited from a longer version.

■ *Máximo R. Colón*

present article identifies these distinct moments in the discourse on Puerto Ricans and "race"/racism since the 1960s. I speak here of "moments" rather than periods, since while these discourses can be marked off chronologically, there is also considerable temporal overlap. In the case of the discourse on Puerto Ricans and "race," dominant, contestatory and emergent models coexist.

There are two main parts to this article. The first seeks to review some of the main discourses and counter-discourses on Puerto Ricans and "race." The second part examines the tenets of the "third movement" of the 1960s and 1970s, and the current dominant discourse on Puerto Ricans and "race" in the United States, focusing on what has become the main intervention on the subject, the theory of the "rainbow people."

■ *First Moment: Race as Sociopathology*

Much of the literature written on Puerto Ricans and race has been generated by North American anthropologists, social scientists, journalists, and policy-makers. For the most part, this literature represents a continuation of earlier formulations of "ethnic" relations literature. Books written in the 1960s, such as *Beyond The Melting Pot* by Nathan Glaser and Daniel Patrick Moynihan[4] and *La Vida* (1965) by Oscar Lewis[5] established a paradigm within the social sciences and political arenas for looking at Puerto Ricans and the question of ethnicity and race. These studies have remained hegemonic in the discourses on the subject to this day.[6] Especially influential is Lewis' culture of poverty thesis, which has lost none of its discursive power despite its being critiqued throughout the first half of the 1970s. (The ethnic relations literature has its counterpart within the historical writing on immigration to the United States. Oscar Handlin's *The Newcomers: Negroes and Puerto Ricans in a Changing Metropolis*[7] is the best known example of this genre.)

These anthropological, sociological, and historical writings were concerned to analyze what was seen as the anomalous case of the Puerto Rican. Puerto Ricans were described as deficient at a number of levels which could be explained as the result of socio-cultural pathologies. In "blame the victim" fashion, Puerto Rican poverty and social stigmatization was explained as a result of Puerto Rican dysfunction. Puerto Ricans were seen as morally lacking, prone to violence, undisciplined, present oriented, devoid of a work ethic, oversexed, etc. This sociopathology was the key to understanding and addressing the failure of Puerto Ricans to assimilate into the "mainstream" of American society, as had been the case with "other ethnic groups," such as Irish, Italian, Jewish, and other hyphenated Americans. In short, Puerto Ricans constituted a problem.[8] An important paradox of the liberal social science literature is that "race" is elided in favor of the notion of ethnicity. Such a deployment veils the racist "common sense" that informs the analysis of poverty and powerlessness among Puerto Ricans and other racialized groups.[9] This writing also tended to be ahistorical, as Puerto Ricans were continuously described as recent or new "immigrants," concealing the fact of a measurable Puerto Rican presence since the turn of the century, and their status as U.S. citizens. There was also a marked tendency to ignore the colonial relationship between the U.S. and Puerto Rico as being in any way related to the condition of Puerto Ricans in the U.S.

This body of writing, addressing what was conceived as the "Puerto Rican problem," promoted strategies that would aid in transforming the dysfunctional aspects of Puerto Rican "community" life. It is important to note that the above literature was authored by individual scholars with decidedly liberal credentials. Moreover, the social context for the strategies proposed by these writers coincided with the second expansion of the U.S. semi-welfare, funded by the War on Poverty program. These programs were the response to demands being placed upon the state by emergent social movements, the most central at this time being the traditional civil rights movement, and their liberal allies. The mid-1960s also saw, in addition to transformations in the African American movement, the birth of movements, including a radical Puerto Rican movement that drew from a number of political and intellectual currents.

Before engaging these writings and their context(s), it is necessary to comment on the Puerto Rican diasporic experience as it relates to race, particularly the relationship between

Puerto Ricans and African Americans in New York City. The experience of Arturo Alfonso Schomburg and his times claim our attention, since that experience demonstrates a need to problematize binary thinking on "race" and identity.

■ *Diasporic Exchanges: Expanding the "Black Atlantic"*
It is important to note here that the social movements generated by the African American people in the United States was, and remains, significant for the Puerto Rican diasporic experience. The process of racialization Puerto Ricans underwent was not totally unlike that of African Americans, especially in the post Second World War era. From the late 1940s on, African Americans migrated in large numbers from the agrarian south to the industrial belt of the Northeast and Midwest. Puerto Ricans similarly settled in cities such as New York, Trenton, Philadelphia, and Chicago. Both groups experienced unemployment, housing discrimination, police brutality, racial violence, and racial devaluation via academic and popular portrayals.[10] In this context it is very suggestive that much of the literature of the 1960s and 1970s in the social sciences concerning Puerto Ricans compare and contrast their situation with that of African Americans.[11] The propensity for such linking could lead anyone unfamiliar with the existence of the two different groups to view them as one, or as a hyphenated signifier, i.e., African American-Puerto Rican. In short, the perceived position of the two peoples vis-a-vis civil society and the state were similar

While it is traditional to think of different groups as hermetically sealed, social interaction includes exchange, borrowing, and transformation. It is a process that can be observed even by the casual observer. The social position of African Americans and Puerto Ricans resulted in a sociocultural and ideopolitical complex of exchanges and transformations not easily reduced to their individual parts. Certainly one can isolate certain ideological currents originating among the African American people, which Puerto Ricans employed for understanding their situation in the U.S. But much of the development of African American thought on these matters was itself generated by the broader experience of appropriation and transformation within the African diaspora.[12]

The actual lived history of interaction between African American and Puerto Ricans in the U.S. has not been seriously explored by scholars. Puerto Rican writers have also tended to be reluctant to explore this experience.[13] The few references lack historical depth and are typically impressionistic.[14] Also, they more often than not pose the relationship between African Americans and Puerto Ricans as either oppositional or united.[15] Again, a complex and constantly changing relationship is understood rigidly and ahistorically. The appropriation by both African Americans and Puerto Ricans of the legacy of Arturo Alfonso Schomburg (1874–1938) richly illustrates this complexity.

Arturo Alfonso Schomburg's biography encompasses the history of Puerto Rico, the Puerto Rican diasporic community of political exiles in New York at the turn of the century, and the history of Black scholarship and culture.[16] To identify him as a political activist, bibliophile, collector, librarian, and figure of the Harlem Renaissance is only to begin to describe this complex individual. What interests us here is that there has been a tendency for Schomburg to be identified simply as an African American by African Americans, and simply as Puerto Rican by Puerto Ricans. In truth, at different stages in his life, Schomburg defined himself both as Puerto Rican and as black. As he became more involved in collecting and documenting the African presence in Europe and the Americas, and as he became active in Harlem's political and cultural life, he began to use the English translation of his name—Arthur A. Schomburg instead of Arturo Alfonso Schomburg. However, during late in his life, he began again to use the Spanish spelling of his name. Schomburg's identification with blackness on the one hand and a Puerto Rican national identity[17] on the other intimates an interaction between the need for social agency and the sociopolitical vehicles for its realization. Moreover, it illustrates processes of racialization at work over time in the U.S., from the turn of the century to the 1940s.

In looking at the biography of Schomburg it becomes clear that what is required is an historically informed analysis, which, rather than reifying genealogies of either group, grasps the shifting terrain of sociocultural interaction in all of its manifestations. For example, an examination of the life of Jesús Colón, a member of the American Communist Party, a journalist, and a fighter for social justice, would provide us with another set of complexities with respect to how "race" was experienced by a black Puerto Rican in the period before and after the Second World War. In the course of Colón's being simultaneously Puerto Rican, black, Red and diasporic? An analysis of his writings on racial discrimination and his active efforts to foster Black-Puerto Rican unity within the context of the twists and turns of Communist Party policy on what was known as the "Negro Question" would add greatly to our knowledge on the question of "race," leftist political culture, and the efforts of Puerto Ricans to exercise human agency.[18] Another example is the biography of a friend and political comrade of Colón, Bernardo Vega. In his memoirs Vega describes himself as "white, a peasant from the highlands (a *jíbaro*)."[19] What did whiteness mean for a Puerto Rican migrating to the U.S. in the first decades of this century? How did his claim to whiteness affect his ability to move within the labor movement, the Socialist Party and the Puerto Rican community as compared to Jesús Colón? How would this whiteness compare with Cuban immigrants who claimed white identities during this period?[20]

These are two examples that speak to us from the past through their writing. But the many different lives of individual Puerto Ricans who cannot speak to us, and in particular the lives of the many Puerto Rican women who migrated, would in all likelihood present us with even more nuanced understandings of the racialization process as Puerto Ricans experienced it before the Second World War. Racialization is also a gendered process. These types of explorations would lay the basis for a richly textured comprehension of how political cultures evolve and of the limitations of binary thinking in accounting for convergences and divergences among and between African Americans and Puerto Ricans. The existence of individuals from both worlds who exist at the different borders and intersections blur the hard and fast lines of demarcation.

During the postwar era, the profound socioeconomic and ideopolitical transformations which took place would also result in a rearticulation of "race." The way in which a Puerto Rican might understand and articulate a racial identity would reflect these transformations. For example, the way in which Schomburg or Colón might view "race" would be somewhat different than black Puerto Ricans such as Antonia Pantoja and Piri Thomas or Pablo "Yoruba" Guzmán, who represent different post–1945 generational experiences.[21]

■ *Second Moment: Countering the Dominant Discourse*
By the late sixties there emerged a "counter-discourse" articulated by Puerto Ricans, both within the academy and in various public spheres that sought to critique conservative and liberal discourses on Puerto Ricans. This response was generated by Puerto Ricans active within the many social movements of the period. The most radical impulse on the question of race came from the independence and left-wing sectors of the movements which emerged in the late 1960s and early 1970s. Deeply influenced by different radical intellectual traditions and by different political cultures, both those past and those being created, the question of "race" as it applied to Puerto Rico and the diasporic Puerto Rican communities in the United States was explored. Below we will look at some of the more significant statements that emerged both from Puerto Rico and the U.S. The influences shaping the discourses under consideration in what we refer to here as the "Second Moment" differ in several respects, though I would argue that they should be grouped together because of their common referent to colonial domination and the eliding of "race" in the nationalist project, as well as their common commitment to an alternative political project.

It is significant that much of the thinking on the question of "race" and Puerto Rican identity was articulated not in systematic academic fashion, but rather in political tracts, manifestos, organizational platforms, and newspaper articles; also, in the debates and discussions that took place among countless individuals in everyday life. That is to say, the debate took place outside of the dominant state ideological apparatuses.[22] This is not to argue that the dominant logics of capitalist modernity in the U.S. were overcome, but rather to suggest that the possibility existed for doing so since what had heretofore been invisible was now being brought into focus.

In reviewing some of the writing of this period it is evident that a key document was Juan Angel Silén's *Hacia una visión positiva del puertorriqueño*,[23] which was translated into English as *We, the Puerto Rican People: A Story of Oppression and Resistance*.[24] Interestingly, Silén did not address the question of Puerto Rican racial identity. Instead, the question of colonialism and the struggle for nationhood are the central coordinates by which Puerto Rican identity is constructed. Following in the tradition of Puerto Rican nationalism, Silén asserts that *"lo nacional"* is the framework for understanding Puerto Ricanness. He believes that the extent to which "race" is an issue, it is one generated by external factors such as Spanish colonialism and U.S. imperialism. Despite his criticism of the literature produced by Creole elites on the "docile Puerto Rican," from the 19th century to René Marqués' writings of the1960s, the question of "race" is not broached in any significant manner.[25] This silence, together with other omissions, will prove significant for the Puerto Rican nationalist project of the1970s.

In his article "The Prejudice of Having no Prejudice in Puerto Rico,"[26] sociologist Samuel Betances influentially addressed the question of Puerto Ricans and "race." Here he addresses the subject of "race" and racism among Puerto Ricans, and challenges the "myth that Puerto Rico is a kind of human relations paradise where racism is nonexistent." Published in the Chicago-based pro-independence journal *The Rican*, Betances' article received mixed responses from various audiences.[27] One response was that Betances was not accurate in his assessment because his historical reflection on and analysis of Puerto Rican society was largely the result of the context in which he was writing. The context was that of the U.S. and the discourse on "race" and racism generated by the struggle of African Americans and other racialized groups in the United States. Therefore, "race" and racism was something that had to be contended with in the U.S., not in Puerto Rico. But this assertion made by critics of Betances was never substantiated. Rather, it rested on two propositions: first, the myth of a non-racial order achieved through racial miscegenation *(mestizaje);* second, the transposition of a paradigm on "race" operative within the context of the United States, but not Puerto Rico. However, for many who read the article, and especially for black Puerto Ricans and others who had reflected on the racism which they had experienced and witnessed within the Puerto Rican diaspora and in Puerto Rico, the article was a confirmation of a lived experience.

In the mid-1970s there were other attempts to address the question of Puerto Ricans and "race" in Puerto Rico, most notably the work of Isabelo Zenón Cruz. The publication in 1974-75 of his *Narciso descubre su trasero: el negro en la cultura puertorriqueña* represents an important benchmark in the ideo-political culture of Puerto Rico with regards to "race."[28] In this book, the traditional silence within the independence movement in particular, and the left in general, on the question of "race" and racism was broached in polemical fashion. Zenon's book provoked debate among the pro-independence left intelligentsia and political activists and the Island's traditional political and cultural elite. The pages of newspapers such as the Puerto Rican Socialist Party's *Claridad*, as well as the daily press such as *El Nuevo Día* and *El Mundo*, debated the contents of the book and what constitute "race relations" in Puerto Rican society.[29] Unlike the response to Betances' article in *The Rican*, it was much more difficult to dismiss Zenón Cruz as an "outsider," since he was not part of the Puerto Rican diaspora. Indeed, his position as an academic and black Puerto Rican within Puerto Rico did not permit such facile dismissal. However, despite criticism by Betances and Zenón Cruz, the myth of the human relations paradise in Puerto Rico remained hegemonic. The social irreverence of Zenón Cruz became in many circles an excuse for ignoring his criticism. To date there has been little serious engagement with this book. However, among black Puerto Ricans and among those who reflected on the question of "race" and racism in Puerto Rico, *Narcisso descubre su trasero* was received with varying degrees of enthusiasm. Many described reading the book as the most significant work on race they had read. Professor Magali Roy Fequere remarks, "For my part, I had never read anything like it. The book forever changed the way I would view Puerto Rican literature and culture." So despite the relatively silent responses, Zenón Cruz's work provided a small opening for looking at the issue of "race" and racism in Puerto Rico.[30]

In the late 1970s and early 1980s several works appeared that reflected both the current trends within intellectual discourse and the fortunes and contradictions of the social movements and political culture(s) of Puerto Ricans in Puerto Rico and the United States. This period marks the decline of the anti-systemic movements that emerged during the 1960s and the1970s. The independence movement and the left began a decline in strength and influence, from which it would not recover. By the first half of the eighties most of the political organizations that made up the organized Puerto Rican left had fragmented or ceased to exist altogether.

During this period three works stand out as the most significant with respect to "race" and Puerto Rican identity. One of the works, authored by the writer José Luis González, created a great deal of controversy and debate within the independence movement left, the literary intelligentsia, and a broad range of cultural elites in the Island, reminiscent of the response to Zenón Cruz's book five years earlier. *El país de cuatro pisos* addressed the question of race/identity within the framework of the "national question."[31] The privileging of the African in the historical process of the making of Puerto Rican identity/nationality proved the most provocative dimension of his thesis. According to González: "It is by now a commonplace to assert that this culture has three historical roots: the Taino Indian, the African, and the Spanish. What isn't however a commonplace—in fact just the opposite—is to say that of these three roots the one that is most important, for economic and social—and hence cultural—reasons, is the African."[32]

Once again, the polemics greeting this work went to great pains to argue that Puerto Rico is a country not divided by "race," and that what existed was a people who were basically Hispanic in heritage and culture. The status of the African and the indigenous people, the Taino, in the making of the Puerto Rican nation was subordinate to its European component. Puerto Ricans, while a racially "mixed" or "mulatto" people, were culturally European.[33]

Another important statement made during the 1970s was Angela Jorge's "The Black Puerto Rican Woman in Contemporary American Society," which appeared in an anthology on Puerto Rican women.[34] Here was a rare attempt to look at the way in which "race" intersects with gender in the case of Puerto Rican women. The question of racism, both within the Puerto Rican community and in the U.S., and its impact on black Puerto Rican women are explored via Jorge's personal observations and reflections as a black Puerto Rican woman. The psychological stress resulting from the denial of blackness is highlighted by Jorge; the social and sexual dimensions of black female devaluation is also reflected upon.

Unlike previous attempts to grapple with the question of race and racism among Puerto Ricans, the position of the author as a black Puerto Rican woman assumes a central place. It is seen as important to conveying the firsthand experience of the social and psychological impact of "race"/racism within Puerto Rican society, the diasporic community and the U.S. Jorge also addresses how relations between Puerto Rican men and women and among other groups are structured by race, as the possible choices for intimate relations are racially circumscribed.

The reception to this article among Puerto Ricans in the U.S. varied. The public "washing of dirty laundry" made some very uncomfortable. It was argued that racism was an external problem and that any attempt to discuss it was destructive for Puerto Rican unity. Others, notably black Puerto Rican women, received the article as a breath of fresh air. However, for the most part, the piece was met with a stony silence. In Puerto Rico the reception of the article was, to say the least, extremely limited as the article was not included in the Spanish language version of the book published on the Island.

Another important work appearing a year after Jorge's article is Juan Flores' *Insularismo e ideología burguesa*.[35] This book critiqued an essentialized Eurocentric version of Puerto Rican identity, articulated most forcefully in the 1930s by Antonio S. Pedreira in his classic statement on the subject, *Insularismo* (1934). In this book Pedreira's Hispanic conceptualization of Puerto Rican cultural identity, his denigration of black people as constituting an inferior "race," and his racial determinism as the central organizing principle in his writing are critiqued by Flores from within a Marxist tradition.

The response to Flores' book were somewhat different than those which greeted previous attempts to criticize racial hierarchy and Hispanophile conceptualizations of Puerto Rican culture and society. The book won the Cuban Premio de Ensayo de Casa de las Américas in January 1979, and it was published in Spanish by Ediciones Huracán that same year. However, despite the enthusiasm on the part of the Cubans, in Puerto Rico the book does not appear to have had the same impact that the work of Zenón Cruz or José Luis González had generated.[36]

○ *Reflecting on the Second Moment*
The literature produced during this second moment of discursive production represented a genuine advance over the literature on Puerto Ricans and "race" generated by the U.S. mainstream academic and policy institutions. "Race" and racism was directly confronted and named, breaking the polite silence imposed by hegemonic ideopolitical and sociocultural forces. The existence of racism in Puerto Rican society, the role of the African in Puerto Rican history and culture, the gendered dimension of Puerto Rican racial experience, and the ideological roots of Eurocentrism in the Puerto Rican context were brought into sharp relief. The central coordinate of ethnicity was abandoned in favor of the differing notions of *lo nacional*. Puerto Ricans writing in the U.S. sought to connect with Puerto Rico as part of a strategy to overcome the discourse on ethnic groups that marked Puerto Ricans as a "minority" and as pathological. These counterhegemonic ideological currents resonated within the U.S.-based independence movement and other anti-systemic, and reformist movements that Puerto Ricans created and participated in. The writings of different currents within Marxism and Third World revolutionary currents, together with the theoretical and political statements elaborated by the black power movements, formed an important part of the discourse of the period for Puerto Ricans in the diaspora.

In Puerto Rico the different sectors of the independence left generated its own ideological matrix from some of the same sources that informed Puerto Ricans in the U.S. in addition to ideopolitical traditions of the nationalist movements from previous decades. The question of "race" and racism proves difficult and problematic within the context of an anti–colonial struggle based on a nationalist imaginary that denied or subordinated the significance of the African, and denied or subordinated the question of racism as it existed within Puerto Rican society.

■ *Third Moment: Obfuscating Racial Formation and Signification*
Since the 1980s, the efforts of Puerto Ricans to analyze "race" has tended to occur within traditional "objective" social sciences and are not linked in any significant way with the social movements of recent decades. Most contemporary writing eschews the polemical style and the sense of political commitment typical of the literature generated by the social movements of the 1960s and 1970s, and much of it is produced by individuals located within the U.S. academy.

The writings of Clara Rodríguez on Puerto Ricans and ethnic/racial identity have come to dominate the way in which the subject is treated.[37] In this work we can see a return to some of the elements of the ethnic/race paradigm elaborated in the 1960s, combined with elements of the "counterhegemonic" discourses elaborated in opposition to mainstream conceptualizations. This eclectic approach can most clearly be seen in Rodríguez's book *Puerto Ricans Born in the U.S.A.*, in particular the chapter "The Rainbow People," which has become the most cited text on the subject since its appearance in 1989.[38]

○ *The "Rainbow People" Thesis*
In reviewing this recent work on Puerto Ricans and race one is struck by the fact that its basic propositions harken back to earlier formulations. In 1974, Clara E. Rodríguez published what was to be the first of several attempts to address the question of Puerto Rican ethnic and racial identity in the United States. In "Puerto Ricans: Between Black and White," Rodríguez presents a thesis which will remain central to her late arguments:

> Perhaps the primary point of contrast is that, in Puerto Rico, racial identification is subordinate to cultural identification, while in the U.S., racial identification, to a large extent, determines cultural identification. Thus when asked the divisive question, "What are you?" Puerto Ricans of all colors and ancestry answer, "Puerto Rican," while most New Yorkers answer, black Jewish, or perhaps, "of Italian descent." This is not to say that Puerto Ricans feel no racial identification, but rather that cultural identification supersedes it.[39]

This argument is repeated, nearly verbatim, fifteen years later in "The Rainbow People" when she states the following:

> Perhaps the primary point of contrast was that, in Puerto Rico, racial identification was subordinate to cultural identification, while in the United States, racial identification, to a large extent, determined cultural identification. Thus Puerto Ricans were first Puerto Rican, then *blanco/a* (white), *moreno/a* (dark), and so on, while Americans were first white or black, then Italian, Irish, West Indian, or whatever. This is not to say that Puerto Ricans did not have a racial identification, but rather that cultural identification superseded it.[40]

For Puerto Ricans, then, "racial identification was subordinate to cultural identification," and for other groups "racial identification, to a large extent, determined cultural identification." It bears mentioning that Rodríguez is not the only author who asserts the primacy of cultural over racial identification. In 1974, sociologist John F. Longres, Jr. published an article titled "Racism and Its Effects on Puerto Rican Continentals"[41] in which he asserts: "In Puerto Rico, the primary source of self-identity is culture or class, not color. Unlike the United States, subgroup identities do not involve considerations of color."[42]

A problem with this formulation is that "cultural identification" is never clearly defined. Is "cultural identification" a reference to an "ethnic" or national identification? Do Puerto Ricans at all times and in all places identify culturally or "ethnically" before identifying racially? It seems rather, that there can be a great deal of variation in the self-identification of a single Puerto Rican, including more than one racial or "cultural" identification. Puerto Ricans in the U.S. have historically had a number of different racial identifications, which result from the racial formation that takes place in diasporic conditions linked to colonialism. It is important to note that the mass migration which racialized the migrants was undertaken by the darker peoples of the global South.

○ *The Census As Measure of Racial Identification: Mis-measuring Puerto Ricans and/or "Race"*
The work of Clara Rodríguez is marked by a reliance upon classificatory schemas. The categories employed by the U.S. Census for Puerto Ricans and the analysis of Puerto Rican responses to this classificatory schema is the central empirical basis for her analysis of Puerto Rican racial self-identification. There are a number of problems with this approach.

First, the conceptual basis for the categorization of human beings in the census is accepted with little reservation. There is no thought given to the origins of classificatory schemes or their functions historically or in the present. The classifying of "natural types" and the typologies of "natural races" emerged simultaneously in what Michel Foucault called the Classical epistime.[43,44]

A further problem is the way in which Rodríguez sees the responses by Puerto Ricans to census categories as signifying racial ambivalence. She does not explore how Puerto Ricans may understand the classifications provided by the census and how they are framed within a system of signification. A certain commonsense understanding as to the responses given by Puerto Ricans is operative in this analysis. In other words, the results are taken to speak for themselves. Rodríguez concedes that there may need to be a greater refinement of the census, or any other instrument used for classifying or measuring self-identification. However, the possibility that the very act of identification constitutes a problem is never acknowledged.

○ *Negotiating the Medical/Scientific Discourse*

Puerto Ricans have negotiated the racialization process inherent in the diaspora experience in a variety of ways over time. One of the common ways in which this is done is by deployment of a national identity in an effort to escape identification as black or as non-white. The identification as Puerto Rican first, which the "rainbow people" thesis presents as evidence for the primacy of "cultural identification," is not itself racially neutral. The negation of racial identification, while potentially representing resistance, relies on an identification that is itself racially constituted. The Puerto Rican nation, as we noted above, has been represented as both white and male. Conversely, in the global context in which national identification occurs, Puerto Rican nationality is identified by the globally hegemonic as non-white. The attempt to deploy a national identity as a shield against racialization collapses on two fronts. Evidence of this is the continued identification of Puerto Ricans as non-white, e.g., as "spics" or as black—in other words, the dark Other—by state ideological apparatuses and in the mass media.[45] At another level the resistance to racial identification is itself based on the acceptance of a racializing logic. This resistance does not undermine racial signification; rather, "race" or blackness is a quality of the "otro Other." The identification of a person as Puerto Rican may serve as a means of identifying that person as non-black, not as a way of identifying as non-white. The hierarchical normative value of "whiteness" is not questioned, much less undermined in this negotiation of identity. Another instance in which Puerto Ricans have contested racialization on its own terms has beesn in response to the racialized discourse on hygiene.

The racist inscription of impurity, uncleanliness and disease onto the bodies of the colonial dark Other can be observed historically and in contemporary life. Puerto Ricans have been depicted as insects, carriers of tuberculosis and AIDS, creators of dirty slums, etc. Much of this discourse has its origins in the medical professions as they evolved during the 19th century and their linkage to the colonial enterprise. The history of immigration offers a clear example of the nexus of medical science, racialization and state power. Alan M. Kraunt makes the following observation:

> The reciprocal influence of immigration and public health in the United States stands at a busy cultural and social intersection, where at least four significant themes converge to shape the relationship. The first theme is the relationship among health, disease, and nativism, those prejudices and policies that express opposition to the foreign-born. The medicalization of preexisting nativist prejudices occurs when the justification for excluding members of a particular group includes charges that they constitute a health menace and may endanger their hosts. While some members of an immigrant group may of may not have a contagious disease that can cause others to become sick, the entire group is stigmatized by medical natavism, each newcomer being reduced from "a whole and useful person to a tainted, discounted one," because of association with disease in the mind of the native-born. Thus there is a fear of contamination from the foreign born.[46]

The discourse which this produced on Puerto Ricans and hygiene is part of a medicalized vision of racial Otherness. At the level of everyday popular racist discourse Puerto Ricans and other groups have been described as "dirty spics," "greasy Porto Ricans," etc. Puerto Ricans often respond by claiming hygienic practices as inherent to Puerto Rican culture. "We are clean. White people are the dirty ones. Have you ever been in a white person's house? It's so dirty...*parece que nunca limpian!*," are some common assertions. Some representations of the Puerto Rican home attest to a near fetishistic preoccupation with cleanliness and hygiene. In the play "Las Ventanas" by Roberto Rodríguez Suárez, which depicts life in a poor Puerto Rican neighborhood in New York City, one of the characters remarks on the obsessive cleanliness of another character and how the dominant racist culture identifies and devalues Puerto Ricans:

Alejandra: (...) Miren al Goyo limpiando la calle, pa' que los gringos no digan que los "espiques" somos unos puercos...Usted no sabe lo que tenemos que pasar aquí, don Juan. Dicen que somos basura, que las mujeres son toas unas putas, que los hombres son tos mirihuaneros y cortadores de cara... Y dicen que la venérea está regá por toa la cuidad proque y que la trajeron los puertorriqueños. Y en un anuncio de la tienda Kassay, de esos que salen en los periódicos, decía que había llegado el producto pa' matar cucarachas puertorriqueñas.[47]

This preoccupation with hygiene is not a simple response to medicalized racial signification and its popular deployments in the U.S. Dating from the later part of the 19th century in Puerto Rico, a discourse on cleanliness and hygiene evolved in the multiple social struggles that took place between the popular classes and the Creole and colonial elites. Central to many of these struggles was the battle over public space between black domestic workers and urban administrators. When the Spanish authorities launched campaigns in the name of improving public hygiene, their actual goals were the regulation of public space and the control of domestic workers, many of whom were black women.[48] One can see an intensification of such campaigns following the U.S. invasion of 1898. The U.S. colonization of Puerto Rico involved the implantation of a new regime. Part of this process meant seeing the colonized as pathological and diseased colonial body, requiring the implementation of social hygiene technologies.[49] Therefore, Puerto Ricans who migrated had already been subjected to a medically sanctioned racial discourse in Puerto Rico.

The "rainbow people" thesis does not view such negotiations as a discursive continuum on "race" and the body, but rather as evidence of the incompatibility of racial paradigms between Puerto Rico's racial order and that of the U.S. Thus it is claimed that since the racial hierarchies in Puerto Rico and the United States have been historically constituted differently, Puerto Ricans would experience a "clash" when confronted with U.S. society: "Given the experiences Puerto Ricans brought with them, and given the U.S. racial context they entered, there was bound to be a clash as the North American system was superimposed on the rainbow people."[50] The main issue for Rodríguez is the misunderstanding of race that Puerto Ricans bring with them to that of the United States, which she identifies as infinitely harsher than that which operates in Puerto Rico in particular, the Caribbean and Latin America generally. The notion of "clash" also implies a psychological dimension resulting from encountering a different racial paradigm which results in a "perceptual dissonance."[51]

As evidence of this difference, she asserts that unlike the United States, which is multiethnic and biracial, Puerto Rico is a culturally homogeneous, racially integrated society:

> Although not without strong class differences, the society in Puerto Rico is basically culturally homogeneous and racially integrated. This contrasts with the more biracial, multiethnic society that has historically existed in the United States. While in the United States ethnic-racial minorities have traditionally been segregated, in Puerto Rico, Blacks were not a distinguishable ethnic group. This is not to say Blacks were evenly distributed throughout the social structure, for there is still debate on this issue. Nor is it to say that Blacks in Puerto Rico were treated in all regards exactly as Whites. But in terms of housing, institutional treatment, political rights, government policy, and cultural identification, it appears that black, white and tan Puerto Ricans were not treated differently.[52]

Professor Rodríguez qualifies her statement a few pages later:

> These descriptions of differing racial ambiances in New York and Puerto Rico should not be taken to mean that Puerto Rico is the ideal racial environment. Indeed, some authors argue that 'Puerto Ricans seem to have developed a Creole ethos tolerant of the mulatto group...but scornful of the black sector' (Duany, 1985: 30; see also Zenón Cruz, 1975; Longres, 1974: 68 ff.). Betances (1972) argues that the

general lack of concern with racial issues on the island constitutes for some 'the prejudice of no prejudice.' He argues that claiming that there is not prejudice may in itself be a prejudicial act. But, 'if racism can be seen in term of degree, then obviously there is much less racism in Puerto Rico than in the United States' (Longres, 1974: 68). This was the situation from which Puerto Ricans came.[53]

These two statements would seem to be at odds with each other, though the relative brevity of the second proposition on "prejudice" in Puerto Rico seems to support the contention that racism in Puerto Rico does not exist. Or rather, while racism in the Puerto Rican context may exist, the issue is one of degree. How should this contradiction be understood? Above all, Rodriguez seems to want to have her cake and eat it too. Racism as a concealed fact in Puerto Rican society is acknowledged but simultaneously subordinated in significance to that of racism in the U.S.

The larger implications of the "rainbow people" notion for U.S. sociology are suggested in Rodríguez's assertion that "the irony was that Puerto Ricans represented the ideal of the American melting pot ideology—a culturally unified, racially integrated people."[54] Similarly Longres Jr. claims that Puerto Ricans are "a culturally homogeneous and racially integrated and mixed group."[55] Here we see the redeployment of a long standing myth concerning the ways in which "race" and racism are experienced by Puerto Ricans in Puerto Rico. The putative absence of hard and fast racial discrimination and racial violence is equated with a softer and more benign racial order. Puerto Rico's racial order, although not perfect since Blacks are not at all treated the same as whites, is nevertheless superior, since institutionalized racism and cultural belonging are not significant questions within Puerto Rican society. Indeed if Americans could learn from the case of Puerto Rico, Glazer and Moynihan's "melting pot" could become a reality in the U.S.

○ *Overlooking Race in Contemporary Puerto Rico*

Another dimension to the "rainbow people" thesis is that it does not concern itself with the present state of affairs with respect to race in Puerto Rico. The few references to Puerto Rico and "race" are not recent ones, and one has the impression that it is not a significant issue in contemporary Puerto Rico. However, an observation that does not comply with the imposed silence on "race" in Puerto Rican politics or culture might draw quite different conclusions.

The statehood party's cynical support for such a class and race marked musical form as "Plena"; the continued existence of blackface comedy on Puerto Rican television; the conflict throughout the 1980s between youth who defined themselves according to musical preference, the *cocolos* favoring *salsa* and Latin-Caribbean music generally, and the *rockeros* favoring rock and roll & U.S. popular music generally; the racist jokes and discrimination against Dominican immigrants on the Island; and more recently, the controversies over rap music are only some of the more glaring instances in which "race" remains salient in Puerto Rican society.[56] Recently Kelvin Santiago-Valles has analyzed the convergence of poverty, "race," and criminalization, arguing that as social polarization increases and "law and order" is demanded by a broad spectrum of the Island's political class and by the colonial state, the racialization of the spaces in which illegal activities occurs is intensified. Within Puerto Rican society crime and criminal activity is increasingly imagined as that which is committed by non-whites.[57]

Thus, in so far as "race" is a problem in Puerto Rico today, it is a problem for black Puerto Ricans. Understood in another way, blackness is a problem. The Creole dream of *blanqueamiento* (whitening) or *mejorando la raza* (improving the race) is hampered by the continued existence of the Other Puerto Rican—that is, *el Puertorriqueño negro*. The presence of black Puerto Ricans and the history of racial formation in Puerto Rico will continue to frustrate the Creole racialist fantasy of exorcising the African dimension of Puerto Rican identity.

○ *Racial Formation in the U.S.: Undermining the "One Drop Rule"*

As for its view of the U.S., the "rainbow people" thesis relies on the formula of the "one drop rule"–"one drop of black blood makes you black." Yet, the racialization of Irish, Italian and Jewish immigrants who were identified as non-white Others was not based on the one drop rule but rather directly related to racialization processes linked to power and domination on both sides of the Atlantic. Similarly, the attempt to establish the corollary "Over there one drop of blood makes you black. Here [in Puerto Rico], one drop of white blood makes you white" becomes untenable.[58]

It is clear that the "rainbow people" thesis is not informed by an awareness of the actual histories of racial formation either in Puerto Rico or the U.S. Furthermore, it does not seek to problematize these racial constructions. This allows for Puerto Ricans, and other groups who are defined as racial others, to be defined against a normative and naturalized whiteness. Whiteness is never questioned or interrogated, rather it is the non-disclosed dominant identity. The dependence on the ethnic paradigm elaborated by American pluralists in the construction of the "rainbow people" thesis is obvious in the description of the U.S. racial order. For Clara Rodríguez, there is a repression of ethnicity rooted in a fear of Otherness: "the fear of 'difference' has been a central, recurring phenomenon."[59] In fact U.S. history is conceived of as "ethnic" history with European immigrants experiencing an ethnic whiteness.[60] Here Rodríguez, while claiming distance from the earlier formulations on Puerto Ricans as an ethnic group, subscribes to an ethnic group model in order to understand social hierarchy in the United States.

In Rodríguez's writing the terms "ethnic" or "ethnicity" are employed as signifying a distinct identity separate from any notion of "race." On other occasions this distinction is not at all clear. Puerto Ricans are viewed as both an ethnic group and as a racial group. Such imprecision in defining and employing concepts and categories makes for a murky picture of the Puerto Ricans' subordinate insertion into U.S. society. It would appear that the failure of Puerto Ricans to achieve integration and upward mobility, as explained by the "rainbow people" thesis, is the result of the contradiction between the ethnic group model for advancement and the problem posed by race. Puerto Ricans at once claimed as an "ethnic" group and as a "mixed" racial group, find difficulty advancing in accordance with the ethnic group model since the system of racial ordering precludes advancement for non-whites.

However, a number of questions arise once this duality is asserted. How accurate is it to claim that Puerto Ricans are an ethnic group, given that the history of Puerto Rican migration to the U.S. does not resemble that of European immigrants, which is what the ethnic relations model is based on? Moreover, the explanatory strength of the ethnic model falters when the actual history of European migration is critically examined. In fact, contrary to Rodríguez's assertion, racial hierarchies in Puerto Rico are actually less fluid than previously imagined. In addition, U.S. racialization processes appear less static than simplistic black-white dichotomies allow for. Very suggestive for reexamining the history of European immigration and claims on white American national identity is the notion of "inbetweenness" and "not-yet-white," which Orsi and Roediger employ in examining the racial histories of Italian and Irish immigrants in the U.S.[61] In the case of Puerto Ricans and other racialized groups the actual relations of power between the sending country and the U.S. must be explored and compared. As E. San Juan Jr. argues:

> Concrete investigation of various historical conjunctures is needed to answer how the reproduction of social relations operate through race insofar as capitalism, for example, articulates classes in distinct ways at each level (economic, political, ideological) of the social formation. In effect, the schematics of race and its use to ascribe values, allocate resources, and legitimize the social position/status of racially defined populations (in short, racism) centrally affect the constitution of the fractions of black, Asian, or Hispanic labor as a class.[62]

In this context it should also be pointed out that while colonialism is mentioned in an earlier section of *Puerto Ricans Born in the U.S.A.*, it does not figure in the section on "race" as at all significant in the process of racial formation or signification. Does the fact that Puerto Ricans are colonial migrants determine their insertion into the U.S. system of racial hierarchy? Obviously not, if one is employing the ethnic model, which does not recognize colonialism as part of the structuring of discursive and material power in Western capitalist democracies such as the U.S.[63] The ethnic model, as elaborated by Gunnar Myrdal in 1944, and traditional American structural-functionalist sociology, which informs Professor Rodríguez's analysis of "race" in the U.S., eschews relations of power as determinant.[64]

By obfuscating and distorting the history of racial hierarchy in Puerto Rico the "rainbow people" thesis confuses the different ways by which Puerto Ricans experience the different racializing processes inherent in the migratory process over time. In the same measure, the thesis also minimizes the complexity of racial formations in the U.S., ignoring how racial hierarchies have been historically constituted and structurally mediated. Instead, two static and historically inaccurate narratives on "race" in Puerto Rico and the U.S. result in a culture clash whichever way they turn. Yet, does moving between racial formations entail a "clash," with its implied psychological dimensions? Or should we instead conceptualize the conflict involved with Puerto Rican self-identification as occurring within a shifting terrain of racial signification, which is then negotiated on differing terms by Puerto Ricans with heterogeneous racial identities, class positions, sexualities etc.?

○ *What's in a Metaphor?*
The "rainbow people," a metaphor intended to signify diversity and inclusion, actually works to deny hierarchy based on race. To say "rainbow people" conjures images of not only of white, black or "tan," but also green, purple, and orange, etc. Therefore the rainbow contains colors that have no correspondence with the sociopolitical construction of "race." These other colors do not have the sociocultural or political salience of "race" and help form a discourse that seeks to evade "race" as evidencing relations of power and subordination.

○ *At the End of the "Rainbow"*
The "rainbow people" thesis thus represents a turn away from the critical counterdiscourses initiated in the 1970s. Reliance on an ethnic paradigm for explaining the social advancement of groups and its empiricist and neopositivist methodological approach link it to the first moment, that is, to the mainstream conceptualizations articulated during the 1960s by liberal and neoliberal academics and public policy analysts. In addition, the mere numeration of social statistics and the mention of colonialism do not add up to a radical critique of imperialism or of a racialized capitalist hierarchy. Moreover, the coincidence of this discourse on "race" in Puerto Rico with that of the Creole mythology of racial harmony also brings it in line with the continuing conspiracy of silence in the Island.

That Puerto Ricans encounter a differently constituted racial field when they migrate to the U.S. is logically consistent. However, this movement, and the racialization inherent in it, must be rigorously examined and analyzed. That Puerto Ricans are not easily contained within the classificatory schemes established in the U.S. by the census or by other state or private agencies is not evidence of an undermining of U.S. racial hierarchy or systems of signification. As long as the concept of "race" remains unchallenged there is no possibility of challenging racial signification. The conceptualizing of Puerto Ricans as a "rainbow people," somehow standing between "black/white," elides what "blackness" or "whiteness" means for Puerto Ricans in the U.S. or in Puerto Rico. Given the concealed, hegemonic status of "whiteness" there is no deconstruction of how "race" is invented—"blackness" becomes the heart of the problem of "race relations."[65] Notions of being "tan" or *café con leche* (coffee and milk) explains little of what it means to be a "racially mixed" Puerto Rican, since the meaning of what is contained or excluded in the "mix" is again obscured.

At the end of the "rainbow," we do not find a theorization which can capture the complexities of Puerto Rican racial formation and signification. The problem of "difference," and "race" has been theorized in an ahistorical and reductionist fashion, which has resulted in a failure to visualize how Puerto Ricans rearticulate what constitutes "race" through such supposed difference. This rearticulation demands a renewed intellectual vision that goes beyond linear and binary thinking, and relies on the functionalist and empiricist methodology that has dominated social theory in the U.S.

■ A Fourth Moment?

Since the mid-1980s in there has begun to emerge a new discourse on "race" and racism. The work of Stuart Hall, Omi and Winant, Alexander Saxton, David Roediger, Theo Goldberg, E. San Juan Jr., Theodore Allen, and Anne McClintock have begun, from different perspectives, to analyze the socially constructed nature of "race" through sociohistorical, textual and philosophical treatments. Much of the impulse for this new theorization has come from different intellectual traditions, e.g., Marxism, structuralism, postmodernism, postcolonial theory, etc. Similarly a number of Puerto Rican intellectuals drawing from these intellectual currents have begun to address the question of Puerto Rican racial identity. This new body of work shares with the above mentioned authors a concern with how "race" is socially constructed and rooting this process in a rigorous reconstruction of historical and structural processes. Coloniality, imperialism and other forces of domination and subjugation are central to this reconstruction, as is the critical examination of the conceptual tools and categories employed in this undertaking. In addition to the above intellectual project(s) there are also a number of academics and students who eclectically draw from the works of the different moments mapped in this article, but in the final instance tend towards the formulations identified in the "rainbow people" conceptualization.

The existence of these two different intellectual trajectories will make for an increasingly complex and contested ideopolitical terrain in the years to come. The debates that will emanate between these, and perhaps other, tendencies point toward a new moment in the discourse on Puerto Ricans and "race." This new moment promises to be both an advance over earlier formulations and revealing of other problematic issues and themes. ■

ENDNOTES

1. Ralph Ellison, *Shadow and Act*, New York: Random House, 1964, p.123.

2. Of course, there have been earlier efforts, both in Puerto Rico and the United States, to address the issue of Puerto Ricans and "race." I hope to analyze this earlier body of writing in the future. Some examples of this literature include José Celso Barbosa, *Problemas de Razas*, San Juan, Puerto Rico: Imprenta Venezuela, 1937; Tomás Blanco, *Prejuicio Racial en Puerto Rico*, San Juan, Biblioteca de Autores Puertorriqueños, 1942; Charles Rogler, "The Morality of Race Mixing in Puerto Rico," *Social Forces*, XXV, October 1946; Joseph P. Fitzpatrick, "Attitude of Puerto Ricans Toward Color," *American Catholic Sociological Review*, Vol 20, No. 3, 1959; and Edwardo Seda Bonilla, "Social Structure and Race Relations," *Social Forces*, Vol. XL, No. 2, December 1961.

3. Ivan Hannaford, *Race: The History of an Idea in the West*, Baltimore: The John Hopkins University Press, 1995.

4. Nathan Glazer and Daniel Patrick Moynihan, *Beyond the Melting Pot*, Cambridge Mass.: MIT Press, 1970, (2nd ed.). The first edition of *Beyond the Melting Pot* received the Anisfield-Wolf Award in Race Relations. Like *La Vida*, *Beyond the Melting Pot* has become part of the established canon within the liberal tradition in the social sciences.

5. Oscar Lewis, *La Vida: A Puerto Rican Family in the Culture of Poverty —San Juan and New York*, New York: Vintage Books, 1966. A runaway best seller, *La Vida* won the National Book Award for nonfiction in 1967. Lewis' work is perhaps the most cited study of Puerto Ricans in traditional social sciences.

6. In the tradition of Oscar Lewis see Philippe Bourgois, *In Search of Respect: Selling Crack in El Barrio*, Cambridge: Cambridge University Press, 1995. For a critical review of Bourgois see Adam Shatz, "Among the Dispossessed," *The Nation*, December 25, 1995, pp. 836-839.

7   Oscar Handlin, *The Newcomers: Negroes and Puerto Ricans in a Changing Metropolis*, Cambridge: Harvard University Press, 1959.

8   The viewing of Puerto Ricans as a problem follows a tradition within U.S. social science which views the very existence of different racial/ethnic groups as itself constituting a problem. The mere presence of diverse groups is seen as giving rise to conflict generated by cultural difference. For a representative statement, see T.J. Woofter, *Races and Ethnic Groups in American Life*, New York & London: McGraw-Hill Book Company, 1933.

9   For a critique of the ethnic paradigm on "race" see Hermon George, Jr., *American Race Relations Theory: A Review of Four Models*, Lanham, New York & London: University Press of America, 1984, pp. 1—48.

10 Andrés Torres, *Between Melting Pot and Mosaic: African Americans and Puerto Ricans in the New York Political Economy*, Philadelphia: Temple University Press, 1995.

11 Today there is a tendency on the part of much of the writings on Puerto Ricans to contrast and compare this experience to that of other Hipanics/Latinos ignoring the historical relationship with African Americans and other members of the Caribbean/African diaspora. This has tended to blur the similarities between African Americans and Puerto Ricans on a number of levels.

12 The African diaspora is not represented by a straight line from Africa to the U.S., but rather encompasses the African continent, Europe, the Americas, and the complex world of the Caribbean. In *The Black Atlantic: Modernity and Double Consciousness*, Cambridge, Massachusetts: Harvard University Press, 1993, Paul Gilroy has referred to the field of meaning created out of this diaspora as the black Atlantic. Puerto Rico, together with Cuba and the Dominican Republic, is part of the world which Gilroy has begun to "re-imagine," although his limited knowledge of the Spanish-speaking Caribbean has tended to obscure his efforts. A consideration of this syncretic culture, described by Alejo Carpentier as baroque, would enhance and further complicate Gilroy's black Atlantic. For a work which presents the complexity of the Caribbean world in iconoclastic and suggestive ways, see Antonio Benítez-Rojo, *The Repeating Island: The Caribbean and the Postmodern Perspective*, Durham & London: Duke University Press, 1992. On Alejo Carpentier's notion of the Baroque, see Roberto González Echevarría, *Alejo Carpentier: The Pilgrim At Home*, Austin, Texas: The University of Texas Press, 1990.

13 Histories of the Puerto Rican communities in New York City and Chicago have inexplicably declined to examine this question. See Virginia Sánchez-Korrol, *From Colonia to Community: The History of Puerto Ricans in New York City*, Berkley: The University of California Press, 1994 (second ed.); and Félix M. Padilla, *Puerto Rican Chicago*, Notra Dame, Indiana: University of Natre Dame Press: 1987. However, one can find a few journalistic pieces that attempt to explore this relationship. See, Barbara Omolade and Angelo Falcón, "Black/Latino Politics...Black/Latino Communities" in *Puerto Rico Libre* Summer 1985, pp. 18—23.

14 In the introduction to Allon Schoener ed., *Harlem On My Mind: Cultural Capital of Black America*, New York: Random House, 1968, p. 4, the argument is made that in their relations with Puerto Ricans, "Blacks are left with only three choices—fight them, ignore them or welcome them." The author betrays an incredible ignorance of the contact between African Americans and Puerto Rican. In addition, such options never present themselves in such neat terms or as options at all. Rather, contact between groups is mediated by historical forces, structural arrangements, and the agency of different collectivities and individuals.

15 For a representative example of the perspective that African American and Puerto Rican relations are antagonistic and inevitably competitive, see Julio Morales, *Puerto Rican Poverty and Migration: We Just Had to Try Elsewhere*, New York: Praeger, 1986, pp. 45—61. More recently this framework has been extended by liberal analysts looking at the relations between African Americans and Latinos in general. See Jac;k Miles, "Blacks vs. Browns," *Atlantic Monthly*, October 1992, pp. 51—60 and Jerry Yaffe, "Prospects and Barriers to Successful Latino and African-American Coalitions," *Harvard Journal of Hispanic Policy*, Vol. 8, 1994-1995, pp. 61—86.

16 For accounts of the life of Schomburg, see Victoria Ortiz, "Arturo A. Schomburg: A Biographical Essay" in *The Legacy of Arthur A, Schomburg: A Celebration of the Past, A Vision for the Future*, New York: New York Public Library, 1986; and Elinor Des Verney Sinnette, *Arthur Alfonso Schomburg: Black Bibliophile & Collector*, Detroit: The New York Public Library & Wayne State University Press, 1989.

17 This national identity is further complicated if we contextualize it within the ambiance of black nationalism in Harlem. Many of the Black activists before the Second World War were immigrants from English-speaking Caribbean countries. Pan-Africanism was articulated by intellec-

tuals from the Caribbean who had immigrated to New York City. With the decline of the 19th century *independentista* movement in Puerto Rico, the most vibrant political movement in New York City was that of labor, which was connected with Socialist and Communist parties and the black Nationalist movements. The best known of the latter is the movement led by Marcus Garvey. This was, in part, the ideopolitical context in which Schomburg, a black Puerto Rican concerned with documenting the African contribution to world history, found himself. The Caribbean connection in the emergence of Pan-Africanism is probably not irrelevant for understanding his turn, together with the Hispanophilic and Eurocentric racism in Puerto Rican society and in diaspora. Moreover, Schomburg, a believer in the notion of an intellectual-class leadership, or "talented tenth," possessed class aspirations that could not be realized within the small Puerto Rican community made up mostly of workers.

18 While a number of interesting studies have appeared on the role of African Americans within the Communist Party and the its role within the Black community, there has not been any major exploration of the Puerto Rican presence within the party or of its activities within Puerto Rican communities such as Harlem's East Harlem. For treatment of the Communist Party's relation with African Americans see Mark Naison, *Communists in Harlem During the Depression*, Chicago: University of Illinois Press, 1983; Robin D. G. Kelly, *Hammer and Hoe: Alabama Communists During the Great Depression*, Chapel Hill and London: The University of North Carolina Press, 1990; and Earl Ofari Hutchinson, *Blacks and Reds, Race and Class in Conflict 1919-1990*, East Lansing: Michigan State University, 1995.

19 César Andreu Iglesias (ed.), *Memoirs of Bernardo Vega: A Contribution To The History Of The Puerto Rican Community In New York*, New York & London: Monthly Review Press, 1984, p. 3. In the Spanish language original, Vega's text explictly links "whiteness" to a masculine national identity: "Jíbaro de la montaña, era blanco, y en mi rostro había un matiz de cera, característico de los hombres del corazón de nuestra patria." César Andreu Iglesias (ed.), *Memorias de Bernardo Vega*, Rio Piedras, Ediciones Huracán, 1977, p. 37.

20 For an interesting memoir on being a white Cuban growing up in Ybor City in the 1930s see Ferdie Pacheco, *Ybor City Chronicles: A Memoir*, Gainsville, University Press of Florida, 1994, pp. 1—26.

21 Antonia Pantoja migrated to the U.S. in the post war era and was a key member of the generation of the 1950s and 1960s known as the "Young Turks." Piri Thomas is best known for his coming-of-age autobiography *Down These Mean Street,s* published in 1967 by Vintage Books. For an interesting reading of this work relevant to the above discussion, see Marta S. Sanchez, "Revisiting Binaries of Race and Gender: Piri Thomas' *Down These Mean Streets* and the Construction of the Puerto Rican Ethnic Nationalist Subject," 1996 (unpublished paper). Pablo 'Yoruba' Guzmán was a leader of the Young Lords Party in New York City during the late 1960s and early 1970s. In his own account of his political education, Guzmán credits the political movement of the African American people as having a major impact on his life. See Pablo Guzmán, "The Young Lords Legacy: A Personal Account" *Crítica*, No. 11-12, April—May 1995, p. 1.

22 See Louis Althusser, "Ideology and Ideological State Apparatuses" in Louis Althusser, *Lenin And Philosophy And Other Essays*, New York & London: Monthly Review Press, 1971, pp. 127—186.

23 Juan Angel Silén, *Hacia una visión positiva del puertorriqueño*, Rio Piedras, Puerto Rico: Editorial Edil, 1970.

24 Juan Angel Silén, *We, the Puerto Rican People: A Story of Oppression and Resistance*, (trans. Cedric Belfrage), New York & London: Monthly Review Press, 1971.

25 Ibid., pp. 36—45.

26 Samuel Betances, "The Prejudice of Having No Prejudice in Puerto Rico: Parts I&II" in *The Rican*, Winter 1972 & Spring 1973, pp. 41—55, 22—37.

27 This assessment is based on discussions with a number of activists and intellectuals active during the period. There did not appear to be much response to the article in writing at the time. However, it has been one of the most frequently quoted article on the subject.

28 Isabelo Zenón Cruz, *Narciso descubre su trasero: el negro en la cultura Puertorriqueña*, Humacao, Puerto Rico: Editorial Furidi, 1974.

29 Juán Antonio Corretjer, "El libro de Isabelo Zenón," *El Nuevo Dia,* February 14, 1975, p. 21; Ernesto Reques, "!Negro no, incierto!" *Claridad,* February 28, 1975, p. 14; Wilfredo Mattos Cintrón, "Racismo e ideologia," *Poder Estudiantial*, February 19 - March 5, 1975, p. 9; Cesar Andreu Iglesias, "El Narciso de Zenón" *Avance*, February 17, 1995, p. 17; Mariano Muñoz

Hernández, "Racismo e imperialismo en Puerto Rico," *Claridad, En Rojo,* May 1, 1995, p. 11; Juan Cepero, "¿Negro Puertorriqueño o Puertorriqueño Negro?", *El Mundo,* March 23, 1975, p. 10; Juan Silén, "Una critica y una contra-critica," *Claridad,* Marzo 27, 1995, p. 17; Luis P. Ruiz Cepero, "Los negros Boricuas," *El Nuevo Dia,* April 25, 1975, p. 23; Manuel Maldonado Denis, "El descubrimiento de Zenón," *Claridad, En Rojo,* May 24, 1975, p. 7; Jorge María Ruscalleda Bercedóniz, "Carta a Isabelo Zenón," *Claridada, En Rojo,* July 5, 1975, p. 7; Amelía Agostini de del Río, "Impresiones sobre *Narciso descubre su trasero,*" *El Nuevo Dia,* October 4, 1975, p. 16; Efraín Barradas, "Narciso descubre su trasero (El negro en la cultura Puertorriqueña)" in *Sin Nombre,* July/September 1975, Vol. VI, No. 1, pp. 73—75; Enrique A. Laguerre, "Identidad Puertorriqueña", *El Mundo,* Noviembre 6, 1975; p. 7A and José Luis González, "Antes y despues de Zenón," *Claridad, En Rojo,* August 16, 1976, pp. 4—5.

30 The work of Zenón Cruz was less known among Puerto Rican left activists in the U.S. Betances' article seems to have been the best-known account on race and Puerto Rico in the U.S.

31 José Luis González, *El país de cuatro pisos y otros ensayos,* Rio Piedras: Huracan, 1980.

32 José Luis González, *Puerto Rico: The Four Storeyed Country and Other Essays,* Princeton & New York: Markus Wiener Publishing, Inc., 1993, p. 9.

33 Manuel Méndez Ballester, "Un ataque brutal" *El Nuevo Dia,* May 12, 1980, p. 21; José Luis Méndez, "La arquitectura intelectual de *El país de cuatro pisos*" *Claridad,* April 22, 1982, p. 16 and April 29, p. 23 and Manuel Maldonado Denis, "En torno a *El país de cuatro pisos,*" *Casa de las Américas* 135, November-December, pp. 151—159. For a sympathetic and appreciative critique see Juan Flores, "The Puerto Rico that José Luis González Built" in *Divided Borders: Essays on Puerto Rican Identity,* Houston, Texas: Arte Público Press, 1993, pp. 61—70.

34 Angela Jorge, "The Black Puerto Rican Woman in Contemporary American Society" in Edna Acosta-Belen (ed.), *The Puerto Rican Woman: Perspectives on Culture, History and Society,* New York: Praeger, 1979.

35 Juan Flores, *Insularismo e ideología burguesa,* La Habana: Casa de las Américas, 1980, Río Piedras: Ediciones Huracán, 1980.

36 Ramon de Armas, "Insularismo a la luz de hoy," *Casa de las Américas,* Vol. XX, No. 117, November-December, 1979.

37 See Clara E. Rodríguez, "Puerto Ricans: Between Black and White," in Clara E. Rodríguez, Virginia Sanchez Korrol and José Oscar Alers (eds.), *The Puerto Rican Struggle: Essays on Survival in the U.S.*, Maplewood, New Jersey: Waterfront Press, 1980, pp. 20—30 (paper originally published in *New York Affairs* vol. I, no. 4, pp. 92—101); Clara Rodríguez, "Racial Identification among Puerto Ricans in New York," *Hispanic Journal of Behavioral Sciences,* Vol. 12, no. 4., pp. 366—379; Clara E. Rodríguez, "Race, Culture, and Latino "Otherness" in the 1980 Census," *Social Science Quarterly* 73:930—937; Clara E. Rodríguez "Challenging Racial Hegemony: Puerto Ricans in the United States," in Steven Gregory & Rodger Sanjek, (eds.), *Race,* New Brunswick, New Jersey: Rutgers University Press, 1994, pp. 131—145; Clara E. Rodríguez et. al., "Latino Racial Identity: in the Eye of the Beholder?", *Latino Studies Journal,* Vol. 2, No. 3., 1991, pp. 33—48; and Clara Rodríguez and Hector Cordero-Guzman, "Placing Race in Context," *Ethnic and Racial Studies,* Vol. 15, No. 4 (October 1992), pp. 523—542.

38 Clara Rodríguez, *Puerto Ricans Born in the U.S.A.*, Boston: Unwin Hyman, 1989, pp. 49—84.

39 Clara E. Rodríguez, "Puerto Ricans: Between Black and White," p. 21.

40 Clara E. Rodríguez, "The Rainbow People," in Clara E. Rodríguez, *Puerto Ricans Born in the U.S.A.,* p. 52.

41 John F. Longres, Jr., "Racism and Its effects on Puerto Rican Continentals," *Social Casework,* February 1974, pp. 67—75.

42 Ibid., p. 69.

43 Michel Foucault, *The Order of Things: An Archaeology of the Human Sciences,* New York: Vintage Books, 1970; Michel Foucault, *The Archaeology of Knowledge,* New York: Pantheon Books, 1972; and Michel Foucault, *The History of Sexuality,* New York: Vintage Books, 1978.

44 Arguing via Foucault, both Cornel West and David Theo Goldberg have attempted genealogies of modern racism—meaning here not contemporary racism so much as the racism of modernism—that link the Western fetishistic practices of classification, the forming of tables, and the consequent primacy of the visible with the creation of metaphysical and moral hierarchies between racialized hierarchies of human beings. Given this genesis, the concepts

of race and racial difference emerge as that which is visible, classifiable, and morally salient. Hence, the utilization of classificatory schemas that are founded on a racialist logic. These schemas emerged as capitalist modernity expanded, and they reproduce, at least discursively, the same racial typologies.

45 See Richie Pérez, "From Assimilation to Annihilation: Puerto Rican Images in U.S. Films," *Centro*, Vol. II, No. 8, pp. 8—27; Blanca Vázquez, "Puerto Ricans and the Media: A Personal Statement," *Centro*, Vol. III, No. 1, pp. 4—15 and Alberto Sandoval Sánchez, "West Side Story: A Puerto Rican Reading of "America," in *Jump Cut*, Vol. 39, 1994, pp. 59—66.

46 Alan M. Kraunt, *Silent Travelers: Germs, Genes, And The "Immigrant Menace,"* New York: Basic Books, 1994, pp. 2,—3.

47 "Alejandra: (...) Look at Goyo cleaning the street, so the gringos don't say that the "spics" are pigs...You don't know what we have to go through here don Juan. The say that we're garbage, that the women are whores, that the men are marijuana smokers and face cutters... And they say VD has been spread throughout the city because Puerto Ricans brought it with them. And there is an announcement at the Kassay store, those that come out in the newspapers, it said that the product had arrived to kill Puerto Rican cockroaches." Roberto Rodríguez Suárez, *Las Ventanas*, San Juan: Instituto de Cultura Puertorriqueña, 1969, p. 204.

48 Felix V. Matos-Rodríguez, "Street Vendors, Pedlars, Shop-Owners and Domestics: Some Aspects of Women's Economic Roles in Nineteenth-Century San Juan, Puerto Rico (1820 - 1870)," in Verene Shepherd, Bridget Brereton and Barbara Bailey (eds.), *Engendering History: Caribbean Women in Historical Perspective*, New York: St. Martin's Press, 1995, pp. 176—193, and Yvette Rodríguez, "Las mujeres y la higiene: la construcción de 'lo social' en San Juan, 1880 - 1920," unpublished paper, 1995.

49 Kelvin Santiago-Valles, "On the Historical Links Between Coloniality, the Violent Production of the "Native" Body, and the manufacture of Pathology," in *Centro*, Vol. VII, No. 1, (Winter 94-95/Spring 95), pp. 108— 118.

50 Clara E. Rodríguez, "Rainbow People," p. 56.

51 Rodríguez approvingly quotes Longres, who asserts that "the experience of being seen in a way different from the way you see yourself, particularly as it pertains to race, is clearly an unsettling experience. Indeed it has often been maintained that for the migrating Puerto Rican, the experience of racial reclassification, and its attendant racism, 'frequently undermines the sense of autonomy and initiative...and leaves a residue of self-doubt and inadequacy.'" Clara E. Rodríguez, Ibid., p. 76. There is no question that racialization involves psychological dimensions. The work of Franz Fanon has clearly demonstrated this. However, two questions should be posed. First, what is the nature of this psychological impact? Second, what is the psychological impact of racism on Puerto Ricans in Puerto Rico? With respect to the first question Rodríguez offers very little by way of an explanation or analysis. With respect to the second, her understanding of racism in Puerto Rico precludes this question as we shall see later on. Thankfully, Rodríguez does not reiterate Longres' position that: "Upon arrival, Puerto Ricans find that they are viewed as a racially mixed group, which for most Puerto Ricans, means that they have been labeled black. Given the Puerto Rican orientation to color, psychological processes, although having their roots in prejudices on the island, are compounded and become destructive to mental health." Longres, Racism and Its Effects on Puerto Rican Continentals," p. 71.

52 Clara E. Rodríguez, "Rainbow People," p. 54

53 Ibid., p. 56

54 Ibid., p. 49.

55 John F. Longres, Jr., "Racism and Its Effects on Puerto Rican Continentals," p. 67.

56 See the documentary by Ana María García, *Cocolos y Roqueros*, 1994; Palmira N. Ríos, "Acercamiento al Conflicto Dominicano-Boricua" *Centro*, Vol. IV, No. 2, pp. 44—49; and Raquel Z. Rivera, "Rap Music in Puerto Rico: Mass Consumption or Social Resistance?" in *Centro*, Vol. V, No. 1, Winter 1992—1993, pp. 52—65.

57 Kelvin Santiago-Valles, "Vigilando, administrando y patrullando a negros y trigueños: del cuerpo del delito al delito de los cuerpos en la crisis del Puerto Rico urbano contemporáneo," *Bordes*, No. 2, pp. 28—42.

58 Eneid Routté-Gomez, "So, Are We Racists????? A Conspiracy of Silence: Racism in Puerto Rico," *San Juan Star Magazine*, December-January, 1996, pp. 54—58. The quote is attributed to clinical psychologist Antonio Díaz-Royo.

59 Clara E. Rodríguez, "Rainbow People," p. 50.

60 Ibid., p. 50.

61 Robert Orsi and David Roediger, *Towards the Abolition of Whiteness*, New York & London: Verso, 1994, pp. 181—198.

62 E. San Juan, Jr., *Racial Formations/Critical Transformations: Articulations of Power in Ethnic and Racial Studies in the United States*, New Jersey & London: Humanities Press, 1992, pp. 47—48.

63 For a recent book in the tradition of the ethnic model, which attempts, following the "rainbow people" thesis, to situate Puerto Ricans together with other groups as ethnics, see Judith Goode and Jo Anne Schneider, *Reshaping Ethnic and Racial Relations in Philadelphia: Immigrants in a Divided City*, Philadelphia: Temple University Press, 1994.

64 Gunnar Myrdal, *An American Dilemma*, New York: Harper, 1944. For a critique of this work, see Robert Blauner, *Racial Oppression in America*, New York Harper & Row, 1972.

65 For an interesting attempt to map the invention of the white race in the U.S. see Theodore W. Allen, *The Invention of the White Race,* New York & London: Verso, 1994.

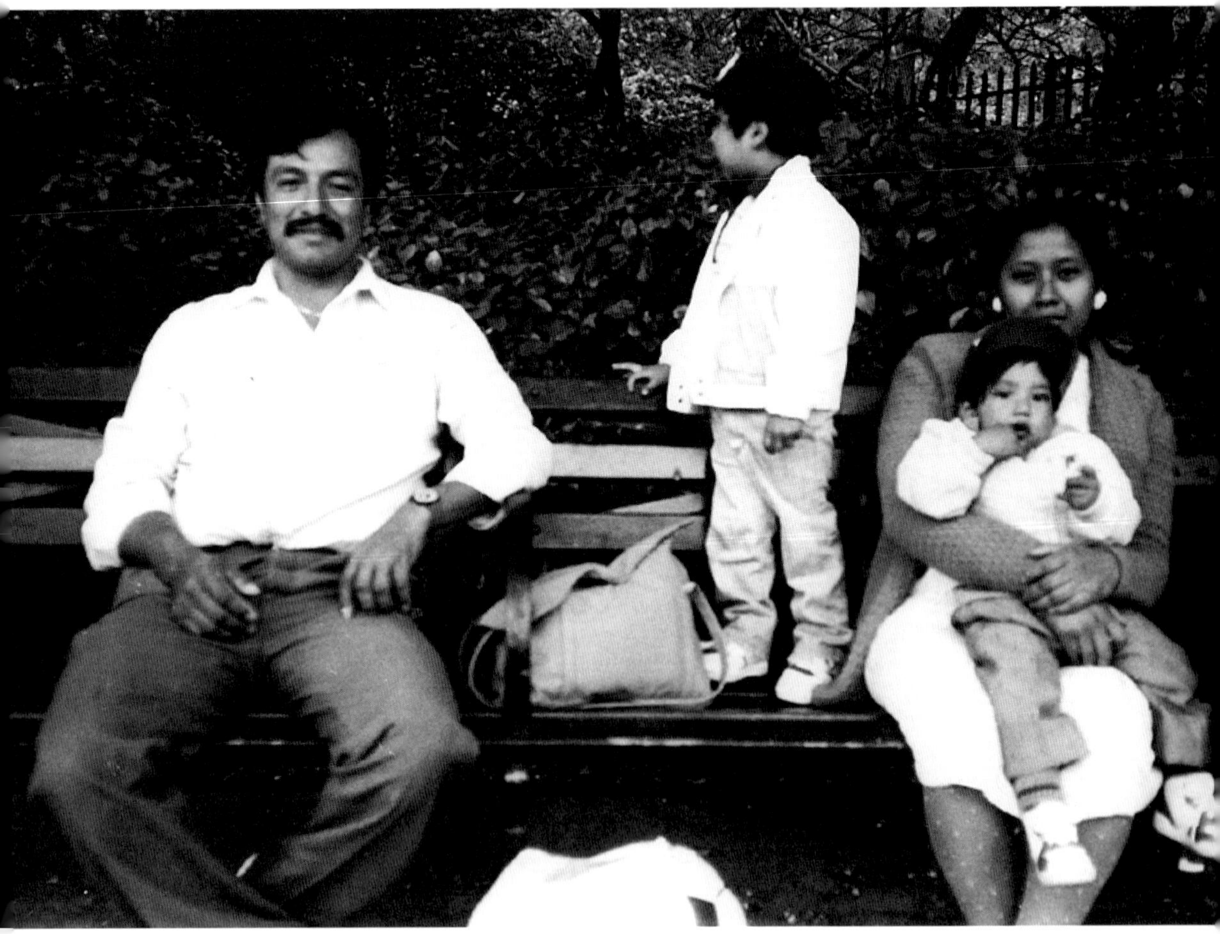

Pan-Latino/Trans-Latino:
Puerto Ricans in the "New Nueva York"

JUAN FLORES

One of the most dramatic and visible changes in the face of New York City over the past 20 years or has been the growing diversity of its Latino presence. Of course Puerto Ricans have never been the lone Spanish-speaking group here; earlier chapters of that history, as told by chroniclers like Bernardo Vega and Jesús Colón, abound with accounts of Cubans, Dominicans, Spaniards, Mexicans, and many other "Hispanos" making common cause with Puerto Ricans in everyday life and in social struggles on many fronts. But over the decades, and especially with the mass migration of the 1950s, Puerto Ricans have so outnumbered all other Latinos that they have served as the prototype or archetype—certainly the stereotype—of Latino/Hispanic/"Spanish" New York. Increasingly since the 20s, and indelibly with influential representations of Puerto Rican culture such as *West Side Story* and Oscar Lewis' *La Vida*, the overlap has been nearly complete, the terms "Latin New York" and "Puerto Rican" ringing virtually synonymous in the public mind.

By the 90s that image—based of course on unambiguous demographic realities—has waned significantly, especially as the media and many research efforts tend to find greater delight in the novelties and anomalies of "other," more exotic newcomers than in the more familiar Puerto Rican culture. And yet, the growth, quantitative and qualitative, of the Dominican community, especially in New York City and in urban Puerto Rico, has been nothing short of sensational; the political and cultural consequences of such growth, for New York, the Dominican Republic, Puerto Rico, and perhaps most of all for the Puerto Rican community in New York, are already highly visible and promise to increase over time.

The "Mexicanization" of New York has also proceeded apace, especially over the past decade; in fact, for some years the proportional arrival rates of migration from the Mexican state of Puebla may even exceed those from the Dominican Republic. Add to them the huge numbers of Colombians, Salvadorans, Ecuadorians, Panamanians, Hondurans, Haitians, Brazilians, and the "new" New Yorkers from nearly every country of Latin America and the Caribbean, and it is clear why "Latinos in New York" no longer rhymes with Puerto Rican.

This momentous pan-Latinization over the course of a single generation makes it necessary to rethink the whole issue of Puerto Rican culture and identity in the United States. How does Puerto Rican/Nuyorican (self) identification and cultural history interface with and elude the pan-ethnic "Latino" or "Hispanic" label? We must remember that such an identification has by now become stock-in-trade of most media, government, commercial, social science, and literary-cultural "coverage," so that Puerto Ricans themselves have constant recourse to the term in extending their political, cultural, and intellectual reach in

---

JUAN FLORES is director of the Centro de Estudios Puertorriqueños and a professor in the Department of Black and Puerto Rican Studies at Hunter College, and in sociology and cultural studies at the CUNY Graduate Center.
■ *Máximo R. Colón*

accord with changing social realities. For while we may be appropriately critical and even suspicious in the face of the catchall categories, a contemporary analysis of Puerto Rican culture and politics in New York necessarily invokes a more embracing term and idea such as "Latino" to refer to what is clearly an ensemble of congruent and intertwining historical experiences. Most of the deliberation over the Latino/Hispanic label thus far has been national (that now all of the United States) in reference, or with a mind to areas, mostly cities, witnessing ample interaction among more or less equally sizeable Latino groups (Chicago is the first example to come to mind, though Los Angeles and Miami are also pertinent). But in many ways it is New York which has become the pan-Latin city par excellence. And it is perhaps here, in the "new," post-Nuyorican Nueva York, that the Latino concept of group association stands its strongest test.

■ *The New Mix*

The first signs of imminent change can be traced to the early 1960s. The aftermath of the 1959 Cuban Revolution brought a huge new influx of Cuban exiles, many of them settling in the New York area. The death of Trujillo in 1961 marked an easing of the restrictive emigration policies that had prevailed in the Dominican Republic throughout the Trujillo era (1930–60). Pressing economic conditions and ongoing political strive, especially the civil war and American military invasion in 1965, have propelled growing numbers of Dominicans to the immigrate to the U.S. ever since. The overwhelming majority of them—by 1990 a full two-thirds—came to New York City.

But what is considered the single most important factor to usher in the "new immigration" was the change in the U.S. immigration law in 1965, which put an end to the national origins quota system, in effect since the 1920s, favoring northern and western Europeans. This policy shift, which placed a ceiling of 120,000 people each for Asia and the Western Hemisphere, literally opened the floodgates to a massive immigration from many parts of Asia and most countries of Latin America and the Caribbean. True to its longstanding historical role, New York City has continued to be a favored destination for these new arrivals, and the figures for the post-1965 period are indeed telling. "In the past two decades," it was reported in 1987, "more than a million immigrants have settled in New York City, most from the West Indies, Latin America, and Asia...." According to the 1980 census, 80 percent of the Asian-born, 82 percent of the Jamaican-born, and 88 percent of the Trinidadian-born residents in the New York metropolitan area had arrived since 1965.[1] That was how things stood a decade before the 1990 count, which recorded an even greater increase of new arrivals.

New New Yorkers from Spanish-speaking countries, increasingly referred to in official parlance as "Hispanics," figure prominently in this demographic explosion, and their numbers are true to the pattern. With the exception of Puerto Ricans and Cubans, representation from nearly all countries of Latin America and the Spanish Caribbean has increased geometrically over the decades since 1960. Already numbering nearly a million according to official count by 1960, the size of the composite New York Latino population has more than doubled by 1990 to make up a full fourth of all New Yorkers, equal in proportion to African Americans. National groups with only a minor presence of one or two thousand in 1960 (for example, Salvadorans, Guatemalans, Hondurans, and Peruvians) have grown to around 20,000 by 1990, while the ranks of Colombians, Ecuadorians, and Mexicans have swelled to well over 50,000 each within the 30-year period. The most dramatic increase, of course, is among the Dominicans, who at 13,293 represented 1.7 percent of the city's Latino population in 1960; by 1990, Dominican New Yorkers totalled 332,713 or 18.7 percent of Latinos in New York, making them by far the largest Latino community after the Puerto Ricans.[2]

But while the legislative change of 1965, and for the sake of statistical contrast the 1960 census, may serve as convenient signposts for marking off the "old" from the "new" immigration period, the most dramatic demographic leaps among New York Latino groups actually occur a decade later and thereafter. The "New Nueva York," as *New York Newsday* titled a lengthy supplement on the city's Latinos in 1991, is really a phenomenon of the

1980s and 1990s, though trends did point clearly in that direction by the later 1970s. If one looks at the overall Latino population, it is true that growth has been roughly the same per decade since 1960. But when it comes to the diversification of New York's Latinos, and the emergence of the "pan-Latino" face by which the city is now recognized, the last quarter of the twentieth century makes for a more accurate time frame. For, to begin with, it was in the 1970s that the Puerto Rican migration, having reaching a benchmark around 1970, levelled off significantly. Puerto Ricans continued to arrive by the thousands, but their numbers were more than offset by a continually growing return migration and by diasporic dispersion in the U.S.

Relative to many other Latino groups, and to the composite Latino population, the proportion of Puerto Ricans has been on a steady decline: over 80 percent in 1960, Latin New York is now only half Puerto Rican, with a full 10 percent drop in the 1980s. Cuban New Yorkers, after doubling in size in the post-Revolution 1960s, have been declining substantially ever since; long the city's second largest Hispanic group, and still so in 1970, they were far surpassed by Dominicans during the 1970s; by 1980 there were twice as many Dominicans as Cubans, and by 1990 over six times as many. By 1990, in fact, Cubans no longer even counted among the five largest Latino groups in the city: in 1980 they were still a comfortable third, but by the latest offical tabulation they have come to be outnumbered by Colombians, Ecuadorians, and Mexicans, with Salvadorans, Panamanians, and Peruvians ranging not too far behind.

This radical reconfiguration of the Latino mix in New York is of course a highly complex, conjunctural process, with layers and levels of explanation as diverse as the range of Latin American nationalities that have come to reside in the city in the present generation. Rather than one, pan-Latino story of arrival and settlement in New York, there are clearly Cuban, Puerto Rican, Dominican, Salvadoran and Colombian stories, each of them bearing varied and sometimes jarring internal narratives of their own. Still, the stories all converge in "Nueva York," achieving full hemispheric representation, including even that crucial Mexican component, by 1990. The common locus of new social experience and identity formation is New York City, just at a time when it is being christened a "global city" in the contemporary sense.[3]

It is in the story of present-day New York City, the restructurings—some would say its rotting, squashing, or slicing of the Big Apple in accord with its global geo-economic role, that it is possible to find a binding thread in the intricate Latino weave, or at least a framework in which to interpret the huge and diverse Latino presence in some more encompassing way. From this perspective, the history of the "new" immigration, and particularly the story of Latinos settling in New York, takes on a different range and contour. Rather than stretching from 1965 to the present, the change-over from "old" to "new" immigration has comprised two periods, corresponding to two phases in the restructuring of the city's economy since midcentury, with the turning point being marked by the fiscal crisis of the mid-1970s. The first phase, from 1950 to 1975, but especially since the early 1960s, amounted to a time of "dashed hopes" for Puerto Ricans; the second, since 1975, is characterized by their "re-placement" in both senses of the word-to other places, and by other groups.

When Puerto Ricans began flocking to New York by the tens and hundreds of thousands in the late 1940s and early 1950s, hopes were high, and expectations only reasonable, that over time they would find their place in the local economy. There would be gaps to fill in the city's postwar labor market, the thinking went, and adequate employment opportunities for newcomers, which in those years meant predominantly Puerto Ricans and African Americans: "Assuming continued regional vitality and an effective educational system, there was no a priori reason to doubt the likelihood of successful incorporation of these groups into the economic mainstream."[4] The shared historical experience between "Latinos" and African Americans warrants particular emphasis: New York's "Negroes and Puerto Ricans" were, after all, the "newcomers" in Oscar Handlin's influential 1959 book of that title.[5]

But "continued regional vitality," presupposing as it does for the "global city" continued national and international economic vitality, was decidedly not in the offing. The stagnation that set in by the late 1950s, combined with the disastrous aftermath of the Operation

Bootstrap experiment, dashed whatever hopes Puerto Ricans might have held to strike a more stable and favorable foothold in New York life. "For Puerto Ricans the principal outcome of this period was labor force displacement, manifested in a sharp decline in labor force participation and a rise in unemployment from 1960 to 1970."[6] In 1976, in what amounts to a taking stock of this phase, the United States Commission on Civil Rights released its alarming report, *Puerto Ricans in the Continental United States: An Uncertain Future*, which put Puerto Ricans on record as the exception to the rule of immigrant incorporation and advancement.[7]

The second phase, beginning in the mid-1970s, brought a continuation of these developments, but at more intense levels and in different ways. Unemployment levels among Puerto Ricans magnified as stable jobs in both the corporate and public sectors became ever scarcer. Public employment opportunities, which had expanded consistently since midcentury and absorbed increasing numbers of Puerto Rican and African American workers, were curtailed sharply as a result of the fiscal crisis of 1975–76, with Puerto Ricans being the heaviest casualties in this shrinkage. The replacement of relocated corporations by service industries and light manufacturing harbored little hope, as both "established a new profile of occupations and labor process" largely inaccessible to African Americans and Puerto Ricans. The reorganization of light manufacturing since the mid-1970s in particular spelled the large-scale "re-placement" of Puerto Ricans by more recent immigrants, mostly other Latinos: "The labor force attached to the earlier manufacturing complex, which had been displaced to a significant extent, was not redeployed into the newly evolving sector. The growth of the new sector was dependent on a lower cost of labor, a condition met by the use of new sources of immigrant labor." And further, "It is a considerably revamped manufacturing sector [in which Puerto Ricans have had a historically high representation], dependent on lower labor costs, that has largely absorbed Dominican labor," though it is added that "since the mid-1980s, the garment industry has suffered a new period of decline."[8]

"Decline within Decline"—the title of the article cited—seems an apt description of what New York's huge Latino population has experienced in recent decades, at least when it comes to its fit into a sharply fluctuating labor market. For the critical socioeconomic hardships confronting the New York's "new" Latinos in the 1990s are an extension, a further stage, in a local, regional, and global restructuring process extending back to the 1950s and experienced at its onset by an overwhelmingly Puerto Rican population. In important ways, adjustments in the city as a postindustrial command center propelled the demographic movements leading to its most recent re-peopling. The emergence of a "pan-Latino" New York comes in the wake of a prior move to import and incorporate Puerto Ricans.

Whatever the parallels and differences, though, the pan-ethnic diversity of the current Latino population is in large measure a reflex of major structural shifts as manifest in the regional political economy of the "global city." The history of this adjustment extends back to the immediate postwar years and has entailed a paradigmatic change in the immigrant experience, from the "old," mainly European, to the "new," mainly Hispanic. Viewed in its full trajectory, the Latinization of New York centers on the congruences and contrasts between Puerto Ricans and the other Latino groups, individually and as a composite. For Puerto Ricans are not only "still the largest and oldest" of the New York Latino populations. With a century of experience here, New York Puerto Ricans actually straddle the "old" and the "new," and their emigration en masse in the 1950s and 1960s was clearly the first wave of the "new," non-European flow. Rather than just one more among the many Latino groups, receding in relative prominence as the others expand and dig in, the Puerto Rican community remains at the crux of any consideration of Latinos in New York, the historical touchstone against which much else that follows must be tested.

Within present-day public discourse it is the embattled concept of "Latino" or "Hispanic" that is once again at issue, and by extension the policy and practices of "pan-ethnic" categorization. Over the same generation in which New York came to join Chicago, Miami, Houston, Los Angeles as "pan-Latino" cities on a contemporary scale, the terms "Latino" and "Hispanic" have established themselves firmly in everyday U.S. parlance, and the debate over their relative validity and limitations—linking as it does the volatile questions of race and immigration—rages close to the combat zone in the culture wars of our time. Before returning to the "New Nueva York," then, and assessing the new issues of Puerto Rican cultural identity raised by its recent reconfiguration, a critical engagement of that discourse may suggest an appropriate theoretical framework.

■ *Ethnic, Pan-ethnic*

The terms "Hispanic" and "Latino" have come into such wide currency since the 1970s, and especially since the official use of "Hispanic" in the 1980 census, that they have the ring of neologisms, fresh coinages for a new, as yet unnamed presence on the social scene. Historical memory seems to stop short at the heyday of the Chicano and Puerto Rican movements, when it comes to a genealogy of these newfangled labels. Yet the people thus labeled have been using these and similar terms, in English and Spanish, to identify themselves at least since the 1920s and probably much earlier. Even in New York, which when compared to the Southwest is the younger and smaller of the two major concentrations of Hispanic peoples, there were through those early decades countless organizations, periodicals, movements, and events with "Latino," *"Hispano,"* "Latin," "Spanish," "Spanish-speaking" in their titles, probably as many as there were *"Puertorriqueño,"* "Puerto Rican" or *"Boricua."*[9] Indeed, what could be more "Latino" in the sense of pan-ethnic solidarity than the Partido Revolucionario Cubano with its "Sección de Puerto Rico," which united the two Caribbean nationalities in joint struggle against Spanish colonialism? The Partido, and its affiliated Club Dos Antillas, which included Dominicans and sundry "others," were active in New York City over 100 years ago.

The sense and practice of a "Latino/Hispanic" unity across national lines thus go way back, as does the recognized need for names to designate such tactical or enduring common ground. Even the government bureaucracy was not without its earlier pan-group usage: before "Hispanic" the traditional entry had been "Spanish Origin," with "Spanish/Hispanic origin or descent" cropping up frequently in explanatory memos prior to the 1980 Census.[10] And there are continuities between the older and the more recent (self-)identifications, not the least of which is their consistently Eurocentric connotation. Though surely outnumbered by the casualties of time and renaming, there are pan-Latino organizations, newspapers, neighborhoods, and of course people that harken back to the earlier decades and attest to the longevity of the cross-ethnic newborn whose baptism we are now asked to celebrate, or at least acknowledge. As has been well argued, the "racialization" of Latin American and Caribbean peoples in the U.S., the "othering" process for which the label "Hispanic" provides an official seal, spans the full 20th century, and if we extend the frame to include hemispheric relations, much of the 19th century as well.[11]

What is new, if not the object or act of signification, is the discursive context, the sociohistorical climate in which the (self-) naming is enacted. The quantum growth, diversification, and dispersal of the Latino populations over a single generation are surely at the base of this change, though the many Latino social and cultural movements since the late 1960s also resonate strongly in the new semantic reality. More than the census count itself, it is the echoing cries of Brown Power and the alarm signals about "America's fastest growing minority" that have set the temper for the present discourse, a collective mood ranging from radical defiance to a national anguish bordering on hysteria. By the 1990s, "Hispanic" and "Latino" are everywhere, the terms, like the people themselves, having proliferated in numbers and locations, and having assumed an emotional charge and connotative complexity unknown in their previous historical usages.

And the "coverage," in the form of media specials and academic studies, also abounds. In the 1980s and 90s most major newspapers and magazines dedicated investigative surveys and extensive portraits of the "new Americans" from south of the border, while in the same period dozens of books and hundreds of journal articles have focused on the "sleeping giant" of U.S. cultural and political life. The subject now is the experience not so much of single national or regional groups—Caribbeans, say, or Mexicans and Central Americans— but of the whole composite, the "Hispanic" or "Latino" experience, with an emphasis on commonalities and interactions across groups. The first half of the 1990s alone saw the publication of the following book titles: *Latinos: A Biography of the People; Latinos in a Changing U.S. Economy: Comparative Perspectives on Growing Inequality; Hispanic Presence in the United States: Historical Beginnings; Out of the Barrio: Toward a New Politics of Hispanic Assimilation; Ethnic Labels, Latino Lives: Identity and the Politics of (Re)Presentation in the United States; The Hispanic Condition: Reflections on Culture and Identity in America;* and even, *Everything You Need to Know about Latino History.*

These varied works—and their variety along political, methodological, and stylistic lines could hardly be more thorough—all tend to take the validity of the pan-category for granted, and proceed to make their analyses, spin their reflections, and set forth their policy proposals on that basis. Disclaimers and qualifiers abound, of course, and a book like Earl Shorris' *Latinos*, subtitled "a biography of a people," actually harps more on differences among the groups than on their similarities, and the promised story line ends up splintering into what are really "biographies of people." Little critical energy goes to scrutiny of the category itself, and what there is of theoretical options often amounts to a stereotyped counterposition of "Hispanic" vs. "Latino," with no evidence of a consensus as to the preferred term.[12] But there is in all of these writings an assumption that the term(s) refer to something real or in the making, whether a demographic aggregate, a voting bloc, a market, a language or cultural group, a "community" or, in Ilan Stavans' grandiloquent phrase, a "condition." Given the xenophobic tenor of mainstream politics in the 1990s, of course, which perceives "Hispanic" and "Latino" most of all as a "problem" ("HisPANIC Causing Panic"), such conceptions are all necessary and contribute to the social construction of a major group identity.

A consensus of these writings would probably settle on "ethnicity" as the concept that most closely approximates the bond among Latinos, and the boundary that marks them off from "others" in U.S. settings. Though the phrase "Hispanic ethnic group" does not always appear as such, the underlying premise throughout America today is that insofar as Latinos comprise a definable group, they are an ethnicity. But even in those scholarly efforts that seem least troubled by lumping Hispanics together and demographers are no less inclined in this direction than are culturalists—there is also an abiding awareness that if anything this is an ethnicity of ethnicities, an "ethnic group" that does not exist but for the existence of its constituent "subgroups."

A more circumspect line of thinking therefore refers to Latinos as a "pan-ethnicity," a group formation that emerges out of the interaction or close historical congruence of two or more culturally related ethnicities. The "pan-ethnic" approach, for which writers like David López, Yen Espiritu, and others have done much to establish a place in contemporary social theory,[13] has the distinct advantage for the study of Latinos of centering analysis on the dialectic between the parts and the whole, the discrete national groups and the "Latino" construct. The focus is necessarily on interaction, while the hypostasized social group itself, along with its "discourse," is understood as process rather than as a fixed entity or meaning.

An early instance of such an approach, though predating concepts like pan-ethnicity by over a decade, is Felix M. Padilla's *Latino Ethnic Consciousness: The Case of Mexican Americans and Puerto Ricans in Chicago*. Published in 1985, the book is actually based on case studies from the early 1970s, when Chicago was still the city with the nation's most substantial multi-Latino population, and the two largest groups, Mexican Americans and Puerto Ricans, at that. Padilla's aim was to analyze "the process of Latino/Hispanic ethnic group formation in the city of Chicago."[14] He is interested in the "conditions that have enabled Mexican Americans and Puerto Ricans to transcend the boundaries of the respective nationally and culturally based communities and adopt a new and different collective 'Latino' or 'Hispanic' identity during the early years of the 1970s." By studying the "interaction process involving Puerto Ricans and Mexican Americans," he seeks to understand the emergence of a "Latino or Hispanic ethnic-conscious identity and behavior, distinct and separate from the groups' individual ethnic identities."

The strength and the weakness of Padilla's book, looked at now with the advantage of hindsight, is its pragmatism. On the positive side, it takes seriously what should be an imperative of "pan-ethnic" analysis, the study of the actual social interaction between and among Latino groups. Focusing on the lived experience of distinct but kindred communities coming together to act, and feel, as one, Padilla avoids cultural essentialism before that pitfall was being talked about, at least in present-day terms. To this end, he argues well for an understanding of Latino unity as "situational"—and also "political" in the sense of being grounded in the recognition of shared social interests.

The problem with this on-the-ground, pragmatic concept of "Latinismo," however, is that it reduces the object of study, "ethnic consciousness," to "behavior" (the words are coupled throughout, often as synonyms). And because the emergent Latino identity is taken in such explicit and deliberate separation from Mexican American or Puerto Rican identity, the process of pan-ethnic formation is disengaged from the historical trajectories of each group. The book is notably sparse, in fact, on such background, and on any sustained attempt to explain how so many Mexicans and Puerto Ricans got to Chicago in the first place. Contrary to his own expressed political sentiments, and to views about "Latinismo" to appear in his subsequent writings,[15] Padilla effectively divorces the formation of pan-Latino unity from its larger international context, Latin America.

Many of these limitations are averted, and the terms of analysis significantly updated, in Suzanne Oboler's recent book, *Ethnic Labels, Latino Lives: Identity and the Politics of (Re)Presentation in the United States*, published in 1995. Here the hemispheric sensibility is more alive, as would befit a Peruvian American writing in the years when "Latino ethnic consciousness" is being infused with perspectives and experiences from all over *"nuestra América."* Oboler treats the conceptualization of Latino identity in much broader theoretical and historical terms than Padilla does. Indeed, her treatment is broader than other writings on the subject to date. And while expansive, her account of "the Hispanic condition" wisely avoids the presumptuousness, and the glaring errors, of Ilan Stavans' in his book of that unhappy title.[16] Most important, Oboler is writing after the term "Hispanic" has been made official as a census category and during commercial circulation as an item of semantic consumption.

Oboler's major contribution, as her title indicates, is the critical scrutiny of that clash between "labels" and "lives" that is, between imposed and assumed identities. She traces the genesis of and motives behind the newfound "policy" toward Hispanics, and relates it to a larger process of "racialization," though her account of these matters is best supplemented by some of the articles in a special 1992 issue of the journal *Latin American Perspectives* on "The Politics of Ethnic Construction," to which Oboler also contributed.[17] In any case, its sharp dramatization of the crisis of Latino "(re)presentation," its inclusive yet critical sense of a fully "pan-Latino" identity, and its sustained attention to gender and class differentiations make *Ethnic Labels, Latino Lives* an important and welcome advance beyond the methodological and theoretical limitations of Padilla's earlier study.

Nevertheless, when it comes to the Latino concept itself, Oboler remains within Padilla's universe of discourse, or at least in close proximity to it. "Ethnicity," as a reliable category of social differentiation, still reigns supreme, as does the inevitable equivocation, when referring to Latinos, about the two "levels" or kinds of ethnic affiliation, the single group and the pan-ethnic. Oboler cautions repeatedly against the lazy relativism and arbitrariness of the ethnic concept, and calls for a historical and structural differentiation among the "Latino" groups. At points she even sides with skeptics, such as Martha Giménez and David Hayes-Bautista and would seem to do away with the "Hispanic" category altogether.[18] But she pulls back from the implications of Giménez's distinction between "ethnics" and "minorities" and, especially in the second, ethnographic half *of Ethnic Labels, Latinos Lives*, lapses into a "Latino" ethnic relativism of her own.

Oboler conducted her fieldwork—her testing ground for the utility of the Hispanic/Latino label—in New York City in 1988–90. While teaching ESL classes for a union education program, she interviewed thirteen women and nine men who worked in the garment industry. Her informants, most of them between thirty and sixty, come from nine different Latin American countries. Significant in the sample, aside from the circumscription of age and other important variables, is that only one male informant, "Juan," was a Puerto Rican born in New York, and that only three of the twenty-two informants were Puerto

Rican. There were four Colombians, three Dominicans, three Nicaraguans, and two each from Peru, Honduras, and El Salvador. Throughout the book, and when introducing her findings, she emphasizes the main crack in the "Hispanic" front, the difference between the Latin American "immigrant populations" and the "more historically established communities of Chicanos and Puerto Ricans."[19] And in concluding her report she reminds us, "Again, the study is not representative of the immigrant populations from Latin America nor of the Puerto Ricans in New York City,"[20] though she fails to mention that when doing her fieldwork more than 50 percent of New York Latinos were Puerto Rican.

Nevertheless, despite her theoretical intentions, the ethnographic part of *Ethnic Labels, Latino Lives* underplays one of the serious perils in using the Hispanic category, a danger that Martha Giménez for one has identified as potentially "racist"; "these labels are racist," she says, "in that ... they reduce people to interchangeable entities, negating the qualitative differences between, for example, persons of Puerto Rican descent who have lived for generations in New York City and newly arrived immigrants from Chile or some other South or Central American country...."[21]

Now Oboler does not exactly "negate" these differences, as is clear from her theoretical caveats and also because such differences are obvious to all but the most casual observer of Latino life in New York. In fact, it is so significant that she even describes her sample as "a small group of twenty-one Latin American immigrants and one U.S.-born Puerto Rican," and when first defining her studys she seems to have been uncertain even about including any Puerto Ricans, especially those from the U.S.[22] And her report itself has repeated recourse to such conditionals as "many Hispanics, regardless of country of origin (and again, with the exception of Puerto Ricans)" or, "leaving aside the U.S.-born Puerto Rican."[23] The irony is that Oboler does not even need these warning signals; her interviews speak for themselves. "Juan," and to some extent "Teresa," her two U.S.-born Puerto Rican informants, make statements and express views about "Hispanic" identity and U.S. society that stand out markedly among all the testimony. Examples abound, as when Juan says, "I'm American only by accident, because Puerto Rico's a territory of the United States. I don't think it's by choice, because they've got American bases there."[24] Even "Jorge," the Puerto Rican from the Island, responds to the "Latino" category in a way unmatched by the other foreign-born informants: "At the beginning, when I arrived, my boss wanted me to speak English, even though I didn't know the language. I think he thought that I was a Latino."[25]

But most revealing of the divide between New York Puerto Ricans and the other Latino views cited is the lengthy statement by Juan about the contemporary labeling of groups. "White people," he says, "have a name for everybody else. From whites you came up with the word Hispanics, and spic. I mean, Puerto Ricans never call each other Hispanic. They never called each other spics.... They just count all Latin people in one bunch. They do it to the blacks, too. I mean, come on, they're more than just blacks. You got your American blacks, you got your African, your Jamaican; then you got your Puerto Rican blacks; some guys are darker than me. Then you got your Dominican blacks, you got white people that are dark skinned.... So you got your Hispanics over here which includes whatever race you want to put in it south of the border. Then you got your blacks, anything from the Congo down. Then you got your whites which is Americans."[26] Oboler notes that Juan is voicing his recognition that the ethnic labeling process in the U.S. context involves the conflation of race and nationality, but she does not acknowledge that he is the only one of her informants to pose the issue in those terms. Nor does she make anything of this "exceptional" perspective. Rather, she is so intent on drawing out contrasting class, and to a lesser extent gender, positions across national lines that she leaves unanalyzed the blatant singularity of the "Nuyorican" among the many Latino voices in New York.

■ *Pan-Latino/Trans-Latino*

Yet this is precisely the most serious challenge facing an analysis of Latino identity in the "New Nueva York": How are we to conceptualize the converging cultural geography of so many Latino lives, and assess the relative validity of a common identificatory term for all, while still giving adequate analytical weight to the special position and standpoint of the largest, oldest, and most structurally different group, the Puerto Ricans? And further, can that qualitative demarcation be drawn without the analysis appearing divisive or "exceptionalist," to the point of ignoring important commonalities and new lines of solidarity suggested by changing historical circumstances?

In the reigning public and social science view, of course, New York Puerto Ricans have long been viewed or construed as the "exception," the extraneous ingredient in the melting pot. The assimilationist thrust involved in ethnic and immigrant analogies has gone accompanied by the social pathologies of the "Puerto Rican problem": one thinks of Glaser and Moynihan and Oscar Lewis, or in more benign terms, of C. Wright Mills and Father Joseph Fitzpatrick. And again in the 1990s, as the Hispanic giant rouses from its slumber, the Puerto Ricans are still the "exception" to the pan-ethnic rule, the "problem" even among their own kind. Derailed from the path "toward a new politics of Hispanic assimilation," U.S. Puerto Ricans are granted a special chapter all their own in Linda Chavez's controversial *Out of the Barrio* (1991). The chapter titled "The Puerto Rican Exception"—says everything. Again the New York Puerto Ricans are stuck in the "*barrio*," mired in their "culture of poverty," while other Latinos are headed for the mainstream. After fifty years of massive presence in New York and other parts of the U.S., Puerto Ricans have gone from being left out of the sauce to being left out of the salsa.

But even Chavez, from her officialist, neoconservative stance, seems at least dimly aware that a dismissive, blame-the-victim account only gets her so far when it comes to explaining her "exception." Speaking of Puerto Rican non-assimilation into American ways as evident in their apparent political apathy, she notes, "Puerto Rico's status, however, cannot help having some effect on the attitudes of Puerto Ricans toward the political process, particularly since they retain a strong identification as Puerto Ricans first and Americans second, according to public opinion surveys."[27] Despite their much longer presence here than other New York Latinos and, as formal citizens, their closer historical relationship to U.S. society, Puerto Ricans have most stubbornly rejected the hyphen, and Chavez, for many of the wrong reasons of course, stumbles onto the key line of explanation. "Puerto Rico," she remarks, "is neither fish nor fowl politically, neither a state nor an independent nation."[28] By relating the Puerto Ricans' "exceptional," unassimilable position to the issue of the political status of Puerto Rico, Chavez is acknowledging that the pan-ethnic concept needs to be aligned with a knowledge of transnational relations if it is to include its most notable "exception." As expected, she sidesteps the deeper implications of this wider conceptual field, concluding her thoughts cursorie on the status options with the comforting notion that, "in any event, it is unlikely that a change in Puerto Rico's status will do much to solve the problems that face Puerto Ricans in the United States."[29]

But the association is made, even when the ideological objective is to deny or minimize its pertinence to generalizations about Latinos as a composite group. The bracketing of Puerto Ricans among the Latino aggregate is necessitated by the abiding colonial relationship between the United States and Puerto Rico, which even the most internally focused, U.S. ethnicity-framed discussion cannot altogether ignore. Interestingly, Oboler's South American informants voice an awareness of this difference at some points in their conversation. When "Soledad," who is from Colombia, hears some of her fellow workers saying that they don't know why Puerto Ricans are "separated" from the other groups, volunteers an explanation: "Oh, I do. It's because they're undecided about Puerto Ricans. They don't really know if they're American or if they're Puerto Rican. See, they have a problem with Puerto Ricans because they can't believe that they can be Americans and still speak Spanish. So they catalogue them as Americans for some things, but for others they're Puerto Ricans. When they count for something they're Americans, but when they don't need them to count for anything they're *boricuas.*"[30] Soledad does not explicitly attribute the ambiguity she notes in the identification of Puerto Ricans in New York to the machinations of colonial control, but she is clear that the ambivalence particular to them results from a political opportunism at levels far transcending the confines of the New York *barrios* and factory floors. Here again, the full range of the pan-ethnic category implies transnational relations and perspectives.

Soledad also recognizes that such treatment is not so particular to Puerto Ricans after all, but is perhaps only more evident and intense in their case. The "exception" may also be the paradigm. "But in different ways," she concludes her remarks, "they do that with all of us who speak Spanish. You know, if an American is running, he's just doing exercise; but if one of us is running, we've just committed a robbery."[31] With this common experience in view, what would seem to distinguish the situation of Puerto Ricans—the direct structured link between their "ethnic" placement and the political reality of their homeland—is actually a more graphic and prominent version of the Latino experience in general. The reason for differentiating, and perhaps privileging, a Puerto Rican perspective when analyzing the pan-Latino concept does not rest, therefore, on an appeal to the size and longevity of the New York community, though a much longer historical view than that provided by Oboler is clearly called for. There is, after all, some solid and heartfelt truth in the angry response of *salsero* Willie Colón to the description of Puerto Ricans in *Out of the Barrio*, which he suggests calling "out of left field." "Perhaps Chavez thinks Puerto Ricans have a genetic problem," he notes, and draws a parallel to the pitiful situation of Native Hawaiians. "Just change Hawaii to Puerto Rico. This is what happens to people who become guests in their own home." Stressing the price Puerto Ricans have paid for their ground-breaking role in the history of Latin New York, Colón goes on: "The fact that, in the east, people tolerate Spanish speakers, the reason there are Spanish newspapers, TV and radio shows, bilingual driver's license tests, and salsa music is because Puerto Ricans gave their hearts and souls to earn their place here. Puerto Ricans created an environment that makes it easy for other Latinos to succeed. I hear many new Latino immigrants say, 'In this country any little job is a profession.' That's because they weren't here when they would beat you with a baseball bat for trying to sell *piraguas* or put you in jail for playing dominoes."[32]

Again, this "we-were-here-first" and "there's-more-of-us" reaction, though a valid response to an ahistorical pathology, is not enough to account for the "Puerto Rican exception" among Latino groups. A more adequate explanation, which addresses the seeming paradox of Puerto Ricans having more, as citizens, yet accomplishing less than other Latinos, is suggested in the response to Chavez's book by another public figure, Bronx Congressman José Serrano: "She…blames us for not capitalizing on our citizenship," Serrano remarked. "How do you capitalize on a second-class citizenship? What she doesn't understand is that in the same way slavery's legacy remains with African Americans, colonialism has affected Puerto Ricans."[33] Serrano insists on the long historical view, and on the enduring impact of international power relations on the life and domestic status of Puerto Ricans in U.S. society. Pan-ethnicity only stands up as a reliable group category if it is recognized that each group making up the aggregate is at the same time participating in a transnational community, the example of the Puerto Ricans, as colonial Latino immigrants, being the most salient.

Losing sight of this exception-as-paradigm location of the Puerto Ricans within the pan-Latino geography can lead to serious misconceptions and omissions, as Oboler's "situational" ethnography illustrates. Such blurring abounds, of course, in the more cosmic, essentialist accounts, usually of a journalistic kind, where *"lo Latino"* appears as a glorious new "race," united by a primordial bond forged of the Spanish language and Catholicism, a glorious spirit on the verge of a cultural takeover of Nueva York. Enrique Fernández, for example, the Cuban-American journalist for the *Village Voice*, *Más* magazine and the *Daily News*, moans that "'Hispanization' was a figure of speech at the beginning of the decade. Today, it's an astonishing reality. We're already a majority in San Antonio and Miami. Ay, Nueva York! How soon before we need a 'Festival Americano' to meet minority needs?"[34] Differentiations of a socioeconomic or political kind are a matter of indifference for such triumphalist rhetoric, with the *"nuestros hermanos boricuas"* being but one more condiment in the festive *sancocho*. (That's *"boricuas,"* for Ilan Stavans' information, or *"borincanos,"* but never "Borinquéns."[35])

But such imprecision in posing the notion of Latino "ethnicity," with its characteristic inattention to particularities and exclusions, is rampant in the abundant empirical work on New York's Latinos as well. Demographic and socioeconomic profiles generally take the "Hispanic" aggregate and other census designations for granted and proceed to amass evidence and generate analysis and policy proposals accordingly. The recent report by Fordham's Hispanic Research Center, for example, promisingly titled "Nuestra America en Nueva York: The New Immigrant Hispanic Populations in New York City 1980–1990" (1995), does disaggregate data findings according to national group; but nowhere does it reflect on the differential placement and historical experience of Puerto Ricans, and consistently takes "non-Hispanic whites" (NHW) as the only operational control variable. This conflation of "racial," national, and ethnic categories does not seem to concern the researchers, nor does the potential value of comparisons and contrasts with other groups, particularly African Americans and Asian Americans. And as for any resonances of the José Martí vision taken as their title, "Nuestra America en Nueva York" lacks a hemispheric, transnational frame of analytical reference.

The same criticism goes to the earlier report by Department of City Planning demographers Evelyn S. Mann and Joseph J. Salvo, "Characteristics of New Hispanic Immigrants to New York City: A Comparison of Puerto Rican and Non-Puerto Rican Hispanics." Though the title of this 1984 paper would suggest a closely focused look at the differences between discrete aggregates, Puerto Ricans and "other Hispanics," their results prove to be of limited value, for they do not make a comparison between Puerto Ricans and each of the "other" groups taken separately, and between Puerto Ricans and the entire "Hispanic" aggregate including Puerto Ricans. Further, the explanatory power of their conclusion is minimal, as is evident in their attribution of the reported differences, which they recognize are "wide," to "basic disparaties in fertility, labor force participation and most of all family structure and composition."[35] Once again, ideological assumptions and ahistorical treatment of the "Puerto Rican exception" land us right back at the culture of poverty.

Even analysis undertaken from an explicitly Puerto Rican perspective, where one might expect a more historical cast to the Puerto Rican–"other Hispanic" comparison, can fall short of the mark. The recent essay "Understanding Socioeconomic Differences: A Comparative Analysis of Puerto Ricans and Recent Latino Immigrants in New York City" (1995), for instance, disappoints not because it fails to foreground the particularities of Puerto Rican experience, but because it slides too easily from a contrastive to a pan-Latino project as a result, the weight of the argument and policy orientation ultimately rests more on a Latino-mainstream contrast than one between Puerto Ricans and "recent Latino immigrants."[37] Admittedly a first stab at the topic, the essay does draw the pertinent data into play. It is helpful in defining a research and policy agenda on some of the most visible issues raised in assessing Puerto Rican–"other Latinos" relations. But the most pressing of these issues, having to do with questions of race, class, gender, and political positioning, are either muddled or sidestepped in the name of an undefined "unity," "progress," and "integration."

Many of the shortcomings of "Understanding Socioeconomic Differences," and indeed how far we are from such an "understanding," are evident in the final paragraph: "The severity of most of the socioeconomic indicators presented above challenges researchers, policy makers, and city officials with a sense of urgency; this is not only a problem for the Puerto Rican or Latino communities. Expected growth in the Latino population coupled with a simultaneous stagnation or decline of socioeconomic position has potentially explosive effects for the entire city—as well as for other areas where Puerto Ricans live. While comparisons between Puerto Ricans and other groups are important to understanding how each group is faring, pitting one against the other does nothing to further the progress of any group—and may actually aggravate intergroup conflicts. It is critical for Puerto Ricans to gain entry into different sectors of the city's economy and regain socioeconomic stability. At the same time, however, lessons learned from the Puerto Rican experience in New York City can be useful in successfully integrating other Latino immigrants into the city's mainstream—and charting the progress of future Latino generations. The problems that affect Puerto Ricans have been identified; understanding their origins is the next step toward devising effective solutions."[38]

Perhaps the central question raised in a comparative inter-Latino analysis of present-day New York is the relation between Puerto Ricans and Dominicans, a question that is generally elided because of the frequent official grouping of Dominicans in the "Central and South American" or "Other Hispanic" categories. This absence of Dominicans as a discrete point of comparison is the case in "Understanding Socioeconomic Differences" and in the sources provided in that most recent study. Yet it is clearly the Dominicans, already by far the second largest group and rapidly approaching the number of Puerto Ricans by unofficial count, that bear closest resemblance to the Puerto Ricans in terms of both cultural history and socioeconomic placement. The two groups together, sometimes even conjoined within the Latino aggregate because of their common Caribbean background, account for well over 80 percent of the whole. They command the public image of the "New York Latino." And in addition to magnitude and cultural affinities, it is in its comparison with the situation of Dominicans that the Puerto Rican experience finds its most direct counterpoint.

Unfortunately, sociologically grounded treatment of the Dominican community has thus far left this kind of contrastive analysis largely unaddressed. Whether the pitch is for the community's bustling "vitality" and rapid progress or for its unequalled "poverty"—accounts tend to oscillate between those two extremes—the reference point is the Latino population as a whole, or non-Dominican society in general. A recent study, *Dominican New Yorkers: A Socioeconomic Profile*, for example, marshals ample tabulations comparing Dominicans with "New York City Overall," "Non-Hispanic White," "Non-Hispanic Black" and "Hispanic, overall," but includes only one parenthetical mention of the Puerto Ricans ("only Puerto Ricans have a greater presence").[39] Among other things, the omission of such group-to-group comparison places in question the authors' repeated claim to Dominicans' worst-off status among all New York Hispanics, indeed on many counts among all New Yorkers.

Of course the point of these comparative analyses cannot be to establish a socioeconomic pecking order of the "most oppressed" or the "fastest achievers." The main problem has more to do with methodology and theoretical perspective than with the unexplored terrain itself. Another recent essay by some of the same authors, in fact, arrives at a more balanced account of the complex socioeconomic reality of the New York Dominican community.[40] But it is another recent publication of the CUNY Dominican Studies Institute, Jorge Duany's *Quisqueya on the Hudson: The Transnational Identity of Dominicans in Washington Heights*, that suggests an analytical framework appropriate to a useful comparative study between the two groups, and to a differentiated consideration of the New York Latino experience overall. Duany does not make much mention of Puerto Rican identity—though he has written widely on the subject from many angles—nor does he draw out any parallels or contrasts; his strictly local, neighborhood sample focus, in fact, is even narrower than that of many other studies. But by placing the issue of "Dominican York" experience in the context of globalization and the formation of "transnational identities," he speaks in terms that, from a historical standpoint, resonate with parallels to social processes lived through by Puerto Ricans. In addition to the usual "socioeconomic characteristics," Duany offers observations and cites attitudes on political and cultural orientation toward the homeland, assimilation, and its resistance, bilingualism and race, and a range of other identity issues long of central interest in the study of Puerto Rican life in New York. He frames his discussion with reference to concepts of "transnational communities," diaspora, circular and global migration processes, and other constituents of contemporary cultural theory. When he describes Dominicans, for example, as a "transnational community," "characterized by a constant flow of people in both directions, a dual sense of identity, ambivalent attachments to two nations, and a far-flung network of kinship and friendship ties across state frontiers,"[41] he could just as well be speaking of Nuyoricans, the prototype of that kind of community among Latinos in New York. Quisqueya on the Hudson, seen in these terms, bears more than a casual resemblance to El Barrio on the East River some thirty or forty years ago, a parallel also noted by other seasoned observers.[42]

■ *The Colonial "Exception"*

"Mex-Yorkers," the latest group to appear en masse on the City's Latino landscape, are also very much a "transnational community," as creative ethnographic research has established in convincing detail[43] and a visit to the old Puerto Rican neighborhoods of El Barrio or Williamsburgh, Brooklyn makes palpably evident. Colombians, Ecuadorians, Salvadorans, all of New York's major Latino groups partake of a "transnational sociocultural system" in their everyday lives, "here" or "there," and in their increasingly hybrid forms of self-identification.[44] Individually and as a composite they are more a "diasporic transnation" than anything resembling an ethnic immigrant group. As much as the familiar immigrant narrative may accompany them as they settle into their niches and enclaves, the prospects of their ready or eventual incorporation into New York life remain dim at best under conditions of global economic restructuring. The formation of systemic transnational linkages with economic, political, and cultural dimensions is thus a matter of historical necessity in both locations; the linkages are structured into the very relations between country or region of origin and the U.S., and into the very conditions of migration in the first place. In this respect, the transnational quality of the Latino presence in New York follows the pattern set over the course of decades, and in the most intricate way, imitates the Puerto Rican emigrant experience.

But even as "Latino transnationals" Puerto Ricans remain the "exception" among the New York groups, distinct even from their closest cousins, the Dominican Yorks. This difference is marked off, in a formal sense, by U.S. citizenship, and in the practical social arena, as Congressman Serrano is quick to add, by the second-class nature of that supposedly privileged status. Direct colonial relations, as an uninterrupted legacy and everpresent reality, govern the motives and outcomes of the whole migratory and settlement process, and fix a consistently low ceiling on the group's expectations and opportunities. For Puerto Ricans, the "blessings" of American citizenship have been even worse than mixed. Under the constant sway of colonial machinations, citizenship has been a set-up for stigmatization and pathological treatment, more than outweighing, over the long haul, any advantageous exemption from the most pressing of immigrant woes. As Willie Colón has it in the title of a recent album, Puerto Ricans are "legal aliens." And other Latinos, most of whom have indeed endured the deathly humiliations of undocumented status, recognize this difference themselves; as a correspondent for the *Christian Science Monitor* reported in a survey of Hispanic communities, "whenever Puerto Ricans came up for discussion, Chicanos and Cubans repeatedly said that Puerto Ricans had an extra burden to bear, in addition to their language, their color, and their poverty. It was, they said, the psychological uncertainty resulting from the limbo which Puerto Rico's commonwealth status had turned out to be. To the average Puerto Rican, the argument goes, commonwealth status means his or her being made a kept man or woman of the US."[45]

Puerto Ricans are perhaps most precisely to be considered "colonial emigrants" (or "[im]migrants" as Clara Rodríguez would have it) in the global metropolis, bearing closer congruences, on an international scale, with counterparts like Jamaicans in London, Martinicans in Paris, and Surinamese in Amsterdam.[46] In rebuffing Linda Chávez, Serrano equates the psychological legacy of colonialism for Puerto Ricans with that of slavery for American Blacks, or at least relates them in the same breath as the unmentioned grounding for her shallow diagnosis of the "Puerto Rican exception." And indeed, it is in many ways their long, profound and complex relation to African Americans, even more than the outward marker of citizenship, that most clearly distinguishes the social position and interactions of Puerto Ricans from those of the other transnational Latino groups in New York. Throughout their century-long sojourn in New York, and especially since the late 1940s, New York Puerto Ricans have been at close living and working quarters with Blacks, perhaps closer than any other national group in the history of this country. In addition to unprecedented cultural fusions, most social indicators point consistently to Puerto Ricans bearing greater similarities to Blacks than to the other Latino groups or to the Latino aggregate.[47] Needless to say, because of the gulf between sociodemographic and qualitative-theoretical analysis, little has been made thus far of those potent and demonstrable realities. And the foisting of a "Latino" construct onto the field of identity options has only further clouded the issue.

As different from transnational diasporic communities in general, the colonial emigrant is organically inserted into the racial divide and the cultural and class dynamic of the metropolitan society. Especially since the 1960s, the issue of Puerto Rican identity has been entwined with the social and cultural experience of African Americans, with the concomitant problems of blackness and "double consciousness"—indeed, more so than is likely even for that of the "blacker" Dominican community for some time to come. Similarly, Puerto Ricans in the U.S. bear closer historical ties to the Chicano population than do their ancestral cultural kin from Central America, and even their Mixteco neighbors in El Barrio. It is the directness of the colonial tie that thus places U.S. Puerto Ricans both inside and outside of U.S. domestic politics, with interests rooted equally in the struggles for justice and equality in the U.S. and in the struggles for sovereignty in the Caribbean and Latin America. The sense of ambivalence generally attributed to the limbo of commonwealth status has to do with this duality of political focus, this simultaneous grounding on two social fronts. But it is not just a "burden," as sympathetic fellow Latinos call it, nor does it necessarily spell dysfunction or identity crisis. Strategically, with an unprecedented half of the nationality living on either side, and with the "sides" constantly intermingling because of an unparalleled circular migration, there is no alternative to a multiple-identity position.

The adequacy of the embattled "Latino" or "Hispanic" concept hinges on its inclusiveness toward the full range of social experiences and identities, and particularly its bridging of the divergence within the contemporary configuration between recent "Latino immigrant" populations and, for want of a better term, the "resident minority" Chicano and Puerto Rican communities. In the context of the "New Nueva York," the toughest test of "Latinismo" is its negotiation of the varied lines of solidarity and historically structured relations informing Puerto Rican social identity—with other, Francophone or Anglophone Caribbean communities, for example, or with African Americans and Chicanos, or with other colonial migrants in "global cities," or of course with other Puerto Ricans, "over there" on the Island, or "out there" in the diaspora. All of these crucial dimensions of New York Puerto Rican self-identification stretch the "pan-Hispanic" idea in different ways, but must be accounted for if Puerto Ricans are not once again, as was reported back in 1958, to "substitute [the terms 'Hispano' and 'Latino'] for that of 'Puerto Rican,' because the latter, in more ways than one, has become a 'bad public relations' identification for New York Puerto Ricans."[48] That is, unless the pan-ethnic net is cast wide enough across and along language, racial, class. and geographic lines, the Puerto Rican component too readily equates with the stigmatized, abject implications of the label. As a result, Puerto Ricans are seen as the stain that the "new politics of Hispanic assimilation" must cleanse.

On the other hand, the influence is of course reciprocal and general, and the perspectives introduced by the new Latino groups are also helping shape the terms of a multigroup identity and social movement. These terms are always provisional and subject to reexamination, as is clear in the ironic reversal of inter-Latino conditions in present-day Chicago, where "Latino ethnic consciousness" was first committed to sociological study by Felix Padilla. By the end of 1995, there are Latino groups calling for a dismantling of the Congressional district they had once fought so hard to create. The reason given was that Mexicans and Puerto Ricans are, in their words, "racially different and have little in common beyond their language."[49] (By the way, the president of Chicago's Latino Firefighters Association Charles Vázquez pointedly responded to the quote, "To those who say we are 'racially different,' what's the difference between a poor Mexican making minimum wage and a poor Puerto Rican making minimum wage?"[50]) Tales of such contention among Latino groups abound, of course, in Los Angeles, Miami and New York. They put the lie to any too facile, wistful, or ominous image of Latinos as a seamlessly knitted tribe or horde. Yet practical disjunctures do not necessarily invalidate the strategic prospects and formative process of Latino unity. Rather, they point up the need for an eminently flexible, inclusive concept based on a clear understanding of historical differences and particularities.

With such a concept in view, one can only agree with Oboler when she argues that "differences in the ways that race and class are understood by more recently arrived Latin American immigrants are important to consider in assessing the issues that contribute toward or hinder the fostering of...a 'Latino Culture' in the U.S. context."[51] The lessons and experiences from Latin America and the Caribbean stand to enrich and broaden the cultural and political horizons of Latinos, notably Mexican Americans and Puerto Ricans, with a longer standing in U.S. barrios and workplaces. They offer grounds for hope that the idea and study of "Latino" might transcend—and transgress—the domestic confines of U.S. public discourse on politics and cultural identity, and engage (or re-engage) it to the global processes of which it is a part. This hope is very much alive in the "New Nueva York," as Puerto Ricans-U.S. citizens and increasingly English-speaking-are impelled in the name of Latino solidarity to reassert their commitment to immigrant and language rights, and to embrace the trans-Latino vision of "nuestra América."[52] ∎

ENDNOTES

1. Nancy Foner, ed. *New Immigrants in New York* (New York: Columbia University, 1987), pp. 1, 3.
2. As cited by Gabriel Haslip-Viera, "The Evolution of the Latino Community in the New York Metropolitan Area, 1810 to the Present," in Haslip-Viera and Sherrie Baver, eds. *Latinos in New York: Communities in Transition* (Notre Dame: Notre Dame University, forthcoming 1996).
3. See for example the influential book by Saskia Sassen, *The Global City: New York, London, Tokyo* (Princeton: Princeton University, 1991). The idea of New York as a "global city" was also an integral part of the mayoral campaign and administration of Ed Koch; see also Robert Fitch, *The Assassination of New York* (London: Verso, 1993), esp. "Global City or Globaloney."
4. Andrés Torres and Frank Bonilla, "Decline Within Decline: The New York Perspective," in *Latinos in a Changing U.S. Economy,* Rebecca Morales and Frank Bonilla, eds. (Newbury Park, CA: Sage, 1993), pp. 98–99.
5. Oscar Handlin, *The Newcomers: Negroes and Puerto Ricans in a Changing Metropolis* (Cambridge: Harvard University, 1959).
6. Torres and Bonilla, op.cit. 99.
7. *Puerto Ricans in the Continental United States: An Uncertain Future* (Washington, DC: U.S. Commission on Civil Rights, 1976). That report concludes (p. 145): "The Commission's overall conclusion is that mainland Puerto Ricans generally continue mired in the poverty facing first generations of all immigrant or migrant groups. Expectations were that succeeding generations of mainland Puerto Ricans would have achieved upward mobility. One generation later, the essential fact of poverty remains little changed. Indeed, the economic situation of the mainland Puerto Ricans has worsened over the last decade. "The United States has never before had a large migration of citizens from offshore, distinct in culture and language and also facing the problem of color prejudice. After 30 years of significant migration, contrary to conventional wisdom that once Puerto Ricans learned the language the second generation would move into the mainstream of American society, the future of this distinct community in the United States is still to be determined."
8. Torres and Bonilla, op.cit. 102–3.
9. For a discussion of pan-ethnic Latino organizations and activities in New York during the early decades, see Ruth Glasser, *My Music Is My Flag: Puerto Rican Musicians and Their New York Communities* (Berkely: University of California, 1995), esp. pp. 94 97. See also Bernardo Vega, *Memoirs of Bernardo Vega: A Contribution to the History of the Puerto Rican Community in New York* (New York: Monthly Review, 1984).
10. See Jack D. Forbes, "The Hispanic Spin: Party Politics and Governmental Manipulation of Ethnic Identity," *Latin American Perspectives* 19:4 (1992), 59–78.
11. For this wider historical perspective, see Forbes, ibid.; Martha Giménez, "U.S. Ethnic Politics: Implications for Latin Americans," *Latin American Perspectives* 19:4 (1992), 7–17; William I. Robinson, "The Global Economy and the Latino Populations in the United States: A World Systems Approach," *Critical Sociology* 19:2 (1992), 29–59; Félix Padilla, "Latin America: The Historical Base of Latino Unity," *Latino Studies Journal* 1:1 (1990), 7–27.
12. On the question of terminology ("Hispanic" or/vs. "Latino"), see David E. Hayes Bautista and Jorge Chapa, "Latino Terminology: Conceptual Basis for Standardized Terminology," *American Journal of Public Health* 77 (1987), 61–68; Fernando M. Treviño, "Standardized Terminology for Standardized Populations," *American Journal of Public Health* 77 (1987), 69–72; Earl Shorris, Latinos: Biography of a People (New York: Norton, 1992), xv-xvii; Ilan Stavans, *The Hispanic Condition: Reflections on Culture and Identity in America* (New York: Harper Collins, 1995), esp. 24–27.
13. See David López and Yen Espiritu, "Panethnicity in the United States: A Theoretical Framework," *Ethnic and Racial Studies* 13 (1990), 198–224: Yen Le Espiritu, Asian American Panethnicity: Building Institutions and Identities (Philadelphia: Temple, 1992); Howard Winant, *Racial Conditions: Politics, Theory, Comparisons* (Minneapolis: University of Minnesota, 1994), pp. 60–62.
14. Padilla, *Latino Ethnic Consciousness: The Case of Mexican Americans and Puerto Ricans in Chicago* (Notre Dame: Notre Dame University, 1985), p.vii.
15. See e.g. Padilla, "Latin America: The Historical Base of Latino Unity," op. cit., n. 9, and "On the nature of Latino ethnicity," in R. de la Garza, ed. *The Mexican American Experience* (Austin: University of Texas, 1985), pp. 332–345.

16 Misguided pomposity and downright errors abound in Stavans' book. They are evident in his use of worings such as like "Latino metabolism," "a five-hundred-year-old fiesta of miscegenation," "Latino assimilation into the melting pot," "our aim is to assimilate Anglos slowly to ourselves," "[s]ociety is beginning to embrace Latinos, from rejects to fashion setters, from outcasts to insider traders," "[y]esterday's victim and tomorrow's conquistadors, we Hispanics," etc.

17 See especially José Calderón, "'Hispanic' or 'Latino': The Viability of Categories for Panethnic Unity," 37–44, and Jack D. Forbes, "The Hispanic Spin: Party Politics and Governmental Manipulation of Ethnic Identity," 59–78.

18 See Oboler, op. cit., pp. 3–6.

19 Ibid., p.102.

20 Ibid., p. 157.

21 Giménez, "U.S. Ethnic Politics...," loc. cit., note 9 above, p. 8.

22 Oboler, pp. 102, 110.

23 Ibid., pp. 111, 122.

24 Ibid., p. 152.

25 Ibid., pp. 152, 154.

26 Ibid., p. 155.

27 Chavez, p. 156.

28 Ibid.

29 Chavez, p. 158.

30 Oboler, op. cit. p. 140.

31 Ibid.

32 Willie Colon "Taking Exception with Chavez," *New York Newsday*, 1991, p. 86.

33 José Serrano, *New York Newsday*, p. 83.

34 Enrique Fernandez, "Estilo Latino: Buscando Nueva York [sic]," *Village Voice* (August 9, 1988), p. 19.

35 Stavans, *The Hispanic Condition*, pp. 42 passim.

36 Mann and Salvo (Abstract).

37 "Understanding Socioeconomic Differences," ms. submitted to *Revista de Ciencias Sociales* (Puerto Rico), 1996.

38 Ibid., ms. p. 35–6.

39 Ramona Hernández, Francisco Rivera-Batiz, and Roberto Agodini, *Dominican New Yorkers: A Socioeconomic Profile* (New York: CUNY Dominican Studies Institute, 1995), p.5.

40 See Ramona Hernández and Silvio Torres-Saillant, "Dominicans in New York: Men, Women, and Prospects," in *Latinos in New York*, op. cit., pp. 30–56.

41 Duany, *Quisqueya on the Hudson: The Transnational Identity of Dominicans in Washington Heights* (New York: CUNY Dominican Studies Insitute, 1994), p. 2.

42 See for example Torres and Bonilla, o.p. cit., p. 102.

43 See Robert Smith, "Mixteca in New York; New York in Mixteca," *NACLA Report on the Americas* 26:1 (July 1992), 39 41. See also Joel Millman, "New Mex City," *New York*, September 7, 1992, pp.37 43.

44 The term "transnational sociocultural system" was used in a study of Caribbeans in New York; see Constance R. Sutton, "The Caribbeanization of New York and the Emergence of a Transnational Sociocultural System," in Sutton and Elsa M. Cahney, eds. *Caribbean Life in New York City: Sociocultural Diemensions* (New York: Center for Migration Studies, 1987), pp. 15–30.

45 Geoffrey Godsell, "The Puerto Ricans," *The Christian Science Monitor* (May 1, 1980), p. 13.

46 The specification of Puerto Ricans as "colonial (im)migrants" and their parallel position to colonial or post-colonial immigrants in other parts of the world is noted but scarcely elaborated by Clara Rodríguez, *Puerto Ricans: Born in the U.S.A.* (Boston: Unwin Hyman, 1989), pp. 18 19. For a fuller discussion see Ramón Grosfoguel, in this issue

47 See, for example, Andres Torres, *Betweeen Melting Pot and Mosaic: African Americans and Puerto Ricans in the New York Political Economy* (Philadelphia: Temple University, 1995).

48 Elena Padilla, *Up from Puerto Rico* (New York: Columbia University Press, 1958), p. 32.

49 See Jorge Oclander, "Latinos Split Over Keeping Their House District," *Chicago Sun Times* (Dec. 13, 1995), pp. 22 3.

50 "Hispanics Must Forget Politics, Focus on Unity," *Chicago Sun Times* (Dec. 27, 1995), p. 30.

51 Oboler, p. 16.

52 For a discussion of the relation of Puerto Ricans to the issue of immigration, see Franklin Velázquez, "Puerto Ricans and Immigrants: La Misma Lucha," *Crítica* 9 (February 1995), 1, 5–6. A valuable assessment of Latino politics in New York City may be found in Annette Fuentes, "New York: Elusive Unity in La Gran Manzana," *NACLA Report on the Americas* 26:2 (September 1992), 27–33.

GLORIA RODRIGUEZ
PORTFOLIO

■ El hijo de Dios, *1995, acrollage, 36" x 24"* / Steven Tucker, Photographer

Gloria Rodríguez *is an accomplished painter, whose numerous awards attest to her talent. Born in Arecibo, Puerto Rico, she has lived most of her adult life in New York. Between commuting from her Brooklyn home and New Jersey studio, she steals time whenever possible to travel to her native island where she studied with the beloved Maestro Lorenzo Homar. She has received grants from the New York State Council on the Arts, The National Endowment for the Arts and a number of awards and honors to mark her impressive artistic trajectory.*

■ Christ of the Christians, *1995, acrollage, 52" x 36"* / Steven Tucker, Photographer

■ Before his time, *1995, acrollage, 42" x 32"* / Steven Tucker, Photographer

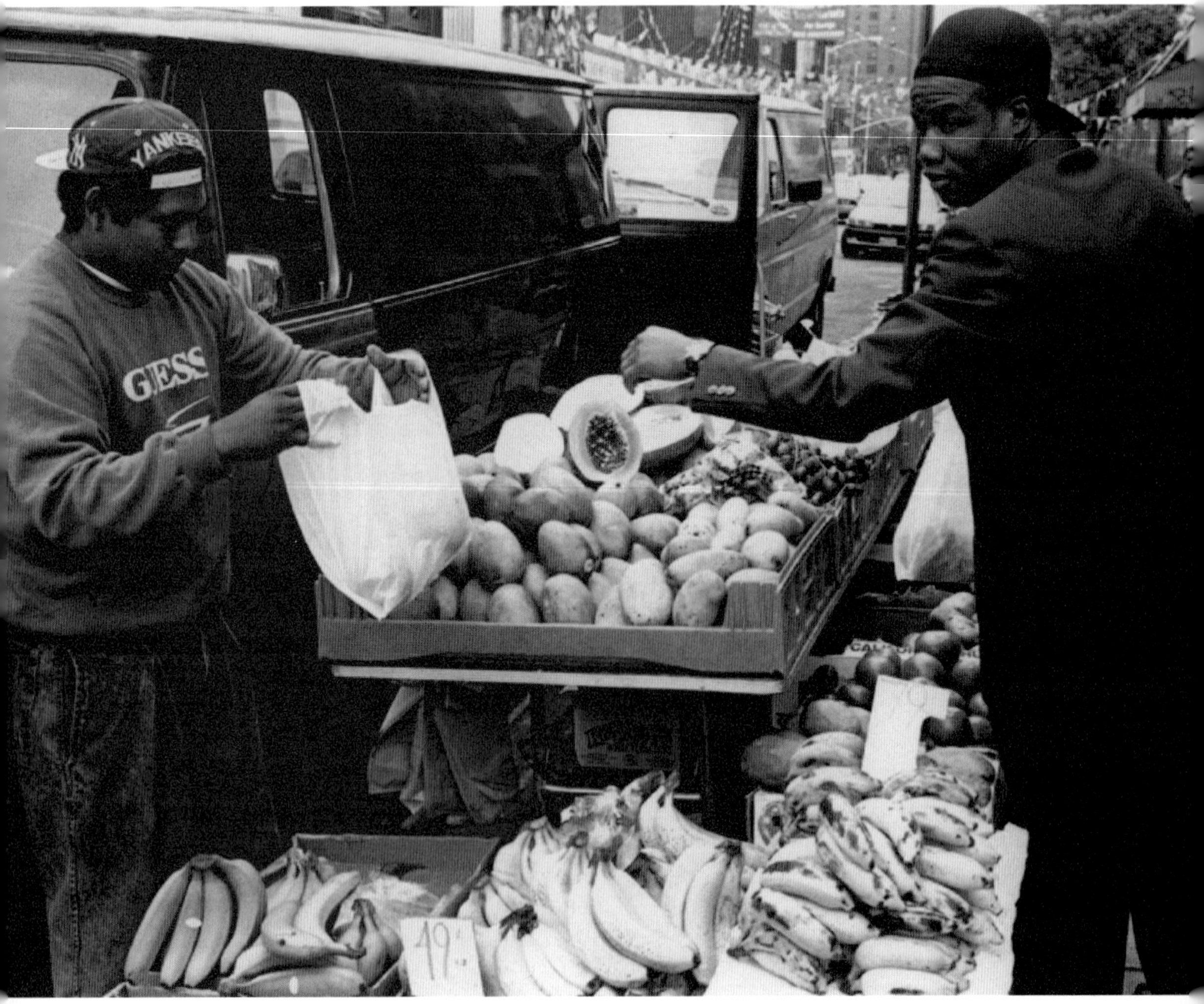
GESS
49

The Racialization of Latino Caribbean Migrants in the New York Metropolitan Area

Ramón Grosfoguel and Chloé S. Georas

Three recent autobiographical novels by authors from the Spanish Caribbean diaspora in the United States make reference to how new Latino immigrants were often confused with Puerto Ricans. In her memoir *When I Was Puerto Rican,* Esmeralda Santiago recalls translating for Spanish-speaking women at a welfare office in New York City:

> Often I would be asked to translate for the other women at the welfare office, since mami told everyone I spoke good English. Their stories were no different from mami's. They needed just a little help until they could find a job again.
> ...Women with accents that weren't Puerto Rican claimed they were so that they could reap the benefits of American citizenship. A woman I was translating for once said, "These gringo's don't know the difference anyway. To them we're all spiks." (1993:250)

Julia Alvarez writes about a Dominican family's difficult adaptation to life in New York in *How the García Girls Lost Their Accents*. Alvarez describes how Carla, one of the four García sisters, was mistreated in her new school:

> And as the months went by, she neglected to complain about an even scarier development. Every day on the playground and in the halls of her new school, a gang of boys chased after her, calling her names, some of which she had heard before from the old lady neighbor in the apartment they had rented in the city. Out of sight of the nuns, the boys pelted Carla with stones, aiming them at her feet so there would be no bruises. "Go back to where you came from, you dirty spic!" (1991: 153)

In Cristina García's *Dreaming in Cuban*, the spirit of Jorge del Pino advises his daughter, Lourdes Puente, to put her name on the sign of her bakery shop in the following manner:

RAMON GROSFOGUEL is an assistant professor in the department of sociology at the State University of New York at Binghamton. CHLOE S. GEORAS is a graduate student in the art history department at SUNY, Binghamton.

■ *Máximo R. Colón*

"Put your name on the sign, too, hija, so they know what we Cubans are up to, that we're not all Puerto Ricans," Jorge del Pino had insisted. (1992: 170)

To be labeled deprecatingly as a "spic," that is, a Puerto Rican, in the racial hierarchy of New York City is a racist marker for a new immigrant. In this article we attempt to address how the construction of Puerto Ricans as a racialized minority adversely affected the incorporation of Dominicans to the New York metropolitan area[1] and why the pre-1980s Cuban migrants were able to escape the same fate.

Puerto Ricans have migrated to New York since the turn of the century, but the largest migration occurred in the 1950s (Centro de Estudios Puertorriqueños 1979, 186–187). The mass migration of Dominicans started quite recently, after the United States' invasion of the Dominican Republic in the mid–1960s (Grasmuck and Pessar 1991, 20–21). Although Cubans have migrated to the United States since the turn of the century, they came in large numbers between 1960 and 1980 as anti-Communist refugees (Boswell and Curtis 1984, 40–42).

The class origin of the post–1950 Puerto Rican migration has been primarily from unskilled/rural labor extraction with low income and low educational levels (Friedlander 1965; Gray 1966; Levine 1987; Grosfoguel 1995).[2] By contrast, the Dominicans that arrived between 1965 and 1985 were mainly from urban middle-sectors of the working classes with higher skill levels than the average workers in the Dominican Republic (Bray 1984, 1987; Grasmuck and Pessar 1991)[3]. However, despite these differences, both the Puerto Ricans and the Dominicans in the New York metropolitan area are at the bottom of the labor market, experiencing the worst economic conditions. Puerto Ricans and Dominicans have the highest unemployment rates, the lowest labor force participation rates and the highest poverty rates in the New York Metropolitan Area (Grasmuck and Grosfoguel 1996). The Cubans that arrived in the New York Metropolitan Area between 1960 and 1980, a group similar to the Dominicans, came from skilled urban middle-sectors (Cronin 1981; Boswell and Curtis 1984, 49), but, contrary to the Dominicans, were able to improve their socio-economic situation. Relevant questions include the following: Given the higher socio-economic background of the Dominicans relative to the Puerto Ricans, why did the former end up in a similar structural position to the latter in New York's labor market? Given the similar class origins of the Dominicans and the pre-1980s Cuban migrants, why did the situation of the former deteriorate and the latter improve?

The contemporary racial/ethnic division of labor in the New York Metropolitan area can only be understood in relation to the historical and structural dynamics of the colonial/racialized migrations to the city. The first part of this article discusses the concept of symbolic capital and its implications for the understanding of a racial/ethnic symbolic field; the second part addresses Puerto Ricans as a colonial/racialized migration; the third part is about the Dominicans experience in New York; and the last part is on the Cuban migration. Our argument is twofold: first, that the racialization of Puerto Ricans conditioned the mode of incorporation of Dominicans to New York's labor market; and second, that Cubans who arrived before 1980 were able to escape the same destiny due to the "European style" welfare programs they received through the Cuban Refugee Program as part of the Cold War strategy of the United States.

■ *Symbolic Capital*

In the symbolic field of New York's racial/ethnic hierarchy, different ethnic groups are invested with different social values. Symbolic capital (Bourdieu 1977), that is, a capital composed of prestige and honor, varies for each group contingent on their position in the racial/ethnic hierarchy of the city. Groups at the top of the racial/ethnic hierarchy enjoy a high or positive symbolic capital, that is, social prestige. Prestige is frequently translated into greater economic opportunities and access to economic capital. On the contrary, groups at the bottom of the racial/ethnic hierarchy have a low or negative symbolic capital, that is, no prestige, and their identities are usually tied to a negative public image. These groups are discriminated against in the labor market, finding barriers for economic opportunities.

Social identities are relationally constructed and reproduced in a complex and entangled political, economic, and symbolic hierarchy that produces an unequal accumulation of symbolic, political, and economic capital for different classes, racial/ethnic groups, genders, and other socially classified groups. The dominant groups of the symbolic, economic and political fields are the ones who hegemonize the social classifications of a society.

In the U.S. the social classification of peoples has been hegemonized by white-male elites throughout a long historical process of colonial/racial domination. The categories of modernity such as citizenship, democracy, and national identity have been historically constructed through two axial divisions: between labor and capital, and between Europeans and non-Europeans (Quijano 1991). White-male elites hegemonized these axial divisions. According to the concept of coloniality of power developed by Aníbal Quijano, even after independence, when the formal juridical/military control of the state passed from the imperial power to the newly independent state, white elites continued to control the economic and political structures. This continuity of power from colonial to post-colonial times allowed the white elites to classify populations and to exclude people of color from the categories of full citizenship in the "imaginary community" called the "nation." The civil, political, and social rights that citizenship provided to the members of the "nation" were selectively expanded over time to white working classes. However, internal colonial groups remained as "second class citizens," never having full access to the rights of citizens and the "imaginary community" called the nation (Gilroy 1987).

Historically, much of the literature on race and ethnicity has been dominated by conceptualizations of identity as fixed essences reduced to micro-level social processes. Here we attempt to treat identity as relational, that is, as a relation of difference with other group's identities, embedded in multiple structural levels (global, state, local). Group identities are shaped through social relations with other groups in a symbolic field of dominant and subordinate groups.

■ *Puerto Ricans as Racial/Colonial Migrants*

In this article ethnicity refers to a distinct cultural group within or across the boundaries of a nation-state. In the United States the word "ethnic" has referred to cultural differences among white European groups (e.g. Italian, Irish, German), while racial categories have been used to refer to people of color (e.g. blacks, Asians), erasing ethnic differences within these racially classified groups. Since the 1960s "ethnic" in the United States has become a code word for race. During the 1960s civil rights movement, there was a shift in the dominant discourses on race. Rather than characterizing groups along racial lines, "ethnic" and "migrant" were coined as the new terms. This emerging dominant discourse was elaborated by Nathan Glazer and Daniel P. Moynihan in their now classic *Beyond the Melting Pot: The Negroes, Puerto Ricans, Jews, Italians, and Irish of New York City* (Cambridge: The M.I.T. Press, 1963). The experience of people of color in the United States is equated with that of the white migration from Europe at the beginning of the twentieth century. By transmuting racial discrimination into ethnic discrimination, Puerto Ricans and African Americans can go through the same experiences as any other ethnic group and eventually be economically incorporated, as happened to the white European migrants.

But this approach obliterates the history of racial/colonial oppression experienced by African Americans and Puerto Ricans: African Americans have a long colonial history of slavery and political/racial barriers thwarting their upward mobility, and Puerto Rico's colonial regime expropriated the land and incorporated the people as cheap labor in sugar plantations first and in manufacturing later in both Puerto Rico and the United States. Puerto Ricans and African Americans are not simply migrants or ethnic groups, but rather colonial/racialized subjects in the United States.

Although there have been Puerto Ricans and African Americans in New York City since the nineteenth century, their mass migration did not occur until the early 1900s, when European migration was restricted and labor shortages increased due to the First World War (Ottley and Iatherby 1967). As part of the war efforts, African Americans and Puerto

Ricans were recruited in manufacturing industries and low-wage services in New York City (Ottley and Iatherby 1967; Centro de Estudios Puertorriqueños 1979; Sánchez-Korroll 1983). Labor agents, aided by the U.S. Labor Department, directly recruited blacks from the south and Puerto Ricans from the island. New York City became one of the main destinations of these racialized/colonial migrants.

The 1924 Immigration Act which restricted European migration to the United States, further accelerated the massive migration of internal colonial subjects to New York. As the white workers became upwardly mobile because of job opportunities and higher skills in higher-wage industries, the low-wage manufacturing jobs in the garment and apparel industries became an undesirable economic sector, one identified with racialized minorities. During the 1920s and 1930s, African Americans became the main source of cheap labor in New York City's manufacturing sector and low wage services. Puerto Ricans were the second largest group, with approximately 30,000 newcomers in the 1920s. The racialization of these colonial subjects was reflected in the low wages they received in the garment industry sweatshops, relative to wages earned by whites of different ethnicities. As early as 1929, Puerto Ricans and African Americans earned $8 to $13 per week, while Jewish and Italian workers earned $26 to $44 per week (Laurentz 1980: 90, 104).

After the Second World War Puerto Rican migrants were incorporated in larger numbers to New York's labor market. Why were Puerto Ricans recruited rather than Chicanos, African Americans, Dominicans, Cubans or Jamaicans? Capitalist accumulation logic can explain the demand for labor in the metropole, but not which ethnic group would be massively recruited. To answer this question, we must understand the ideological/symbolic global state strategies of the United States during the Cold War.

■ *Puerto Rico: A Capitalist Showcase of the United States*

Immediately after the Second World War, newly independent countries emerged in the periphery of the world economy. National liberation movements defeated the European colonial administrations. The inter-state system was bipolarly divided under two spheres of influence, namely, the United States and the Soviet Union. The main preoccupation of the superpowers concerning the geo-political periphery was how to control the elites of the newly independent countries once the colonial means of domination had been destroyed. The Truman administration's response to this challenge was to develop the most ambitious foreign aid and technical training programs to ideologically co-opt third world elites.

The purpose of these programs was to improve the symbolic capital, that is, the social prestige, of the United States' model of development vis-à-vis that of the Soviet model. One of these programs was the Point Four Program run by the State Department of the United States. The Point Four Program was established to give third world elites technical skills, purportedly to help them break the chains of underdevelopment. Needless to say, the underlying agenda was propaganda favoring the American model of development for the Third World, better known as "industrialization by invitation." This model was based on the strategy of opening the local economy to U.S. foreign investments by offering tax exemptions and cheap labor.

As part of a long negotiation process between the Truman Administration and Muñoz's colonial government during the late 1940s, the international training ground for the Point Four Program was located in San Juan (Grosfoguel 1992). The idea was to make of Puerto Rico a symbolic showcase of the American capitalist model of development for the Third World. However, in order to use San Juan without causing major embarrassment to the United States, it would first be necessary to eliminate San Juan's huge shanty towns (50 percent of the city's housing as of 1950), improve the economic conditions of the islanders-most people lived under conditions of extreme poverty-and conceal Puerto Rico's colonial status. Thus, the late 1940s Truman-Muñoz negotiations led to the following agreements:

1. Conceal the colonial status of the Island by creating a more subtle form of colonial relationship called Commonwealth.
2. Include Puerto Rico in the United States' Federal Programs for Health, Education,

Housing, and other infrastructural programs without paying federal taxes.
3. Support the Operation Bootstrap program, which consisted of attracting United States labor-intensive industries by offering tax exemptions and a low-wage labor force.
4. Reduce the cost of air fares between the Island and the mainland to foster mass migration.

Puerto Rico became part of the core state's geopolitical symbolic strategy to gain symbolic capital vis-à-vis the Soviet Union. For the next twenty years more than 30,000 members of the Third World elites visited the Island and stayed from six months to two years as part of the Point Four Program. The visitors were shown the industrialization program, the housing projects, the health system, and other construction projects. The purpose of this program was to sell the Puerto Rican model of development to the Third World elites who would, in turn, sell it to their fellow citizens. The geopolitical symbolic strategy of showcasing Puerto Rico was intended to encourage the migration of the poorest sectors of the Puerto Rican society, many of them mulattos, to the urban centers of the United States.

After the Second World War there was a great demand for cheap labor in manufacturing industries in urban centers such as New York, Chicago, and Philadelphia. However, to understand why Puerto Ricans rather than Jamaicans or Chicanos were recruited, we must understand the global ideological/symbolic strategies of the United States and Puerto Rico's concomitant role. The elimination of the lower strata of the Island made possible the upward mobility of those who remained. By reducing airfare between the Island and the mainland, the Truman Administration provided a highly important institutional mechanism promoting the flight of young men and women. This policy paved the way for the first mass airway migration in world history. Approximately 600,000 Puerto Ricans, mostly rural unskilled workers, migrated to the mainland in twenty years. Since the Puerto Rican showcase was the Island rather than the migrants, the United States channeled its resources to the Island. Those who migrated ended up in the urban ghettos of the metropole with one of the highest poverty rates in the United States.

■ *Puerto Ricans: A New "Race"?*

Unable to place Puerto Ricans in a fixed racial category, either as white or black, due because of the mixed racial composition of the community, white Americans increasingly perceived them as a racialized Other. Puerto Ricans became a new racialized subject, different from whites and blacks, sharing with the latter a subordinate position to whites. The film *West Side Story* probably marked a turning point where Puerto Ricans became a distinct racialized minority, no longer to be confused with Asians, African Americans or Chicanos in the national imaginary of white America. This racialization was the result of a long historical process of colonial/racial subordination in the Island and in the mainland (Santiago 1993; Vázquez 1991). In many instances the racism experienced by Afro-Puerto Ricans is more profound than that experienced by lighter-skinned Puerto Ricans. However, no matter how "blonde or blue-eyed" a person may be, and no matter how successfully he can "pass" as white, the moment that person self-identifies as Puerto Rican, he enters the labyrinth of racial Otherness. Puerto Ricans of all colors have become a racialized group in the imaginary of white Americans, whose racist stereotypes cause them to see Puerto Ricans as lazy, violent, stupid, and dirty. Although Puerto Ricans form a phenotypically variable group, they have become a new "race" in the United States. This highlights the social rather than biological character of racial classifications. The demeaning classification of Puerto Ricans as "spiks" in New York designates the negative symbolic capital attached to being Puerto Rican.

In New York's racial/ethnic division of labor Puerto Ricans occupied a bottom-rung economic niche, often working in low-wage manufacturing jobs. By 1960, more than 50 percent of Puerto Ricans in New York were employed as low-wage laborers in this sector. During the 1960s, Puerto Ricans' successful struggles for labor rights made them "too expensive" for the increasingly informal manufacturing sector. Simultaneously, the de-industrialization of New York led to the loss of thousands of manufacturing jobs. Most of the manufacturing industries moved to peripheral regions around the world, while those that stayed in New York informalized their activities. The manufacturing industry, in constant need of cheap labor, relied heavily on new Latino immigrants, legal or illegal, that had even less rights than did internal colonial subjects such as Puerto Ricans. The expulsion of Puerto Ricans from manufacturing jobs and the racist educational system that excluded Puerto Ricans from the best public schools produced a redundant labor force that could not reenter the formal labor market. This led to the formation of what some have called the Puerto Rican "underclass," which we prefer to call a displaced or redundant population. Unable to find jobs, many Puerto Ricans developed popular strategies, legal or illegal, to survive the crisis. Currently, only 14 percent of Puerto Ricans are in manufacturing, and more than 50 percent are either unemployed or out of the labor force (Grasmuck and Grosfoguel 1996).

■ *The "Puerto Ricanization" of Dominicans in New York*

There was hardly any Dominican migration to the United States during the Trujillo dictatorship. Only after 1961, following the United States-backed military coup against Trujillo, did emigration take off. The out-migration process was politically induced by the political elites of the United States and the Dominican Republic as a safety valve against social unrest and political instability. Several studies on Dominican migration have mentioned this geopolitical strategy designed to perpetuate a stable pro-United States government (Báez-Evertsz and D'Oleo Ramírez 1986: 19; Mitchell 1992: 89–123; Grasmuck and Pessar 1992: 31–33). The United States' foreign policy toward the Caribbean concentrated on avoiding another Castro-style regime because American government officials were very aware of what had happened during the Cuban revolution (Grasmuck and Pessar 1992: 32–33). The United States' military forces invaded the Dominican Republic to defeat the Constitutionalist' forces in 1965 as part of this containment strategy. The amount of out-migration increased after this intervention. From 1961 to 1965, 35,372 Dominicans were legally admitted to the United States. During the 1966–70 post-invasion period, the number of legally admitted Dominicans increased to 58,744 (Grasmuck and Pessar 1992: 20). Most of the migrants came from urban middle-sectors, and many of them were politically active against the regime.

The United States guaranteed political stability in the Dominican Republic by admitting persons who could pose a political threat. This coincided with the Immigration Act of 1965, which facilitated skilled-labor immigration to the United States. Compared to other countries in the Western Hemisphere, the Dominican Republic, with a total population of less than five million people, has one of the highest rates of legal immigration to the United States. There was no deliberate legislation but rather an actively permissive policy encouraging Dominican entry to the United States. Beyond the active fostering of Dominican migration to guarantee political stability, no other policies addressed the incorporation of Dominican immigrants to the United States. The U.S.'s geopolitical interest in fostering migration to achieve security in the Dominican Republic did not translate into a policy of active incorporation. Instead, Dominican immigrants were left to fend for themselves.

Dominicans in the New York metropolitan area initially settled in Puerto Rican communities located in the Lower East Side, the South Bronx, and Brooklyn (Guarnizo 1992; Grasmuck and Pessar 1991). They relied on Puerto Rican social networks to find jobs, to acquire information about services in the city, and to avoid the migra[4] by assuming a "Puerto Rican identity." Similar to Puerto Ricans, Dominicans are racially mixed, probably with more people of African descent than Puerto Ricans. Moreover, most Dominicans could not speak English well, and their "accent" while speaking English was not significantly different from that of Puerto Ricans speaking English. Thus, Dominicans remained indistinguishable from Puerto Ricans in the white imagination. Even Dominicans who made an effort to distinguish themselves from Puerto Ricans to avoid being associated with their negative symbolic capital were unsuccessful. Whites could not distinguish them from the Puerto Rican "race." Thus, even though Dominicans came predominantly from an urban, middle-sector class/educational background, that is, a higher class background than that of Puerto Rican migrants, it was not an accident that Dominicans came to occupy the same economic niche of the Puerto Ricans in the racial/ethnic division of labor of New York City. As racialized non-citizens, Dominicans were an even cheaper source of labor than were Puerto Ricans. Dominicans replaced the so-called "expensive" Puerto Rican labor force in the manufacturing sector. Many Dominicans worked in New York City's sweatshops, earning wages below the federal minimum wage.

The story of Jamaicans in relation to African Americans helps illustrate that of Dominicans in relation to Puerto Ricans in the New York Metropolitan area. Jamaicans initially settled close to African-American communities. Questions include the following: How did the Jamaicans avoid being identified as African Americans? Why did they escape the labor market marginalization of African Americans in New York? Although they initially relied on African American social networks for job opportunities, a large number of the post-1965 Jamaican immigrants in New York City came from the more educated and skilled population of Jamaica (Grasmuck and Grosfoguel 1996). Many professionals, managers, secretaries, administrative personnel, and skilled workers formed the bulk of the Jamaican migration to New York. Moreover, the West Indian English "accent" of Jamaicans distinguished them from the negative symbolic capital of African Americans. The Jamaican community's strategy was to emphasize ethnic over racial identity. The fact that Jamaicans were not subsumed under the categorization "African American" avoided offsetting the positive impact of their skilled background. Thus Jamaicans were successfully incorporated into the host labor market in well-paid public and private service jobs. Jamaicans are currently portrayed by the white establishment in New York as a model minority vis-à-vis African Americans. Jamaicans' mastery of the English language as their native tongue and their cultural capital, evident in the form of high educational background, led to their positive symbolic capital and successful incorporation into American society, while the Dominican's subsumption under the Puerto Ricans led to their stagnation.

By 1980 Dominicans had formed their own ethnic community in Washington Heights. They started to be identified by whites as a "racialized other" distinct from Puerto Ricans. However, the "Puerto Ricanization" of the Dominican migration in New York's racial/ethnic division of labor was an accomplished fact by then. Around 50 percent of the Dominican labor force worked as cheap labor in manufacturing.

During the 1980s Dominicans experienced the largest migration flow to New York City. However, the de-industrialization of New York accelerated during these years. Many Dominicans either lost their jobs or were replaced by even cheaper sources of labor-namely Ecuadorian, Mexican, and Chinese immigrants. This displacement, plus the large numbers of new Dominican immigrants entering the labor force who were unable to find jobs in their traditional economic niche, formed a large redundant labor force. As a result, the labor-market marginality of the Dominican community reached proportions similar to those of Puerto Ricans. It seems that the Dominican community is presently experiencing the same processes the Puerto Rican community experienced, but in a shorter length of time.

■ *Cuban Migration*

Most of the Cuban migrants in the New York metropolitan area arrived between 1960 and 1980 and settled in Union City, New Jersey. Many Cubans came to New York by way of the Havana-Miami "freedom flights" between 1965 and 1973. These Cubans were part of an urban skilled-labor migration (Prieto 1984, 7). Similar to the Dominican experience in New York City, Cubans were also confused with Puerto Ricans. Given the similar class/educational/Latino origin of Cuban and Dominican migration, how did Cubans avoid ending up at the bottom of the labor market with the Puerto Ricans? First, most of the Cuban refugees before 1980 were "white" (Pedraza-Bailey 1985a, 23). However, being phenotypically white does not necessarily preclude racialization in the white imaginary; association with the Puerto Ricans is a racializing factor irrespective of a person's color. Ethnic social practices and a Puerto Rican accent can also "color" a person. The pre-1980s Cuban migrants managed to escape the negative symbolic capital of Puerto Rican racialization with an infusion of over one billion dollars from the U.S. government's Cuban refugee program[5]. Every city where Cubans settled received millions of dollars in government assistance to cover refugee costs in education, welfare, hospitals and other public services. This made the Cubans' situation radically different from that of Puerto Ricans. Every local government perceived Cuban settlement as a financial gain for a city rather than a burden, "whitening" the perception of their difference in the imaginary of white America. As a Puerto Rican from East Harlem once told us, "The federal government dipped the Cuban refugees in Clorox." The media as well as the government represented Cubans as a "model minority" that managed to lift themselves by their "bootstraps" (Pedraza-Bailey 1985b).

The development of a positive symbolic capital for the Cubans was part of a global strategy of the United States during the Cold War. The United States made Cuban refugees a symbol of the superiority of capitalism over socialism in its efforts to influence politics in Cuba. The Cuban "success story" in the United States was a symbolic win for the United States government vis-à-vis the Soviet model of Cuba. Thus, the Federal services Cubans received were superior to those available for citizens or residents of the United States and, for that matter, other immigrants at the time (Dominguez 1992: 31). Cubans were the only ethnic group in the United States that received "European style" welfare. As a result, Cubans received bilingual training, educational loans, health care, legal recognition of their professional degrees from Cuba, assistance in seeking jobs, welfare, and many other services through the Cuban Refugee Program. This massive assistance increased after 1965 when President Johnson created a Task Force that included the Departments of State, Labor, Agriculture, Commerce, Housing and Urban Development, the Office of Economic Opportunity, and the Small Business Administration to coordinate Federal assistance to avoid burdening local communities where these refugees were concentrated and other communities where they were resettled (see Johnson 1966, *Miami News* 1966).

In addition to their role as demonstrating the advantages of capitalism, Cubans were used as a model minority against the civil rights movement of the internal colonial/racial minorities during the 1960s. In Miami as well as in Union City and New York City, cities with a large concentration of Cubans, the Small Business Administration (SBA) practiced institutionally racist policies against Puerto Ricans and African Americans, favoring disproportionately the Cubans in the provision of loan programs. For example, the SBA in Miami gave Cubans 66 percent of its total loans between 1968 and 1979; 8 percent was given to African Americans (Grosfoguel 1994: 358–359). Similarly, successful entrepreneurship among the Cubans in Union City can be correlated to assistance from the SBA [Cronin 1981]. A survey done of more than one hundred and twenty Cuban-owned firms in Union City found that 73 percent had acquired their initial capital through the SBA's direct or guaranteed bank loans (Crown 1981). Approximately 80 percent of the total initial capitalization of these Cuban-owned firms consisted of SBA direct and guaranteed bank loans.

The study found that the SBA in New Jersey and New York City favored Cubans over Puerto Ricans in their loan programs even though approximately 70 percent of the Cuban entrepreneurs had completed only eight years or less of formal education and came from class origins similar to those of Puerto Ricans. The study raises the following question: If current Union City Cuban small business owners shared a similar educational and economic profile to Puerto Ricans in the metropolitan area, why did Puerto Ricans not experience the same entrepreneurial success? The study found that when Puerto Ricans called the SBA offices in New Jersey and New York City, 75 percent and 80 percent of the callers, respectively, were misinformed and disoriented. When Cubans called the same SBA offices, 84 percent of the callers in New Jersey and 70 percent in New York received the correct information. The study concluded that there was a broad institutional discriminatory policy favoring Cuban refugees and excluding Puerto Ricans. Cubans, who numbered approximately 700,000 people in the U.S. by 1975, received approximately 1.3 billion dollars in "European-style welfare" assistance between 1961 and 1974 (only a 15-year period), close to half of the total foreign aid of the United States to Brazil, a country of more than a 100 million people, between 1945 and 1983 (a 38-year period) (Grosfoguel 1994: 359). This privileged treatment of Cubans was based on geopolitical symbolic strategies of the Cold War. As Pedraza-Bailey states:

> While the Cuban state utilized the exodus to externalize dissent, on our shores the question remains: Why should the United States so eagerly receive the exiles? Because in America during the Cold War years, all the political migrations-the Hungarians, Koreans, Berliners, and Cubans-served a symbolic function. When West and East contested the superiority of their political and economic system, the political exiles who succeeded in the flight to freedom became touching symbols around which to weave the legitimacy needed for foreign policy (1985b: 154).

This global symbolism translated into greater economic resources for the Cuban refugees, increasing their ethnic symbolic capital. The most dramatic representation of how Cuban identity was associated with positive symbolic capital was the 1969 movie, *Popi*, in which a Puerto Rican from a New York City ghetto, holding three jobs, decided that the only way he could give his sons a better life was to turn them into Cuban refugees arriving in Miami. He trained his sons to be Cuban and put them off the coast of South Florida to pass them off as refugees. After their rescue by the Coast Guard, they received all the benefits for Cuban refugees. This sadly hilarious film documents the positive symbolic capital associated with Cuban identity and its relation to state resources.

During the 1980s thousands of Cuban refugees from the Mariel migration went to New York from Miami. These migrants were from a more popular class background relative to the pre-1980s Cuban migrants. Moreover, a large number of the Mariel migrants were Afro-Cubans and mulattos. When the Cuban Refugee Program was fazed out in the late 1970s, these migrants did not have access to state assistance and in turn were not cushioned against racial discrimination. As a result, the Marielitos suffered a marginalization in the labor market similar to that of Puerto Ricans and Dominicans.

■ *Conclusion*

We need to account for the diverse historical, cultural, and structural experiences of different Caribbean migrants to understand the different social and economic conditions of their communities today. Global state ideological and symbolic strategies as well as the racial/ethnic symbolic field of New York City are crucial determinants to understand the differences among these migrants. An important distinction for Caribbean migrants is whether they come from colonies or nation states. Colonial migrants have a longer history of racialization in the white metropolitan imaginary due to the U.S.'s long colonizing history. The racialization of immigrants affected their incorporation into the United States. This was the case of Dominicans, who were adversely affected through their association with a "Puerto Rican racial/ethnic identity" in the white imaginary. Dominicans participated in Puerto Rican social networks, sharing a similar fate in the New York racial/ethnic hierarchy.

However, there are also factors at the global level that determine who migrates and how they are received in the metropolitan society. The United States developed symbolic and military/security strategies in the Caribbean during the Cold War, and these strategies differentially affected migration processes. Mass migration of the Dominican urban-middle sectors was fostered by the United States as part of a strategy to gain political stability and to avoid the emergence of another Cuba. Puerto Rico and Cuba waged by proxy a symbolic Cold War battle between the United States and the Soviets. In the case of Puerto Rico, the showcase was the island itself and not the migrants. The migration of rural, unskilled labor was the basis of success of Puerto Rico as a showcase for American capitalism. Thus, state resources of the United States were channeled to the islanders rather than to the migrants. In the case of Cuba, the showcase the migrants, not the island was showcased. Thus, state resources of the United States were channeled to the migrants, while the islanders suffered a trade embargo. Thanks to the assistance of the federal government, local communities did not perceive the Cubans who settled in them as a burden. This happened because wherever Cubans settled, the federal government sent millions of dollars in assistance. Thus, Cubans developed a positive symbolic capital that neither Dominicans nor Puerto Ricans enjoyed. This helps explain why, in contrast to the Dominicans, Cubans were able to escape the networks of, and the racialization attached to, the Puerto Rican community in New York. ∎

ENDNOTES

1. The unit used in this article is the New York metropolitan area, which is larger than New York City. We sometimes used New York or New York City interchangeably to refer to the New York metropolitan area.
2. Most of the unskilled rural migrants from Puerto Rico came between 1950 and 1970. By 1970 Puerto Rico had changed from a rural to an urban society, and while most migrants came from unskilled labor backgrounds, they came from urban rather than rural areas. During the 1980s there was a skilled labor and middle-class migration from Puerto Rico to Florida and Texas. However, most of the Puerto Rican migrants to the New York metropolitan area came from unskilled labor backgrounds (see Grasmuck and Grosfoguel 1996).
3. As time passed, the Dominican migration has included large numbers of people from poor sectors of the Dominican Republic. This is especially so during the 1980s (see Grasmuck and Grosfoguel 1996).
4. As the Immigration and Naturalization Service is known in Latino communities.
5. This section refers only to the pre-1980 Cuban refugees. It does not refer to the 1980 Cuban migration, better known as "Marielitos," which was largely composed of mulattos and Afro-Cubans. By the time the Marielitos came to the United States, most of the federal assistance programs for Cuban refugees were over. Thus, the Marielitos, like the Cuban refugees before 1980, were unable to escape being racialized.

REFERENCES

Báez-Everszt, Franc and Frank D'Oleo Ramírez (1986) *La Emigración de Dominicanos a Estados Unidos: Determinantes socio-económicos y consecuencias.* República Dominicana: Fundación Frederich Ebert.

Boswell, Thomas and James R. Curtis (1984) *The Cuban-American Experience: Culture, Images, and Perspectives.* New Jersey: Rowman & Allanheld Publishers.

Bourdieu, Pierre (1977) *Outline of a Theory of Practice.* Cambridge: Cambridge University Press.

Bray, David (1984) "Economic Development: The Middle Class and International Migration in the Dominican Republic." *International Migration Review* 18 (2): 217–236.

_____. (1987) "Industrialization, Labor Migration and Employment Crises: A Comparison of Jamaica and the Dominican Republic" in Richard Tadarnico (ed.) *Crises in the Caribbean Basin.* Beverley Hills: Sage Publications.

Centro de Estudios Puertorriqueños (1979) *Labor Migration under Capitalism: The Puerto Rican Experience.* New York and London: Monthly Review Press.

Cronin, Denise Margaret (1981) "Ethnicity, Opportunity and Occupational Mobility in the United States." Ph. D. Dissertation. State University of New York, Stony Brook.

Dominguez, Jorge I. (1992) "Cooperating with the Enemy?: U.S. Immigration Policies toward Cuba" in Christopher Mitchell (ed.) *Eastern Hemisphere Immigration and United States Foreign Policy.* University Park, PA: The Pennsylvania State University Press.

Friedlander, Stanley L. (1965) *Labor Migration and Economic Growth: A Case Study of Puerto Rico.* (Cambridge, MA: M.I.T. Press).

Gilroy, Paul (1987) *'There Ain't No Black in the Union Jack': The Cultural Politics of Race and Nation.* Chicago: Chicago University Press.

Grasmuck, Sherri and Ramón Grosfoguel (1996, forthcoming) "Islanders in the States: A Comparative Account of Caribbean Migrants" in Refugio Rochín (ed.) *Immigration and Ethnic Communities: A Focus on Latinos.* East Landing: Michigan University Press.

Grasmuck, Sherri and Patricia Pessar (1991) *Between Two Islands: Dominican International Migration.* Berkeley: University of California Press.

Gray, Lois Spier (1966) "Economic Incentives to Labor Mobility: The Puerto Rican Case." Ph. D. Dissertation. Columbia University.

Grosfoguel, Ramón (1992) "Puerto Rico's Exceptionalism: Industrialization, Migration and Housing

Development, 1950–1970." Ph. D. Dissertation. Temple University.

_____ (1994) "World Cities in the Caribbean: The Rise of Miami and San Juan" *Review,* Vol. 17, No. 3 (Summer): 351–381

_____ (1995) "Depeasantization and Agrarian Decline in the Caribbean" in Philip McMichael (ed.) *Food and Agrarian Orders in the World-Economy.* New York: Praeger.

Guarnizo, Luis (1992) "One Country in Two: Dominican-Owned Firms in New York and the Dominican Republic." Ph. D. Dissertation. Johns Hopkins University.

Johnson, Lyndon B. (1966) Letter Establishing a Task Force on the Impact of the Cuban Refugee Program (November 18, 1965), *in Public Papers of the Presidents of the United States: Lyndon B. Johnson* (Washington, D.C.: U.S. Government Printing Office).

Laurentz, Robert (1980) "Racial/Ethnic Conflict in the New York City Garment Industry, 1933–1980." Ph. D. Dissertation. State University of New York, Binghamton.

Levine, Barry B. (1987) "The Puerto Rican Exodus: Development of the Puerto Rican Circuit" in Barry B. Levine (ed.) *The Caribbean Exodus.* New York: Praeger.

Miami News (1966) LBJ Keeps A Promise To Greater Miami: Federal Task Force August 12: 6A

Mitchell, Christopher (1992) "U.S. Foreign Policy and Dominican Migration to the United States" in Christopher Mitchell (ed) *Eastern Hemisphere Immigration and United States Foreign Policy.* University Park, PA: The Pennsylvania State University Press.

Ottley, Roi and William J. Iatherby (1967) *The Negro in New York: An Informal Social History, 1626–1940.* New York: Praeger.

Pedraza-Bailey, Silvia (1985a) "Cuba's Exiles: Portrait of a Refugee Migration." *International Migration Review,* Vol. 29, No. 1 (Spring): 4–34

_____ (1985b) *Political and Economic Migrants in America: Cubans and Mexicans.* Austin: University of Texas Press.

Prieto, Yolanda (1984) "Cuban Migration of the '60s in Perspective." Occasional Papers No. 46. Center for Latin American and Caribbean Studies. New York Universtiy.

Quijano, Aníbal (1991) "Colonialidad y Modernidad/Racionalidad" *Perú Indígena,* Vol. 29: 11–21.

Sánchez-Korrol, Virginia E. (1983) From Colonia to Community: The History of Puerto Ricans in New York City, 1917–1948. Istport: Greenwood Press.

Santiago, Kelvin (1994) "Subject People" and Colonial Discourses. Albany: State University of New York Press.

Vázquez, Blanca (1991) "Puerto Ricans and the Media: A Personal Statement" *CENTRO* Vol. 3, No. 1: 5–15

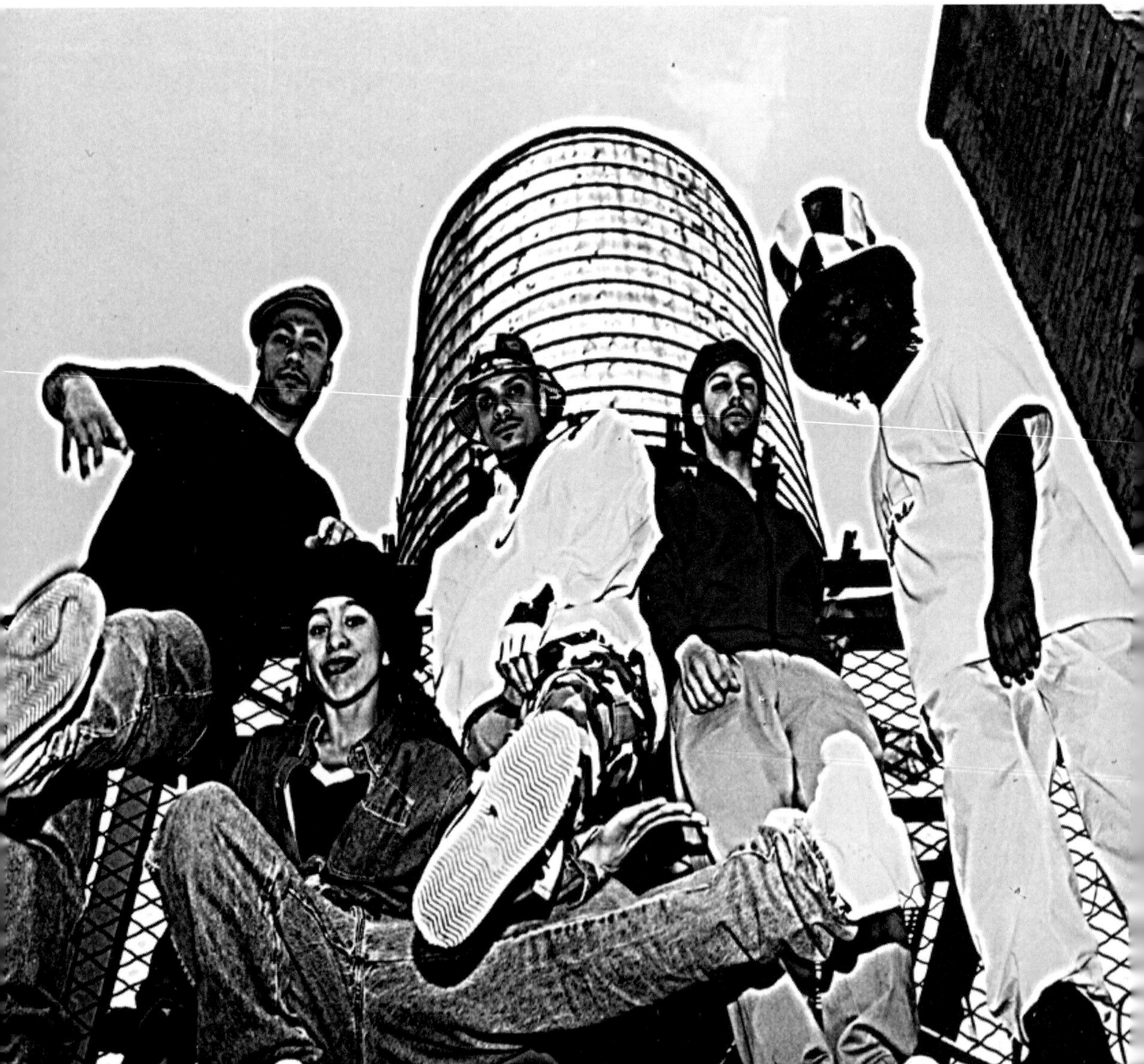

Boricuas from the Hip Hop Zone: Notes on Race and Ethnic Relations in New York City

Raquel Z. Rivera

para José Raúl González (poeta del Chamaco's Corner)

Yo, yo, yo. What's up? This is Pee Wee Dance of the legendary Rock Steady Crew and here's what I want you to do. Yo, over this funky track you're hearing right now, check the lyrics. Understand Hip Hop culture is a Black and Latino manifestation of an oppressed creativity. But understand also that rap is a White manifestation of a desire to package and sell that expression. So while you're thinking about what I just said, let this rhythm get to your head. Peace.
Tony Touch #45, 1995

Hip hop has been most commonly construed in the mainstream media as an African-American cultural form that has crossed over into mainstream U.S. culture and has had wide international acceptance. It is widely understood to have emerged during the early 1970s in the South Bronx. What is not as often recognized is that it was cultivated by both African-American and Afro-Caribbean youth. The historical and present role played by youth of the Spanish-speaking Caribbean, particularly Puerto Ricans, has been sometimes completely disregarded and often underplayed. Puerto Ricans are frequently marginalized and ignored within a culture in which they were co-creators (Flores, 1992–93; Flores, forthcoming). Puerto Ricans in particular and Latinos in general end up being seen as latecomers who have taken up this African-American cultural form in the late 1980s with the advent of "Latin rap" or "Latino Hip Hop."

The main questions that I seek to address here are the following. Why is hip hop, although historically a joint African-American and Afro-Caribbean cultural expression (Rose, 1994; KRS-ONE, 1995), often understood to be an "African-American thing"? Is there something about black-Puerto Rican relations that might explain this phenomenon? Does it have to do more with the position that Puerto Ricans and blacks, respectively, occupy with respect to the larger U.S. society? Is it a combination of factors?

To attempt to answer these questions I will begin by exploring the controversy surrounding the position of Puerto Ricans within hip hop culture. Then, I will discuss the socioeconomic and cultural context in which hip hop culture emerged. Finally, I will turn to how race and ethnic relations among Puerto Ricans and African Americans have had an impact on hip hop.

■ *Whose Hip Hop?*
Contrary to the mainstream media, more specialized accounts of hip hop such as those by David Toop and Tricia Rose, acknowledge the pivotal role of Latinos—most of them Puerto Ricans—in the culture. These historically oriented accounts recognize hip hop as heir to an

---

RAQUEL Z. RIVERA is a doctoral student in sociology at the City University of NY Graduate Center. Her master's thesis for the Centro de estudios avanzados de Puerto Rico y el Caribe was entitled "Para rapear en puertorriqueño: discurso y politica cultural" (1996).

■ *Full Circle (left to right) Siame, Rockafella, Kwikstep, Bam Bam, Shake*
Photo courtesy of Raquel Z. Rivera

Afro-diasporic tradition that includes decades of joint musical production by African-American and Latino musicians in New York City (Toop, 1991; Rose, 1994).

Toop, for example, emphasizes the impact that the Latin soul movement of the mid 1960s had on hip hop. He recognizes the Latin flavor going into the hip hop brew. During the introductory chapter, he interchangeably refers to the creators of hip hop as "blacks," "African Americans and Hispanics," and "blacks and Puerto Ricans." It is important to note that in his subsequent account of the early stages of hip hop, Toop does not make a point of differentiating African Americans from Puerto Ricans. He does, however, introduce ethnicity into his analysis when he explains the Caribbean influences of hip hop and calls to attention that Kool DJ Herc was raised in Jamaica and that Grandmaster Flash is of Barbadian parentage. Nevertheless, the fact that other well-known pioneers whom he mentions are also of Caribbean, most specifically, Puerto Rican background, goes unmentioned. Among these artists are Rock Steady Crew's Crazy Legs, DJ Charlie Chase of the Cold Crush Brothers, Devastating Tito and Master O.C. of the Fearless Four, and graffiti artists Lee and Futura 2000.

Toop's treatment of Black and Latino ethnicity within the hip hop zone implicitly follows the logic that Tricia Rose explicitly espouses. In a footnote to the chapter dedicated to discussing the emergence of hip hop culture, Rose explains:

> My arguments regarding Afro-diasporic cultural formations in hip hop are relevant to African-American culture as well as Afro-diasporic cultures in the English and Spanish-speaking Caribbean, each of which has prominent and significant African-derived cultural elements. Although rap music, particularly early rap, is dominated by English-speaking blacks, graffiti and breakdancing were heavily shaped and practiced by Puerto Ricans, Dominicans, and other Spanish-speaking Caribbean communities that have substantial Afro-diasporic elements. (The emergence of Chicano rappers took place in the late 1980s in Los Angeles.) Consequently, my references to Spanish-speaking Caribbean communities should in no way be considered inconsistent with my larger Afro-diasporic claims, particularly those that dominate future chapters devoted specifically to rap music. (Rose, 1994: 189)

I have quoted at length because the explanation reveals the ambivalence and confusion surrounding the cultural heritage and socio-political solidarities of people of the Spanish-speaking Caribbean. Rose is clear that Puerto Ricans, Cubans, Dominicans and others are part of the African diaspora; the claim is far from being common knowledge, however, and is likely to be received with skepticism or outright rejection, thus forcing Rose to explain the foundations of her position.

Rose's main purpose is to analyze rap as part of African-American cultural history and contemporary life. Although she acknowledges the critical role of Puerto Ricans and other "young people of color" in cultivating this cultural expression, her main concern and matrix of understanding and exploring is based on the African American community. The particularities of the Latino experience within the hip hop zone are thus subsumed under the African American experience.

Boricua and other Latino hip hoppers who have been fighting and negotiating respect and recognition are quite exasperated at such accounts. Q-Unique, an m.c. affiliated with the world-famous Rock Steady Crew, is very blunt in his judgment, starting with the title of Rose's book:

What the fuck is that?: "Black Noise." If anything she should have named it "Ghetto Noise." (Q-Unique, 1995)

As Q. explained, he is not one to deny that Puerto Ricans are part of the African diaspora. What he objects to is the presumption that the "black" experience, as it has been defined until now, can properly address the particularities of Puerto Rican life in the United States. Behind inclusion lies the specter of subsumption and dismissal. Q. wants to see the history and culture of Puerto Ricans addressed directly. He says, "I don't wanna be under anybody's umbrella."

Even though Puerto Ricans were active participants in hip hop from its beginning, even then Puerto Ricans held a somewhat precarious and ambivalent position in the culture. DJ Charlie Chase recalls that, on seeing him, people would refuse to believe that as a light-skinned Puerto Rican, he could indeed be the famous Cold Crush Brothers' DJ. He recalls times when ethnic animosity ran high, such as the time at a DJ Breakout and Baron jam in the late 1970s when the only thing that saved Chase from a hard "ass-kicking" was his friend Tony Tone. "What the fuck are you doing here, Puerto Rican," was the question posed to him for venturing too deep into black territory (Flores, 1992: 1009).

Puerto Rock from Latin Empire explains how "Puerto Rock" was the pejorative term that some African Americans used to refer to Puerto Ricans who were into hip hop. Those who mocked "Puerto Rocks" thought these Puerto Ricans were "trying to be down" with a culture to which they did not belong. Puerto Rock decided to use this derogatory label as his artistic name to turn it on its head, take away its power as an insult and "shut everybody up."

> They used to see the Hispanics dressing with the hat to the side and all hip-hop down and some assume that we're just supposed to stick to our own style of music and friends. They thought rap music was only a black thing, and it wasn't. (Flores, 1991: 85)

Charlie Chase speaks of his experience in the late 1970s and early 1980s; Puerto Rock elaborates on the mid to late 1980s. Are Puerto Ricans in the 1990s faced with similar concerns? Unfortunately, the answer seems to be yes. Sun Doobie, of Funkdoobiest, believes this is the case.

> I've always been a strong nationalist as far as hip hop, 'cause ain't no one has emphasized the contributions made to hip hop as far as Latinos are concerned. We was there from the fuckin' start, that was from the get go. They can talk all this we started this and blase blah, that's the bullshit, can't nobody say black nothin'. But as far as they were black Puerto Ricans, they were there from the get go, there was high yellow Puerto Ricans and they was Puerto Ricans that came as white as you. In hip hop there was no black or white thing, if you was dope, you was dope... writers, rappers, breakdancers, if you was white and you was dope you could get mad respect. (Cross, 1993: 281)

Puerto Ricans' legitimacy as part of the grassroots hip hop culture has been frequently put in doubt; they have not fared well in the rap industry, either. In a recent conversation with Hurricane Gee, an m.c. who has collaborated in albums with widely acclaimed African-American rappers Eric Sermon, Redman, and Keith Murray, she expressed her frustration at the difficulties she faces as a Puerto Rican artist (Hurricane, 1995). Puerto Ricans face obstacles both at the streets and grassroots level, as well as at the level of the music industry.

That is not to say that Puerto Ricans have had no influence within the rap industry. DJ Charlie Chase from the Cold Crush Brothers, Master O.C. and Devastating Tito from the Fearless Four, Rubie Dee and Prince Whipper Whip of the Fantastic Five, Prince Markie Dee Morales of the Fat Boys and The Real Roxanne are all famed figures of the early rap period. Among well-known 1990s artists, Funkdoobiest's Son Doobie, Black Sheep's Dres, Hurricane Gee, Kurious Jorge, Frankie Cutlass, and Fat Joe are all Puerto Rican.

Prominent rap artists like these aside, the New York underground hip hop scene has always been thriving with Puerto Ricans. Currently distinguished m.c.s and d.j.s in that underground include: Bobbito the Barber, DJ Tony Touch, Doo Wop, G-Bo, Joe Fatal Prince from Powerule, Main One, and the Arsonists Crew. Also in the underground, to attest that breaking did not die out after media attention waned, are b-girls Honey Rockwell of the

Rock Steady Crew and Rock-a-fella of Full Circle, and veteran b-boys Prince Ken Swift, Mr. Wiggles, Fabel, Kwikstep, and Crazy Legs. Graffiti also thrives in the underground, where scores of Puerto Rican aerosol artists cultivate their craft. Even though this list of names indicates the extent of Puerto Rican involvement in hip hop, the fact still remains that Puerto Ricans have led a somewhat marginal existence in the rap industry.

As opposed to the grassroots, where notions of community and cultural ownership are at stake, the music industry is concerned primarily with packaging what sells. To their further chagrin, Puerto Rican rappers have never been a particularly hot item for the mainstream U.S. market. An m.c. who shall remain nameless was shopping for a record deal in 1993. His manager spoke to an A&R at the now defunct Hollywood Basic, who informed him that the label was not interested in signing this rapper because "Puerto Ricans don't sell."

Although operating in two distinct spheres, there is a history of interaction between the hip hop communities in New York and in Puerto Rico, particularly at the underground level. Puerto Rico's political status as a United States colony is directly related to the tight economic, political, and demographic ties between the island and the U.S. The constant migratory flow to and from Puerto Rico has provided a direct link between both communities. The Nuyorrican connection has been vital in the development of hip hop in Puerto Rico.

The underground connection notwithstanding, mainstream Puerto Rican rap artists from the island have barely had an impact on the larger rap audience in the United States. Vico C., Lisa M., Francheska, D.J. Playero, and D.J. Adam, although highly recognized in Puerto Rico, have only had brief moments of popularity in the U.S., and their appeal has been confined to pockets within the "Latino" market. The factors which account for the lack of popularity of Puerto Rican rap artists from the island are quite different from those which affect the standing of Nuyorrican artists. Addressing such issues is an important matter, but not in the scope of this paper. In this article, I will concentrate on Nuyorricans and the New York hip hop scene.

■ Boricuas and Blacks in the 1970s South Boogie Down

Hip hop was born and cultivated in marginalized communities of color. To the present day, it is a cultural expression with vital ties to those communities. Although closely related to consumer culture and the music industry, its creative energy and ways of understanding the world are, to a great extent, still strongly rooted in the ghetto.

Hip hop is a culture with a rich history. It arose during the early 1970s in the South Bronx, mainly among African-American and Afro-Caribbean youth (Cross, 1993; Flores, 1988; Rose, 1994; Toop, 1991). Hip hop is an Afro-diasporic cultural form that encompasses music, rhyming, dance, and graffiti writing. Ask any committed and historically conscious hip hopper about the culture, and he'll most likely emphasize the importance of recognizing and cultivating the "four elements of Hip Hop": d.j.ing, m.c.ing, b-boying/b-girling, and graffiti writing.

As is the case with any other culture, hip hop was intimately related to the socio-economic and political realities of the time. The social conditions and economic prospects for young people of color living in poor communities during the 1960s and 1970s were appalling. African-Americans and Puerto Ricans, in particular, shared similar conditions and, quite often, the same dilapidated neighborhoods and were served by the same decaying schools and hospitals. As Bronx d.j., producer and m.c. KMX-Assault explained of blacks and Puerto Ricans in New York during the 1960s and 1970s: "You lived next door; you shared the same cockroaches" (Vázquez et al., 1992–93: 41).

Government "urban renewal" projects of the 1960s and early 1970s, like the construction of the Cross-Bronx Expressway, entailed the dislocation of communities of color in the South Bronx. Although there was a substantial Jewish population in these neighborhoods, most of the people affected by the construction of the Cross-Bronx Expressway were black and Puerto Rican (Rose, 1994: 31). To top things off, this was an expressway whose purpose was to make commuting easier for suburban residents, not to improve the quality of life in inner-city ghettoes.

The South Bronx saw during these two decades an unprecedented flight of jobs and residents and a great decrease in housing options. In the decade beginning in 1970, the South Bronx lost 27,763 housing units-the equivalent of 10.5 percent of total housing available. The demographic composition of the area also changed radically. During that same decade, 87 percent of the white population moved. In 1970, 20.2 percent of the population was white, 33.9 percent black and 35.1 percent Hispanic; by 1980, 91 percent of the population was black and Hispanic. Puerto Ricans were the largest group in the South Bronx throughout the decade (Rodríguez, 1991: 109).

The plight of the South Bronx was connected to economic changes at both the city and the global level. New York as a whole experienced a serious economic downturn in the 1960s and 1970s. This downturn was tightly linked to the shifting position of New York-as well as to other U.S. cities-with respect to the global economy (Wilson, 1987). Historically a manufacturing center, the New York economy was turning more towards the financial and service sectors. The ensuing loss of manufacturing jobs had the most intense effects among racial minorities, particularly blacks and Latinos, whose livelihood depended heavily on industry.

As living conditions in the city deteriorated, there was a tremendous amount of middle-class flight towards the suburbs. As the primarily white middle class left, the city's tax base suffered a great setback. To compound the situation, these new suburbanites became commuters, keeping their jobs in the city and thus not opening up positions for city residents. Between the postwar and the 1970s, the New York City white population decreased by 25 percent. Blacks and Puerto Ricans made up 33 percent of the city population by 1970 (Torres, 1995: 44-45).

These changes for the worse in economic and social conditions in New York City had the greatest impact on people of color. Blacks and Hispanics disproportionately occupied the bottom fifth of the income scale in the period from 1978 to 1986. The proportion of households living at or below the poverty level during the same period was 40 percent for Puerto Ricans (30 percent for Hispanics) and 25 percent for African Americans (Rose, 1994: 28). Whereas these numbers remained virtually the same in 1989, the white population, by comparison, had 12.3 percent of its population living in poverty (Torres, 1995: 187).

Tricia Rose explains that "early Puerto Rican, Afro-Caribbean and black American hip hop artists transformed obsolete vocational skills from marginal occupations into the raw materials for creativity and resistance." Graffiti writer Futura 2000, for example, attended a trade school that specialized in printing skills. He wound up working at a MacDonald's after graduation, however, since much of the work he was trained to do could be performed by computers (Rose, 1994; 34).

Hip hop culture was born out of deprivation. It arose amid dwindling income and job opportunities, and the dislocation of neighborhood and local support institutions. D.J.s, m.c.s, b-boys, b-girls and graffiti writers busted the lock of their—to borrow Pee Wee Dance's phrase—"oppressed creativity," extracting poetry out of urban decay. They constructed a booming soundscape out of old records and beat-up turntables; they converted drab subway cars into vibrant masterpieces that loudly testified to their skill and ingenuity; they made nimble bodies and quick tongues into weapons for a ghetto cultural reconstruction.

■ *Nigger-Reecan Blues II*

"*He's not so bad,*" *said a shy, timid voice.* "*He's a polite guy and seems to be a good athlete. And besides, I hear he's a Puerto Rican.*"

"*Ha, he's probably passing for Puerto Rican because he can't make it for white,*" *said the thin voice. Ha, ha, ha.*" [...]

"*...no, really!*" *a girl was saying.* "*I heard he's Puerto Rican, and they're not like Neg-*"

"*There's no difference,*" *said the thin voice.* "*He's still black.*" (Thomas, 1967: 85-86)

The above conversation was overheard by a young Piri Thomas, the author of *Down These Mean Streets*, in 1944. A Puerto Rican born and raised in Harlem, Thomas had just moved with his family to Long Island and was shocked, confused, and incensed on hearing his classmates' disparaging dialogue.

Puerto Ricans and African Americans have been the object of a vicious racial contempt. Some times, they have been ranked slightly differently, "I heard he's Puerto Rican, and they're not like Neg—." Other times, they have been lumped together in an undifferentiated non-white mass: "There's no difference. He's still black."

The 1990s social landscape that Nuyorrican poet Willie Perdomo describes is in many ways strikingly similar to Piri Thomas's recollections of the 1940s. Like Thomas, Perdomo painfully recognizes not only the racial prejudice but also the similar socio-economic circumstances that surround African Americans and Puerto Ricans.

> I'm a Spic!
> I'm a Nigger!
> Spic! Spic! No different than a Nigger!
> Neglected, rejected, oppressed and depressed
> From banana boats to tenements
> Street gangs to regiments...
> Spic! Spic! I ain't nooooo different than a Nigger. (Santiago, 1995: 93)

Since Puerto Ricans began arriving in New York in large numbers after the 1940s, blacks and Puerto Ricans have been linked through what Andrés Torres has termed an "alliance of survival." Their geographical proximity, high poverty levels, and similar historical experiences and cultural legacies have made evident the commonalities of their struggles.

African Americans and Puerto Ricans worked together throughout the 1960s and 1970s in the civil rights movement and the black power movement. Among the joint endeavors were the efforts to increase community control over public schools and anti-poverty programs, as well as the welfare rights movement (Torres, 1995: 78–82). Many black Puerto Ricans were part of the black power movement, not as merely sympathetic allies but also as core members (Rodríguez-Morazzani, 1991–92: 109).

The movement also provided an ideological and organizational framework from which Puerto Rican activists of the time drew on. The Young Lords Party, for example, was modeled after the Black Panthers (Young Lords Party and Abramson, 1971). Denise Oliver remembers that it was through the Black Panther newspaper that the group of activists who eventually became the Young Lords in New York first learned of the existence of young Puerto Rican activists from Chicago, who called themselves the Young Lords Organization. Oliver, who was Minister of Economic Development in the Young Lords Party from 1970–71, is an African American, one of many who participated in Puerto Rican organizations.

In the cultural realm, blacks and Puerto Ricans also have a history of joint endeavors. Latin music benefited from an interest by African-American audiences on the wane of the Harlem Renaissance (Glasser, 1991: 39). In the 1930s and 1940s, Puerto Ricans participated along with African American and Cuban musicians in the production of Afro-Cuban Jazz and Latin Jazz. There was also a collaboration of African Americans and Puerto Ricans in rhythm-and-blues music of the late 1950s. One example is the greatly successful Frankie Lymon and the Teenagers. This group had two African-American members, two Puerto Ricans and one Dominican (Rodríguez-Morazzani: 110).

The Latin bugalú of the 1960s, which mixed mambo with early black rock-and-roll, has been described by John Storm Roberts as "a genuine reflection of the impact of 1960s black music on young Latins" (Roberts, 1979: 167). Ricardo Ray and Willie Colón, both New York-born Puerto Ricans, were among its exponents. Hits like Joe Cuba's "Bang Bang," which sold over a million copies, and Héctor Rivera's "At The Party" were very popular both among black as well as Latino teenagers. Latin soul, an offshoot of bugalú, became popular in the mid-1960s. Joe Bataan, a musician of Filipino and African-American ancestry and ex-leader of El Barrio gangs the Young Copasetics and The Dragons, and Jimmy Castor, an African American, were both central figures in Latin soul. Jimmy Castor's music later became a pivotal component of the hip hop soundtrack. "It's Just Begun," a b-boy and b-girl classic of the early 1970s, mixed timbales breaks with Sly Stone bridges—a further profession of Afro-Rican hybridity (Toop, 1991: 22).

Hip hop culture is yet another testimony to African American-Puerto Rican cultural production and socio-political action. Just like previous generations had done before them, Puerto Rican and African American youngsters in the 1970s transformed their forced joint segregation into a chosen partnership. Although still shunned as Spics and Niggers, they refused to fall pray to the "Nigger-Reecan Blues."

■ *Rifts*

Despite their long history of cooperation and alliances, African Americans and Puerto Ricans also have a parallel history of rifts and conflicts. hip hop is not an exception. Although hip hop is a culture cultivated extensively by both African American and Latino youth, ethnic and racial harmony between the two groups has not always existed.

For Puerto Ricans in the United States, cultural identification is of greater importance than racial identification (Rodríguez, 1991: 52). A multiracial, culturally distinct group, Puerto Ricans have resisted compliance with the reigning system of racial classification in the United States, according to which, any known African ancestry makes a person black.

Whereas, historically, American culture developed what has been termed a hypo-descent or one-drop rule (one drop of "black blood" makes a person black), the system of racial classification that evolved in Latin America depends more on phenotype than on genotype (Degler, 1986; Davis, 1991; Omi and Winant, 1991). Put in other terms, Latin American racial categories depend more on "color" (and other physical characteristics) than on "race" per se (Betances, 1974: 428). In Latin America, skin tone, facial characteristic and hair type, along with class markings such as dress, body language, and speech patterns, all have bearing on race (Rodríguez, 1991: 52). Members of the same family may actually be categorized differently. Another great difference between the two systems of racial classification is the white-black dichotomy in the U.S. which contrasts with the recognition of a wide variety of intermediate racial possibilities in Latin America (Degler, 1986; Davis, 1991).

Puerto Ricans believe themselves to be the product of interbreeding between Africans, Taínos, and Europeans (primarily of Spanish descent). Miscegenation is built into the language of community and nationality (Blanco, 1985; González, 1989; Pedreira, 1992). But to choose one race over the other -which is the way in which race is thought of in the United States has been perceived as denying a part of one's self. Thomas gave voice to this sentiment by writing,

> It wasn't right to be ashamed of what one was. It was like hating Momma for the color she was and Poppa for the color he wasn't (Thomas, 1967: 121).

Further impeding Puerto Rican identification as white or black was their ethnic distinctiveness. As Clara Rodríguez expresses, "Puerto Ricans, racially speaking, belonged to both groups; however, ethnically, they belonged to neither" (Rodríguez, 1991: 51). When faced with the black-white dichotomy, Puerto Ricans balked.

But there is yet another reason why Puerto Ricans have refused to accept the one-drop rule and identify as blacks. Although a multiracial people, Puerto Ricans are still the bearers of strong anti-black prejudice (Zenón Cruz, 1975; Díaz Quiñones, 1985; Jorge, 1986; González, 1989). Therefore, not only have a lot of them, regardless of color, not considered themselves black, but they have held their "blacker" African American neighbors with contempt. Anti-black sentiment was brought on the trip from Puerto Rico and bread within Puerto Rican communities in the continent; these attitudes were compounded with the adoption of U.S. prejudices against African Americans (Blanco, 1985: 102; López, 1980: 324).

For many African Americans, the Puerto Rican insistence on identifying culturally and not racially, combined with Puerto Rican racism, have not made Puerto Ricans dependable partners in race-based struggles. Suspicion and prejudices have run both ways.

Early hip hop, in some senses, transcended the interethnic rifts. Puerto Ricans participated along with African Americans right from the start. Nevertheless, particularly in terms of record-spinning and rhyming, the predominant sense seemed to be that Puerto Ricans were participating in a black cultural expression. DJ Charlie Chase talks of having to disguise the Latin music that he sampled and recalls that m.c.s held back from writing rhymes in Spanish, knowing that the audience would disapprove (Flores, 1991). They were Puerto Ricans in a predominantly black medium, and it wasn't to their advantage to make too many waves.

So the question still remains, why has hip hop become conceptualized as African-American cultural property? Why have Puerto Ricans, although co-creators, been considered junior partners? Why is this still the case more than two decades after the birth of hip hop?

■ Lost in the Shuffle

U.S. race relations have gone through profound changes in the postwar period. This has been largely the legacy of the civil rights and black power movements of the 1950s and 1960s—a period which Omi and Winant have termed "the great transformation" (Omi and Winant, 1994: 95). Another important factor in the changing significance of race in the United States has been the large-scale migration of people of color after the national origins immigration quotas were suspended in 1965 (Davis, 1991; Kasinitz, 1992). The increasing visibility and politicization of multiracial people whose presence in the U.S. predated or did not hinge on the post 1965 migration (such as Puerto Ricans, Mexicans and self-identified "biracial" or "multiracial" people) has also played a part on the changing of U.S. racial politics and categories.

One of the reasons—though certainly not the only one why immigration has had an impact on race relations in the U.S. has been the increasing number of non-compliants with the hypo-descent rule of racial classification. Before the "great racial transformation" of the 1950s and 1960s, race relations had traditionally hinged on a black-white axis, with groups like Mexicans and Puerto Ricans taking the role of blacks (Davis, 1991:115). The post 1965 immigrants, aided by a transformed racial landscape, contested the black-white racial dichotomy of the U.S. Political mobilization and pressure, particularly by Asians and Latinos, called into question the lumping of all "others" as blacks or, at least, as non-white. This led to the creation of pan-ethnic categories like "Asian" and "Hispanic," which finally appeared in the census in 1980. The present racial classifications in the U.S. are thus a mixture of both racial and ethnic categories.

Although the post-1965 migration and the increasing number and politicization of self-identified "biracial" or "multiracial" people have brought about changes in the racial, political and cultural realms, these changes should not be overestimated. Even though the U.S. racial imaginary has expanded, it is still by and large dominated by the black-white dichotomy.

Black welfare mothers and young black drug dealers are used constantly as the symbols of the national ills. The so-called "underclass" is virtually synonymous with "the black underclass." In cities like New York, where "other" groups (not black and not white) are highly visible,[3] the ghetto is sometimes thought of as black and Latino; however, often Latino ghetto residents are subsumed under the black category.

African Americans and Puerto Ricans in New York share a similar socioeconomic status. There are, however, differences between the two groups. With respect to unemployment and labor force participation the differences are not too astounding, but they are with respect to median family income. Although African Americans are the group most closely associated and stereotyped in terms of poverty, Puerto Ricans fare even worse in terms of one of the principal indicators of socioeconomic status.

Puerto Ricans have been, in this three decade period, consistently at the bottom of the income scale. Furthermore, the gap between the median income levels of African Ameri-

TABLE 1

New York City Median Family Income: Total White, Black, Puerto Rican, 1960–1980

	1960	1970	1980
Total	$6,091	$9682	na
White	$6365	$10,378	$21,515
Black	$4,432	$7,150	$12,210
Puerto Rican	$3,811	$5,575	$8,705

Source: Andrés Torres, Between Melting Pot and Mosaic: African Americans and Puerto Ricans in the New York Political Economy, Philadelphia, Temple University Press, 1995, 63.

cans and Puerto Ricans has progressively widened. The same pattern is evidenced with respect to wages and salaries -Puerto Ricans rank below African Americans (Torres, 1995: 89–103).

Andrés Torres offers some explanations why Puerto Ricans, although a group ravaged by poverty, are frequently out of sight in national policy discussions. First of all, Puerto Ricans evidence a greater regional concentration and a smaller population size when compared to African Americans. But more interestingly, Torres suggests that another reason may be that Americans [sic] don't want to hear of yet another ethnic group living in poverty when the society is still consumed by talk of black-white racial inequality. Furthermore, some African Americans may feel that a focusing on Puerto Ricans might take resources and attention away from their own community. Therefore, they too might not be interested in exploring the plight of the Puerto Rican community (Torres, 1995: 5).

Another reason for the relatively greater prominence of African Americans in national policy discussions may be their long history in the United States, which dates back to the early colonial period. Puerto Ricans, in comparison, have a shorter history, which began shortly before the United States' invasion of Puerto Rico in 1898. Furthermore, the continental Puerto Rican community did not start reaching substantial numbers until the 1940s.

Just like policy discussions regarding poverty frequently still hinge on a black-white axis, plenty of other aspects of contemporary life still operate accordingly. In "Rice & Beans," an unreleased hip hop track, Q-Unique bitterly points out how Puerto Ricans have seen themselves pushed to the margins and lost in the black-white bipolarity. As he puts it, Puerto Ricans have gotten "lost in the shuffle."

> What does it mean to be born Puerto Rican?
> Minority, Spanish-speaking, rice & bean eating?
> Welfare recipients, living in the slums of the city
> Hidden past so the future looks shitty
> Avoid all the muffle and scuffle
> In this black and white world we got lost in the shuffle

Q-Unique's phrase reminds me of a comment made by another m.c., Krazy Taíno of Latin Empire, who lamented that a lot of young Nuyorricans either do not know or do not want to know about their Caribbean heritage. He described these youngsters as being "lost in the sauce" (Flores, 1992–93).

Gina Amaro, Latina community organizer and fellow hip hop enthusiast, pointed out to me the crucial importance of our generation, namely, Latinas and Latinos in our twenties, reaching out to the younger generation. Amaro recalls growing up black-identified and not speaking Spanish. She attended a Catholic school, Mother Cabrini, where the students were, by and large, light-skinned Dominican girls who spoke fluent Spanish. A black Puerto Rican who spoke no Spanish, she related much better to her African-American classmates. As Amaro explains, there was great stigma attached to being Puerto Rican. Thus, "you either were an upwardly mobile white Puerto Rican, or you identified as black, or you were stigmatized" (Amaro, 1995).

Amaro believes that despite the greater visibility and organization of the Latino community, and the proliferation of Latino businesses, publications, clubs and restaurants, the generation of Puerto Ricans now in their teens is faced with similar dilemmas to those Amaro's generation faced. In many senses, New York has witnessed a great Latino rebirth in the last few years. El Puente's "hip hop Ambassador" Edgar Miranda calls it the Latino Rennaissance. However, "Latinoness" is, more often than not, conceptualized in reductive terms; group identity is argued to be based upon Spanish language and Latin American culture. Given their cultural hybridity and frequent lack of fluency in Spanish, the "Latinoness" of Nuyorricans is often put into question. Many Nuyorricans are thus not only caught between black and white, but they are also shunned by "their own."

The way in which Puerto Rican hip hoppers have been singled out as a culturally alienated generation is a prime example. Peter Manuel, in a recent publication devoted to developing a sociological history of Caribbean music, includes a section on "Latin rap." Considering the notions of purity that frequently guide discussions of national culture and the distaste with which rap is often regarded by Latin American intellectuals, I was pleased to see the inclusion of this musical genre. I was disturbed, however, by the references to the young Latinos who have "drifted away" from salsa and into rap as "alienated youths" (Manuel, 1995: 91). Manuel recognizes that nowadays rap has "replaced salsa as the real voice of the barrio." Rap is, to him, the real voice of the *barrio*, but it is nonetheless an alienated voice. Manuel explains:

> Among English-speaking Newyorricans in the 1980s who were growing up with ghetto blacks and inundated with hip-hop culture, there developed a widespread tendency to adopt contemporary Afro-American dress, mannerism, and music.

The history and richness of African American-Puerto Rican musical cross-fertilization is absent from this account. Nuyorrican hip hoppers are portrayed as having been "inundated" by this "Afro-American" culture, when in fact they were the willful, skillful, and enthusiastic co-originators of this culture.

Manuel is not the only one suggesting that Latino hip hop artists and audiences are somehow alienated by "black music." Percussionist Johnny Almendra agrees with the same premise.

> I tell you, we're losing a lot of the kids to hip hop, because a lot of them don't speak Spanish... These kids are being influenced by other musics, so was I, but I chose to listen to my music. And I listened to Elvis Presley, too, but something was calling me. (Salazar, 1995: 21)

Although Sergio George, producer[4] and head of Sir George Entertainment, does not consider hip hop a source of cultural alienation, shares Manuel and Almendra's assumption that hip hop is a "foreign" or "outside" influence on Latino youths.

George grew up in East Harlem. He recalls that before he got into Latin music, such as that made by Willie Colón, Héctor Lavoe, and the Fania All Stars, he was "strictly into black music." The following is an excerpt of an interview conducted by Jorge Cano-Moreno.

> J.C.M.: As a black Latino what are your feelings on Latino roles in black Music or rather should we be limited to just Latin music?
>
> Sergio George: That's a difficult question. Personally, it is tough but I have decided to stick to my own people and use the influences I like from black music.[...] I feel I have to stick with my people and by that I just don't mean Puerto Ricans that includes Dominicans, Cubans, Colombians; it has to include all Latinos. We all share the same kind of struggles and hopes. (Cano-Moreno, 1995)

George does not suggest that Latinos have no business doing "black" music. On the contrary, he mentions R&B and even hip hop as some of his largest musical influences. What George does is accept the dichotomy Latin music-black music. This dichotomy reaches beyond musical categories to the realm of lived relations, manifesting itself in definitions of community and political solidarities. He has opted to deal with these rifts between the African American and the Latino community by "stick[ing] to my own people."

Manuel, Almendra, and George all share the assumption that hip hop is "Black music." Although Latinos may enjoy and be influenced by this black music, Latin music is somehow presumed to hold the key to the true Latino essence.

These appeals to cultural legitimacy or genuine roots is nothing new. Many Latino musicians shunned the Latin bugalú movement of the 1960s for being, as bandleader Willie Rosario said, "American music played with Latin percussion." The problem then resided in the disrespectful innovations of a younger generation that paid no mind "to the sacred cows of Cuban-derived orthodoxy" (Roberts, 1979: 167).

The appeals being made to the Latino hip hop generation in the name of cultural awareness have a foundation in judiciousness. Puerto Rican hip hoppers may often get "lost in the sauce" and/or "lost in the shuffle" out of a lack of information regarding the culture and history of the Puerto Rican community. Greater knowledge and appreciation regarding one's cultural roots can only bring about positive results. I wholly agree with Almendra that music is a good vehicle to introduce young people to other issues.

> As these kids get to know this music, maybe some of them will be sparked to get curious about their culture and one of the best ways is through music (Salazar, 1995: 21).

That shouldn't mean, however, that to be culturally aware one has to fit into a narrowly defined Latino cultural mold or stick to reductionist notions of "our own people."[5] Rap should be considered a further development in the history of Latin music and not simply an offshoot of black music where culturally alienated defectors have gone to seek refuge. Rap also has to be understood in its own terms and not squeezed into a prescribed "Latin music" mold. For example, due to the notion that true Latin music has Spanish lyrics, many seem to regard the fact that some Latinos are making rap in Spanish or Spanglish as a vindicating factor that lends it greater legitimacy. In Peter Manuel's view,

> [...] because going hip-hop could mean forsaking Spanish language and identity an inevitable development was the emergence of Latin rap, mixing Spanish and English languages and musical identities in various proportions.

There is nothing "inevitable" or even necessary about incorporating Spanish into rap. It might be welcome, desirable, and refreshing, but not indispensable. Besides, "Latinizing" rap does not automatically make a good rap song. Gerardo's song "It's a Latin Thang" was lauded by Manuel as "an exemplary barrio product, with its 'Spanglish' text, funky boogaloo vamp, and whimsical urban-life interjections" (Manuel, 1995: 93).

Ironically, Gerardo is held by the hip hop core with as much respect as MC Hammer or Vanilla Ice. The "Rico Suave" has been dissed explicitly and implicitly in several rap tracks by artists like Puerto Rico's Vico C. and New York's Kurious Jorge. DJ Charlie Chase says he has mixed feeling about Gerardo's success: "I say power to the guy because he's Latino, he's succeeding and he's just helping to open doors for us, which is cool." Yet Chase is skeptical about the quality of Gerardo's music. "But his stuff is corny, man. I can't get with that. ... His looks are what's selling for him" (Flores, 1992: 1005). Cuban DJ and producer Skatemaster Tate is harsher in his judgment: "Gerardo is straight up candy ass, pansy muthafucker, get a haircut" (Cross, 1994: 225). The virtue of a rap song, if done by a Latino artist, does not reside in its being "Latinized."

Hip hop has been understood as a "black culture" by most Latinos. This has been due, partly, to a lack of knowledge regarding the history of hip hop and the central role that Latinos played in its masterminding. Another reason why hip hop has been conceptualized as black and thus, non-Latino, is related to the persistence of reductive notions of cultural purity and true "Latinoness." The hip hop-centric generation is thus perceived as composed of alienated defectors from the Latino community.

Hip hop has also been regarded as exclusively black by African Americans. The long history of segregation, economic deprivation, and cultural expropriation of African Americans make Latino claims to cultural co-authorship subject to skepticism and/or rejection.

Another reason why hip hop is conceptualized as solely African American has to do with the invisibility of Puerto Ricans at a national level. The smaller population numbers and the regional concentration of Puerto Ricans promote their inconspicuousness (DJ Tony Touch, 1995). The long history of black-Puerto Rican interaction in New York remains largely untold and unknown. Also, as Tricia Rose has noted, the stronger presence of Puerto Ricans in breaking and graffiti art—as opposed to the hip hop elements of greatest mainstream visibility, namely d.j.ing and m.c.ing (Rose, 1994: 189), also contributes to the perception of Boricuas as marginal in hip hop. Further, Puerto Ricans are sometimes considered virtual blacks, both by the mainstream and by the African-American community, so that their specificities are erased to give way to a "black" common ground.

New York Puerto Ricans who consider themselves heirs to hip hop culture have often been perceived as "just like blacks," or "wanna-be-black," or "not black enough." Getting hit from so many sides at once, it is indeed a wonder how Puerto Ricans have negotiated and insist on claiming their spaces within hip hop.[6]

This is not to say that it is all an uphill and constant struggle. There is also a strong current within hip hop, particularly among those who consider themselves part of the "true school," that upholds the culture as a joint endeavor of black and Latino urban youth. KRS-ONE and Afrika Bambaataa, for example, are two well-known and respected figures who constantly refer to hip hop as a black and Latino cultural expression.

This ethnic and racial dimension of hip hop culture is closely related to political and economic matters, as the quote from Pee Wee Dance at the beginning of this article shows. The distinction that Pee Wee draws between the rap industry and hip hop culture has both ethnic/racial as well as political/economic dimensions. The rap industry, controlled by the "white" other, has pimped an element of hip hop culture to no end. The answer, for Pee Wee and for a great many others, seems to be to reclaim hip hop as a holistic and complex Afro-diasporic cultural form that extends far beyond the music industry. The point does not seem to be to shun commercialization in favor of a mythical underground purity or to claim hip hop as exclusive black and Latino cultural property. Instead, the point is to denounce that the oppressive conditions out of which hip hop emerged are still in effect. The point is also to reclaim hip hop in all its dimensions, ethnic, racial, economic, political, so that the creative energy that gave birth to hip hop not loose its subversive strengths.

■ *Who Runs New York? (epiloguito)*

A while back, I was listening to Redman's Dare Iz a Darkside (Rush Associated Labels, 1994) and on track #18 entitled "We Run New York" a tough and piercing female voice started booming through the speakers: *The Hurricane Gee is live and in color/We run you motherfuckers.*

Her skilled lyrical flow and her smoothly splayed inflections caught my attention right away. My question to myself was: "Who is this female deemed hard enough, thus worthy enough to do a track like 'We Run New York' with a hard-core rapper like Redman?" Then, a few lines later, when she gives a shout out to "my big dick Boricuas in the back," I was overjoyed. Well, to be frank, my first reaction was a resigned "Great! female phallocentrism and big-dick worship with an ethnic twist." But that pang of annoyance took a back seat to my joy.

The pleasure was double, for here is an excellent female m.c. who also happens to be Puerto Rican making inroads in a male-dominated medium where Puerto Ricans frequently exist only as shadows. And to top it off she is in an album with one of the most popular East Coast rappers of the 90s! The last Puerto Rican woman to make some noise as a rapper was The Real Roxanne in the mid–eighties. Another Boricua female m.c. was long overdue. *Latin Queens in the house!*

"We Run New York," say Redman and Hurricane Gee. Although it would be interesting to ask why they run New York or what exactly does "running New York" entail, the main question is "Who is 'We'?" Do they mean "we" as Redman and Hurricane Gee? Or do they mean "We" as in the segment of the population that they represent? Or do they mean to say that they, as Redman and Hurricane Gee, "run New York" on behalf of the population which they represent?

My feeling is that their "We" operates at all three levels. They constantly affirm their skill and power as individuals, at the same time, they refer constantly to "their people," those who they represent. "Their people" also operates as a multi-level category which may include gender, ethnicity, generation, social class, race, musical culture, neighborhood, and different combinations of these.

I'm representin' bitches universal!

Hurricane explicitly claims to represent "Brooklyn, Flatbush," "Boricuas," "bitches," and "Latin Queens" in this track. Redman, being from Jersey, not being a Boricua and, presumably, not considering himself a Latin Queen or a bitch, is unspokenly admitting to sharing in "running New York" with groups which he does not personally represent.

So, where are the points of conjuncture? Again, who is "We"? "We," in this case, runs the gamut of categories from the personal to different variations on the communal. "We" can be Hurricane and Redman, or African Americans and Puerto Ricans, or young people of color, or all ghetto youngsters -regardless of racewho are into hip hop, or.... The possibilities for intersections and alliances inside that "we" are numerous. What is clear and highly significant is that both men and women, as well as both Boricuas and African Americans, are indispensable units in that "We."

The above interpretation, so full of optimism with regards to gender and ethnic solidarities, gets quite muddled if we read the text in light of the lived situation that brought this song to fruition. Hurricane's collaboration with Redman can be considered as an honor, in some sense. We might interpret her inclusion in this track as a way to give exposure to an aspiring artist.[7] However, we cannot pretend that Redman is on the same artistic standing as Hurricane. The male half of the unit that "runs New York" gets most of the recognition and money.

Not everyone can be a cacique[8]. True. Hurricane may be a guest artist in this production because she has to start somewhere, and not necessarily in the spotlight. But why is it always so hard for women to reach the spotlight? (Guevara, 1987; Rose, 1994; Smith, 1995). T-Love, an m.c. from south central Los Angeles, believes that women have to work doubly hard to get any recognition. The only way she was able to get on the mic was by "elbowing my way past the muthafuckers" (Cross, 1993: 299).

It is good to know that this highly skilled m.c. is currently on contract with Columbia Records and that her album is due in early 1996. The process has not been easy, however. She recognizes that being a woman has precluded a lot of people from taking her seriously.

> If you're not [having sex with everyone], it's hard. If they cannot be personally involved with you, then they're not interested in working with you (Hurricane, 1995).

Being Puerto Rican does not make her life as a struggling artist any easier either. Hurricane acknowledges the difficulties she faces in rap as a genre dominated at the artistic level by African Americans and by "white" people in the upper reaches of the music industry (Hurricane, 1995).

My musings regarding "We Run New York" do not intend to confuse hyperboles and metaphors with community organizing and political activism. However, I do think that, at an abstract textual level, this track points toward conjunctures with regards to gender and ethnicity that shed light upon African- American-Puerto Rican relations as they play themselves out within the hip hop zone. It is highly unlikely, if not outright impossible, that Redman could have recorded "We Run New York" with someone not black or Latino.

"Realness" is in vogue in rap. But regardless of how much the "real" street hardness is stretched and manipulated in order to bolster sales, a part of the real that cannot be changed or forgotten is that New York ghettoes have for decades been and still remain black and Latino. And, as Fat Joe notes in "Envy,"[9] it is the black and Latino "brothers" that the Giuliani-Pataki administration intends to "fry" with the re-establishment of the death penalty in New York.

Rhymes and lyrics are but just one version of the story. Musical alliances do not immediately equate real lived commitment. But words can influence the world of knowledge and knowledge can influence the sphere of action. An African- American man and a Puerto Rican woman claiming to run New York together and considering themselves a unit signified by the word "We" points to cognitive perceptions that harbor the seeds for political alliances. The question is, When are we going to come together for real, make some changes in the New York power structure, and really take care of our own? ∎

ENDNOTES

1. B-boys and b-girls are the original terms for the dancers that later became known as "breakdancers." Rock Steady Crew leader Crazy Legs, among many other hip hoppers, shuns the term "breakdancer" as a media–fabricated misnomer and insists on the necessity of using the original terms.
2. Taken from Willie Perdomo's poem of the same title in Roberto Santiago (ed), *Boricuas: An Anthology of Influential Puerto Rican Writings,* (New York: Ballantine Books, 1995): 91–92.
3. Puerto Ricans are the largest ethnic group in New York, with numbers around 900,000. Nevertheless, they no longer account for the majority of the Latino population. The second largest Latino group is made up of Dominicans who (including estimates of undocumented immigrants) number around 800,000 (Fernández et al., 1994).
4. George has produced songs for La India, Marc Anthony, Tito Nieves, and Orquesta de la Luz.
5. Who, after all, is part of "our people"? Are Rudolph Giuliani appointees Rubén Franco and Herman Badillo part of the the caetegory "our people" that we should stick to and defend from "others"? Ene, o. "Our people" is better exemplified by the multi-ethnic (but largely Black and Latino) Zulu Nation, founded by DJ Afrika Bambaata, that the Giuliani administration has decided is no more than a gang and a public threat.
6. I have concentrated here on exploring these issues by focusing on notions of community, race, ethnicity, and identity and have skirted, for the most part, the impact of the rap music industry. Such a topic merits careful and detailed discussion, which I will leave for future development.
7. Hurricane had previously done a track with Redman on his first album. She also collaborated on a song on Keith Murray's "The Most Beautifullest Thing In This World."
8. A *cacique* was the leader of a Taíno village.
9. From Fat Joe, "Jealous One's Envy" (Relativity, 1995).

REFERENCES

Betances, Samuel. 1974. "Race and the Search for Identity." In María Teresa Babín and Stan Steiner, *Borínquen: Anthology of Puerto Rican Literature*. New York: Vintage Books.
Blanco, Tomás. 1985. *El prejuicio racial en Puerto Rico*. Rio Piedras: Ediciones Huracán.
Cano-Moreno, Jorge. 1995. "La nueva visión/The New Vision," *Urban: The Latino Magazine*, 4, (Fall), 8–9.
Cross, Brian. 1993. *It's Not About a Salary: Rap, Race and Resistance in Los Angeles*. New York: Verso Books.
Davis, F. James. 1991. *Who is black?: One Nation's Definition*. Pennsylvania: Pennsylvania State University Press.
Degler, Carl. 1986. *Neither black Nor White: Slavery and Race Relations in Brazil and the United States*.

Wisconsin: The University of Wisconsin Press.
Díaz Quiñones, Arcadio. 1985. In Tomás Blanco, *El prejuicio racial en Puerto Rico*, pp. 13–91. Rio Piedras: Ediciones Huracán.
Fernández, Enrique, Juan González and Silvana Paternostro. 1994. "Latin Rainbow: New Arrivals Create a Changing City Scene," *Daily News* (March 6), 36–37.
Flores, Juan. forthcoming. "Puerto Rocks: New York Ricans Stake Their Claim." In Eric Burkins and Juan Flores, ed. *Droppin' Knowledge: Essays on Rap Music and Hip Hop Culture*. Philadelphia: Temple University Press.
——. 1992–93. "Puerto Rican and Proud, Boyee!: Rap, Roots and Amnesia," *Centro de Estudios Puertorriqueños Bulletin*, 5, 1 (Winter), 22–32.
——. 1992. "'It's a Street Thing!': An Interview with Charlie Chase," *Callaloo*, 15, 4, 999–1021.
——. 1991. "Latin Empire: Puerto Rap," *Centro de Estudios Puertorriqueños Bulletin*, 3, 2, (Spring), 77–85.
——. 1988. "Rappin', Writin' & Breakin'," *Centro de Estudios Puertorriqueños Bulletin*, II, 3 (Spring), 34–41.
Glasser, Ruth. 1991. "The Backstage View: Musicians Piece Together a Living," *Centro de Estudios Puertorriqueños Bulletin*, III, 2 (Spring), 24–49.
González, José Luis. 1989. *El país de cuatro pisos y otros ensayos*. Rio Piedras: Ediciones Huracán.
Guevara, Nancy. 1987. "Women Writin', Rappin', Breakin'." In Mike Davis (ed), *The Year Left*, pp 160–175. London: Verso Books.
Jorge, Angela. 1986. "The Black Puerto Rican Woman in Contemporary American Society." In Edna Acosta Belén, ed. *The Puerto Rican Woman: Perspectives on Culture History and Society*, pp. 180–187. New York: Praeger.
Kasinitz, Philip. 1992. *Caribbean New York: Black Immigrants and the Politics of Race*. Ithaca: Cornell University Press.
KRS-ONE. 1995. *The Science of Rap*. New York: A Street Publication.
López, Adalberto. 1980. "The Puerto Rican Diaspora." In Adalberto López, ed. *The Puerto Ricans: Their History, Culture and Society*. Vermont: Schenkman Books.
Manuel, Peter. 1995. *Caribbean Currents: Caribbean Music from Rumba to Reggae*. Philadelphia: Temple University Press.
Omi, Michael and Howard Winant. 1994. *Racial Formation in the United States: From the 1960s to the 1990s*. New York: Routledge.
Pedreira, Antonio S. 1992. *Insularismo*. Rio Piedras: Editorial Edil.
Perdomo, Willie. 1995. "Nigger-Reecan Blues." In Roberto Santiago, ed. *Boricuas: Influential Puerto Rican Writings, An Anthology*, pp 91–93. New York: Ballantine Books.
Roberts, John Storm. 1979. *The Latin Tinge: The Impact of Latin American Music in the United States*. Oxford: Oxford University Press.
Rodríguez, Clara. 1991. *Puerto Ricans: Born in the U.S.A.*. Boulder: Westview Press.
Rodríguez-Morazzani, Roberto. 1991–92. "Puerto Rican Political Generations in New York: Pioneros, Young Turks and Radicals," *Centro de Estudios Puertorriqueños Bulletin*, 4, 1, (Winter), 96–116.
Rose, Tricia. 1994. "Black Noise: Rap Music and Black Culture" in *Contemporary America*, Hanover: Wesleyan University Press.
Salazar, Rodrigo. 1995. "Afro-Cuban Music 101," *Urban: The Latino Magazine*, 4, (Fall), 21.
Smith, Danyel. 1995. "Ain't a Damn Thing Changed: Why Women Rappers Don't Sell." In Adam Sexton, *Rap on Rap: Straight-Up Talk On Hip Hop Culture*, pp.125–128. Delta Books: New York.
Thomas, Piri. 1967. *Down These Mean Streets*. New York: Vintage Books.
Toop, David. 1991. *Rap Attack 2: African Rap to Global Hip Hop*. London: Serpent's Tail.
Torres, Andrés. 1995. *Between Melting Pot and Mosaic: African Americans and Puerto Ricans in the New York Political Economy*. Philadelphia: Temple University Press.
Vázquez, Blanca, Juan Flores and Pablo Figueroa. 1992–93. "KMX Assault: The Puerto Rican Roots of Rap," *Center for Puerto Rican Studies Bulletin*, 5, 1 (Winter), 38–51.
Young Lords Party and Michael Abramson. 1971. *Palante: Young Lords Party*. New York: McGraw-Hill.
Wilson, William Julius. 1987. *The Truly Disadvantaged: The Inner City, The Underclass and Public Policy*. Chicago: The University of Chicago Press.
Zenón Cruz, Isabelo. 1975. *Narciso descubre su trasero*. Vol II. Humacao, PR: Editorial Furidi.

Discography
Fat Joe, Jealous One's Envy (Relativity Recordings, 1995).
Redman, Dare Iz a Darkside (Rush Associated Labels, 1994).
Q-Unique, "Rice and Beans" (unreleased).

Interviews
DJ Tony Touch a.k.a. The Taíno Turntable Terrorist (d.j., member of the Rock Steady Crew), October 12, 1995.
Gina Amaro (community organizer), December 16, 1995.
Hurricane Gee, a.k.a Gloria Rodríguez (m.c.), October 10, 1995.
Q-Unique (m.c., member of the Arsonists Crew and Rock Steady Crew), October 13, 1995.

38 UNDERGROUND PLAYERO

ADVISORY — **EXPLICIT LYRICS**

PUERTO RICAN UNDERGROUND

Mayra Santos

Yo también perdí quimeras pero me hice buen voyeur Fito Paez

In July of 1994, the editor of *Diálogo*, Peri Coss, published a controversial essay in *El Nuevo Día* that discussed what in Gringoland has been dubbed as "Generation X." This generation is made up of the children of the Reagan era, and it has widely popularized many cultural annunciations, such as grunge music, reggae-rap, fashions inspired by K-mart and prison uniforms, body piercing, and tattoos. According to Coss, "political apathy" characterizes this group and the cultural and social response that it has given to its historical moment, in contrast to the reply of the 1970s.

Here in Puerto Rico, some of these styles have taken root and gained momentum, particularly the new fusions of Caribbean and African American music that reach us from New York and Miami and that we have reshaped. This is the origin of *Boricua*[1] underground rap, one of the most important cultural phenomena in contemporary Caribbean music. Reggae-rap in Spanish serves as a means of expression for millions of young people while avoiding complete co-optation by the aboveground market. Thus, an entire, almost invisible, youth culture exists that operates between the social fringes (either as a chosen lifestyle or sole option) and criminal illegality, and whose emblems—marijuana, fashion, music, and cars—create a series of encounters that in turn set the criteria comprising an "identity."

However, this identity has been under assault in a public sphere that openly declares war on it. During the month of February, the Puerto Rican police launched a raid against underground rap, confiscating every cassette of this music being sold in the country's record shops and applying those sections of the penal code known as Laws 112 and 117 against obscenity. Fines were levied, material confiscated, and throughout the following months, radio, television, and newspaper media took up the task of "demonizing" rap and rappers, characterizing them as immoral, instigators of violence, and irresponsible corrupters of the public order. This brought to the public eye a cultural phenomenon already underway in Puerto Rico since approximately 1983. What has changed is not the content of the music, but rather its sphere of influence.

The acts of aggression and political repression against rappers now also target other social groups and the meeting places of the country's youth, particularly two bars in Río Piedras and San Juan, "El estudiante" and "El escenario" respectively. Although the usual pattern of aggression from the Puerto Rican police may be discerned here, this aggression is specifically directed at three marginal groups: those of gays, rap, and youth. It is important to note that these are the groups that during the decade of the 1980s acted as the focal points of greatest political contention and opposition to the official and social status quo. Since 1983 and above all from 1985 to 1990, the struggles against AIDS of the activist gay group ACT-UP were the unifying agent for a gay presence and action throughout the entire planet. The emergence and global influence of African American rap and other Afro-American music manifested itself in the Rodney King case and the Los Angeles rebellion and in greater public exposure for black groups in England, France, the Caribbean, and

---

MAYRA SANTOS is a professor in the department of Hispanic Studies at the University of Puerto Rico, Río Piedras campus. Her book *Pez de vidrio* received the Letras de Oro award (1993–1994) given by the Spanish government and the University of Miami.

The article was translated from the original Spanish by Félix Cortés.

South America.[2] The emergence of grunge as a movement of protest and social criticism of marginalized poor white youth in the United States has definitely been incorporated into the international social iconography through the music and fashion industries. Now, with the "return" of the Republicans to the U.S. Congress and the new Puerto Rican Senate, there is an attempt to control these groups and take back the gains they have made, most importantly that of winning a presence in the public sphere. Their existence and their freedom of movement in terms of presence, cultural products, and meeting spaces are made "illegal" to once again marginalize and silence them. The conflict lies in the experience gained and in the spaces, even within the marketplace, that they have already opened up for themselves.

Frankly, it is at the point where state control and marketplace meet that the most interesting aspects of this struggle are waged. Neo-liberalism has drawn the coordinates that allow these groups access to the market, creating companies or even marginal business circuits that give them autonomy and ways of increasing profits and their social presence. Through the buying and selling of fashion and music articles, cultural modes of conduct and practice are promoted that lend cohesion to or create an "imaginary community" (to loosely apply Benedict Anderson's terminology) no longer mediated by the printed word or legal publicity, but rather by the digital, visual, and auditory technologies of music and video. These are the means that set and propagate stereotypes and serialized modes of behavior and that concurrently enjoy a relative freedom, given the fact that they may be produced independently and at small cost in living quarters converted to small recording or video editing studios, a rather common practice in Puerto Rico. Underground music cassettes are recorded in studios in housing complexes such as Villa Kennedy and Jurutungo. These cassettes are makeshift but of high quality. And rap video clips aired on the two music video channels, channels 52 and 18, are accessible because they are mostly produced with hi-8 and super VHS video camera equipment at very little cost, and edited mainly with equipment set up in the *marquesina*.[3] The proliferation of these independent outfits surges at the moment that digital video and audio equipment become economically and generally available to the public and further results from the market's need for new products for public consumption.

In "Art Ideology and Pop Practice," the British critic, Simon Frith, explains:

> Pop music has become an ideological issue again (the BBC banning records with the same bizarre logic of "offensiveness" as in the mid '60s) because the problem of leisure and unemployment has arisen just as the leisure industry is being acclaimed as the solution to Britain's economic problems. The transformation of electronic goods into consumer goods, the development of cable TV, video recording, home computers, and so on, have put an economic premium on people's leisure tastes (and, in some respects, threaten state and oligopolistic manipulation of those tastes). Pop's leisure significance is thus being fought for again-hence Britain's newest youth subculture, the "casuals," whose aggressive, stylistic celebration of leisure goods and "life-style" conceals both continuing dole queues and continuing "hooliganism"—the street-corner menace now comes from such nice, clean-cut, Tory looking boys and girls! (p. 471)

It is precisely this fear of losing the ability to manipulate "taste" that has lead the state in England as well as in Puerto Rico to intervene against underground rap and other youth culture groups. The relative autonomy of the cultural postulates produced by these groups exposes the state in its inefficient role of social administrator by putting forth other focal points of identities that separate themselves from those programmed by civil society for the "smooth" functioning of the market and civil apparatus.

Another interesting feature of the phenomenon is evident in that the demarcations of this new culture, increasingly diluted and paying less attention to national identity as the primary constituent of the multiple identities that arise. In the past, the question was who were the assimilated *Boricuas* and who were the authentic ones while today, the same approach is inadequate for understanding the emergence of the multiple, intertwining identities that make up international youth culture and, by extension, Puerto Rican youth culture. One must turn to concepts other than alienation, authenticity, nation, popular culture, and citizenship in order to capture what, before the public eye, races dizzingly by.

This once again leads us to the question of how identities are produced in the 1990s, particularly at the meeting point of the state and the market. Peri Coss' concern about individualism as the preferred emblem of youth culture in the 1990s is here again pertinent. The "apathy" towards collective and political action arises precisely with the changes in the very nature of what is considered to be and defined as the public sphere. In place of the old identity of the "citizen," another identity has consolidated in the 1990s, that of the "consumer" who in a new manner links the private and the public, the regional and the global, the individual and the collective. It is impossible to understand the response in social and cultural practices to our historical moment without at least trying to explore this system of interactions in which young people enter social life.

■ *Identity '90: The citizen is dead, long live the consumer*
"No estoy solo, puedo salir a comprar" Argentinean rock group Dividos

One of the major problems facing sociologists, anthropologists, historians, and other students of contemporary youth culture is how to explain the supposed "individualistic apathy" characteristic of this decade. In the more informal critiques, including the Coss article and Pantojas' performance piece last year, "Rompeforma," an entire generation is branded as individualistic and "sold out" without taking into account the permutations undergone by the concept of "commitment" as a result of the historical changes, nor the manner in which individualism today functions as a paradigm for new political transformations. Many commentators assert an oppositional relation between the social and the individual, which no longer suffices to discuss the field of interrelations between the subject and society at the close of the millennium. A reappraisal of these concepts is without question in order from the perspective that, far from satanizing or glorifying the capitalist individual, examines the transformations in the creation of identities and the new ways of negotiating between the individual and the collective.

In his book *La sociedad de los individuos* Norbert Elias details the precedents for the dichotomization of the concepts of individual and society:

> We already find in the seventeenth century, possibly beginning with the English Puritans, the distinction between that which is done in an individual manner and that which is done collectively. This represented a prior step to the subsequent elaboration of the concept, which finally in the nineteenth century, accompanying a growing need for a verbal means for designating opposing socio-political movements and ideals, lead to the formulation of terms such as individualism, on the one hand, and socialism and collectivism on the other. In more recent periods, these terms have contributed to the use of individual and social as if they entail a set of opposites (180–81).

This process of dichotomization between the social and the individual accelerated as the twentieth century unfolded and national identities consolidated, as well as in the political theories of the so-called social contract. Subsequently, transportation, print, and film, among other technologies, laid the foundations for a field of identity.[4] In the words of José Manuel Valenzuela, "they shaped stereotypes and reconstructed images of daily life"[5] that propagated and consolidated this identity.

With the third technological revolution, that is, massive national and international migrations, production on a global scale, economic integration, etc., the production of culture and identities multiplied and took off. However, they also contradictorily became similar. North American cultural imperialism laid the basis or the common language for an entire generation almost throughout the entire planet. However, this language or cultural substratum, was seen as a commodity, or as market products that were assimilated in different ways according to the space in which the consumer placed them. For these reasons, the processes of cultural consumption and production are very different from the manner in which they were traditionally understood and, therefore, they cannot be analyzed through the old discourse of cultural syncretism, transculturation, assimilation, or the Marxist concepts of alienation.

The neo-liberal language continues to define as individual something that, strictly speaking, no longer exists. The traditional nineteenth century concepts of individualism and its corollaries, while defending the market place as the locus where the individual took shape, were founded on the legal basis of the civil rights and social identity of the citizen, guaranteed at the very moment of birth. The fundamental relation between the individual and the social was mediated by the State, which fulfilled the singular and utopian function of defending the individual rights of the citizen.

In the 1980s and 1990s, neo-liberal discourse has managed to continue to name this new reality, a social reality in which individualism, although based on the socio-political underpinnings of the citizen's identity, moves closer to the identity of the consumer. The legal discourse on civil rights has considerably disappeared from the public forum. Business propaganda and political-state strategies for the privatization of social services have succeeded in convincing people that their first right is the right to purchase, the best means for expressing one's state of being is to purchase things, the only way to defend and achieve rights is to buy them. For this reason, especially in the 1980s and 1990s, contemporary identity is not forged solely through work or at the core of the individual-means of production relation or the individual-State relation, but rather in the relation between the individual and the market.[6] However, the polarization of social classes and the significant reduction in industrial production (replaced by a service economy) increasingly exclude more people from consumption and threaten the buying capacity of millions of people throughout the planet. The drug trade and other illegal trade activities that create work and monetary benefits for those individuals typically displaced from legal activity take advantage of this tension.

The individuals of the 1990s begin with an internationalist consciousness that results from telecommunications, the market, and the famous "deterritorializing of culture" about which Deleuze and Guatari speak so much. In their philosophical treatise, "Imagologies," Mark C. Taylor and Esa Saarinen[7] argue that "while Marx developed a sophisticated interpretation of the relation between socio-cultural processes and economic dynamics, his analysis is not directly applicable to post industrial capitalism. With the advent of consumer society, culture itself becomes commodified." Those concrete things found in the marketplace and advertised on TV are able to thread together a common identity at the individual level, while simultaneously articulating multiple tribal identities. The youth know that culture/identity can be bought, that a subjectivity is constructed through the interaction between market products and people, either at the point of legal economic exchange-the shopping mall of Plaza de las Americas—or illegal exchange-the favorite copping grounds. The differences multiply because those articles that are for sale have the same exchange value, but they do not have the same use value. Being a member of certain social groups then becomes a matter of recombining different market products that could be used to delineate the social configuration of ethnic identities, ideological groupings, distinct sexual orientations or sexual practices, or age divisions. For this reason, identities may be conceived as multiple, variable, and even contradictory, just as membership in different groups is no longer an organic question and becomes contingent, transitory, or "translocal" (see Puerto Rico, the Translocal Nation).[8] For example, Dock Maartens boots and the bald look used to identify skinheads and that were appropriated by gay activists of ACT-UP are today symbols of the anti-yuppie youth of Generation X. Jamaican rasta dreadlocks were appropriated by radical anti-racist rappers in the United States and are now one of the principal marks of distinction among fans of underground reggae-rap in Spanish in Puerto Rico, as well as among black intellectuals, women and men, throughout the Caribbean, Africa, and the Afro-Americas. A single set of articles or discourses, in numerous recombinations, evokes differing identities. It is for this reason that the identities of the 1990s seem so uniform and at the same time, so fragmentary. Just like the marketplace.

Another main characteristic of the 1990s is the link between agency, i.e. political, social, cultural, and the marketplace. At no moment is the attempt made to go against the circuits of distribution and consumption of post industrial capitalism. With the fall of the Soviet block, the defeat of the international left, and the creation of common markets such as Mercosur, Nafta, the European community, and the revised Caricom, a centralized, contentious flow of data, stereotypes, and everyday life images does not exist. What has been produced is a multiplicity of more or less underground circuits that exist outside of the market until it seizes and domesticates them. For some, this domestication implies a real tragedy that leads to self-destruction (the suicide case of "Nirvana" singer Kurt Cobain). But for others, en masse commercialization means greater economic independence and, therefore, greater social intervention, as in the case of gangsta rap in the U.S. and Puerto Rico. Greg Tate, the noted critic of North American hip-hop culture, asserts:

> Unlike avant-garde art movements of the past, hip-hop does not teach anti-capitalism but rather übercapitalism. In a strange twist, hip-hop has resisted market forces by subverting capitalist marketing tools to its own end. (Tate, Greg. "Above and Beyond Decibels: a Defense of Rap," *New York Times*, 6 March 1994: 36)

In this manner, the hip-hop cultural circuit has achieved a freedom from the market not by challenging it, but rather by using its very logic. This is one of the most radical strategies emerging in the 1980s and 1990s to respond to the globalization of the market, and it should be taken into account in the articulation of new discourses of cultural and political resistance.

With the fall of the alternative system of circulation and distribution that the socialist block and its subsidiaries provided, the stereotypes and collective images of what was supposed to be a socialist-communist identity also went on to become products for sale, appropriated by the post industrial international market. Let us recall for a moment the stores that opened in New York after the fall of the wall, in which hammer and sickle pins, Soviet uniforms, berets, Che and Mao T-shirts are sold. Back home, we have a startling example—the festivals of the socialist newspaper, *Claridad*, sponsored by Budweiser. I do not intend to draw attention to the political hypocrisy of this case. I do, however, want to point out how the left no longer has any other recourse, in order to survive, than to participate in the logic of the international market, which does not respect ideological borders or establishes itself in a system of binary power following the old logic of purely national or class identities. The weak and besieged niches of the traditional left increasingly participate less in consumer society and, contradictorily, increasingly form a greater part of it. And they participate not as undercover agents, spies or terrorists attempting to infiltrate in order to destroy, but as open social spokespeople and as consumers.

On the other hand, one could argue that one identity, capitalist individualism, won over the other, socialist collectivism, in a complete and unique manner. Neo-liberalism has not been able to achieve a standard identity, outside of the yuppie identity of the baby boomers that have already disappeared after a brief life span during the 1980s and then being expelled from the social iconography by the marvelous anti-AIDS activists, the battles between the defenders and enemies of abortion, the National African Congress and the freeing of Nelson Mandela, Tianenman Square, the L.A. rebellion, and Chiapas. In fact, the business agents of the international underground act as collectives, beginning with Dr. Dre and ending with Falo or Playero or even DJ Negro, who gather around themselves a whole series of people, relatives, and friends that comprise the force of production of their business and who benefit from it.

Identity shaped at the heart of the marketplace has given rise to multiple discourses that define social belonging according to race, ethnicity, sexual orientation, gender, key social concerns, such as the environment, public policies on abortion, etc. The international phenomena of the decade of the 1980s can largely be explained through these discourses on identities that appeared in the face of the fall of the society of production and the onset of consumer society. Each neo-primitive tribe versus the neo-liberal one found a stereotype, a mythical image, to project and construct with the objects that the market subsequently propagated for its own benefit. The same logic of consumption is used, then, to create oppositional identities and to claim rights, not as state citizens, but rather as consumers. The boycotts of South Africa, and much of the logic and the offensive strategy of environmental groups and of anti-AIDS activism, are founded precisely upon the rights and powers of the consumer.

■ *Techno-Aborigines: Neo-primitive Aesthetics as a Reply to the Third Technological Revolution.*
It is already a well known cliché. Before the implacable advances of technology, one of the most common responses of the cultural paradigms of the nineteenth and twentieth centuries is that of invoking the natural, the savage. The resistance to technology has often been waged in this manner. Rimbaud did as much in *"une saison en Enfer"*; Dario did so in the short story, "El rey burgués"; and the Renaissance discourse on the *belle ile*, Rousseau and Picasso also did as much. However, the neo-primitive aesthetics of the 1990s is very much related to a conception of the urban primitive, that is to say, the dichotomy between the rural and the metropolitan is broken in order to get to the primitive, the savage, within the strongholds of the city. This savagism is found in the most violent of the socially marginalized: criminals, punks, pushers, leather homosexuals, transvestites, bikers, illegal or semi-legal immigrants, and poor workers. From this starting point, and with the cultural emblems of these actors, new aesthetics of the urban-primitive are established. Body-piercing, nose rings, Salvation Army clothes, Dock Maartens boots a la skinhead aesthetics, rasta dreadlocks, baggy pants inspired by prisons and pushers, Irie (Rasta colors) colors, punk hair dyes, all flow into this new aesthetic syntax. Even technology itself is primitivized as it serves as an emblem of social illegality. Such is the case with cellular phones and beepers, mixers and turn tables for scratching records. The common denominators in these aesthetics are violence on the one hand and articles of facile mass consumption on the other. The consumption of kitsch, of industrial garbage, or of the residues of the hypertechnologization of the market: all these also end up in the hands of the new cultural enunciators of the 1990s.

Of all these cultural enunciators, one of the most feared is the rapper. There are two types of rap, commercial rap and underground rap. In both, rap identity is constructed as a social menace. If in the commercial sphere, rap speaks of life in the barrio and offers advise on how to end drugs and unemployment, in the underground market it speaks about life in the barrio in its own terms. Rap lyrics and music offend public morality. They are violent, explicitly sexual, and vulgar. Its sexual discourse includes the homophobia and misogyny characteristic of Boricua culture. But the reason for its persecution is its use of a language that lays bare these prejudices in a violent manner. The main themes of rap songs are, among others, marijuana, crime, sex, the glorification of gun culture, and criticism and transgression of state control, especially as personified by the police force. This music also denounces social hypocrisy and class exploitation. It identifies racial prejudices and exposes the supposed racial democracy that characterizes Puerto Rican society. And, as a last straw, it does not respect national identities neither in musical terms nor linguistically. For these reasons, it is evident that rap is at the present moment the most threatening musical expression in urban Puerto Rico.

Rap takes up violence as a lifestyle and develops aesthetic and thematic strategies to incorporate it. It occupies at present a position similar to that of salsa in the 1970s. It is the genre that represents life in the streets, the gangstas, the volatile girls, death always lurking just around the corner, and the struggle to make it economically. Just like salsa in its beginnings, rap is accused of being solely an exported genre, poor in musical talent and a mere commercial gimmick. And just like salsa, rap gives a collective response to daily life as it is lived by "the people in the street." It, therefore, articulates a discourse of identity that defines the parameters of this community's cultural responses, from the clothing style to the key gestures and elements. It is through rap that a stereotype is presented to be emulated and a vital daily practice is established. Moreover, a cultural space is defined—the streets, the drug corner—that determine the source of these cultural annunciations.

Rap forms part of technoculture. This fact subverts its categorization as a musical genre and even the academic categories of "autochtonous popular music." Turn tables and mixers replace musical instruments and the rapper replaces fine singing. This, in addition to the musical collage that serves as the mix or background for the rapper, points to a new mode of making art, that of juxtaposing, or hybridization. Now lacking orchestras, given that rappers lack access to the means for putting together formal musical groups, the door is open to experimentation with technology. This use of technology has its own history. The use of the voice in place of song also has its precedents. It is not mere coincidence that homegrown rap shares its roots with Jamaican dubpoetry and ragamuffin, African American preaching and bragging rights. They are ancestral traditions of the African griot that join with technoculture to register oral and visual meeting spaces. In an interview with the agent of Prime Records, Marién Gelpí, she points out that "Rap expresses the preoccupations of Puerto Rican youth. The great voice or virtuosity in playing a musical instrument is not necessary for its creation. These limit the possibilities of expression of young people. The rapper witnesses and composes. The important thing is to have good mixing and to sound good."[7]

For all of these reasons, rap in Spanish has become something like the most popular musical stamp of spaces associated with delinquency, violence, illegality, and transgression in contemporary Puerto Rico. Rappers are a social group from juxtaposed social fringes. They are typically young men, blacks and mulattos (although here again, there are exceptions of racial phenotype) between the ages of 14 and 25 from the "lower" classes of the unemployed and underemployed. The customary spaces of rap are the public schools, drug spots, television, and *marquesina* parties. Additionally, rap forms part of an entire, well articulated cultural system that includes fashion, posses, linguistic expressions, a discourse of identities, and an economics of violence.

These spaces require codes to assert legitimacy and to expand. Clothes, dance, vocabulary create particular meanings that appeal to a specific audience, that are identified visually, emotionally, and territorially with the rapper and his crew. In an interview with Carlitos Andujar from the old program "Rap Fridays" on Carolina's channel 18, he tells us "for every hour of recording, we would spend three hours breaking up fights between the rappers from Fajardo and the rappers from Carolina." There are enemy territories-each with its own code that both unites and distinguishes them.

The urban aesthetics of rap thus impose a violence that also aims at the irreverent recycling of images and words. Rappers do not care for purity. They mix English and Spanish, refined voices with vulgar ones, local fashions with the imported, homegrown rhythms with rhythms from abroad, all the while modifying them all to create an expressive collage. The juxtaposed violence suggested by the collage is exaggerated auditorily, through the employment of screams, the shattering of bottles, and scratching, that assault on the record placed on the turn table that also produces rhythms.

However, all that violence does not occur by accident. On the contrary, the rapper presents himself or herself as the author of this "offense." He or she is the one who brings together and integrates all the levels that make up the rap event. And consequently, the rapper is the strongest, the most gangsta, and the one who knows best the philosophy of the street. The rapper's subjectivity feeds on fragmentation because it allows him to transgress the hierarchies ordering the senses. Not showing them any respect, the rapper mixes references to Christopher Columbus with "I Dream of Genie" and references to Flash Gordon with God. His or her own public identity becomes a publicity billboard.

It is precisely in the emergence of this new identity, that of the male or female rapper, that I want to dwell. This identity is expressed through the discourses of bragging, explicit sex, and marijuana. It is thus identified as a criminal, primitive, techno-aboriginal identity that removes it from the parameters of civilization and the moderation of legal civil society.

In the specific case of Puerto Rico, these discourses, through which rap identity is forged, are solidly linked to the construction of masculinity. The critic Rafael Ramírez, in his important book, *Dime, capitán: reflexiones sobre la masculinidad*,[9] defines it as an identity that is constructed through might and competition in the social sphere. Similarly, rap bragging, that rhetorical trick of challenges between troubadour men that is also practiced in other genres and other traditions of popular song, is produced here by using masculinity's own language for laying foundations. And this laying of the foundations of masculinity is inextricably tied to the urban primitive, that is, to violence. It is in the space of violence that manhood is tested. Crude sexuality and the use of marijuana are also incorporated in this space.

"My piece is already going off for you" (Playero #37), "The blonde, the hole, the one I like" (Falo), and "Poke her" (Playero #37, Franky Boy), as well as many other reggae-rap songs in Spanish testify to this. In his article on underground rap, "Entre la censura y la ingenuidad" *(Diálogo,* March 1995: 16), José Luis Ramos Escobar has already collected several of the lyrics with the more violent, extreme language from a range of underground rap that is heard and produced in the Island. Homophobia and misogyny, as parameters contrary to masculinity, glow as important signposts in many of these lyrics. Another important stamp is the possession of luxury items that make evident the rappers buying power. If it is through the relation between the individual and the market that the identities of the 1990s are established and through violence and competitive superiority that masculine identity is established, when the two are combined we have the figure of the gangsta, of the rapper with a beeper, cellular phone, gold chains, a hooked-up BMW, a mansion, etc., although these figure more in the rapper iconography than in daily reality.

We should not forget that the rapper identity is defined by society as pertaining to a group of identities that are three-fold criminal. Because of his or her gender, race, and class position, the rapper is from the start a gangsta. If not in reality, then potentially. And it is precisely as a result of falling into this social position thrice criminalized by the state that the rapper develops responses, some rhetorical, others real, to establish himself or herself and confront his or her marginalization.

One of the most misunderstood responses on the part of the general public, intellectuals, and the mass media is the way in which rap shifts the criminal space to its own performance stage. The discourse of rap lyrics regularly employs metaphors such as pistols, pieces, grenades, shots, in order to move to the club dance floor the violent challenges taking place in the street. These also serve as auditory metaphors, as explosions, shots, screams, alarms, and the familiar scratching are mixed into the music of the cassette tape. This rhetorical operation presents the very act of rapping as a rhetorical crime. That is to say, the rapper, by the mere act of singing his or her genre, is already a criminal, a gangsta, and a "terrorist" against social well-being. This much is demonstrated in the rap number "Prieto" from the underground cassette Chiclín #1 from Carolina:

> *Prieto, Prieto[10] está guillao de maleante/*" " *solo quiere cantarte/*" " *comunal pa' demonstrarte/*" " *como suena mi arte/*" " *no es ningún terrorista/*" " *y yo me esfuerzo en la pista/*" " *solo quiere cantarte/prieto, prieto y dice así/*" " *ey, quisite salvar algo/algo en pie y no vas a lograrlo/si quieres guerra pues guerra tendrás/si quieres tregua, saca tu bandera/pasaste la raya/se acabó el pariseo/no quiero problemas, Prieto no pelea/ pero si me buscas tú me vas a encontrar/así que mamabicho, no me jodas más. (Chiclín #1)*

Here, the vulgar language is limited to superiority in violence, shifting in the Boricua reggae-rap space to the verbal sphere. For this reason, vulgar words frequently appear in underground rap. Through the deft insult and brilliant combinations a superior linguistic violence is exhibited. The most common insults, as one can imagine, are that of "cocksucker" and "faggot" and all those that "reduce" the man to the category of woman. These insults are synonymous with coward in rap discourse.

However, Prieto, as well as many other Puerto Rican rappers unmask their violent act as a simulation, as a performance. For that reason, the rapper explains that he "is no terrorist" and that he "makes like he's a gangsta." That is, the rapper recognizes violence as a rhetorical violence, transferred to the realm of the word as part of an artistic expression. But, beware, for this textual practice is always followed by a warning about the rapper's ability to defend himself if he is messed with:

Juni en la calle viene muy loco/no lo cuques, no lo mires que te viro y te destrozo/
oye, ***, que pasó dímelo/cogiste miedo, canto de maricón/
en corillo eras muy guapito/y ahora que pasó que te cogí solito/
lo miré a la cara, las lágrimas bajaban/
gritarle, no callarme, a mierda ya apestaba,/
no hay, no hay, no hay, claro que no/no hay liga para mi/
que cuando Juni comienza a cantar,/
las chicas te lo pueden decir (Juni, Chiclín #2)

Dirty language, ingenuity in improvisation (or freestyle), self-promotion or bragging or insults are the rhetorical practices for establishing superiority in the space of rap. Many times, a rapper declaring himself or herself "in control" has to be tested in these terms. That is, rap discourse operates within the coordinates of linguistic violence at several planes, those of the insult, precociousness, and finally the metaphorical discourse of criminality displaced to the verbal realm:

no me importa tu amistad,/ni tu lengua larguilla/ni que tu te guilles de terrorista/
porque mi corillo te tiene en la miras
****
soy un maleante, soy un matón/mî lirica es el fuego/que escupe mi cañón. (Chiclin #2)

These rhetorical practices establish a discourse in which killing and defeating the opposing rapper in improvisation and verbal violence is one and the same thing; to shoot and to rap are one and the same. That is, the language that designates violence in the streets and the language of rap become one in order to equate the space of the streets to the virtual spaces of underground rap. In this way, an imaginary community is created that goes beyond the physical limits of the barrio and the crew while asserting them as the organizations of choice to challenge the state.

In fact, underground rap remixes themselves function as techno-aboriginal crews. Each cassette compiles rap numbers of one crew, Carolina's (Chiclín #1 and #2), Bayamón's Puerto Nuevo's, and Jurutungo's (Playero #37, #38), and so on. These are crews that proclaim their superiority and challenge other underground rap crews. In terms of the music, the songs are not separated. They are sung at times by one rapper, other times by more than one, in dialogue and in challenges, denouncing one crew or another for copying their style, each rapper proclaiming that he or she is the best, and asserting at the same time the crew's unity as an important major organization and their DJ as the best. The songs do not follow just one theme and they interweave just as the rappers do in singing. For this reason, it becomes difficult to identify them by a title or a singer. Once again, the supremacy of the crew is shown as definitive. The important thing is that they appear in Playero #38 or Noise #3, in these underground cassettes that play the role of crews that protect and contain tensions within and between groups and that serve to provide order, a place that establishes an identity and offers protection to the individual.

Crews and women then are the other spaces that validate the rapper as a man. In many lyrics of Boricua underground rap, the theme of competition between machos over a woman appears. As in all pop songs, these also reduce the woman to the source of provocation. They are either the partying slut or the desired one. But in contrast to the legal romantic song, in underground rap, the lover seems more sexual than spiritual. She is a loved one with a body and desires. This could serve to explain, at least partially, why many female rap lyricists are sexually explicit -not only because of the role of verbal violence and superiority in improvisational skill in rap, but also because of the proclamation of a type of relationship between couples mediated by sex. If in legal popular discourse all relationships between couples are necessarily mediated by a "spirituality" that validates desire, in underground discourse, the rapper does away with all spirituality, leaving sexual desire without the palliative of spiritual meditation to legitimize it.

> *Brinca pa' arriba/salta y rebota/como si fueras una gran pelota/*
> *********
> *nunca vi mujer con el cuerpo de vedette/que me haga a mi brincar/*
> *como lo hizo esa girl/*
> *******
> *Con Juni en la casa/la nena no pasa/porque el pai no la deja salir/*
> *ella se encierra en el cuarto/se pone a llorar/y se seca con una bounty*
> *******
> *nena dame deso/dame deso, nena nena dame deso de tu amor/*
> *que quiero estar contigo, oye nena/aunque sea un minuto por favor*
> *******
> *tu me lo ligaste/ no digas que no/tu me lo viste grande pelú y cabezón*

In the end, sexual prowess establishes masculine superiority. In masculinity's iconography and rap's macho discourse, it overcomes all other tests of manhood. To be able to seduce the girls, after proving improvising power and courage and counting on the crew's support is primary.

> *Oye man, tengo algo mejor que tu/por eso es la nena está conmigo*
> *(coro)*
> *la tratas mal,/la tratas mal/por eso la nena/no me puede dejar*
> *(coro)*
> *no la vas a obligar/no me va a soltar/y yo con mi labia*
> *me la voy a llevar*
> *(coro)*
> *yo no tengo carro/ni money pa gastar/solo le doy mi bicho*
> *y con eso basta/*
> *(coro)*
> *caricia y besos/siempre yo le doy/y quiero que sepas/que no soy un* playboy.

Another sign of rap identity is marijuana. Given the reigning discourse of the war against drugs that has muddled all critical analysis of legalizing drugs such as marijuana, this defense and wide support for the consumption of pot is one of the most problematic characteristics of underground rap in the Island. Many of the songs of this thematic circuit refer to smoking marijuana, ganja, green, brown, or Thai stick. In the Playero #37 and #38 underground cassettes, there are numerous songs that refer to smoking weed. "Light up a Joint 'Cause I Wanna Smoke" and "Boom Boom Marijuana" are two of the most popular ones. In "Light up a Joint," Playero and Master Joe tell the adventures of their crew, facing cops to cop and smoke weed. Street bravado, as well as camaraderie between crew members, whose primary and communal activities are mixing, singing, hanging in San Juan and smoking, are put on display. At one moment of a rap number, Playero pronounces himself in favor of using ganja and converts the term to an adjective, not as a particularly criminal practice, but rather as a personal matter.

> *Es que yo amo la ganja/la que me arrebata/no me aborchorno de aceptar/*
> *que me gusta fumar/simplemente para mí/es bien personal/*
> *mientras más y más y más/es que yo puedo tripear (Playero #37)*

Here, and in other rap numbers, smoking ganja is a personal activity, a consumer's act, a rite among men in a crew. Just like in the practice of drinking, which was glorified in trio group songs made famous by Felipe Rodriguez, the Panchos, and other interpreters of the 1940s and 1950s, rap glorifies smoking pot. This practice establishes camaraderie between men and their strength next to women. In Playero #37, another rapper argues:

*Ella es predilecta/y digo tiene belleza material, Marijuana/
Todos la quieren fumar/y digo marijuana es lo que quiero fumar*

*Ella tiene lo que yo busco/y es la materia ideal/tiene un crudo degustado/y es también medicinal/
fili, fili yo vengo a promocionar/la trayectoria que lleva no está mal/
viene de la tierra/por eso es natural...*

As I stated earlier, this apology for ganja is not solely Playero's. There are other rappers that defend marijuana and it's widespread use, joining a broad movement that crosses national boundaries and lays bridges to black communities in the United States (such as the California rappers Insane in the Brain) and Jamaica (the whole circuit of rasta culture). This theme, although responding to the rhetorical practices of rap to establish itself in illegality, also responds to techno-primitive aesthetics and to something else that I tentatively would refer to as urban pan-Caribbeanism. That is, the discourse in favor of marijuana is framed by two important signifiers-Jamaica and reggae culture and discourses on the race.

■ *Boricua Rap as an Urban Pan-Caribbean Discourse*

*Ya yo me voy de aquí
me voy pa' Jamaica
marijuana buena quiero fumar...*

If before, *"Cocolos"*[11] (salsa fans) were the ones looked upon as the biggest delinquents in the community, and the ones to develop the discourse of a "Latino" and "black" identity, now they are the rappers, the ones who, through their songs, create a new identity designated with the epithet of "the race." In order to understand this new discourse, we have to review the history of the genre in Puerto Rico.

The history of Boricua rap is very complex, precisely because it unfolds underground. It is, to a certain point, a history that erases itself. The first rap cassettes to appear around 1983 very seldom had copyright labels, or dates, even of the year in which they were produced. Few of the first rappers to appear and give shape to the new urban cultural phenomenon remain active, outside of the central figures of Vico C and DJ Negro. These two were able to not only go beyond the limits of the barrio and become underground rappers known Island-wide, but they were also able to cross over into the mainstream and become international figures. Among the first rappers to produce their own material at home were Piro DJ, EZD, Los Intocables, Bule Buzzy Bee, Brewley MC, MC Base, and Jacob D. Many of these rappers rapped in Spanish, in Spanglish, and/or in English, setting the linguistic tone of the cultural phenomenon. Boricua rap was going to be created in the three languages of the barrio, i.e. among the sectors of the population with the highest migratory rates to the United States.

In the beginnings of Boricua rap, one could note the prevalent influence of New York rap. The explanation is clear. In addition to the commercialization of this style of rap and of North American cultural imperialism, that privileges and idealizes it in the eyes of the mass of Boricua rappers, direct contact with North American urban reality for many of these youth makes this music a familiar one for them, present in and associated with their daily experience. But this influence has been mediated and reshaped by Boricua reality to the point of intensely and/or intimately existing side by side with Caribbean rhythms that figure preponderantly in this music. I am referring to merengue, the Puerto Rican salsa beat, and (primarily) Jamaican reggae-dancehall. Thus at this very moment, one cannot talk about a singular current of influences on Boricua rap, given that the phenomenon has multiple sources.[12]

Our rap's international nature and multiple origins reflect very clearly the globalization of the market. In addition to African American rap that many young Puerto Ricans listened to in Chicago, Philadelphia, or New York, extremely important roots can be traced back to two points of the Caribbean, Panama and Jamaica. The door to an important mainstream for this phenomenon is opened with the commercialization of rap music created by the

Panamanian singer, El General, with his 1990 hits "Bien buena" and "No me va a matar." Immediately after this musical advent and his success in the market, the commercialization of Boricua rap begins with figures such as Vico C, Lisa M, DJ Negro, Brewley MC, and Francheska with the old DJ's Company, presently the Prime Records label. Convinced that a market for rap music in Spanish existed, this company, that was already hiring and offering a stage to (and exploiting) homegrown underground rappers in disco parties that it organized with DJs and MCs throughout the Island, widened its business activity by becoming a recording company. Thus, it established itself commercially.

This commercial move reflects a trend that reaches Puerto Rico from two places that mediate the Jamaican reggae-dancehall boom in the international market, Panama/Miami and New York. It would be too complicated to explain the link between African American rap and Jamaican music in this essay, a link that was established in the '70s but that consolidated toward the end of the 1980s with the emergence of dancehall in the Jamaican musical community of the Island and the exiled community in Panama, Miami, and New York.[13] I do want to emphasize the possibility of greater cultural contact among urban Caribbean communities as is made evident in Boricua rap.

This transition from African American influences to Jamaican influences set important guidelines in the development of the musical genre in the Island. Its key developments are marked by this transition and by a greater criminalization of the genre, which suggests to me evident racial links between Boricua rap and its growing illegality.

It is in its racial demarcation that rap is related to another neo-primitive urban group of the big metropolises, the Jamaican rastas. In Playero #38, rap is introduced as "this is black music" and other rappers present themselves as "being in the house for the race." In the commercial rap circuit, Vico C himself, in the song bearing the album's title, "Explosion," denounces racism in a clear and evident manner. The black presence in Vico's, Taino's, Ranking Stone's, and Falo's, Lisa M., and Francheska are ways in which a profile of the rapper is drawn that sets norms and is serialized. In this manner, rap and race are definitively viewed as akin to one another.

Boricua underground rap employs the exterior emblems of rasta culture and Jamaican reggae dancehall to give form to these new meanings. Now marijuana does not mean union with God, Jah, nor a spiritual escape from Babylon. The signs of this culture, deterritorialized by the global economy, have been turned into articles of consumption. Thus, marijuana, dreadlocks, rasta colors (yellow, green, and red) have become new signifiers that in Boricua reggae-rap mean race and social and legal marginalization as in the case of Jamaican rastas. The values of the "leisure-consumer" society or of getting high come before those of working, as occurs in rasta songs, but here without a deeper motivation than to assert power in the hangout and the crew. Nevertheless, the defense of smoke and its link with the racial construct and the critique of social and institutional racism-classism continue as the most direct annunciations of anti-racist social criticism in Puerto Rico during the past ten years from non-intellectual and non-academic quarters.

Precisely for this reason, I read this link as a pan-Caribbean link. The use of club dance floors, the prevalent use of black fashions and people in music videos, and the cultural connection with exiled Jamaicans (via New York and Miami) (that reflect a criteria of selection in face of the onslaught of North American cultural imperialism) create a community, practices, and an iconography that are specifically black. The names of many rappers — Blackie, DJ NEGRO, Prieto, el Negro— also tend to name the race in a challenging vein that breaks with the reigning discourse of supposed racial democracy. The Jamaican presence, the explicit naming of a black Puerto Rico, and the direct denunciation of racism raise important bridges to reflect upon and analyze.

I consider that this study of rap and of many phenomena in contemporary youth culture call for a revision of categories. The meanings of "political action," "left," "right," "individualism," and "agency" have to be revised. The so-called "political apathy" of Boricua youth has to be closely looked at to see what signs it provides, what keys it offers to better understand the current social conflict. To accuse rap discourse of being apolitical, after discerning its denunciation of racism, its challenge to and repudiation of the police state, and the approach to and recombining of other urban Caribbean cultures would be an act of political myopia. Such would also be the case if the ways in which rap participates in homophobia and misogyny prevalent in this and other Caribbean cultures are not emphasized. To define it as just another discourse of cultural assimilation would also be an mistake. It seems to me that the political apathy that Peri Coss and other social critics perceive originates in the assumption that all political and progressive struggles in Puerto Rico should begin with the defense of the national and not from other social experiences such as racism or sexual repression.

Although there are millions of other themes taken up by rap discourse-satires on the media, feminine rap, and preaching or constructive advice from the rapper to his crew-the themes we have chosen are important in order to understand how underground rap works rhetorically. I address the call to study its multiple manifestations without apologies. This is not a false objectivity, because by studying it I validate and support this genre that is far from being free of presenting ideological problems for me. But a polemic that is based on the criteria either of censorhip or of unconditional support of underground rap, that, ultimately, does not need the approval of intellectuals for its existence, seems innocuous to me. I think that rap is an important subject for study that anyone interested should take up. I, a young black women of working class background, who listens to underground rap, but who also is a university professor, a writer, and a student of popular urban Caribbean culture, approach rap with all the respect and all the fury that it provokes in me. This work is an attempt at healing that cleft of class and race in the two worlds that I inhabit. ■

ENDNOTES

1. Translator's note: *Boricua,* or Puerto Rican, is a term derived from the indigenous name for the Island, Boriken or Borinquen.
2. Rap's popularity has given momentum to the global marketing of musical products such as Jamaican dance-hall, a derivative of reggae and rap. This rhythm has taken deep root in South America, the Caribbean, and Europe to the point of influencing samba, Spanish rock (that already had a solid basis in ska, another off-shoot of reggae), merengue, and salsa. Among the studies made (few in comparison to the impact of the genre) see George Yúdice, "The Funkifation of Rio" in Microphone Fiends, New York: Routledge, 1994. I wish to make clear that the politicizing of many African American communities was the result of numerous influences other than rap and its repression by the North American state. Another factor to be taken into consideration is the impact of the struggle against apartheid and the freeing of Nelson Mandela and his subsequent election to the presidency of South Africa. But anti-racist movements have developed independently, according to the requirements of each country in which they have emerged.
3. Translators note: The *marquesina* in Puerto Rico is a space adjacent to the main body of the house akin to the North American house garage but typically partially open and often furnished for family and social gatherings.
4. This term is employed by Julio Ramos in the introduction to his book *Desencuentros de la modernidad: literatura y política en el siglo XIX* Puerto Rico: Ed. Cultural (1989). For him, it designates the constructs in discourse and practice that fashion the norms of an identity for a social group. It seems a very useful term to me to apply in the discussion on Boricua youth culture precisely because of the number of market, consumer, discourse, and everyday life circuits that come into play in the production and consolidation of these identities in the '90s.
5. Bibliographical note of José Manuel Valenzuela. *¡A la brava ese!: Cholos, Punks y Chavos Banda.* Mexico: El Colegio de la Frontera Norte eds., 1988.
6. For more, see María Milagros López article "Post-work Selves and Entitlement Attitudes in Peripheral Post-industrial Puerto Rico" *Social Text.* No. 38, 1994, 111–133.
7. London: Routlege, 1994
8. Mayra Santos Febres. Doctoral thesis, Cornell University, 1991
9. Interview with Marien Gelpi, Prime Records, October, 1991.
10. Río Piedras, Puerto Rico: Ediciones Huracán, 1993
11. Translator's note: *Prieto* is a common term meaning "black [male]" with a range of affective associations and at times employed with pejorative intent. Here, it serves as a *street nom de guerre.*
12. Translator's note: Like *prieto, cocolo* is popularly synonymous with a "black person." The term was adopted by fans of salsa, recognizing its roots in Africa and the Afro-Caribbean, in contrast to rockeros , or the followers of rock.
13. It is in the identification of a single origin—the North American—that I differ from the thesis of my colleague, Raquel Rivera, in her stimulating thesis "Para rapear en puertorriqueño: discurso y política cultural" (CUNY, 1995). In this work, Rivera proposes it as the sole source of Puerto Rican rap, although she defends very solidly the individuality of the genre in Puerto Rico. This thesis represents the first systematic attempt at studying rap in the Island, outside of the unpublished works of Ivy Rivera. It seems to me to be an obligatory source for anyone wishing to look closely at this cultural phenomenon in Puerto Rico.
14. In *Bring the Noise: A Guide to Rap Music and Hip-hop Culture.* New York: Harmony Books(1991) this link is studied in detail.

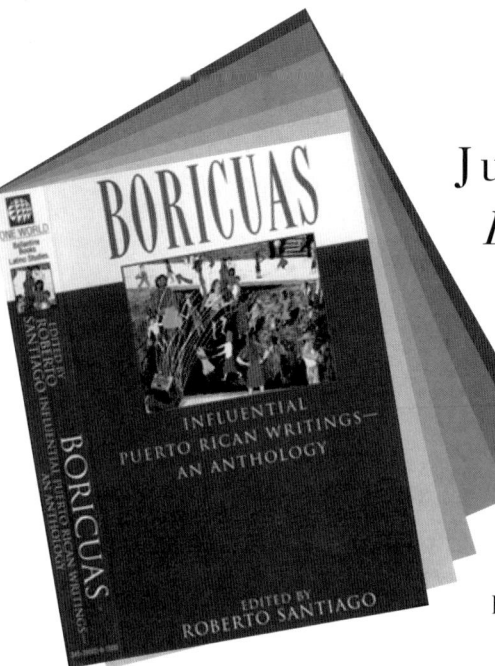

Juan Flores, review of *Boricuas: Influential Puerto Rican Writings — An Anthology*

edited by Roberto Santiago
(New York: Ballantine, 1995)

Boricuas: Influential Puerto Rican Writings—An Anthology, edited by Roberto Santiago (New York: Ballantine, 1995)

¡*Por fin!* At last, an anthology of Puerto Rican writing by and for U.S. Boricuas of the present generation. It's readable, accessible, and touches on all the right issues: colonialism, nationalism, racism, sexism, identity, assimilation, urban reality, pride and transcendence. And so many favorite writers together in one book, from trusty standard-bearers like José de Diego, Pedro Albizu Campos, Julia de Burgos and Jesús Colón, to Nuyorican classics Piri Thomas, Pedro Pietri, Sandra María Esteves, Nicholasa Mohr and Victor Hernández Cruz, to newer voices like Abraham Rodríguez, Ed Morales and Esmeralda Santiago. Poems, stories, letters, speeches, plays, movie scripts—whatever form the written word has taken to give expression to Boricua life and spirit has its place in this new collection.

Roberto Santiago's *Boricuas* is sure to become the most popular introductory textbook for classes in Puerto Rican studies. Its selection, thematic and stylistic range, and emotional blend of anger and celebration, will strike a chord in today's young readers, and make the book a welcome replacement for its long-outdated predecessors: María Teresa Babín's *Borínquen, An Anthology of Puerto Rican Literature* and Adalberto López's *The Puerto Ricans: their history, culture and society.* For one thing, *Boricuas* is interdisciplinary, including everything from a love poem to a political tract, whereas Babín's and López's collections are represented strictly by creative literature or social science writing respectively. More important, perhaps, is the difference in topicality and generational sensibility: when the two earlier anthologies were compiled, the "Nuyorican modality" as Babín called it was still at a formative stage, and the "search" for Puerto Rican cultural identity appeared more straightforward and decidedly Island-based, still relatively uncomplicated by thorny questions of globalization and translocality, racial and sexual affirmation, and crises of representation. Such contemporary themes and perspectives figure prominently in Boricuas, which happily leaves behind many of the literary clichés or turgid sociology characteristic of those previous textbook choices.

But what most distinguishes Roberto Santiago's collection from other presentations of Puerto Rican writing, including those from the Island, is its emphasis on "race" and blackness as an integral aspect of cultural struggle and affirmation. "Black and Latino" is the title of his own piece in *Boricuas*, an essay first printed in *Essence* magazine in 1989. "There I proudly declared to the entire world," he explains in the introduction to the anthology, "that I was both of these things, because to deny any side of my race or my culture would be to deny my very being." How new and refreshing to find that "other," suppressed dimension of Puerto Rican identity, "our third root" as the African presence is euphemistically labelled, standing in the foreground of the cultural debate. And many of the writers included, notably Jesús Colón, Julia de Burgos, Piri Thomas and Victor Hernández Cruz, join Santiago in accentuating this racial aspect of the Puerto Rican experience. Boricuas, then, is first-of-its-kind in offering a portrayal of Puerto Rican cultural and intellectual expression from a Black, or "Black Latino," perspective. Or so it would seem ...

Criticizing an anthology, of course, always seems to entail begging a new one into existence, and to rest on the unfair advantage of hindsight and personal preference. "He had to include something" or "If you don't like it do your own" are built-in responses, or simply "*¡Qué cómodo criticar*, after the fact!" And it's true: why not appreciate what we have and the energy the editor has devoted to compiling and publishing his favorite writings by his fellow Puerto Ricans? Indeed, thanks must go to Roberto Santiago for giving us the best Boricua book around for use in classroom and community settings, partly because it is based so strongly on his own lived experience.

But when he subtitled *Boricuas "Influential Puerto Rican Writings"* Santiago was not just referrring to their influence on himself personally. His aim, as he states it, is "to present an overview of a select group of nineteenthand twentieth-century authors whose writings bring new understanding to our recurring cultural themes." With this more objective claim in mind, the omissions become glaring, and serious in consequence for a critical perspective on Puerto Rican culture. Where for example, to begin with the old-timers, are Ramón Emeterio Betances, Eugenio María de Hostos and Lola Rodríguez de Tió, not to mention Manuel Alonso, Alejandro Tapia y Rivera, Salvador Brau or Manuel Zeno Gandía? Even veering off from the canon, but vital for historical background on issues of gender, race and life in the U.S., how about Arturo Alfonso Schomburg, Luisa Capetillo or "Pachín" Marín? If we're going to include Jesús Colón how about Bernardo Vega, and if José de Diego and Julia de Burgos represent modern Puerto Rican poetry, where is Luis Lloréns Torres, Luis Palés Matos and Juan Antonio Corretjer? And doesn't everyone agree that composers of immensely popular songs like Rafael Hernández, Pedro Flores and Tite Curet Alonso are some of our finest, most "influential" poets of the 20th century?

Representation of Nuyorican and recent writing is more complete and balanced, but I can't help missing such powerful, special voices as those of Tato Laviera and Louis Reyes Rivera, especially when the emphasis is so refreshingly strong on African and Black perspectives. Here though, in this closer-to-home part of the anthology, the problem is not so much the omissions as the selections themselves. However well they might fit into his thematic scheme, Santiago's choices from the work of Victor Hernández Cruz, Martín Espada and José Luis González leaves those important writers poorly represented, and I would also question his selections of Yoruba Guzmán and Felipe Luciano from *Palante* and not Iris Morales, David Pérez and Juan González. But those are omissions again, as is the replacement of Samuel Betances on the issue of race (which was after all in Babín's collection) with the sociological essay by Clara Rodríguez. And then there are the questionable inclusions, most notable in the more journalistic, mass media pieces: cracking up with Freddie Prinze is great (though I don't know about "the best Puerto Rican comedian there ever was"), but for Gerardo Rivera's coverage of the Bernard Carabello case to be the longest inclusion in the book, taking up a full 25 pages, is clearly out of proportion.

What is most objectionable about Boricuas to a contemporary sensibility, and most at odds with the spirit of this new book, is the inflated and poorly informed stature reserved for José de Diego. True to the most conservative, canonical view of Puerto Rican culture, de Diego stands at the pinnacle of the national pantheon, as poet, orator, essayist, lawyer and political visionary. But, first of all, in his contributors' notes Santiago mistakenly dates de Diego (1866–1918) in the 18th century, when he was active in the early decades of the present century. (While we're on faux pas, the great 19th-century composer was Juan Morel Campos, not Juan Morel Fields.) More important, though, "El Caballero de la Raza"—as de Diego was known—was anything but a champion of the black "race," to use the term loosely, nor even of a "Puerto Rican race" for that matter. What Roberto Santiago doesn't mention to his readers is that de Diego was a thoroughgoing Hispanophile and Eurocentric in his opposition to "American" cultural imperialism, an opposition which despite his high-blown rhetoric was equivocal at best. Readers of Boricuas are also left uninformed that as a lawyer and politician de Diego consistently represented the interests not of the Puerto Rican nation, much less of the struggling masses, but those of the hated Guánica Central and the owning elite, even in their collusion with U.S. corporations and politicians. (And on the subject of women, forget it!) If we are going to stay with anything from the canons and pantheons, we can do better than to leave the likes of José de Diego so comfortably in place.

Thus the search for Boricua historical and cultural identity goes on, and Roberto Santiago has done much to illuminate that background and signal the paths ahead. (Santiago's translations, by the way are passable, but that brings me to my final beef: I would have included the original Spanish texts, at least of the poetry. I'm sorry, but Juliá's *"grifa"* just doesn't cut it as "my kinky negress.") Many Puerto Ricans and others, young and old, will be reading *Boricuas*, which makes it especially important not to overlook key landmarks, and all the more necessary not to mistake diversity for inconsistency and confusion. ■

BIBLIOGRAPHY

Selected bibliography on racial relations, racism and negritude among Puerto Ricans[1]

This selection presents mostly journal articles, chapters and books on racism, racial relations and negritude among Puerto Ricans. Because of the authors' research, it is strong in history and the social sciences. Given space limitataions, it has few newspaper articles, speeches and archival materials and excludes theses, dissertations, conferences and other unpublished materials. The selection includes references to points of view that raised debate and discussion.

Alegría, Ricardo. *La Fiesta de Santiago Apóstol en Loíza Aldea.* Madrid: Aro, Artes Gráficas, 1954.

Alvarez Nazario, Manuel. *El Elemento Afro-Negroide en el Español de Puerto Rico.* San Juan: Instituto de Cultura Puertorriqueña, 1961.

Arana Soto, Salvador. *Puerto Rico: Sociedad sin Razas y Trabajos Afines.* San Juan: Asociación Médica de Puerto Rico, 1976.

Armstrong, Robert G. "Intergroup Relations in Puerto Rico." *Phylon: Quarterly Journal of Race and Culture* 10, no. 3 (1949): 220-5.

Barbosa, José Celso. *Problema de Razas.* San Juan: Imprenta Venezuela, 1937.

Betances, Samuel. "The Prejudice of Having No Prejudice. Part 1" *The Rican* no. 2 (1972): 41-54.

—. "The Prejudice of Having No Prejudice. Part 2" *The Rican* no. 3 (1973): 22-37

Blanco, Tomás. *El Prejuicio Racial en Puerto Rico.* With a preliminary study by Arcadio Díaz Quiñones. Río Piedras: Huracán, 1985.

Bryan, William S., ed. *Our Islands and Their People.* 2 vols. St. Louis: Thompson Publishing Company, 1899.

Carrión, Juan Manuel. "Etnia, Raza y la Nacionalidad Puertorriqueña." *La Nación Puertorriqueña: Ensayos en Torno a Pedro Albizu Campos,* edited by Juan Manuel Carrión, Teresa C. Gracia Ruíz and Carlos Rodríguez Fraticelli, pp. 3-18. San Juan: Editorial de la Universidad de Puerto Rico, 1993.

Conde, Eduardo. "Cuestión de Razas." *Unión Obrera,* 14 June 1903, p. 1.

Diego Padró, José Isaac de. *Luis Palés Matos y su Trasmundo Poético: Estudio Biográfico-Crítico.* [Río Piedras]: Ediciones Puerto, 1973.

Denton, Nancy A. and Douglas S. Massey. "Racial Identity Among Caribbean Hispanics: The Effect of Double Minority Status on Residential Segregation." *American Sociological Review* 54 (1989): 790-808.

"Documentos para la Historia de Puerto Rico: Documento 1 [Matrimonios Interraciales]." *Anales de Investigación Histórica* 9, nos. 1-2 (1982): 68-71.

Ezponda, Eduardo. *La Mulata: Estudio Fisiológico, Social y Jurídico.* Madrid: Imprenta Fortanet, 1878.

Falcón, Angelo. *Black and Latino Politics in New York City: Race and Ethnicity in a Changing Urban Context.* New York: Institute for Puerto Rican Policy, 1985.

Fitzpatrick, Joseph. "The Problem of Color." In *Puerto Rican Americans: The Meaning of Migration to the Mainland,* Joseph Fitzpatrick, pp. 101-14. New York: Prentice Hall, 1971.

Flores, Juan. "Cortijo's Revenge." *Centro de Estudios Puertorriqueños Bulletin* 3, no. 2 (1991): 8-21.

—. Divided Borders: Essays on Puerto Rican Identity. Houston: Arte Público Press, 1993.

González, José Luis. *El País de Cuatro Pisos y Otros Ensayos*. Río Piedras: Huracán, 1980.

González, Lydia Milagros. *La Tercera Raíz: La Presencia Africana en Puerto Rico*. San Juan: CEREP, 1992.

Gordon, Maxine. "Race Patterns and Prejudice in Puerto Rico." *American Sociological Review* 14, no. 2 (1949): 294-301.

—. "Cultural Aspects of Puerto Rico's Race Problem." *American Sociological Review* 15, no. 3 (1950): 382-92.

Haslip Viera, Gabriel. "Puerto Ricans and the Afrocentrism Debate." *Crítica: A Journal of Puerto Rican Policy and Politics* 2 (1994): 1, 6.

Hernández Colón, Rafael. "Mensaje del Gobernador del Estado Libre Asociado de Puerto Rico." Speech delivered at a banquet in his honor, Madrid, Spain, 17 May 1988. It aroused controversy in terms of negritude and hispanic identity. *El Mundo* published Tite Curet Alonso on 21 June, Manuel Maldonado Denis on 13 July and Salvador Tió's intervention on 1, 15 June 1988. *El Nuevo Día* carried Rafael Castro Pereda on 24 June, Rafael Hernández Colón on 6 June and Antonio Martorell on 10 June.

Hoetink, Harmannus. *The Two Variants in Caribbean Race Relations, a Contribution to the Sociology of Segmented Societies*. London: Oxford University Press, 1967.

—. "'Race' and Color in the Caribbean." In *Caribbean Contours,* edited by Sidney W. Mintz and Sally Price, pp. 55-84. Baltimore: The Johns Hopkins University Press, 1985.

Hollister, Frederick. "Skin Color and the Life Chances of Puerto Ricans." *Caribbean Studies* 9, no. 3 (1969): 97-94.

Jorge, Angela. "The Black Puerto Rican Woman in Contemporary American Society." In *The Puerto Rican Woman,* edited by Edna Acosta Belén with Elia Hidalgo Christensen, pp. 134-41. New York: Praeger, 1979.

Kantrowitz, Nathan. "Algunas Consecuencias Raciales: Diferencias Educativas y Ocupacionales entre los Puertorriqueños Blancos y No Blancos en los Estados Unidos Continentales, 1950." *Revista de Ciencias Sociales* 15, no. 3 (1971): 387-97.

Kinsbrunner, Jay. "Caste and Capitalism in the Caribbean: Residential Patterns and House Ownership Among the Free People of Color of San Juan, Puerto Rico, 1823-1846." *Hispanic American Historical Review* 70, no. 3 (1990): 433-61.

La Ruffa, Anthony L. *San Cipriano: Life in a Puerto Rican Community*. New York: Gordon and Breach Science Publications, 1971.

Liga para promover el progreso de los negros en Puerto Rico. "Artículos de Incorporación." 1939. Archivo General de Puerto Rico, Fondo del Departamento de Estado, Serie de corporaciones sin fines de lucro, Caja 58A, Expediente 1015.

Longress, John F. "Racism and Its Effects on Puerto Rican Continentals." *Social Casework* 55 (1974): 67-99.

López Llano, Jorge. A series of nineteen articles on racism. *El Reportero,* 16 June 1982 to 9 July 1982

Mills, C. Wright, Clarence Senior and Rose Kohn Goldsen. *The Puerto Rican Journey: New York's Newest Migrants*. New York: Harper, 1950.

Mintz, Sidney W. "The Role of Forced Labor in Nineteenth Century Puerto Rico." *Caribbean Historical Review* 2 (1951): 134-41.

—. "Groups, Group Boundaries and the Perception of 'Race:' Review of H. Hoetink, The Two Variants in Caribbean Race Relations." *Comparative Studies in Society and History* 13, no. 4 (1971): 437-50.

Montero Seplowin, Virginia. "Análisis de la Indentificación Racial de los Puertorriqueños en Filadelfia." *Revista de Ciencias Sociales* 15, no. 1 (1971): 143-48.

El Negrito. "A mis Hermanos de Raza." In *Ruptura Social y Violencia Política en Puerto Rico, 1898-1904: Antología de Documentos,* edited by Mariano Negrón Portillo, p. 146. [Río Piedras]: Centro de Investigaciones Sociales, Universidad de Puerto Rico, 1991.

Palés Matos, Luis. *La Poesía de Luis Palés Matos*. Critical edition by Mercedes López Baralt, San Juan: Editorial de la Universidad de Puerto Rico, 1995.

Pedreira, Antonio S. *Insularismo*. Río Piedras: Edil, 1978.

Picó de Hernández, Isabel. "The Quest for Race, Sex, and Ethnic Equality in Puerto Rico." *Caribbean Studies* 14 , no. 4 (1975): 127-41.

—. Discrimen por Color, *Sexo y Origen Nacional en Puerto Rico*. Río Piedras: Centro de Investigaciones Sociales, Universidad de Puerto Rico, 1981.

Picó, Isabel and Idsa Alegría. *El Texto Libre de Prejuicios Sexuales y Raciales (Guía para la Preparación de Materiales de Enseñanza)*. Río Piedras: Centro de Investigaciones Sociales, Universidad de Puerto Rico, 1983.

Picó, Fernando. *Vivir en Caimito*. Río Piedras: Huracán, 1989.

Quintero Rivera, Angel G. *Historia de unas Clases sin Historia (Comentarios Críticos al País de Cuatro Pisos)*. Cuadernos De CEREP, Avances Para Discusión, no. 6. Río Piedras: Centro de Estudios de la Realidad Puertorriqueña, 1983.

—. "The Somatology of Manners: Class, Race and Gender in the History of Dance Etiquette in the Hispanic Caribbean." In *Ethnicity in the Caribbean: Essays in Honor of Harry Hoetink,* edited by Gert Oostindie, pp. 152-81. London: Macmillan, forthcoming.

Rodríguez, Clara E. "Racial Classification Among Puerto Rican Men and Women in New York." *Hispanic Journal of Behavioral Sciences* 12, no. 4 (1990): 366-79.

—. "Challenging Racial Hegemony: Puerto Ricans in the United States." In *Race,* edited by Stevens Gregory and Roger Sanjek, pp. 131-45. New Brunswick: Rutgers University Press, 1994.

Rodríguez, Clara E. and Héctor Cordero Guzmán. "Placing Race in Context." *Ethnic and Racial Studies* 15, no. 4 (1992): 523-42.

Rodríguez Cruz, Juan. "Las Relaciones Raciales en Puerto Rico." *Revista de Ciencias Sociales* 9, no. 4 (1965): 373-86.

Rogler, Charles. "The Role of Semantics in the Study of Race Distance in Puerto Rico." *Social Forces* 22, no. 4 (1944): 448-53.

—. "The Morality of Race Mixing in Puerto Rico." *Social Forces* 25, no. 1 (1946): 77-81.

—. "Some Situational Aspects of Race Relations in Puerto Rico." *Social Forces* 27, no. 1 (1948): 72-77.

Rosario, José Colombán. *El Negro: Haití, Estados Unidos, Puerto Rico*. [Río Piedras]: División de Impresos, Universidad de Puerto Rico, 1951.

Rosario, José Colombán and Justina Carrión. *Problemas Sociales: El Negro*. Río Piedras: Universidad de Puerto Rico, 1951.

Sagrera, Martín. *Racismo y Política en Puerto Rico*. Río Piedras: Edil, 1973.

Santiago, William Fred. "Problemas de Reificación y Conciencia: Propuesta de Investigación Sobre Etnia, Clase y Nación." *Revista de Ciencias Sociales* 26, nos. 1-4 (1987): 409-34.

Scarano, Francisco. *Inmigración y Clases Sociales en el Puerto Rico del Siglo XIX*. Río Piedras: Huracán, 1981.

Seda Bonilla, Eduardo. "Social Structure and Race Relations." *Social Forces* 40, no. 2 (1961): 141-48.

—. *Los Derechos Civiles en la Cultura Puertorriqueña*. Río Piedras: Editorial Universitaria,

Universidad de Puerto Rico, 1963.

—. "Dos Modelos de Relaciones Raciales: Estados Unidos y América Latina." *Revista de Ciencias Sociales* 12, no. 4 (1968): 569-97.

—. "Ethnic Studies and Cultural Pluralism." *The Rican,* no. 1 (1971): 56-65.

Sereno, Renzo. "Crypotmelamnism: A Study of Color Relations and Personal Insecurity in Puerto Rico." *Psychiatry* 10, no. 3 (1946): 261-69.

Siegel, Morris. "Race Attitudes in Puerto Rico." Phylon*: The Atlanta University Review of Race and Culture* 14, no. 2 (1953): 163-78.

Silva Casona, Manuel. A series of three articles on racism. *Avance* 1, nos. 40-42 (April and May 1973).

Tió, Salvador, Roberto Alejandro, Juan Manuel García Passalacqua, Rafael Castro Pereda and Julio A. Muriente. A Controversy on Hispanic Identity. *El Nuevo Día,* 28 February to 21 October 1985. Tió's articles appeared on 28 February; 27 March; 1, 8, 15, 22 April, and 21 October. Alejandro intervened on 25, 27 July; 7, 19, 24 August and 14 September; García Passalacqua on 19 and 21 March; Castro Pereda on 26 May and Muriente on 12 to 18 April. *El Nuevo Día* published all but Muriente's article that appeared on *Claridad*.

Thompson, Lanny. *Nuestra Isla y su Gente: La Construcción del 'otro' Puertorriqueño en 'Our Islands and Their People'*. Río Piedras: Centro de Investigaciones Sociales and Departamento de Historia, Universidad de Puerto Rico, 1995.

Tumin, Melvin with Arnold S. Feldman. *Social Class & Social Change in Puerto Rico*. 2 ed. Indianapolis: The Bobbs-Merrill Company, 1971.

Vizcarrondo, Fortunato. *Dinga y Mandinga: Poemas.* 4th. ed. San Juan: Instituto de Cultura Puertorriqueña, 1983.

Zenón Cruz, Isabelo. *Narciso Descubre su Trasero.* Humacao: Furidi, 1975.

NOTE ON THE AUTHORS

[1]Juan José Baldrich, a professor of sociology at the University of Puerto Rico, holds a Ph.D. from Yale University. He has done research on populism in Puerto Rico, democracy in Jamaica, and tobacco growing and manufacture in Cuba and Puerto Rico. Isar Pilar Godreau is a Ph.D. student of cultural anthropology at the University of California, Santa Cruz. She is conducting fieldwork on racism in Puerto Rico and is currently elaborating the concept of strategic ambiguity in a black community of Ponce. Heymar I. González is a graduate student of sociology at the University of Puerto Rico. She is presently working at her master's thesis on racial relations and interracial marriages in nineteenth century Puerto Rico. Limarie Nieves-Rosa finished her undergraduate work in sociology at the University of Puerto Rico in 1995. She is currently in the graduate sociology program at the State University of New York, Albany. *The authors acknowledge the suggestions of Juan Guisti.*

bordes

lo conocieron, el borde es aquello a partir de lo que algo comienza a presenciarse

El borde no es eso en lo que algo cesa, sino, como los griegos

Aponte • Jiménez • Santiago-Valles

Pérez • Cámara • Chaluisán

Suárez • Negrón • Silén

Aronowitz • Magas • Virno

Lazzarato & Negri • Torrecilla

Rodríguez-Morazzani • González

Meléndez • Pabón • Material Girl

2 núm.

bordes

Para inventarse el Caribe **'Xiomara mi hermana' Diplo y el travestismo racial** Del cuerpo del delito al delito de los cuerpos **La agonía y el éxtasis del intelectual finisecular** Feminismo vs totalitarismo: textos y contextos femeninos en Cuba contemporánea **Cuerpos firmes y peleítas mongas; notas para bajar de peso** Dibujos **Fábula del olvido** Los discípulos, Poemas **El socialismo ya no es un imaginario político** Ex/Yugoslavia: las causas de la guerra **Cuando la cultura es el centro de la producción, la vida es una gran puesta en escena** Trabajo inmaterial y subjetividad **No future** Hegel contra Nietzsche **El posmoderno y los fantasmas de la modernidad** La NET desde los bordes

subscripciones

1 año (dos números) **$15** individual **$40** bibliotecas e instituciones.
Contribuciones $25 - $50 - $75 - $100 - otras ____

P.O. Box 21971, Estación U.P.R., **Río Piedras**, Puerto Rico 00931 **Fax** (787) 727-6951